PEOPLE AND PLACES

A 21st-century atlas of the UK

Danny Dorling and Bethan Thomas

P

First published in Great Britain in 2016 by

Policy Press
University of Bristol
1–9 Old Park Hill
Bristol
BS2 8BB
UK
t: +44 (0)117 954 5940
pp-info@bristol.ac.uk
www.policypress.co.uk

North America office:
Policy Press
c/o The University of Chicago Press
1427 East 60th Street
Chicago, IL 60637, USA
t: +1 773 702 7700
f: +1 773 702 9756
sales@press.uchicago.edu
www.press.uchicago.edu

British Library Cataloguing in Publication Data
A catalogue record for this book is available from the British Library

Library of Congress Cataloging-in-Publication Data
A catalog record for this book has been requested

ISBN 978 1 44731 137 9 paperback
ISBN 978 1 44731 136 2 hardcover

Typeset and cover design by Soapbox, www.soapbox.co.uk
Printed and bound in Great Britain by Cambrian Printers, Ceredigion, Wales
Policy Press uses environmentally responsible print partners

For Beth and Mick,

and new beginnings...

Acknowledgements and data sources

Our thanks go to all the people at Policy Press who enabled us to create this atlas: Ali Shaw, Laura Vickers, Laura Greaves and Dave Worth. Thanks are due to Dawn Rushen who was, once again, a superb copyeditor. Our gratitude goes to John Schwartz and Paulien Hosang at Soapbox, who turned our very ordinary graphs and typescript into the volume of visual excellence you now hold in your hands. And many thanks are due to David Dorling and Mark Fransham for ploughing through our turgid prose and making many suggestions for improvements. Finally we would like to express our heartfelt thanks to all the people who filled out their Census forms: without you, this atlas would not have been possible.

The 2001 Census data was obtained via the CASWEB portal at UK Data Service Census Support. For 2011, Census data was obtained from a variety of sources. We used UK-wide tables available from the Office for National Statistics (ONS), where they existed. Otherwise we had to obtain the different countries' data from the different agencies, and amalgamate them together. We used ONS or NOMIS (for England and Wales), the Northern Ireland Statistics and Research Agency (NISRA) and Scotland's Census.

Additional data was obtained from the Annual Population Survey/Labour Force Survey (APS/LFS) via NOMIS; from Vital Statistics datasets at ONS; from the mid-year population estimates from ONS; from Standard Area Measurements data at ONS; from Her Majesty's Revenue and Customs (HMRC) (inheritance tax statistics; personal income statistics); Department for Transport (road accidents and safety statistics; bus, rail, light-rail and tram statistics); Department for Communities and Local Government, Welsh Assembly Government and Scottish Government (dwellings statistics); Understanding Society (UK Household Longitudinal Study, health statistics); National Association for Language Development in the Curriculum (NALDC) (bilingual statistics); and What Scotland Thinks (Scottish voting intentions).

Contents

Introduction

Introduction

People and places 2011 is an atlas designed to show how the social geography of the UK is changing as revealed by the UK 2011 Census of Population and Housing. By comparing the latest Census to the previous Census in 2001, and combining that information with more recent data on trends revealed since 2011, up to and including 2015, it is possible to gain a sense of how the UK is slowly transforming in terms of the people who live in each place as well as the places themselves, the families, households, flats and houses they live in, the cars they drive or buses, cycles and trains they use to get to work (or to study), whether they work or study (or both, or neither), for whom they work, who they care for, if they are ill, and so on (and on in bewildering detail), to build up a picture of how millions of people in thousands of neighbourhoods in hundreds of towns and cities interact, survive, prosper, suffer, and – above all else – are changing.

Ever since the *second* UK Census was taken, just over two centuries ago in 1811, this 10-yearly survey of the entire population became interesting because one Census could be compared to the previous Census to see how the population had altered in number, and later, as Censuses became more sophisticated, in its characteristics. Without the ability to compare and contrast, very big or very small numbers have limited significance. And to see any significance of a large volume of numbers relating to many areas it helps to map them. Very little mapping of Census data was done, however, until it became possible to use computers to both tabulate and aggregate Census data, and also to draw the numerous possible maps that could be produced. Automation also turned out to be vital, along with the development of new computer algorithms. These were needed to reorder space itself, creating new map projections that are required if most Census data is to be seen at all clearly and if the rest is to be seen undistorted. Until the 1960s almost all mapping of Census data that was conducted was undertaken by hand, and Census maps were drawn using map projections in which the information about most of the population was hidden in just a few small densely populated places on the map. This was true of all such mapping worldwide.

In 1959 Waldo Tobler, a geography PhD student at the University of Washington, US, published a paper in Volume 49 of the *Geographical Review* titled 'Automation and cartography'. Tobler would go on to pioneer new map projections for showing Census populations and electoral mapping in the US that were later copied across the world and which came to include revelatory new projections of the world and all of humankind. Census mapping spans the whole gamut, from revelation as to our common humanity and distribution, through to who has a kitchen sink that drains, and who goes cold in their home or not.

In the 1960s computing had advanced sufficiently, along with human imagination, so that the UK 1971 Census came to be organised by being punched into a computer, tabulated by another computer, and the results plotted by yet another computer. At the same time, social advancements in the 1960s meant that many more interesting questions were asked in the UK's 1971 Census, including whether people had a sink that drained in their kitchen, and any hot running water anywhere in their home. This was the first Census to be mapped by computer in the UK. Back then we could put people on the moon and map a Census by passing electricity through computer chips, but we were still struggling to ensure adequate plumbing in many homes, and to keep many people warm, well and securely sheltered, living without fear of homelessness. On 16 November 1966 the BBC play *Cathy Come Home* was broadcast concerning homelessness. Its impact was wide enough to alter what questions were asked in a Census. The 50th anniversary of *Cathy Come Home* is later this year, and homelessness is again an acute issue in the UK.

Census mapping of the UK by computer has a history that now spans more than 50 years, with the UK experiments beginning in the 1960s. The first national digitally produced atlas of the 1971 Census was published as *People in Britain: A Census atlas*, with the authorship jointly credited to the Census Research Unit of Durham University (UK) and the Office for Population Censuses and Surveys (OPCS), the predecessor of the Office for National Statistics (ONS). Published by the government, through Her Majesty's Stationery Office (HMSO), it appeared in print just before the 1981 Census was being collected. A copy was purchased by the city of Oxford's public library. That copy sat on a shelf and was untouched for several years, sealed in its brown cardboard packaging. Then, on a rainy Saturday afternoon, a bored schoolboy opened it up, saw what it was possible to map, and applied to Newcastle University to study Geography, Maths and Statistics. That boy is one of the two authors of this atlas.

Progress in Census mapping was rapid in the 1970s. By the end of that decade printing maps on hard-copy paper was considered old fashioned by some. The 1981 Census was made available to schoolchildren as part of the 1986 BBC Domesday project. This was an attempt to replicate the first Domesday Book that was published 900 years earlier, in 1086. Census data from 1981 was embedded in a newly invented 12-inch laser disc that the BBC Domesday computer read. Unfortunately only very well resourced schools could afford to purchase the new laser readers for these discs. The 1981 Census data was held at Newcastle University, where the data had been assembled to be placed on the disc. In effect, the BBC Domesday laser disc contained a Census atlas, one that also mapped data by grid square, as had been done with the 1971 Census, but now 1981 data, and now directly onto the screen, rather than to a pen-plotter driven by a computer program reading data from a magnetic tape.

By the early 1990s the centre of Census mapping in the UK had moved from Durham University and then Newcastle University down to the University of Bristol. Using software developed at the University of Edinburgh called GIMMS (Geographic Information Mapping and Management System), David Gordon and Ray Forrest at Bristol published two Census atlases in quick succession. These were both of the 1991 Census data and published as Forrest, R. and Gordon, D. (1993) *People and places: A 1991 Census atlas of England*, by SAUS Publications, the predecessor to Policy Press (established as an academic publisher in 1996); and as Gordon, D. and Forrest, R. (1995) *Class and economic distinctions in England 1991*, Bristol; SAUS Publications.

The second author of this atlas, Bethan Thomas, moved to Bristol to start work on her doctoral thesis shortly after the publications by Gordon and Forrest were produced. It is partly this series of coincidences that meant that Bethan and Danny authored the 2001 *People and places* atlas for Policy Press, and then this publication for 2011. At the time we began writing this atlas, the only other Census atlas of 2011 data was created to exist online with maps generated automatically according to code written by Alex Singleton of the University of Liverpool. That atlas has far more maps than are shown here, and almost no commentary on each because there are so many maps that could be commented on. Now a second online Census resource exists, http://datashine.org.uk, created by James Cheshire and Oliver O'Brien. This contains almost endless maps, and because of that, almost no commentary – but the maps are fascinating and were the result of a huge amount of hard work allowing the users to alter the map seen. Perhaps one day commentaries will also be semi-automated!

Census mapping keeps on changing. In this atlas all the maps used are of the population cartogram variety, and a particular kind that was first created using a computer by Waldo Tobler in the early 1970s, called *population cartograms*. Every district is drawn in proportion to its population. The same base map is used throughout this atlas, using the population as it was enumerated in 2011. A few years ago it would have taken several paragraphs of text to explain these types of map, and in a publication like this we would also have had to include traditional maps. Today, these population cartogram maps are now known well enough that all you need know is that they are topologically correct, that is, everywhere districts touch where they should and nowhere that they shouldn't, and the districts shown are the 406 Local Authority districts of the UK that existed in 2011. The locator maps, which appear in the pages immediately following this introductory text, show and name each of those districts. We map at the level of district as this simplifies the patterns shown, and allows broad generalisation to be made more easily. However, there is no reason why in future, data for smaller neighbourhoods could not be depicted within each district. Each neighbourhood would have an area equal to its population, and would look very much like it looks on a traditional map, except that the parkland and countryside would shrink away.

Finally, the only other information you need to know to be able to understand this atlas is that unless otherwise specified, all the proportions are reported as a share of the entire Local Authority district population, and wherever possible, everything is counted in units of (or shares of) people. Thus unemployment rates are described as the number of people who are out of work and looking for work for every 100 people living in each place. The denominator 'all people' includes children who would not be allowed to work and people too old or infirm to work, as well as many others whose existence in any district would not normally be used in calculating an unemployment rate. The advantage of calculating all rates in this way is that they can all be compared to each other. It is also easier to understand change over time statistics when proportions are calculated this way. Thus, an increase in unemployment of 0.1% is one extra person becoming unemployed for every 1,000 people living in a place. If two had been unemployed in every 1,000 and now there are three, or if 102 had been and now 103 were, in both cases the increase is measured as 0.1%.

So, sit back and enjoy the view. So much has changed in just over 200 years after the first change between two Censuses was calculated in the UK, 150 years after a Census was first mapped, 100 years after social classes and housing issues were first recorded in the 1911 Census, and half a century since Census data began to be routinely placed on computer tape, rather than punched card, and what could only be imagined before became not just possible, but normal. Today we depict the results of the Census with maps that were once seen as discoveries and great innovations. Today the maps used in this atlas are now just another 'population projection'. To introduce this atlas, we first show the regions and countries of the UK and selected towns and cities. As an aid to easy navigation we reproduce these two maps on the inside front and inside back covers. These are followed by locator maps of Local Authorities. On these locator maps, Unitary Authorities in England are coloured purple. The English District Councils within each county are distinctly shaded, and Scotland, Wales and Northern Ireland are individually coloured. We then begin our commentary by looking at population density, explaining and looking at what population potential is, before moving on to show distributions of poverty, wealth, riches, and those who are neither rich nor poor.

Many of these introductory maps are measures that Census data helps us make, but which cannot be constructed simply by using the Census. There is still much missing from the UK Census form, and just as questions about sinks and hot water had to be added in the 1960s, so there are new questions we should be asking in future Censuses about the most pressing problems of today. Hopefully the maps that follow will help highlight some of those problems.

For those readers less familiar with the administrative geography of the UK, the Appendix presents Local Authorities in the standard geographical order used by ONS, as well as an alphabetical list. We use ampersands where a council name includes an 'and', thus Kensington & Chelsea, Redcar & Cleveland and Dumfries & Galloway refers to three places.

REGIONS AND COUNTRIES

TOWNS AND CITIES

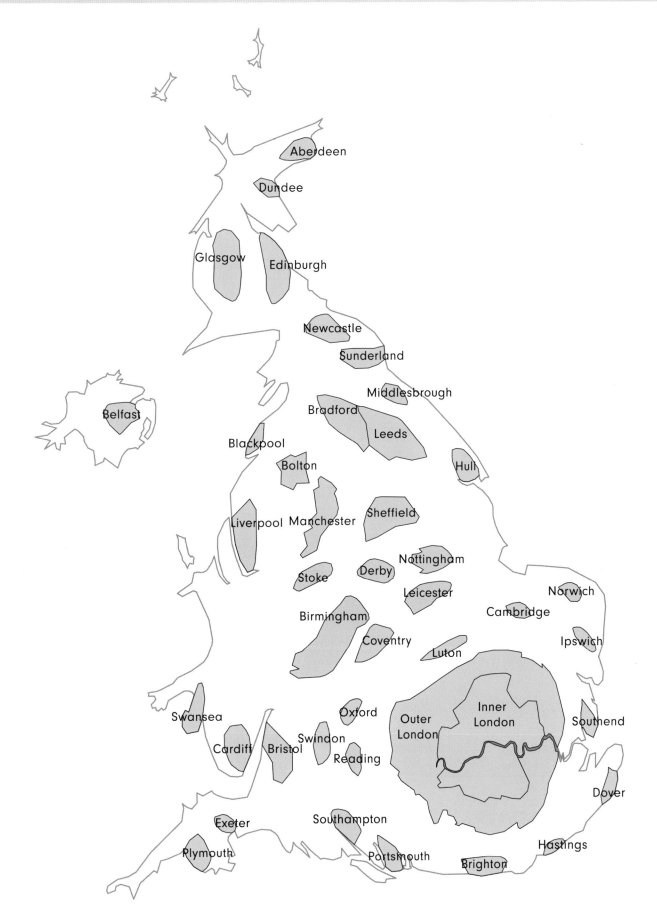

NORTH EAST, NORTHERN IRELAND AND SCOTLAND

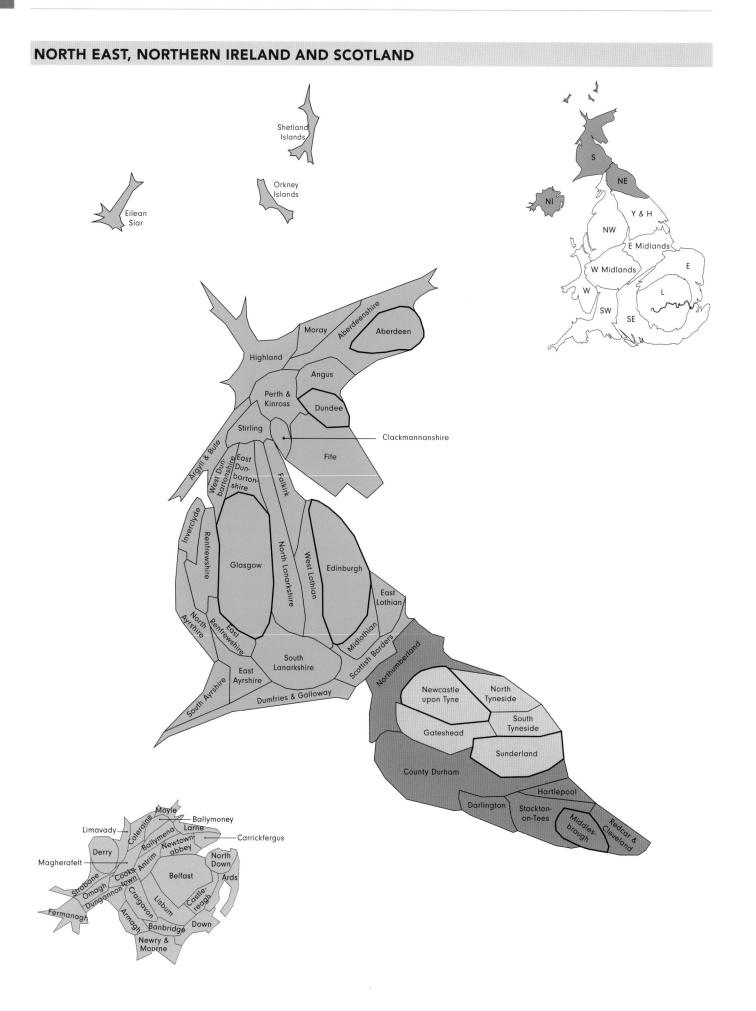

EAST MIDLANDS, NORTH WEST AND YORKSHIRE & HUMBER

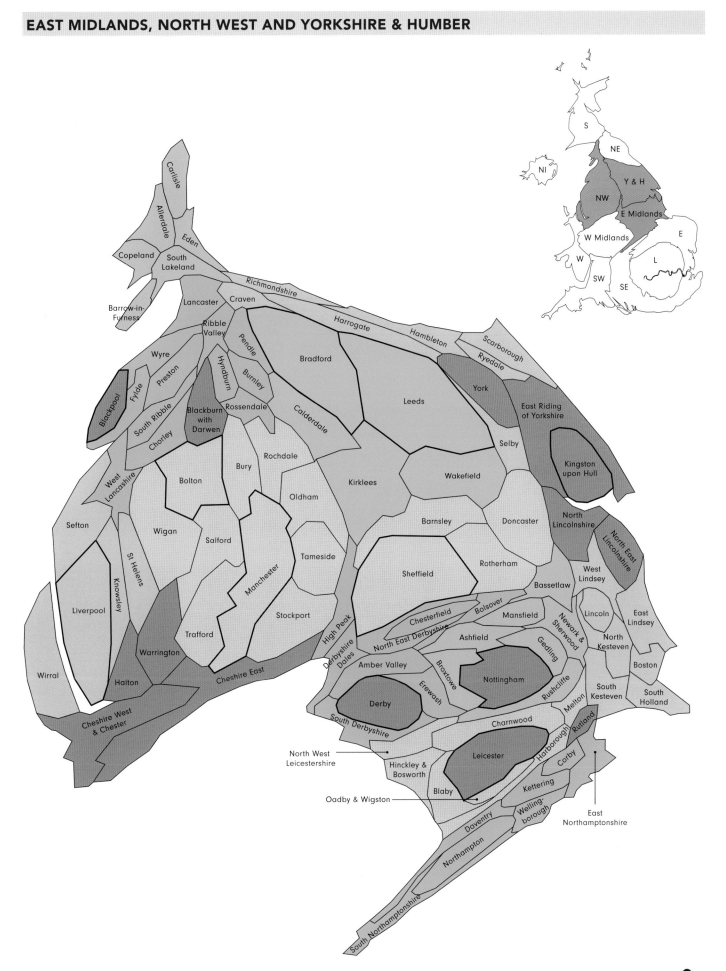

SOUTH WEST, WALES AND WEST MIDLANDS

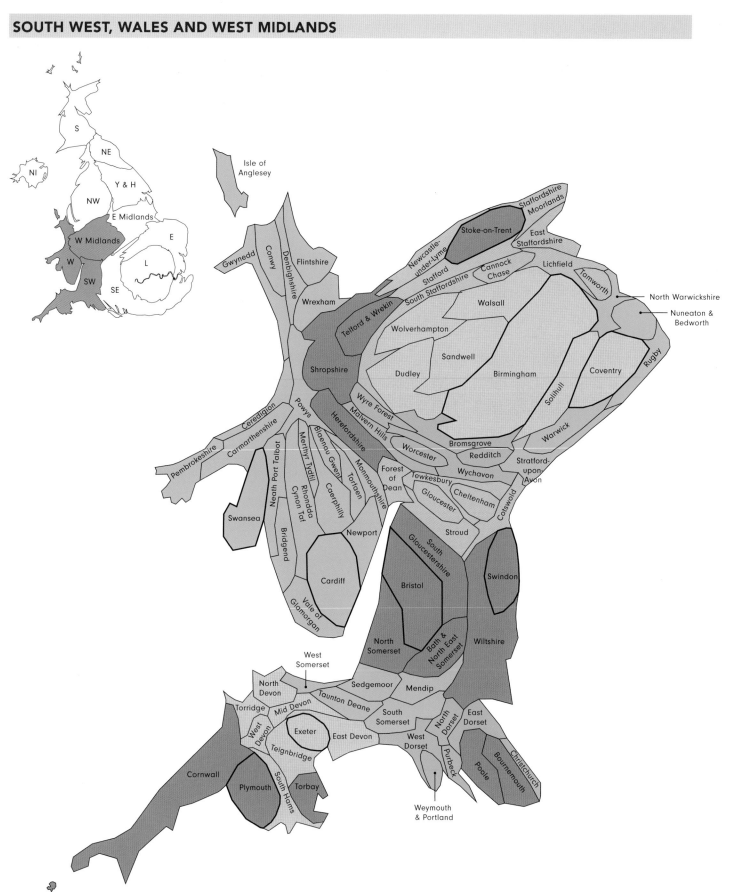

S

NE

NI

Y & H

NW

E Midlands

W Midlands

E

W

L

SW

SE

Isle of Anglesey

Gwynedd

Conwy

Denbighshire

Flintshire

Staffordshire Moorlands

Stoke-on-Trent

East Staffordshire

Newcastle-under-Lyme

Stafford

Cannock Chase

Lichfield

Tamworth

North Warwickshire

South Staffordshire

Walsall

Nuneaton & Bedworth

Wrexham

Telford & Wrekin

Wolverhampton

Shropshire

Dudley

Sandwell

Birmingham

Solihull

Coventry

Rugby

Wyre Forest

Malvern Hills

Bromsgrove

Warwick

Ceredigion

Powys

Herefordshire

Worcester

Redditch

Stratford-upon-Avon

Carmarthenshire

Blaenau Gwent

Monmouthshire

Forest of Dean

Tewkesbury

Wychavon

Pembrokeshire

Merthyr Tydfil

Torfaen

Gloucester

Cheltenham

Catswold

Neath Port Talbot

Rhondda Cynon Taf

Caerphilly

Swansea

Bridgend

Newport

Stroud

South Gloucestershire

Cardiff

Bristol

Swindon

Vale of Glamorgan

North Somerset

Bath & North East Somerset

Wiltshire

West Somerset

North Devon

Sedgemoor

Mendip

Torridge

Mid Devon

Taunton Deane

South Somerset

North Dorset

East Dorset

West Devon

Exeter

East Devon

West Dorset

Cornwall

Teignbridge

Purbeck

Poole

Bournemouth

Christchurch

Plymouth

South Hams

Torbay

Weymouth & Portland

Isles of Scilly

EAST, LONDON AND SOUTH EAST

POPULATION DENSITIES

By 2011 the population density of the UK was 2.6 people
for every hectare of land available (a hectare is an area
of land equivalent to a square with sides 100 metres
long, and thus with an area of 10,000m²). In 2001 the
UK population density had been 2.4 people per hectare
(lower than in some other European countries and many
parts of Europe). No significant amounts of new land have
been created or have disappeared. What has happened
is that the population has risen by 7.4%, and so the
overall density of the population has risen by 7.4%, an
extra 0.2 people for every 10,000m² in just 10 years. Most
people in the UK have not experienced this rise, however,
with 68% seeing a fall or no noticeable rise in population
density where they live. In contrast, 5% of the population
in 2011 lived in areas that had seen an additional
10 people or more per hectare since 2001.

A traditional map version of the population density
cartogram shown above right would look mostly red. This
would coincide with the countryside, and there is a great
deal of countryside in the UK. However, most residents in
those red areas do not live in the countryside, but in towns
within the countryside. Towns are tiny dots hardly visible
on a map of the size that could be included in this book.
While traditional maps are good for showing agricultural
information (crops, livestock grazing, forestry) where
you are interested in acreage, information about people is
best shown on a cartogram where the areas represent the
numbers of people.

By 2011 the four most densely populated areas of the
UK were Islington (139 people per hectare); Kensington
& Chelsea (131 per hectare); Hackney and Tower Hamlets
(both 129 people per hectare). All had experienced
increases in density of over 20 people per hectare since
2001, except for Kensington & Chelsea, which had
experienced a remarkable population *decline* as house
prices in that borough rose quickly and 'investors'
bought mansions or flats to leave empty (or use as their
occasional 'London residence'). Kensington & Chelsea
contrasts greatly with the other areas of the 2001–11
population (and hence density) decline: South Tyneside
(-0.7 people per hectare); Sefton (-0.6); Knowsley
(-0.5); Sunderland (-0.4); Barrow-in-Furness (-0.3);

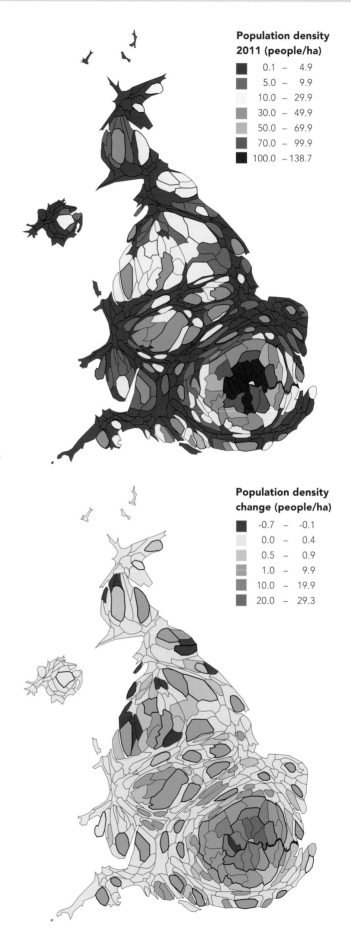

**Population density
2011 (people/ha)**

- 0.1 – 4.9
- 5.0 – 9.9
- 10.0 – 29.9
- 30.0 – 49.9
- 50.0 – 69.9
- 70.0 – 99.9
- 100.0 – 138.7

**Population density
change (people/ha)**

- -0.7 – -0.1
- 0.0 – 0.4
- 0.5 – 0.9
- 1.0 – 9.9
- 10.0 – 19.9
- 20.0 – 29.3

and Burnley, East Dunbartonshire, Redcar & Cleveland, West Dunbartonshire and Inverclyde (all -0.2 people per hectare). In contrast to Central London, the population has declined in these other areas in recent years partly because of deindustrialisation decades earlier, and the deaths of the elderly and their spouses who used to work in those industries and who stayed in those areas.

All the areas of greatest density increase are in London, except for Manchester (+9.5 people per hectare) and Leicester (+6.8). The lowest densities in 2011 were recorded in Eilean Siar (Outer Hebrides), Highland and Argyll & Bute – all with just a net additional 0.1 person per hectare. The Shetland Islands had been in this group in 2001, but population density there had risen by one person per hectare by 2011. The graph below shows that most people in the UK have not been living in areas of population growth during 2001–11. Only a small proportion of the UK population were living in the places in which population numbers and hence density had risen greatly since 2001.

Population experiencing a rise in population density since 2001, UK 2011 %

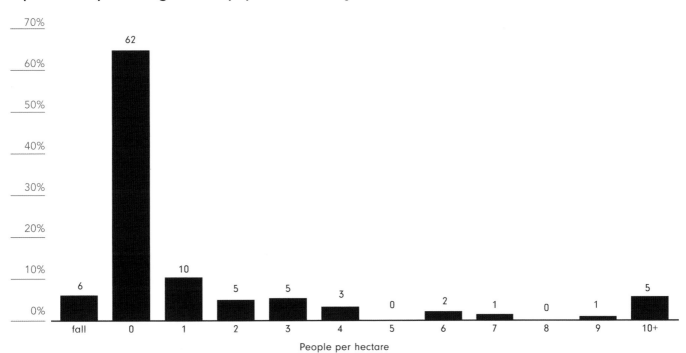

People per hectare

POPULATION POTENTIAL

Population potential is a measure of how near you are to everyone else. The formula to measure potential is the sum of all people in every other district when each group of people are divided by how far away they are from the centre of your district, with distance here measured in metres. The population of your district is not included, but every other district in the UK is. A low population potential is a measure of remoteness. The place with the highest population potential in the UK in 2011 was the City of London, with a surrounding pressure of 1,292 people per metre away from its centre. This is 149 people per metre higher than the measure recorded in 2001, and shows how population growth was concentrated in London in the 2000s. It is almost exclusively within London that people have experienced the arrival of large numbers of additional people, far more than have left overall.

In 2011 the lowest population potential in the UK was recorded in the Shetland Isles at 79.2 people per metre, five higher than in 2001. Nowhere has population potential fallen. Since 2011 the population of the UK has risen by 0.7% in the year to mid-2012, 0.6% to 2013, with those increases then accelerating slightly to 0.8% in the year to mid-2014 when a combination of more births (777,400) than deaths (551,200) and high net migration increased the total UK population by 491,000 in just 12 months. However, deaths will soon increase as the population ages: the median age of people in the UK by mid-2014 was 40, the highest ever recorded.

The most recently released statistics show population potential to be rising fastest in the very heart of London. In the year to mid-2014, the following 10 areas were estimated to have had the greatest population increases in just one year: City of London (+5.5%); Tower Hamlets (+4.1%); Westminster (+2.8%); Forest Heath (+2.6%); Islington (+2.5%); Coventry (+2.3%); Hackney and Camden (both +2.2%); and Oxford and Exeter (both +2.1%). The greatest falls were smaller, but also all a long way from London, being recorded in Richmondshire (-2.2%); Ceredigion (-0.7%); Blackpool, Harrogate, Inverclyde and Eilean Siar (all -0.6%); Argyll & Bute, Blackburn with Darwen and Oadby & Wigston (all -0.4%); and North Ayrshire (-0.3%). The graph below

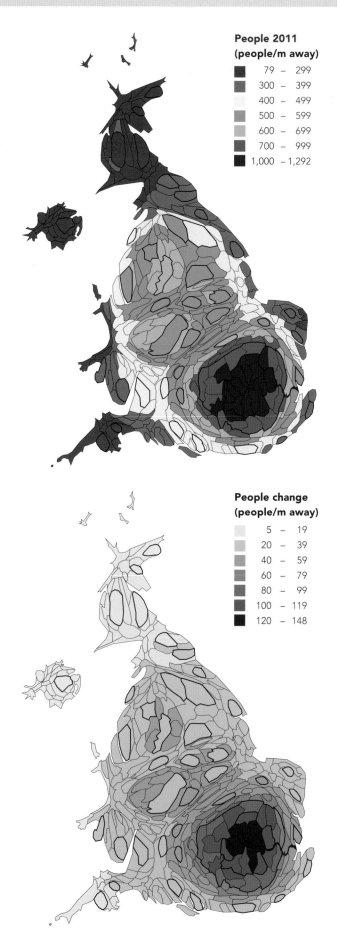

**People 2011
(people/m away)**

■	79 – 299
■	300 – 399
□	400 – 499
■	500 – 599
■	600 – 699
■	700 – 999
■	1,000 – 1,292

**People change
(people/m away)**

□	5 – 19
■	20 – 39
■	40 – 59
■	60 – 79
■	80 – 99
■	100 – 119
■	120 – 148

shows that 80% of the population live in areas where the population potential has increased by less than 50 people per metre. Only a few people in a few parts of the UK with increases of over 50 people per metre are feeling much more actual population pressure.

Population experiencing a rise in population potential since 2001, UK 2011 %

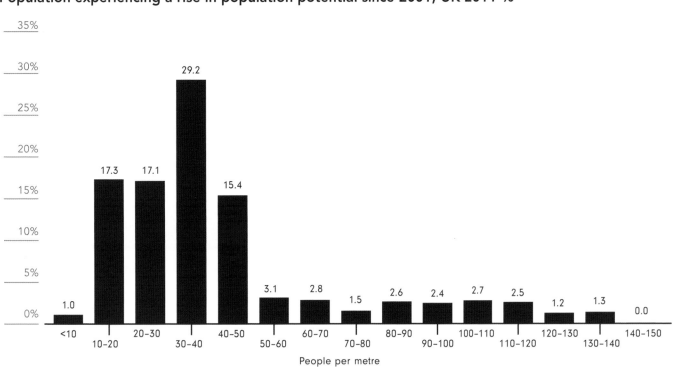

People per metre

BREADLINE POOR

Population counts are the very simplest things the Census provides. The Census is also the basis for making estimates of the distribution of poverty in the UK. A formula was used following the 2001 Census to estimate how many people were poor in each area (see the Appendix for details of the formula). Using that same formula with 2011 data will tend to underestimate the numbers of people who are 'poor': people who cannot partake in the normal activities of society by dint of having too little income or wealth. Poverty has risen in the UK since 2001, as indicated by the rise in people having to resort to food banks. The conservative estimate shown here reveals that the greatest concentration of poverty remains in London, where poverty is strengthening its grip.

The 20 areas with the highest rates of poverty as a proportion of local households in 2011 were Hackney (51.1%); Newham (49.3%); Tower Hamlets (49.0%); Southwark (47.4%) followed by 10 nearby London boroughs; Glasgow (43.2%); Manchester (40.9%); Liverpool (39.9%); West Dunbartonshire (39.4%); Nottingham (39.0%); and Belfast (38.6%). It is remarkable that by 2011 there were 14 London boroughs with higher poverty rates than Glasgow and Belfast. In 2001 there were just five such London districts with greater poverty rates than Glasgow: Tower Hamlets, Hackney, Southwark, Newham and Islington.

By 2011 poverty was most rare in the following areas, often near to London and all in the South, but in all it had risen slightly since 2001: Hart (13.8%); Wokingham (14.0%); Surrey Heath (15.6%); Harborough and East Dorset (both 16.1%). The largest increases in poverty have been in Outer London and just outside London: Enfield (+5.6%); Slough (+4.6%); Brent (4.2%) and Croydon (+4.1%). There have been large falls in poverty, most significantly where poverty was highest in 2011 in Tower Hamlets (-4.2%); but also in Liverpool (-3.8%) and Glasgow (-3.0%). Here unemployment fell, central heating was installed in many homes and housing stock was improved between 2001 and 2011.

Sometimes poverty falls because the poor are moved out of an area. The graph below shows that those areas that have seen poverty rates fall by 5 percentage points

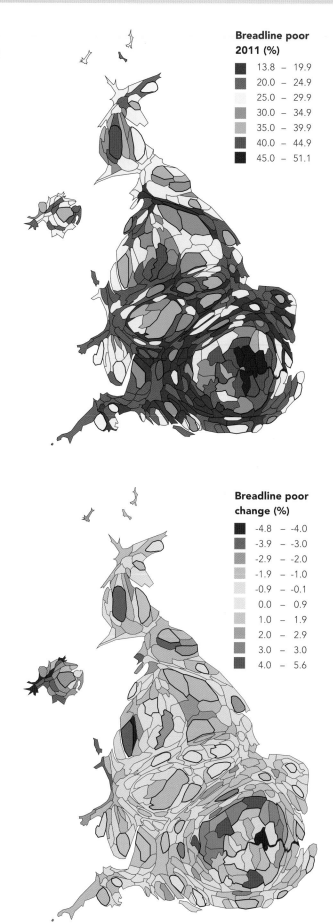

Breadline poor 2011 (%)

- 13.8 – 19.9
- 20.0 – 24.9
- 25.0 – 29.9
- 30.0 – 34.9
- 35.0 – 39.9
- 40.0 – 44.9
- 45.0 – 51.1

Breadline poor change (%)

- -4.8 – -4.0
- -3.9 – -3.0
- -2.9 – -2.0
- -1.9 – -1.0
- -0.9 – -0.1
- 0.0 – 0.9
- 1.0 – 1.9
- 2.0 – 2.9
- 3.0 – 3.0
- 4.0 – 5.6

since 2001 still have an average of 40% of all households within their boundaries living in poverty. Unsurprisingly, those areas where poverty is rising the fastest have some of the highest poverty rates now, but not quite as high as where it has fallen. The graph below makes this clear, and also reveals that the lowest rates of poverty are a quarter of households being poor in areas of almost no change in that rate since 2001. The bimodal nature of the distribution of poverty change in that same graph below suggests that new areas of greater poverty are being formed in the South, while the falls in poverty in the poorest parts of the North have been too small to ensure these are not still some of our very poorest of places. The Y-axis of the graph does not start at zero because then the trend would be far harder to see, and we have never had any area in the UK with poverty rates of zero.

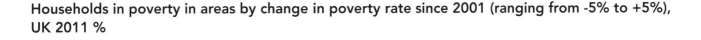

Households in poverty in areas by change in poverty rate since 2001 (ranging from -5% to +5%), UK 2011 %

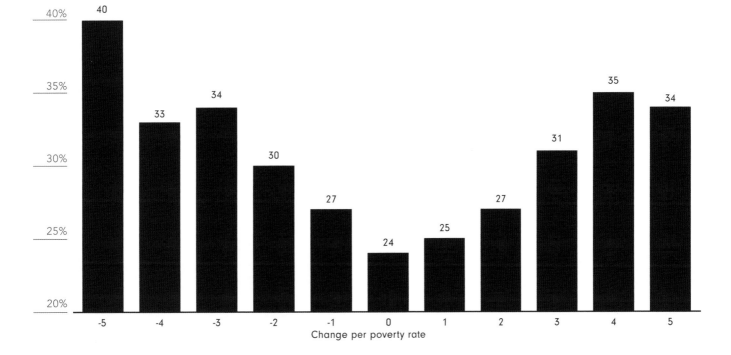

AVERAGE

The Census is extremely poor at measuring many things, mostly because the questions asked in it have not been greatly updated since the early 1970s. Permanent illness preventing work was first asked in 1981, ethnicity in 1991, and religion added in 2001. In 2011 the main new questions were about nationality and immigration, reflecting the obsession of the government and of much of the media. For many decades in the US people have been asked about their incomes on the Census form, while in the UK that question has never been asked. However, we can now use tax data to reveal what such a question might have revealed in 2011 had it been asked! The 10 areas with the highest and lowest mean incomes from employment, self-employment or a pension are given in the table below. This also shows how much less income middle (median) earners receive each year, with what percentage of the mean that is.

Average annual income, Local Authorities, 2010/11 £

	Mean	Median	%
Top 10			
Kensington & Chelsea	128,000	31,700	25
City of London	127,000	61,300	48
Westminster	83,400	31,400	38
Camden	67,100	29,400	44
Elmbridge	57,200	27,000	47
Richmond upon Thames	56,300	30,600	54
Hammersmith & Fulham	52,000	27,100	52
Wandsworth	50,700	29,000	57
South Bucks	50,600	26,700	53
Islington	47,600	26,100	55
Bottom 10			
Moyle	20,200	14,300	71
Leicester	20,100	16,200	81
Weymouth & Portland	20,100	17,000	85
Boston	20,100	15,900	79
Kingston upon Hull	19,900	17,100	86
Sandwell	19,800	17,000	86
Blackpool	19,500	16,600	85
Stoke-on-Trent	19,500	16,600	85
Strabane	19,100	15,600	82
Blaenau Gwent	18,000	16,500	92

The above areas are the extremes: 97% of people live in places where the median income is between £15,000 and £25,000, although it should be noted that this is

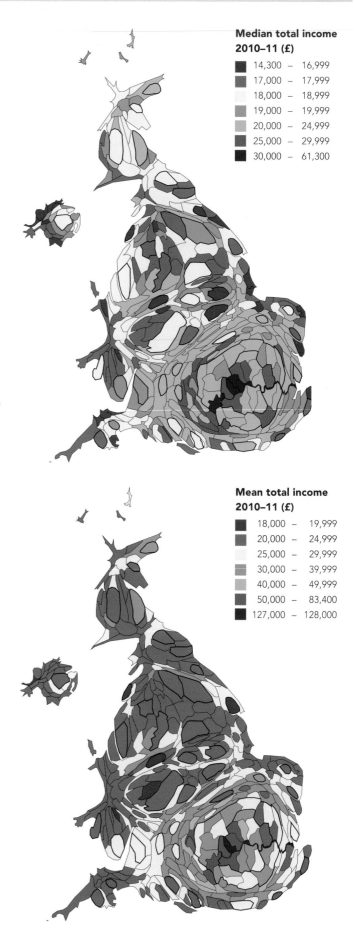

Median total income 2010–11 (£)

■	14,300 – 16,999
■	17,000 – 17,999
□	18,000 – 18,999
■	19,000 – 19,999
■	20,000 – 24,999
■	25,000 – 29,999
■	30,000 – 61,300

Mean total income 2010–11 (£)

■	18,000 – 19,999
■	20,000 – 24,999
□	25,000 – 29,999
■	30,000 – 39,999
■	40,000 – 49,999
■	50,000 – 83,400
■	127,000 – 128,000

still a huge income range. This is of individual incomes in a year of all those in work or receiving a pension. The graph below illustrates that most people (97%) live in areas where median incomes are below £26,000 a year, and over a quarter of the UK population (26.4%) live in areas where the median annual income is £18,000 (£49 a day), to the nearest £1,000. Households relying solely on benefits are not included here, and so real total median household incomes will be lower in most areas than the figures shown below. Most people in most of the UK are getting by on what the very rich would consider a pittance.

Population living in areas by median annual income of local employees and pensioners, UK 2010/11
£ thousands per year

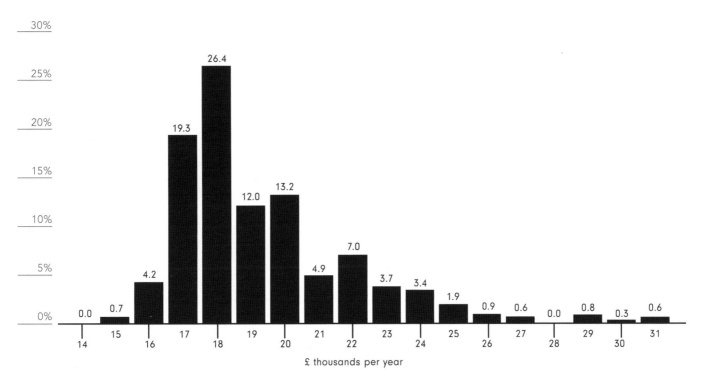

£ thousands per year

RICH

There are two ways in which people can be very well off, and occasionally they are well off in both ways. One is to be rich, to have a high annual income; the other is to be wealthy and to hold a lot of money in various forms. The extremely wealthy also tend to be rich as their wealth holdings generate an income without them having to work at all. Below these extremely wealthy people are the very highly paid but not yet wealthy. These two maps give a hint as to where the rich are concentrated. They show the mean average income received by people who are either self-employed or employees in each Local Authority district according to Her Majesty's Revenue and Customs (HMRC) records for the 2010/11 tax year.

Self-employed people who were residents of the City of London paid tax on a mean income of £160,000 in the Census year 2011. That same year in Kensington & Chelsea the arithmetic mean income of the self-employed was £128,000, and in Westminster it was £101,000. Even in these three areas, because of the skewed nature of income distributions, most people will be earning far less; in fact, the reported median earnings for the self-employed in these three districts was £79,400, and then just £12,500 and £12,800 respectively – so just a tiny proportion of even the residents of the City of London, Kensington & Chelsea and Westminster are very high earners.

The lowest mean average self-employed income reported is of £10,700, recorded in Blackpool that same year. The four areas with the lowest recorded mean employee incomes were Strabane (£17,200 a year); Limavady (£17,500); West Somerset (£17,700); and Blaenau Gwent (£17,800). In contrast, the highest mean employee incomes were recorded in the City of London (£121,000); Kensington & Chelsea (£113,000); and Westminster (£70,300). Again, the respective median employee annual pay in each of those three districts is much lower, at £57,600, £28,700 and £27,500 a year per person respectively. Outside of these places are found the 99.4% of people in the UK who live in areas depicted by the following graph. The rich really are very rare – even in rich areas.

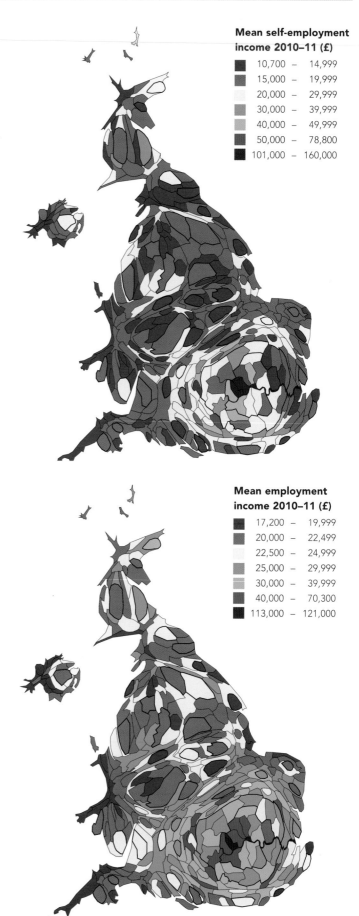

Mean self-employment income 2010–11 (£)

10,700	– 14,999
15,000	– 19,999
20,000	– 29,999
30,000	– 39,999
40,000	– 49,999
50,000	– 78,800
101,000	– 160,000

Mean employment income 2010–11 (£)

17,200	– 19,999
20,000	– 22,499
22,500	– 24,999
25,000	– 29,999
30,000	– 39,999
40,000	– 70,300
113,000	– 121,000

Population living in areas by mean annual income of local self-employed, UK 2010/11 £ thousands per year

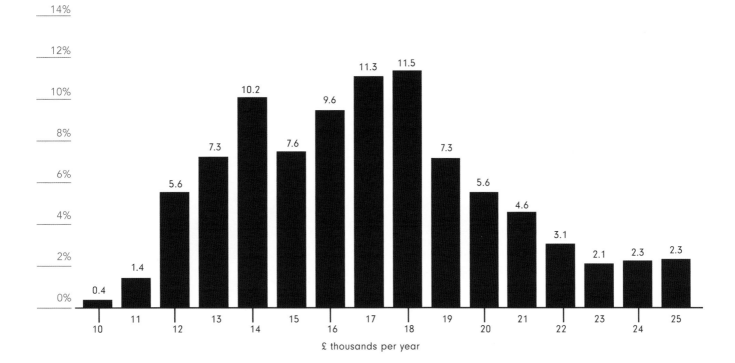

£ thousands per year

WEALTHY

In the past we have tried to use Census data to estimate the numbers of wealthy people living in particular areas. However, proxies such as outright ownership of detached homes with seven or more rooms and multiple car ownership have becomes less good indicators of extreme wealth as even a small two-bed flat within Central London has become worth a fortune and cars have become cheaper to purchase. Because of these changes, we rely here on records published by HMRC, of the number of people's estates that became liable for inheritance tax in the 2010/11 tax year as a proportion of all those who died in that year. Most people leave little in way of 'an estate' when they die.

In only a tiny number of districts are more than 10% of estates liable for inheritance tax on death: Kensington & Chelsea (18%); Elmbridge, Chichester and Richmond upon Thames (all 14%); Westminster (13%); Epsom & Ewell (12%); Guildford and Windsor & Maidenhead (both 11%); and South Bucks, Waverley, Barnet and Camden (all 10%). In great contrast, in 220 Local Authority districts too few people died with enough wealth for any inheritance rate to be recordable. Another way of seeing how little wealth most people have is to look at the median income of pensioners. Most people in the UK (88%) live in areas where the median pension is an annual income of between £10,000 and £12,000 a year – or about £30 a day. This illustrates how little wealth most of the elderly in the UK have. And the elderly have more wealth than the rest of the population.

The lowest (median) pensions are found in Northern Ireland, in Magherafelt, where the middle-income pensioner lives on £6,160 a year, or £17 a day. The highest median pension income is found in the City of London, at £16,800, or £47 a day. Although the median-income pensioner in the City of London has almost three times as much a year to live off compared to the median in Magherafelt, even pensioners in the City of London are not rich. In fact, just 2.9% of those who live out their lives and die in the City of London are rich enough to pay inheritance tax (although most very rich people would be likely to leave the City when they retire). The really rich are a very small proportion of the population living

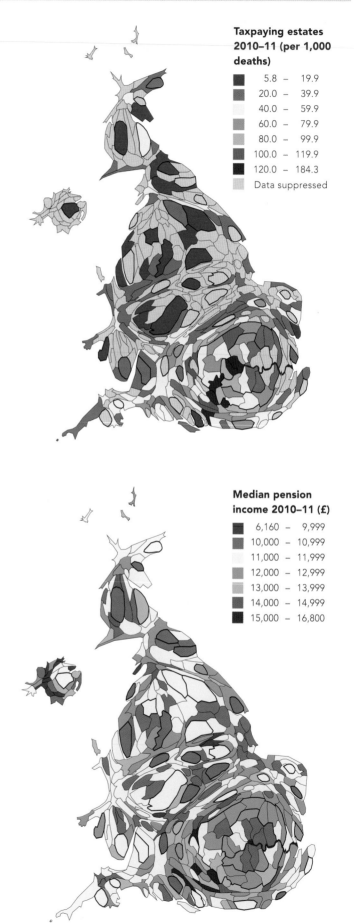

Taxpaying estates 2010–11 (per 1,000 deaths)

- 5.8 – 19.9
- 20.0 – 39.9
- 40.0 – 59.9
- 60.0 – 79.9
- 80.0 – 99.9
- 100.0 – 119.9
- 120.0 – 184.3
- Data suppressed

Median pension income 2010–11 (£)

- 6,160 – 9,999
- 10,000 – 10,999
- 11,000 – 11,999
- 12,000 – 12,999
- 13,000 – 13,999
- 14,000 – 14,999
- 15,000 – 16,800

in a small and select set of areas. And even there they are unusual. Most are only just in the 'really rich' bracket, only just rich enough to possibly have to pay inheritance tax when they die. However, the wealth held by those both a little and a lot richer than them is truly enormous. One day the Census, or future surveys, might begin to ask about assets and wealth – about people's pension pots and how many other properties they may own.

Population living in areas by median annual income of local pensioners, UK 2010/11 £ thousands per year

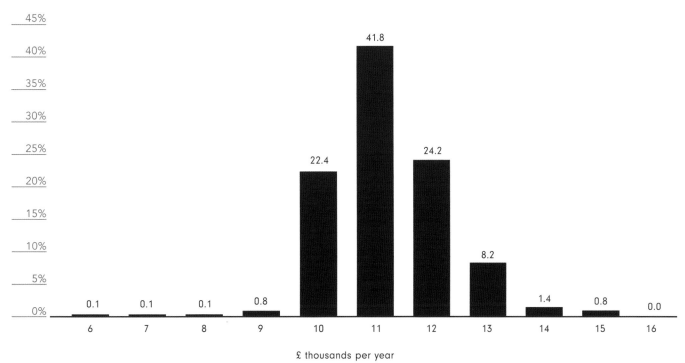

£ thousands per year

ONS CLASSIFICATION

Our final map, offered by way of introduction, is the ONS'
own classification of areas based on the data collected
in the 2011 Census. In the conclusion to this atlas we
present our own alternative classification, but as a simple
introduction to Census mapping, the one shown here can
be useful to consider how the body that collects Census
data both understands and describes it. We can also use
the ONS classification to look at other data. For example,
there are 77 Local Authority districts labelled by the ONS
as 'Mining Heritage & Manufacturing' centres. On average
in these places just 0.3% of the population were affluent
enough to qualify for paying inheritance tax on their
deaths in 2011; that proportion rose to 0.4% in 2012 and
to 0.5% in 2013. Slightly better off are the 53 areas labelled
'Scottish & Northern Irish Countryside' in the map, in
which those respective proportions were 0.6%, 0.7% and
0.9%; still less than one person in every 100 had been dying with enough wealth to qualify to pay inheritance tax.
Here we combine Census and tax data to show just how
few people are very rich by the 2011 ONS classification
of areas.

Next in the wealth ranking using the ONS classification
come the 31 'Business & Education Centres', mainly in
Northern cities. Here, by 2013, 2.2% of the population
were paying inheritance tax on deaths. Contrast that
with the 100 Local Authority districts in the 'English
& Welsh Countryside' cluster where 2.6% were eligible
to pay inheritance tax on their deaths in 2013. This is
significantly lower than the 3.1% of residents in the 27
'Coast & Heritage' Local Authorities, which is lower in
turn than the 3.4% proportion in the 39 'Suburban Traits'
areas, which is lower than the 5.9% of people in the 59
so-called 'Prosperous England' Local Authority districts
where still some 94.1% of the population die leaving too
little money to qualify for paying the tax; until finally we
come to the 20 'London Cosmopolitan' areas in which
6.6% of people pay that tax on their deaths and 93.4%
do not.

In 2015 one person in every 15 paying inheritance
tax in the most prosperous areas of London was seen
as too many by the government, and the threshold was
announced to be rising in the near future, so that unless

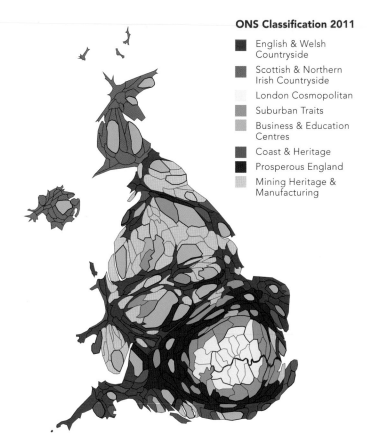

ONS Classification 2011

- English & Welsh Countryside
- Scottish & Northern Irish Countryside
- London Cosmopolitan
- Suburban Traits
- Business & Education Centres
- Coast & Heritage
- Prosperous England
- Mining Heritage & Manufacturing

you left wealth in excess of £1 million (including equity in property), you would not pay the tax as long as you died after 2020. All the percentages quoted here will have now fallen as a result of the rise in that threshold. Hardly anyone pays inheritance tax now, and fewer will in the future, but the Census can be used to tell us much more about the places where the few who do pay the tax live. The Census can illuminate this by showing the underlying context – and highlighting what is normal and what is not. For instance look at the variation in the graph below.

People paying inheritance tax, ONS area %

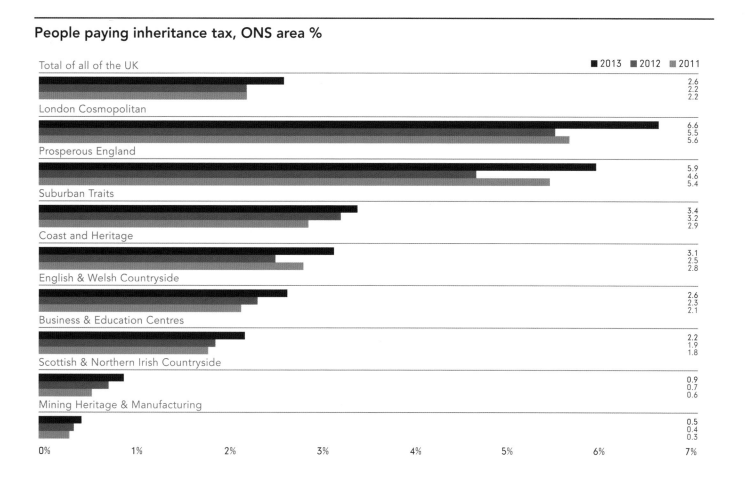

	2013	2012	2011
Total of all of the UK	2.6	2.2	2.2
London Cosmopolitan	6.6	5.5	5.6
Prosperous England	5.9	4.6	5.4
Suburban Traits	3.4	3.2	2.9
Coast and Heritage	3.1	2.5	2.8
English & Welsh Countryside	2.6	2.3	2.1
Business & Education Centres	2.2	1.9	1.8
Scottish & Northern Irish Countryside	0.9	0.7	0.6
Mining Heritage & Manufacturing	0.5	0.4	0.3

Rise in population in the UK
from 2001 to 2011.

MEN
WOMEN

Sex, Age and Marriage

+2.5 million

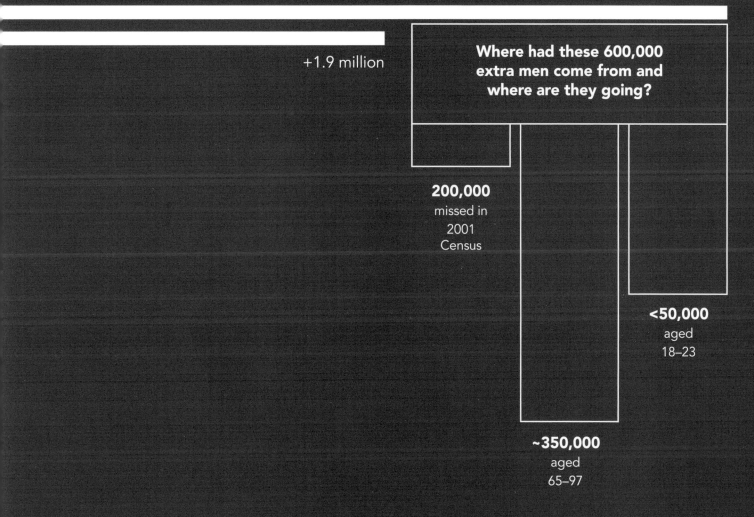

+1.9 million

Where had these 600,000 extra men come from and where are they going?

200,000
missed in
2001
Census

<50,000
aged
18–23

~350,000
aged
65–97

Sex, Age and Marriage

The Census shows a particular moment in time. When we compare one Census to previous ones, it helps us to understand how places are changing. Take, for example, trends in the age of mothers giving birth, which are reported separately for the four countries of the UK.

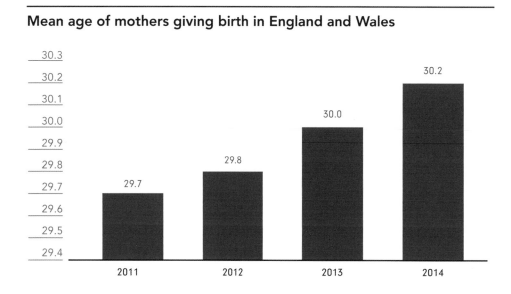

Mean age of mothers giving birth in England and Wales

Births in England and Wales peaked in the year after the 2011 Census, before falling quickly in 2013 and 2014. In 2012 they had reached their highest total since 1972, and the total fertility rate, the number of children each woman was expected to have, hit 1.94, its highest point since 1973. By 2014 total fertility was down to 1.83. Fertility was not falling because there were fewer people of childbearing age; the mean age at which women were giving birth rose from 29.7 in 2011 to 30.2 in 2014, and the graph above shows that this increase has been accelerating. Births within marriage fell from 9.1% of married women under age 45 giving birth in 2011, to 8.8% in 2014. Those same figures for women of the same ages, but not in a marriage, fell from 5.2% to 5.0% over the same period. If marriage rates increase, births can rise, but many other factors influence how the population of the UK is changing.

All these statistics are readily available although difficult to access if you do not know where to look. These shown in the graph above come from the ONS 'Birth summary tables, England and Wales 2014', published in July 2015. Very little commentary and analysis of these tables is provided, however, and if you want to know what is happening across the UK as a whole, you need to find separate statistics for Northern Ireland and Scotland, and work out how to combine them.

The last detailed analysis of trends in cohabitation, marriage, age and number of births appeared in the autumn 2011 145th edition of *Population Trends*, and charted the situation up to 2007, almost a decade ago.[1] A great deal has changed since then, but ongoing and growing government cuts to spending since 2010 mean that most key trends are no longer studied and reported on.

For 126 years, from 1849 through to 1975, the Registrar General published quarterly returns on aspects of the UK population. In 1975 these returns were replaced by the then Office of Population, Censuses and Surveys' (later ONS') quarterly publication *Population Trends*. A total of 145 volumes of demographic interest were issued all the way through from 1975 to the autumn of 2011, when the series was abruptly ended. Official demographic publications ceased to be routinely issued due to the imposition of some of the 2010 coalition government's very first cuts in public spending. At the time, Chris Smith, the editor of the government's official demographic publication, wrote that:

Last year the journal moved to a web-only format as print output was ended. Now, with the introduction of a new and more versatile web system, the ONS is replacing the journal with a mode of delivery that points the way to the future.

Sadly that did not happen. Rather than be replaced by online alternatives, the material that was usually included in *Population Trends*, including a great deal of analysis of the annual population estimates, simply ceased to be created. Instead, just the most basic series of statistics have been continued, and not all of these. These and many other cuts to our national statistical service have made the creation of this atlas far harder, but also all the more necessary.

This atlas was harder to produce because we could not simply look up the most recent analysis to see what was most interesting, and to confirm our initial impressions of what the data was showing us. So it has become more important to do this analysis, because what is shown in the following pages is almost always now not easily available.

The UK population is rapidly changing, and far fewer people are aware of how these changes are occurring in detail than has been the case for many years. The implications of this lacuna of information are great. Without knowing what is going on, there is a temptation to believe that what has happened before is simply continuing along its course. Do that, and you will soon find that you do not have enough schools and hospitals where they are most needed. Or think of a far simpler assumption – is London *still* filling up with more young women than young men? The answer is 'no', but only the Census provides enough detail to know that.

SEX

The City of London, nearby gentrifying Newham, and the long-ago gentrified borough of Westminster head the league table of areas that experienced an influx of men during the 2000s. Within London, only the borough of Kingston upon Thames did not see a greater influx of men than of women, in the decade that saw the finance industries rise up, and then crash. The fourth highest rise in men was recorded in Bournemouth. This was telling because men's mortality in old age has been falling faster than women's. By 2011 there were more men alive to retire to such areas, and to alter the national picture too. By 2011, 32.3 million people in the UK were women and 31.0 million were men. Ten years earlier the gap was wider.

Between 2001 and 2011 the number of men living in the UK rose by 2.5 million and the number of women by only 1.9 million. So where had the extra 600,000 men come from and where are they going? The ONS suggests that 200,000 were here all along, but had been missed by the 2001 Census. Most of the rest were aged 65–97. These were men who had not died in the 2000s as older male mortality improved faster than older female mortality at that time. Less than 50,000 of these extra men were aged 18–23, and many of them may have been student in-migrants. The parts of the country dominated by older populations remain more female, but now the direction of change over time is beginning to smooth the picture out rather than exacerbate the differences, as it did between earlier Censuses.

The higher map shows that a greater proportion of people are female in the far South of England and some other coastal areas. Some cities have very low proportions of people who are female. The lower map shows that the proportion of people who are female has risen in many areas surrounding London, surrounding Belfast, and in the far North of Scotland. The proportion who are female has fallen most in East London.

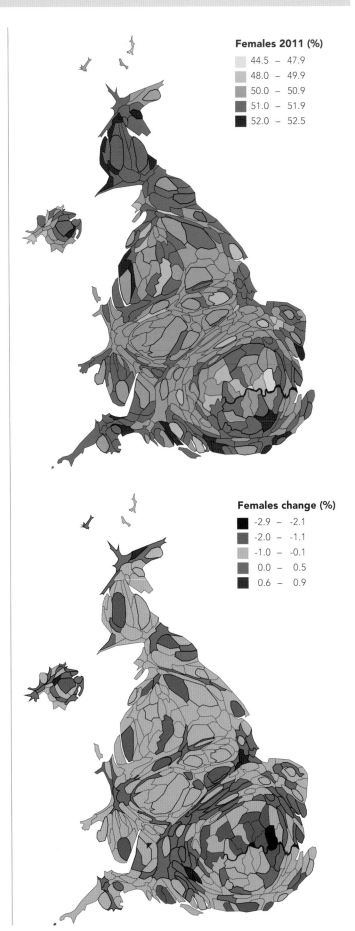

Females 2011 (%)

	44.5 – 47.9
	48.0 – 49.9
	50.0 – 50.9
	51.0 – 51.9
	52.0 – 52.5

Females change (%)

	-2.9 – -2.1
	-2.0 – -1.1
	-1.0 – -0.1
	0.0 – 0.5
	0.6 – 0.9

People who are female, UK %

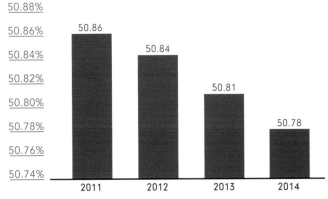

BABIES AND TODDLERS

In 2011 there were 2.4 million children aged 0–2, compared to 2.0 million counted in the 2001 Census, a huge rise on the numbers recorded just a decade earlier. This 20% rise in very young children is partly accounted for by more people being of typical childbearing age by 2011. There was a 10% rise in those aged 25–29 in the UK over that same time period (whose numbers rose from 3.9 million to 4.3 million), but more children is also the product of a rapid rise in childbearing among older adults up until 2011, especially those living in London. The largest rise in the country was recorded in Barking & Dagenham, where an additional 1.7% of the population were aged under three by 2011, amounting to over 4,000 extra children needing schooling by 2016. Nearby, Slough and Reading experienced the second and third greatest proportionate rises, and an increase of over 5,000 extra children in a decade for those two areas combined.

By 2011 the housing market in the UK had been stagnating for three years. Families who might have normally moved home as their young children aged often found they could not move as easily as before. The fall in births after 2012 resulted in a sharp decline in the proportion of those in the UK who were babies and toddlers by 2014. It is very possible that the fall in births since the Census was taken is also related to changes in housing that, as we show in the *Homes and Commuting* chapter, were already evident in that latest Census when it is compared to the situation in 2001. As housing became less and less affordable after 2012, the number of people becoming parents fell.

People aged 0–2, UK %

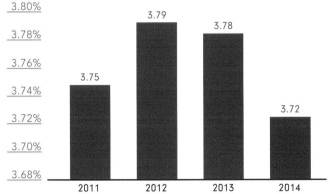

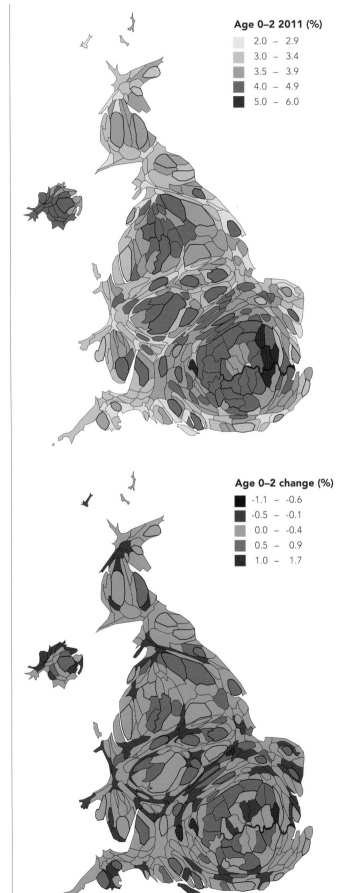

Age 0–2 2011 (%)
- 2.0 – 2.9
- 3.0 – 3.4
- 3.5 – 3.9
- 4.0 – 4.9
- 5.0 – 6.0

Age 0–2 change (%)
- -1.1 – -0.6
- -0.5 – -0.1
- 0.0 – -0.4
- 0.5 – 0.9
- 1.0 – 1.7

CHILDREN

The number of children aged 3–17 fell slightly, from 11.3 million in 2001 to 11.1 million by 2011, due to fewer births during 2002–05. However, a rise in births in the UK after that point almost completely reversed the effect of that fall. The oldest children in the comparisons made here, those aged 17 in 2001, would have been born in 1984.

In 2001 the seven districts with the highest proportion of their populations being children were all to be found in Northern Ireland. By 2011, both Blackburn & Darwen in Lancashire and Bradford in Yorkshire had entered the top seven. Birmingham was 11th. First placed was Barking & Dagenham, where 22.8% of all people were children aged 3–17 in 2011. In London in this period many children who would normally have migrated with their families out of London did not do so before 2011 due to the 2008 housing market crash. By ages 12 and 13 they were still living where they had been at ages 8 and 9. Having not moved at those ages many families then try to stay put, at least until the children become young adults.

During the 2000s there was gentrification in many parts of London, which made staying in some boroughs very hard for families who were renting privately. Two of the areas recording the largest falls in children and probably the greatest rise in gentrification in this period were Tower Hamlets and Hackney. Since the Census the proportion of those aged 3–17 declined in 2012, stabilised in 2013, and showed a slight increase in 2014, this increase being due to the peak in births in 2011. We now know that in future the size of this age group will soon decline as that birth rate peak has passed.

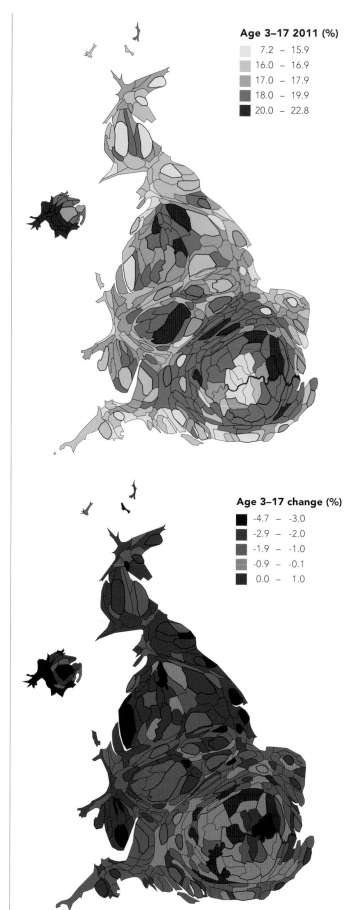

Age 3–17 2011 (%)

	7.2 – 15.9
	16.0 – 16.9
	17.0 – 17.9
	18.0 – 19.9
	20.0 – 22.8

Age 3–17 change (%)

	-4.7 – -3.0
	-2.9 – -2.0
	-1.9 – -1.0
	-0.9 – -0.1
	0.0 – 1.0

People aged 3–17, UK %

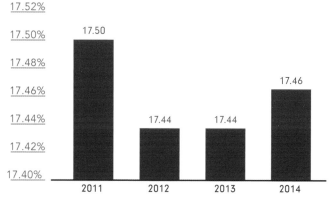

COMING OF AGE

There were 2.2 million people aged 18, 19 or 20 in the UK in 2001; this rose to 2.5 million by 2011. Half of the rise was due to more people being born 18–20 years before the 2011 Census compared to 2001. The other half of the rise was due to more people of those ages having migrated to the UK than had migrated out. A large number of those migrants were overseas students who had arrived to study in UK universities in the three years prior to the 2011 Census being held. By 2011 the largest proportions of the population being of these ages were in Nottingham (9.5%), Ceredigion, where Aberystwyth University is located (9.3%), Oxford (9.3%) and then Cambridge (9.1%). The very lowest proportions were found in the Isles of Scilly (45 people, or 2.0% of the population) and the City of London (162 people, or 2.2%).

In the 10 years to 2011 the largest increases had been where universities had been built or greatly expanded: Lincoln (+3.0%); Canterbury (+2.8%); and Newcastle upon Tyne (+2.2%). In general, the more 18-year-olds there were in a district in 2001, the greater the rise has been since. The two exceptions are Oxford and Cambridge – both only recorded a 0.1% increase in this age group. Since the Census the proportion of young adults has very slightly decreased, and that decrease should be expected to continue in the long term, unless there is a rise in overseas students coming to study in the UK.

People aged 18–20, UK %

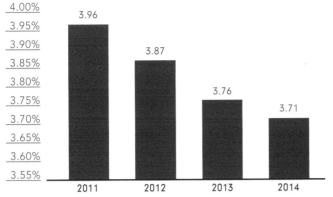

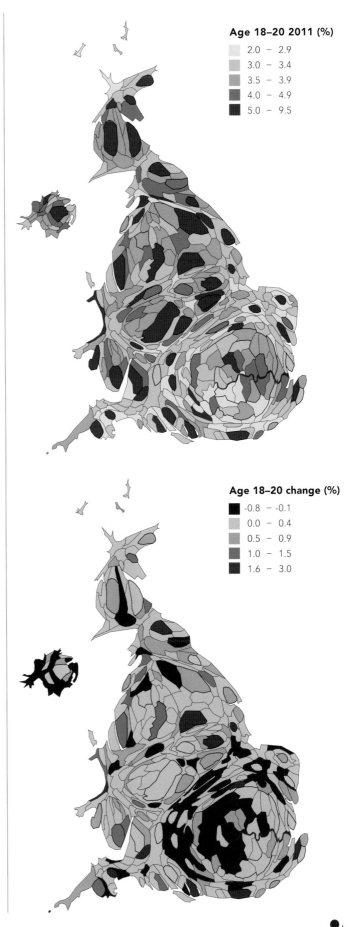

Age 18–20 2011 (%)
- 2.0 – 2.9
- 3.0 – 3.4
- 3.5 – 3.9
- 4.0 – 4.9
- 5.0 – 9.5

Age 18–20 change (%)
- -0.8 – -0.1
- 0.0 – 0.4
- 0.5 – 0.9
- 1.0 – 1.5
- 1.6 – 3.0

EARLY TWENTIES

Immigration still only accounts for just over half of the increase in the population of 21- to 24-year-olds recorded in the UK between 2001 and 2011. The other half of the reason for there being more young adults in 2011 was that women had so few babies in the late 1970s – some of the lowest numbers ever recorded. The total fertility rate fell to 1.66 in 1977. By 1987 it had risen again to 1.81 children per woman. In 2001 there were 2.8 million people aged 21–24 in the UK; by 2011 there were 3.4 million. Some 258,000 more people were in this group by 2011 due to the ageing of the larger birth cohort born in the late 1980s. On top of that, a further 335,000 of the increase was attributed to net migration.

More than a tenth of the entire populations of the following cities and boroughs are made up of people of these four years of age: Oxford (11.0%); Cambridge (10.0%); Tower Hamlets (10.2%); Manchester (10.1%); and Nottingham (10.0%). The proportion in Oxford and Cambridge had actually fallen by 0.5% and 0.7% respectively in the 10 years preceding 2011. Oxford and Cambridge may be taking more postgraduates, but both cities are pushing out an even greater number of other young adults, possibly as a result of going to university elsewhere coupled with green belt control. The only larger reductions to those of Oxford and Cambridge were found in Westminster (-1.3%) and Wandsworth (-1.4%).

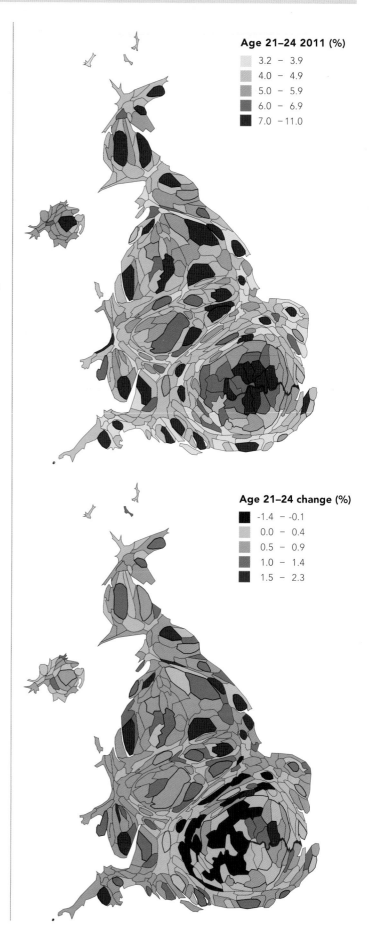

Age 21–24 2011 (%)
- 3.2 – 3.9
- 4.0 – 4.9
- 5.0 – 5.9
- 6.0 – 6.9
- 7.0 – 11.0

Age 21–24 change (%)
- -1.4 – -0.1
- 0.0 – 0.4
- 0.5 – 0.9
- 1.0 – 1.4
- 1.5 – 2.3

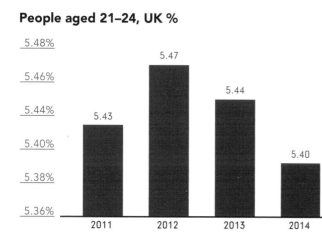

People aged 21–24, UK %

	2011	2012	2013	2014
	5.43	5.47	5.44	5.40

LATE TWENTIES

The number of people in their late twenties, those aged 25–29, rose from 3.9 million in 2001 to 4.3 million in 2011. This entire rise was due to immigration. In fact, had it not been for immigration, this age group would have fallen in size by 240,000. Because of immigration, 640,000 more people are in the UK in their late twenties, at the ages after most have finished tertiary education and when people are often fittest and at their most productive.

Eleven London boroughs recorded the highest proportions of people in this age group (of 11.8% to 15.8%), followed by Oxford (11.3%) and Manchester (11.2%). The lowest proportions were recorded in East Dorset and West Dorset. The largest increases in the decade were in gentrifying Newham (+3.8%); Hackney (+3.5%); Manchester (+2.6%); and Tower Hamlets (+2.4%). Affluent areas in a ring around London, from St Albans (-1.1%); to East Hertfordshire (-1.3%); to Wokingham (-1.3%); to Runnymede (-0.9%), have seen falls as younger adults who may have moved out of London to such areas in the past either chose not to during these years, or were unable to afford to make such moves.

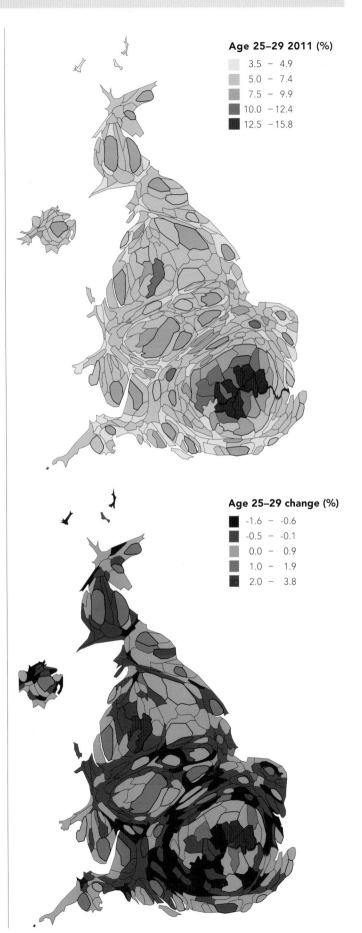

Age 25–29 2011 (%)
- 3.5 – 4.9
- 5.0 – 7.4
- 7.5 – 9.9
- 10.0 – 12.4
- 12.5 – 15.8

Age 25–29 change (%)
- -1.6 – -0.6
- -0.5 – -0.1
- 0.0 – 0.9
- 1.0 – 1.9
- 2.0 – 3.8

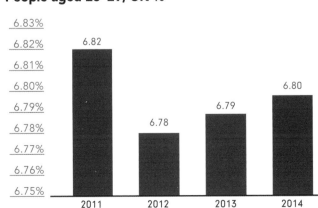

People aged 25–29, UK %

Year	%
2011	6.82
2012	6.78
2013	6.79
2014	6.80

EARLY MIDDLE AGE

There were 12.9 million people aged 30–44 in 2011, 400,000 fewer than in 2001. If it had not been for net immigration of people who are now at these ages, the fall in early middle-age population would have been almost 900,000 more. Over time this age group has come to be more and more concentrated in London, and a few other places mostly commutable to London. Part of the fall in the numbers of early middle-aged people living in rural areas is due to this age group becoming unable to afford to buy their own homes, and remaining renting in cities. The lowest proportion of people in early middle age are found in parts of the South of England from which it is harder to get to London, such as West Somerset, Rother (Bexhill-on-Sea) and North Norfolk. These were the three districts with the lowest proportions of people in this age group. It has tended to be in those areas that have had the smallest fall in the proportion of the population of these ages where the proportion of babies and toddlers has increased the most.

There was one district with a 4% increase in people aged 30–44, but almost no change in the proportion of toddlers and babies: Tower Hamlets. Tower Hamlets has become a London borough typified by a form of gentrification that tends not to also increase birth rates. Since 2011 the share of the national population aged 30–44 has fallen steadily as in-migration at these ages has not outweighed the effects of fertility being so much lower in the 1970s and 1980s compared to the 1950s and 1960s. And as more people live to older ages, we should expect this proportion to continue to fall.

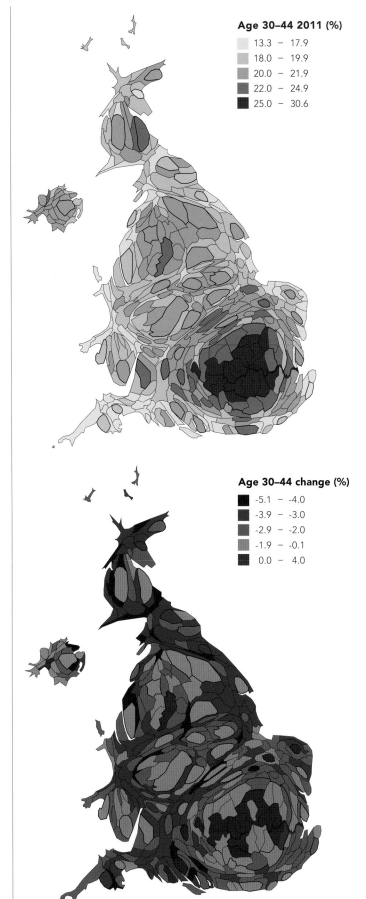

Age 30–44 2011 (%)

- 13.3 – 17.9
- 18.0 – 19.9
- 20.0 – 21.9
- 22.0 – 24.9
- 25.0 – 30.6

Age 30–44 change (%)

- -5.1 – -4.0
- -3.9 – -3.0
- -2.9 – -2.0
- -1.9 – -0.1
- 0.0 – 4.0

People aged 30–44, UK %

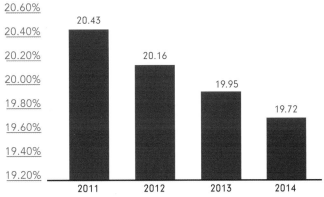

LATE MIDDLE AGE

In 2011 there were 12.4 million people in their late middle age, aged 45–59, a rise of over a million compared to a decade before, and a rise mostly due to the baby boom continuing through 1952–66 births and lower mortality at these ages in the 2000s compared to earlier years. The Local Authority districts with the highest proportions of people of these ages were rural areas, but often those located near to a major centre of employment. The five most popular areas in the UK to be late middle aged are: East Dunbartonshire, Derbyshire Dales, East Renfrewshire, South Hams and the Scottish Borders.

Over the course of the 2000s there was an increase in the proportion of people in late middle age living in more remote areas. The areas with the least people of these ages by 2011 were Islington (15.3%); Camden (15.2%); Hammersmith & Fulham (14.9%); Cambridge (14.8%); Hackney (14.4%); Manchester (14.3%); Oxford (14.3%); Wandsworth (14.2%); Newham (14.0%); and Tower Hamlets (only 11.5%). Both of the authors of this atlas fall into this category and live in two of the 10 areas where people of their advanced years are least frequently found. The 10 areas with the largest increases in the proportions of people of these ages may well be areas where job opportunities for younger people have deteriorated over the course of the last 10 years. These were Knowsley, Castlereagh, Stevenage, Derry, Carrickfergus, South Tyneside, West Dunbartonshire, Inverclyde, Omagh and Lambeth. Since 2011 the size of this age group has grown quickly, as more people become 45 than 60 each year. These are the children of the post-Second World War baby boomers, and of those who were children in that war.

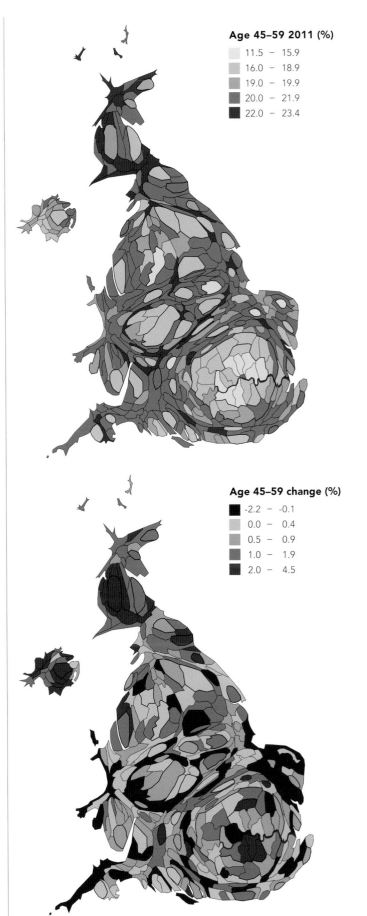

Age 45–59 2011 (%)

- 11.5 – 15.9
- 16.0 – 18.9
- 19.0 – 19.9
- 20.0 – 21.9
- 22.0 – 23.4

Age 45–59 change (%)

- -2.2 – -0.1
- 0.0 – 0.4
- 0.5 – 0.9
- 1.0 – 1.9
- 2.0 – 4.5

People aged 45–59, UK %

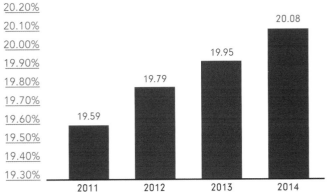

	2011	2012	2013	2014
	19.59	19.79	19.95	20.08

EARLY OLD AGE

In 2001 there were 7.8 million people aged 60–74 living in the UK. By 2011 that number had risen to 9.3 million. The increase was mostly due to the postwar baby boom of 1946–51, but mortality rates have also improved rapidly for this age group, especially for men. Nevertheless, net emigration (and deaths) resulted in there being almost a million fewer people of these ages in 2011 than those aged 10 years younger in 2001. The UK exports almost as many people as it imports, and it exports many to sunny climes just as they are beginning to enter what are traditionally their less productive years. Despite this retirement emigration, because 2.5 million extra babies were born long ago, this remains a large birth cohort, and so the age group it is passing through does not decline in size. Furthermore, the number of men in this age group has increased by 21%, whereas the number of women rose by 17%, reflecting the slightly faster improvement in the mortality of men in the 2000s.

Many past influences shape the demography of older age groups. Retirement migration – increasing because of anticipated longevity and large house price differentials – in particular shapes the geography to our demography. By 2011 West Somerset (in which 23.8% of all people were of these ages in 2011) was the most favoured early retirement location, and Tower Hamlets (5.5%) the least favoured. The largest increases have been recorded in Maldon (Essex), Wyre Forest (Worcestershire), South Hams (Devon) and Castle Point (Essex). In general, demographic changes have been greater in all directions in the South than elsewhere in the UK over the course of the 2000s. The growth of this group since 2011 has been rapid as more people turn 60 than 75 each year.

Age 60–74 2011 (%)
5.5 – 9.9
10.0 – 13.9
14.0 – 15.9
16.0 – 19.9
20.0 – 23.8

Age 60–74 change (%)
-3.1 – -0.1
0.0 – 1.9
2.0 – 2.9
3.0 – 3.9
4.0 – 5.9

People aged 60–74, UK %

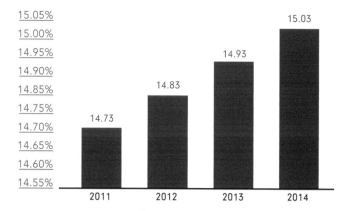

LATE OLD AGE

Between 2001 and 2011 the number of people aged 75–89 living in the UK fell from 5.9 million to 4.4 million. Improving mortality rates were more than offset by a rapid and dramatic decline in the birth rate between 1922 and 1936, the years between which those reaching these ages in 2011 would have been born. These are the babies of the roaring twenties and depressed thirties. A few of this cohort will have been among the youngest to fight in the Second World War, but most were war children. By 2011 the highest proportions of people of these ages were found in Christchurch (Dorset, 14.2%); Rother (East Sussex, 12.9%); East Dorset (12.9%); and East Devon (12.8%). In contrast, the lowest proportions were, unsurprisingly, all found in London: in Lambeth (3.2%); Hackney (2.9%); Newham (2.7%); and Tower Hamlets (2.7%). There appears to be no consistent pattern to the changing proportions of the population of these ages over time, other than greater falls in cities, where elderly people are more often poorer and die earlier.

The proportions of people in late old age are rising in some districts where they are already most numerous (such as North Norfolk), or where they are currently few (East Dunbartonshire); the numbers are falling the most in some places where they were highest (Worthing) and also where they are already quite low (Manchester). One in ten of all people aged 75–89 live in Birmingham, Leeds, Cornwall, County Durham, Sheffield, Glasgow, Wiltshire, Edinburgh, Bradford, Cheshire East and the East Riding of Yorkshire. This is another group growing rapidly in size each year since 2011, as more people in the UK turn 75 than 90 each year.

Age 75–89 2011 (%)

	2.7 – 4.9
	5.0 – 6.9
	7.0 – 7.9
	8.0 – 9.9
	10.0 – 14.2

Age 75–89 change (%)

	-2.1 – -1.0
	-0.9 – -0.1
	0.0 – 0.4
	0.5 – 0.9
	1.0 – 2.4

People aged 75–89, UK %

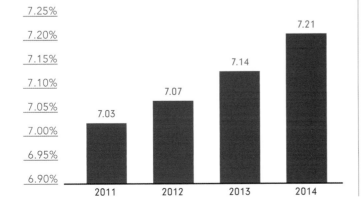

2011	2012	2013	2014
7.03	7.07	7.14	7.21

THE LAST DECADE

Between 2001 and 2011 the number of people aged 90 and above living in the UK rose from 0.4 million to 0.5 million. There has been a huge amount of interest in the growing numbers of very elderly, but it is worth remembering how few they are and how few they will remain to be for some time to come, given the fall in fertility that continued through to the 1930s and early 1940s. By 2012 there were 13,350 people aged over 100, but only 660 of these were aged over 105. For the very few who get to live so long there is thus a 95% mortality rate during those almost always final five years of life after age 100. The bulk of the increase in population numbers at these ages is due to reductions in mortality.

There is very little immigration or emigration past the age of 90. There is also very little internal migration past age 80. Those aged over 90 tend to live in much the same places as those aged 75–89. The proportion of the population aged 75–89 in an area in 2001 tends to be a very good predictor of the numbers aged over 90 living there 10 years later, except that there are roughly 10 times fewer people alive by then. In 2002 there were 7,740 people aged 100 or over in the UK, 2.0% of the 90–99 age group. By 2012 that number had risen to 13,350, or 2.6% of the 90–99 age group. The rise in the very elderly population stalled slightly after 2012 when there was an absolute increase in deaths among elderly women, but larger numbers of additional people turning 90 after 2012 means it continued to grow rapidly in 2014.

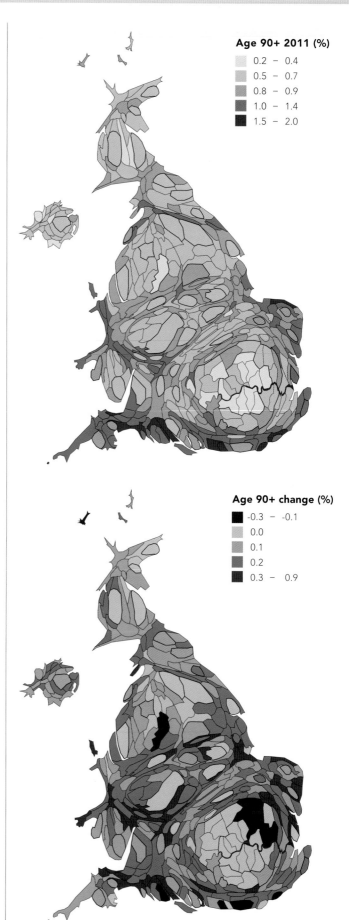

Age 90+ 2011 (%)

- 0.2 – 0.4
- 0.5 – 0.7
- 0.8 – 0.9
- 1.0 – 1.4
- 1.5 – 2.0

Age 90+ change (%)

- -0.3 – -0.1
- 0.0
- 0.1
- 0.2
- 0.3 – 0.9

People aged 90+, UK %

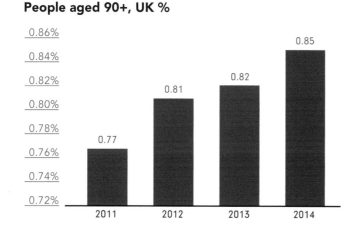

Year	Value
2011	0.77
2012	0.81
2013	0.82
2014	0.85

MARRIAGE

The number of people who are married is falling almost everywhere. More people who are married are dying or divorcing compared to the numbers of newly-weds each year. These marriages only include mixed-sex couples because same-sex marriages were not introduced in Great Britain until 2014 and are still illegal in Northern Ireland. The area of the UK where it was most common to be married by 2011 was East Dorset, which was also the only place in the country where 50% of the population were married by that date. Most children cannot be married, and so this proportion would be a little higher were they excluded. Marriage is now most rare in Islington, where just a fifth (20.8%) of people are married.

Over the course of the 2000s the largest increases in marriage have been in Kensington & Chelsea (+2.3%) and the City of London (+2.2%). The largest falls have been in places that have attracted in many young people, often expanding new university towns and cities such as in Lincoln (-5.0% married); Welwyn Hatfield (-5.0%); and Blackpool (-4.7%), which was also the divorce capital of the UK in 2011 (9.9% of all people there then were divorced). Today Blackpool remains the UK divorce capital (but now as many as 10.8% of all people living there are divorced). In 2011 the lowest rates of divorce were recorded in 14 districts of Northern Ireland, and the next lowest in Harrow in London, all areas with a high proportion of people adhering to religions especially opposed to divorce. Connected to this, people are least likely to be separated, but not divorced, in Belfast (4.4%). Up until 2009 the number of marriages being held in England and Wales was falling, but that trend abruptly reversed in that year. At the time of writing (December 2015), no mixed-sex marriage statistics were available for 2013 or 2014 due to delays in the processing of these official statistics.

Married 2011 (%)
- 20.8 – 29.9
- 30.0 – 34.9
- 35.0 – 39.9
- 40.0 – 44.9
- 45.0 – 50.0

Married change (%)
- -5.0 – -4.1
- -4.0 – -3.1
- -3.0 – -2.1
- -2.0 – -0.1
- 0.0 – 2.3

Marriages held in England and Wales

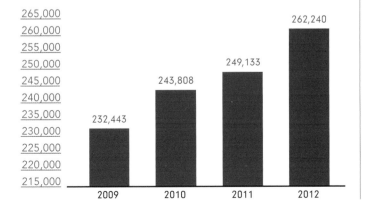

- 2009: 232,443
- 2010: 243,808
- 2011: 249,133
- 2012: 262,240

CIVIL PARTNERSHIPS / LEGAL COUPLES

By 2011 the Census had begun to record civil partnerships. The highest proportions of people in such a partnership were living in the City of London (1.6%) and the lowest in the Isles of Scilly (the only area to record none). Brighton & Hove (0.9%) and Southwark (0.7%) were the second and third most likely places to live in a civil partnership in the UK. When civil partnerships are combined with marriages, the pattern is little altered from that of marriage; however, it is smoothed a little as civil partnerships are dramatically more common in areas where to be married is more rare. There were 113,000 people recorded as being in a civil partnership by 2011, 0.5% of all people in a legal couple.

Just over a third of all people in civil partnerships live in the following 35 districts, which include most of the capital cities of the UK (apart from Belfast): Brighton & Hove, Southwark, Lambeth, Birmingham, Camden, Westminster, Wandsworth, Islington, Manchester, Edinburgh, Leeds, Haringey, Tower Hamlets, Lewisham, Bristol, Hackney, Glasgow, Kensington & Chelsea, Ealing, Sheffield, Cornwall, Kirklees, Croydon, County Durham, Hammersmith & Fulham, Waltham Forest, Greenwich, Hounslow, Richmond upon Thames, Brent, Newham, Wiltshire, Liverpool, Salford and Cardiff. The first marriages of sex-same couples took place on 29 March 2014, and numbers rose after that, with the latest statistics referring to June of that year.

The map of legal couples shows the proportion of people who were either married or in a civil partnership in 2011.

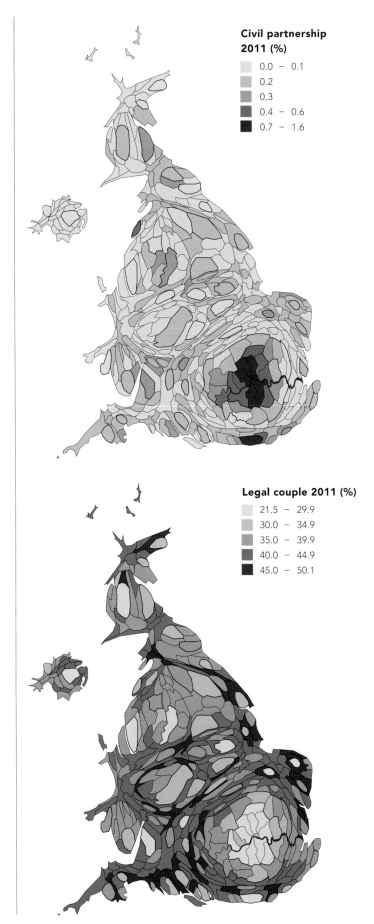

Civil partnership 2011 (%)
- 0.0 – 0.1
- 0.2
- 0.3
- 0.4 – 0.6
- 0.7 – 1.6

Legal couple 2011 (%)
- 21.5 – 29.9
- 30.0 – 34.9
- 35.0 – 39.9
- 40.0 – 44.9
- 45.0 – 50.1

Same-sex couple marriages in England and Wales in 2014

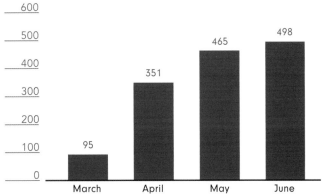

Of the 56.1 million people who
lived in England and Wales, some
30.8 million (55%) stated their
ethinicity was White and their
religion was Christian.

White and Christian

55%
(30.8 million people)

ENGLAND & WALES

Religion and Ethnicity

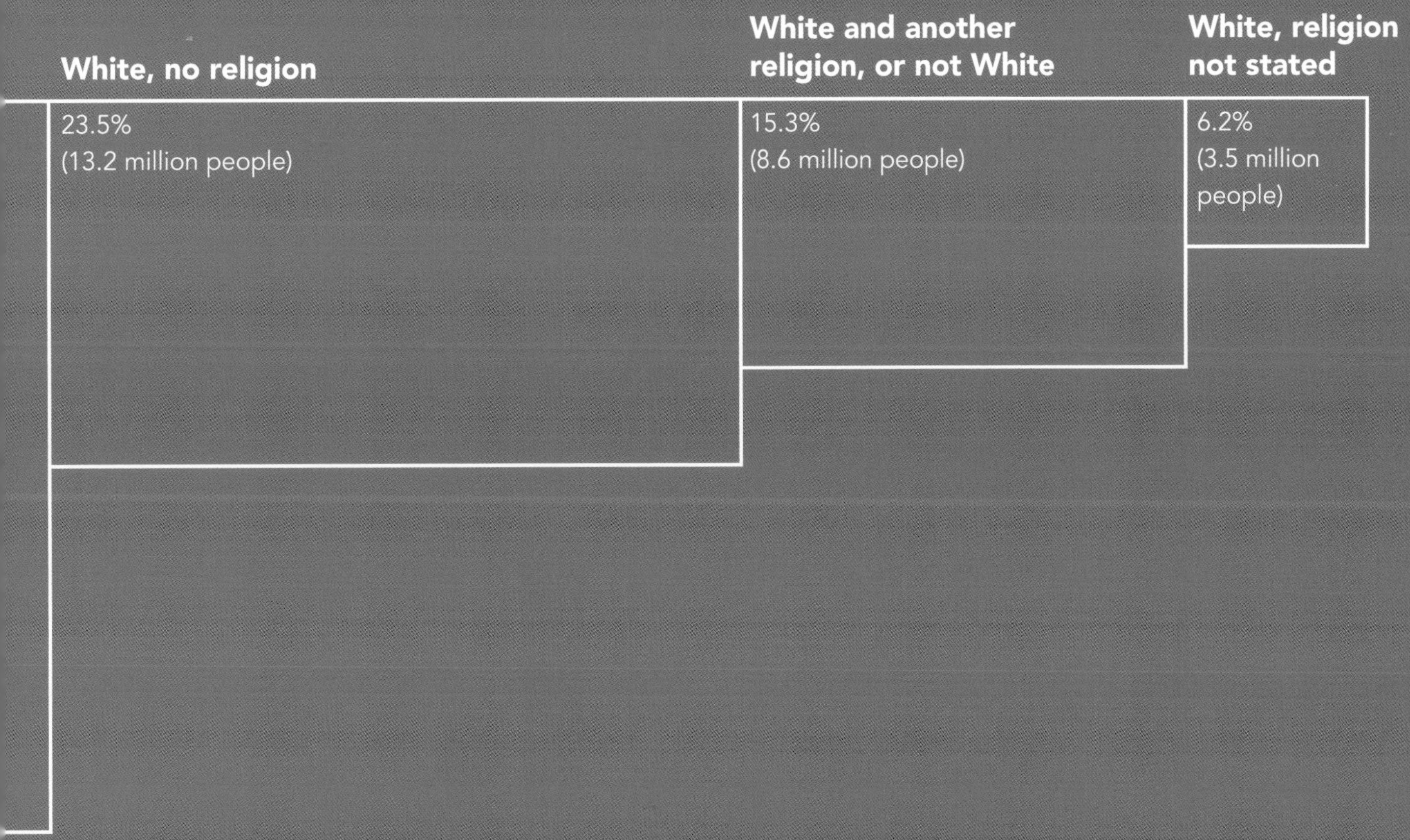

White, no religion

23.5%
(13.2 million people)

White and another religion, or not White

15.3%
(8.6 million people)

White, religion not stated

6.2%
(3.5 million people)

Religion and Ethnicity

The advantage of an atlas over individual maps is that you can
see how the maps relate to each other. This is especially important
when it comes to looking at religion and ethnicity because,
although most minority groups are (by definition) small, taken
together in certain places they are no longer, in aggregate,
a minority.

Of the 56.1 million people who lived in England and Wales in 2011, 30.8 million
stated that their ethnicity was White and their religion Christian on the Census
form – 55.0% of the population. The proportion in the rest of the UK was even
higher. A further 13.2 million (23.5%) said they were of White ethnicity and had
no religion, and another 3.5 million (6.2%) said they were White and would not
state a religion, leaving 15.3% of the population, or two in every 13 people, either
White and of another religion, or not White.

People by religion and ethnicity, England and Wales 2011

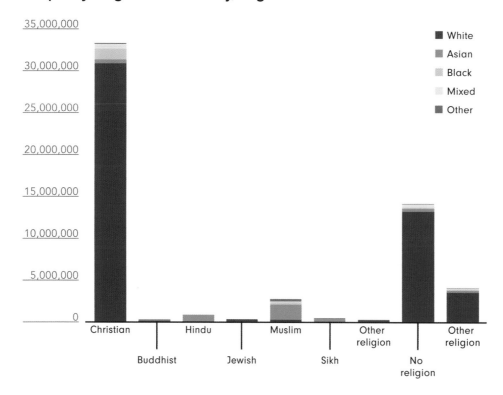

Minorities have traditionally been defined in Britain as 'people not of White
ethnicity, or adherents to a religion other than Christianity'. In Scotland and

Northern Ireland many different kinds of Christianity are distinguished, which will have an effect on the overall numbers of people saying they are Christian, and so they are not included in the graph shown opposite. In Wales, being Welsh-speaking is another way in which a significant proportion of the population may be considered part of a minority and so, towards the end of this chapter, we look at languages spoken as another form of identity and affiliation. However, what matters most is to first recognise just how dominant the dominant groups are, which includes people in the UK who can only speak English.

By ethnicity the proportion of the population of the whole of the UK describing themselves as White has been falling in recent years and between the Censuses, and fell in 2012 to 89.48%, in 2013 to 89.25%, and in 2014 to 89.22% of the entire population. A larger proportion of very elderly people are White than the proportion of the population as a whole, and so simply by ageing, the population partly caused the proportion who are not White to rise by 2014 to 10.75% of the entire population. Just as Christians are divided up, so too is the White ethnic group, into White English, Scottish, Welsh, Irish and White Other. There are also an increasing number of people of Mixed ethnicity or who state they belong to an ethnic group that it is not one of the main minorities, either from the Indian Subcontinent or Black, most often with ancestry in Africa and/or the Caribbean. The rise in Mixed and Other ethnicities between 2013 and 2014 was almost identical to the fall in White ethnicity over that most recent year. The 2011 survey statistics are not included in the graph below because they have not been re-weighted by Census estimates, and because the ONS deliberately did not release them because of a slight change to the annual survey question and categorisation on ethnicity.

Non-white ethnic groups, UK 2012–2014 %

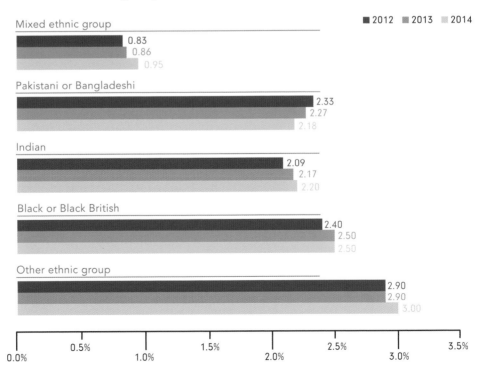

Questions of identity on Census forms change over time. Only a few decades ago minorities were identified by country of birth. The phrase 'New Commonwealth-born' was Census-speak for 'born in the old Empire but not in Canada, Australia or New Zealand'. It meant, 'probably have darker skin'. A century ago the 1911 Census was used to infer that about 120,000 Ashkenazi Jews fleeing pogroms in Eastern Europe who had arrived in the UK.[2] The implementation of the Aliens (Registration) Act 1919 meant that from 1920 onwards, foreign citizens were for the first time not permitted to land in the UK without permission from an immigration officer, and would need to arrive with a work permit obtained from the Ministry of Labour after that date, should they wish to work. Censuses in the UK have a long history of being used to bolster arguments for immigration control and to try to raise fears over the numbers of people belonging to particular ethnicities or religions. It has only been in very recent decades that the Census has also been used to show how much the different population groups were mixing: mixing geographically as segregation has fallen almost everywhere, mixing socially, and mixing sexually, as more and more people with parents with different ethnic, birthplace, religious or other identifiers come together to produce children who are increasingly harder to categorise.[3]

CHRISTIAN

In 2011, 36.1 million people declared that they were Christian on a Census form (or had that declared for them eg parents declaring for children), a drop of over 10% from 40.1 million in 2001. This was despite the population as a whole growing and ageing. Many people who died between 2001 and 2011 will have said they were Christian in the 2001 Census. Saying you are Christian was most common in Knowsley, the only place in the country where over four out of five people were still Christian by 2011. However, in England fewer than a million people attend a Church of England service on a typical Sunday.[4] It is likely that fewer people are becoming Christians compared to those who have decided that they are no longer Christians, but Christianity in all its many forms remains by far the most dominant religion in the UK.

Just below 80%, but more than three-quarters of all people, said they were Christian quite near to Knowsley in Allerdale, Chorley, Copeland, Halton, Ribble Valley, Sefton, South Ribble, St Helens, West Lancashire and Wigan. Something about North West urban (but not too urban) England now equates with Christianity still being the professed norm for a large majority. In contrast, Christianity fell the most in popularity in towns East of the Pennines and on the South coast, most often in places that had successfully attracted a large number of young people to university campuses in recent years. But it also fell rapidly in popularity across South Wales and in many of the more peripheral parts of the UK.

Numbers of Christians had fallen least between 2001 and 2011 in Knowsley (-4.8%) and Inverclyde (-5.1%), but then also in the London boroughs of Haringey (-5.1%); Lambeth (-5.7%); Barnet (-6.1%); Brent (-6.2%); Newham (-6.9%); and Ealing (-7.0%). In contrast, the largest fall in professed Christianity was in Kingston upon Hull (-16.8%). By 2011 Black people were more likely to be Christian than any other group, but only 4% of Christians in England and Wales were Black, 2% were of Mixed ethnicity and 1% were Asian.

People of Christian religions by broad ethnic group, England and Wales 2011 %

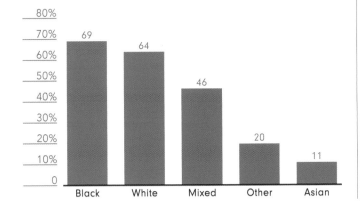

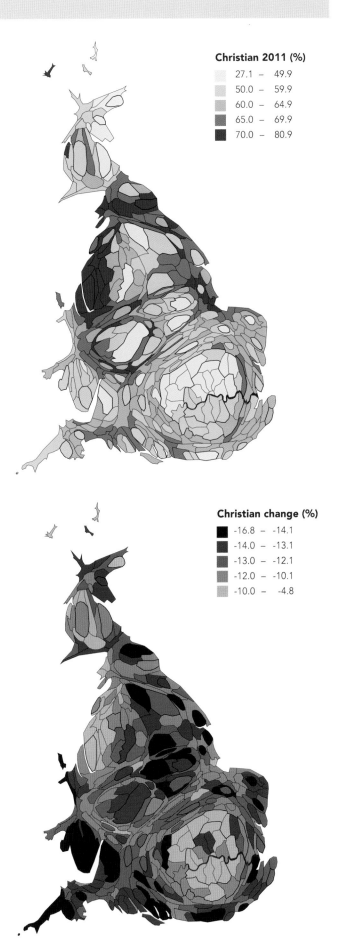

Christian 2011 (%)
- 27.1 – 49.9
- 50.0 – 59.9
- 60.0 – 64.9
- 65.0 – 69.9
- 70.0 – 80.9

Christian change (%)
- -16.8 – -14.1
- -14.0 – -13.1
- -13.0 – -12.1
- -12.0 – -10.1
- -10.0 – -4.8

RELIGION IN NORTHERN IRELAND

Of the 1.8 million people living in Northern Ireland in 2011, 1.5 million professed to currently holding a religious faith. Of these, 0.7 million were Catholics, and 0.7 million Protestants. The Protestants were divided into 0.3 million Presbyterians, 0.2 million Church of Ireland, 0.1 million Methodists and 0.1 million professing to other denominations and religions. Ten years earlier there had been 0.1 million fewer Catholics, a few more Protestants and fewer people who held no belief; 1.7 million had professed to currently holding a religious faith in Northern Ireland in 2001, and that had dropped by 0.2 million, so that by 2011 the number with no religion or not stated had risen to 0.3 million, up 0.1 million in the decade. The largest increase in people professing no belief was in Belfast (+5.5%). The Catholic proportion ranges almost tenfold, from being very high in Newry & Mourne (72.1%) and Derry (67.4%) to very low in Carrickfergus (7.6%) and Ards (10.9%). Presbyterians vary even more – highs are in Ballymena (40.7%) and lows in Fermanagh (3.0%). Segregation is falling, partly because belief of any kind is becoming slightly less common almost everywhere in the province, possibly partly because Catholics are more prepared to move into Protestant areas and vice versa, since the Good Friday Agreement was signed and while it still holds.

People by religion, Northern Ireland 2001 and 2011

■ 2001   ■ 2011

No religion or religion not stated
- 305,416
- 233,853

Other denominations and religions
- 119,239
- 107,249

Methodist Church in Ireland
- 54,253
- 59,173

Church of Ireland
- 248,821
- 257,788

Presbyterian Church in Ireland
- 345,101
- 348,742

Catholic
- 738,033
- 678,462

100,000   300,000   500,000   700,000
0   200,000   400,000   600,000   800,000

Catholic

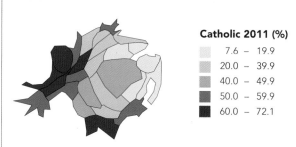

Catholic 2011 (%)
- 7.6 – 19.9
- 20.0 – 39.9
- 40.0 – 49.9
- 50.0 – 59.9
- 60.0 – 72.1

Methodist Church

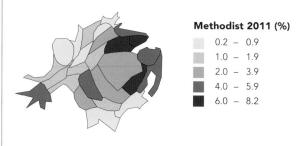

Methodist 2011 (%)
- 0.2 – 0.9
- 1.0 – 1.9
- 2.0 – 3.9
- 4.0 – 5.9
- 6.0 – 8.2

Catholic

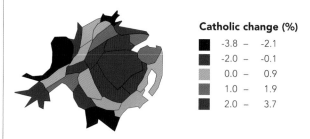

Catholic change (%)
- -3.8 – -2.1
- -2.0 – -0.1
- 0.0 – 0.9
- 1.0 – 1.9
- 2.0 – 3.7

Methodist Church

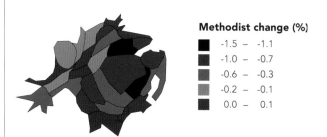

Methodist change (%)
- -1.5 – -1.1
- -1.0 – -0.7
- -0.6 – -0.3
- -0.2 – -0.1
- 0.0 – 0.1

Presbyterian Church

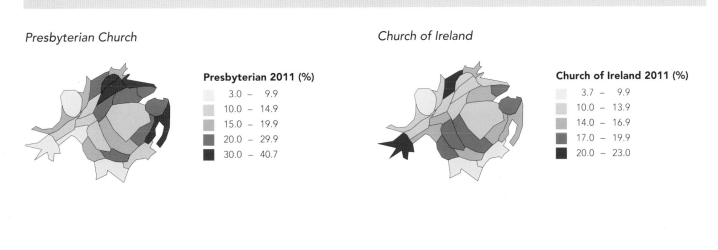

Presbyterian 2011 (%)
- 3.0 – 9.9
- 10.0 – 14.9
- 15.0 – 19.9
- 20.0 – 29.9
- 30.0 – 40.7

Church of Ireland

Church of Ireland 2011 (%)
- 3.7 – 9.9
- 10.0 – 13.9
- 14.0 – 16.9
- 17.0 – 19.9
- 20.0 – 23.0

Other denominations and religions

Other denominations 2011 (%)
- 2.3 – 3.9
- 4.0 – 5.9
- 6.0 – 7.9
- 8.0 – 9.9
- 10.0 – 11.0

No religion or religion not stated

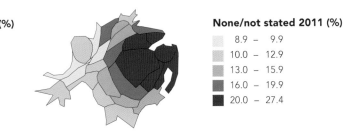

None/not stated 2011 (%)
- 8.9 – 9.9
- 10.0 – 12.9
- 13.0 – 15.9
- 16.0 – 19.9
- 20.0 – 27.4

Presbyterian Church

Presbyterian change (%)
- -4.0 – -3.1
- -3.0 – -2.1
- -2.0 – -1.1
- -1.0 – -0.6
- -0.5 – -0.1

Church of Ireland

Church of Ireland change (%)
- -2.9 – -2.1
- -2.0 – -1.5
- -1.4 – -1.1
- -1.0 – -0.1
- 0.0 – 0.5

Other denominations and religions

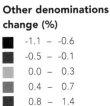

Other denominations change (%)
- -1.1 – -0.6
- -0.5 – -0.1
- 0.0 – 0.3
- 0.4 – 0.7
- 0.8 – 1.4

No religion or religion not stated

None/not stated change (%)
- -1.2
- 0.0 – 1.9
- 2.0 – 2.9
- 3.0 – 3.9
- 4.0 – 5.5

NO RELIGION

Professing no religion is becoming increasingly common in the UK – 16.0 million people declared they were of no religion in 2011, not quite double the 9.1 million in 2001, but possibly the fastest ever rise in non-belief in British history. This probably reflects the increasing acceptability of saying you have no religion. Northern Ireland's religious statistics were tabulated separately as different questions were asked there.

In Britain the rate of no professed religion appeared to be highest on the East coast of Scotland, where there may have been a campaign not to reveal religious affiliation to the state. The question is optional, so not completing it is an easy act of protest. Outside of that area Norwich (42.5); Brighton (42.4%); and Blaenau Gwent (41.1%) have populations with the least belief. In great contrast to these areas people are least likely to profess to no religion in or near London: Slough (12.1%); Redbridge (11.0%); Brent (10.6%); Harrow (9.6%); and Newham (9.5%).

Not believing in any religion has grown everywhere. By ethnicity, having no belief is most common among people of Mixed ethnicity and least common among those describing themselves as Black.

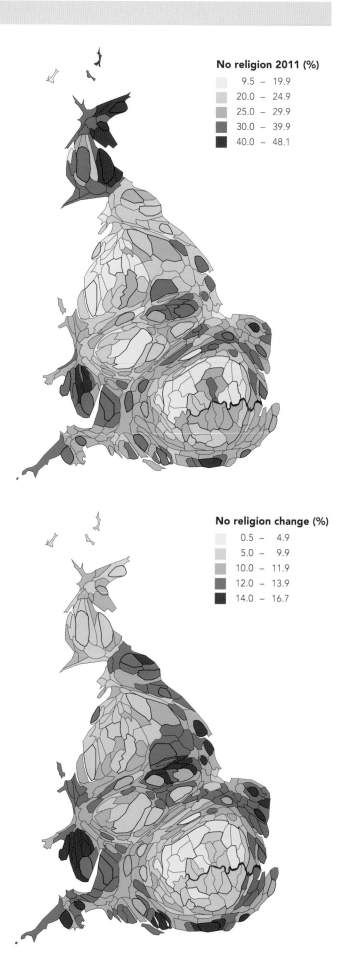

No religion 2011 (%)

	9.5 – 19.9
	20.0 – 24.9
	25.0 – 29.9
	30.0 – 39.9
	40.0 – 48.1

No religion change (%)

	0.5 – 4.9
	5.0 – 9.9
	10.0 – 11.9
	12.0 – 13.9
	14.0 – 16.7

People of no religion by broad ethnic group, England and Wales 2011 %

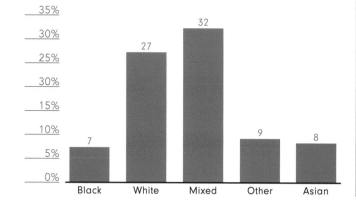

MUSLIM

In 2011, 2.8 million people declared their religion to be Islam, up from 1.6 million in 2001. As a proportion of the local population, a person was most likely to be Muslim in Tower Hamlets (34.5%); Newham (32.0%); Blackburn (27.0%); and Luton (24.7%). The greatest increases in Muslims were found in areas that already had much higher than average proportions, such as in Redbridge (+11.4%); Luton (+10.0%); Slough (+9.9%); Barking & Dagenham (+9.4%); and Bradford (+8.6%). The one area that had seen a small but significant decline in the Muslim population was Tower Hamlets (-1.9%), as in some neighbourhoods there gentrification has forced Muslim families East and North of that borough. A small decrease (-0.1%) was also reported in the neighbouring City of London and in the Rother district of East Sussex (-0.1%), which surrounds Hastings, where there was a slight rise. A lower increase in Inner London boroughs in general suggests that Muslim families were either choosing to move out to the suburbs or being financially forced to move further away than that. A minority of people of Pakistani, Bangladeshi and Indian ethnicities living in England and Wales are Muslims, but a very narrow majority of those identifying with other ethnicities, which includes 'Arab' and 'Any other ethnic group', are Muslims.

Muslim 2011 (%)

- 0.1 – 4.9
- 5.0 – 9.9
- 10.0 – 14.9
- 15.0 – 19.9
- 20.0 – 34.5

Muslim change (%)

- -1.9 – -0.1
- 0.0 – 1.9
- 2.0 – 3.9
- 4.0 – 5.9
- 6.0 – 11.4

People of Muslim religion by broad ethnic group, England and Wales 2011 %

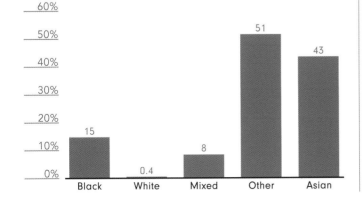

Bar chart values: Black 15; White 0.4; Mixed 8; Other 51; Asian 43.

HINDU

The number of Hindu adherents in Britain rose from 0.6 million in 2001 to 0.8 million in 2011. By 2011 the greatest concentrations of Hindu believers were found in Harrow (25.3%); Brent (17.8%); and Leicester (15.2%). The largest increases in the proportions of local populations being Hindu have been recorded in Harrow (+5.7%); Redbridge (+3.5%); Hillingdon (+3.4%); Oadby & Wigston (near Leicester, +3.1%); and Watford (+3.1%). Adherents to Hinduism are suburbanising rapidly, especially to more distant suburbs and outlying towns, and in some cases to nearby villages, the three largest falls in Hindu proportions being in Lambeth (-0.2%); Haringey (-0.3%); and Barnet (-0.5%). Among the districts with some large but not the largest increases are Welwyn Hatfield (+1.4%); South Bucks (+1.3%); Hertsmere (+1.2%); Kingston upon Thames (+1.1%); Charnwood (+1.0%); Solihull (+0.9%); Windsor & Maidenhead (+0.8%); Epsom & Ewell (+0.7%); Oxford (+0.6%); and Cambridge (0.5%). Not all Hindu out-migration is to areas that tend to be more affluent, although a noticeable amount is.

We cannot look at change in religious affiliation over time since 2011 because surveys large enough to detect the slight changes that occur year by year are not conducted. This is why the data in the graph below are only for 2011. The large majority of Hindus in Britain are of Indian ethnicity. This will almost certainly be the case for several decades; what is less certain is whether there will be Censuses in the future of the kind that allow these changes to be studied.

People of Hindu religion by broad ethnic group, England and Wales 2011 %

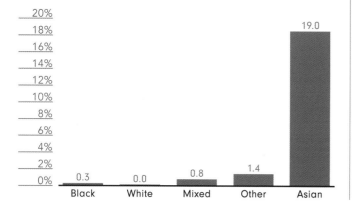

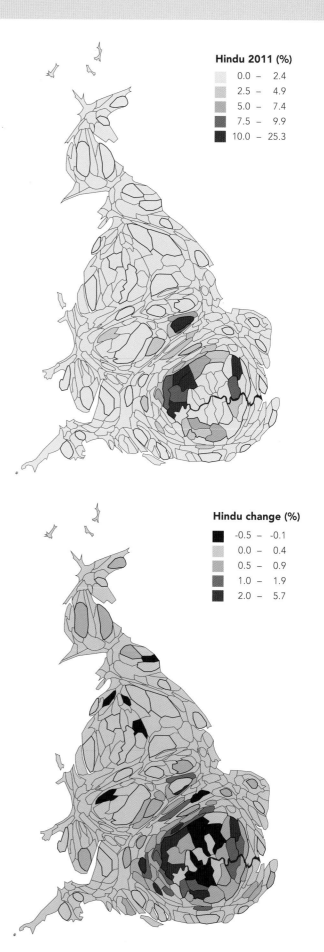

Hindu 2011 (%)
- 0.0 – 2.4
- 2.5 – 4.9
- 5.0 – 7.4
- 7.5 – 9.9
- 10.0 – 25.3

Hindu change (%)
- -0.5 – -0.1
- 0.0 – 0.4
- 0.5 – 0.9
- 1.0 – 1.9
- 2.0 – 5.7

SIKH

In 2011 0.4 million people defined their religion as Sikh, up from 0.3 million in 2001. Sikh 'Central' is the cluster of Slough (10.6%), Hounslow (9.1%) and Ealing (7.9%), while 'Northern Sikh' is centred on Wolverhampton (9.1%) and Sandwell (8.7%). In contrast, the areas where there are no Sikhs reads like a who's who of remote rural, island and coastal districts. However, even in some of the places where there are hardly any other Sikhs, there is, in general, a very slow and steady (if still minuscule) overall increase. The same could not be said of the more central London boroughs where the proportion that are Sikh has fallen between 2001 and 2011: Greenwich (-0.8%); Newham (-0.7%); Ealing (-0.6%); and Brent, Waltham Forest, Hackney and Islington (all -0.1%). The greatest percentage point increases meanwhile were in South Bucks (+3.2%); Oadby & Wigston (+2.4%); and Hillingdon (+2.1%).

More than one in 12 (8.7%) of all people of Asian ethnicity living in England and Wales are Sikh. In contrast, only one in every 6,500 people of White ethnicity in England and Wales are Sikh. It is possible that a number of people whose religion is Sikh also wrote 'Sikh' for their ethnicity which would be classed as 'Other', and that could partly account for why 7.2% of all people of 'Other' ethnicities are Sikh.

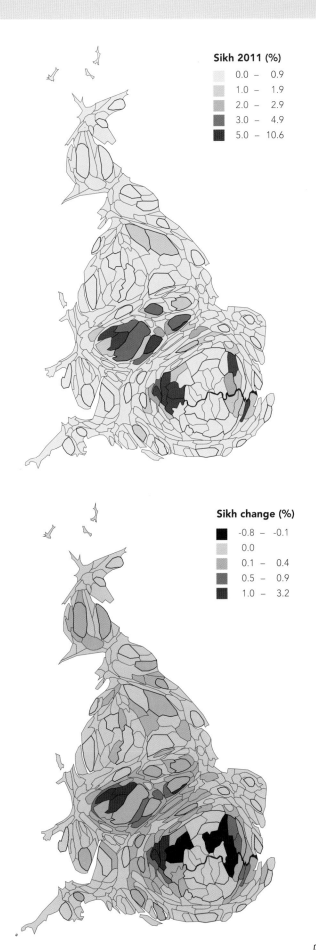

Sikh 2011 (%)
- 0.0 – 0.9
- 1.0 – 1.9
- 2.0 – 2.9
- 3.0 – 4.9
- 5.0 – 10.6

Sikh change (%)
- -0.8 – -0.1
- 0.0
- 0.1 – 0.4
- 0.5 – 0.9
- 1.0 – 3.2

People of Sikh religion by broad ethnic group, England and Wales 2011 %

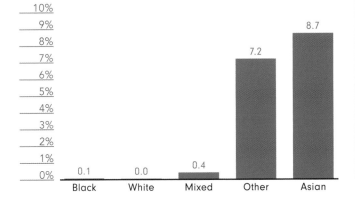

Black	White	Mixed	Other	Asian
0.1	0.0	0.4	7.2	8.7

JEWISH

In 2011 slightly under 0.3 million people were declared to be Jewish by religion. This was a number almost identical to that reported in 2001, just a few thousand people higher. The highest proportions were in Barnet (15.2%) and neighbouring Hertsmere (14.3%), just across the Greater London boundary. Much smaller centres were located around the North West in Bury (5.6%), Salford (3.3%) and Trafford (1.1%); in East Renfrewshire (2.6%); in Gateshead (1.5%); and in Leeds (0.9%). The largest increase has been outer-suburbanisation to Hertsmere (+2.9%). However, the next two largest increases both reversed a century-old process of moving out of the inner city. These were in Hackney (+1.0%) and Salford (+0.9%). The fourth and fifth largest rises were in Gateshead (+0.7%) and Bury (+0.6%).

Numbers rise due to high birth rates in some areas and in-migration in others. All the largest falls were in London: Redbridge (-2.5%); Harrow (-1.9%); Camden (-1.2%), Brent (-1.1%); Westminster (-1.0%); and City of London (-0.9%). By ethnicity, the broad ethnic group with the highest proportion of its members who are of the Jewish religion is 'Other', which includes 'Arab' and 'Any other ethnic group' – which could, of course, include writing in 'Jewish' as an ethnic group on the Census form. However, 92% of people of Jewish religion state their ethnicity as White, while only 0.5% of White people state their religion as Jewish.

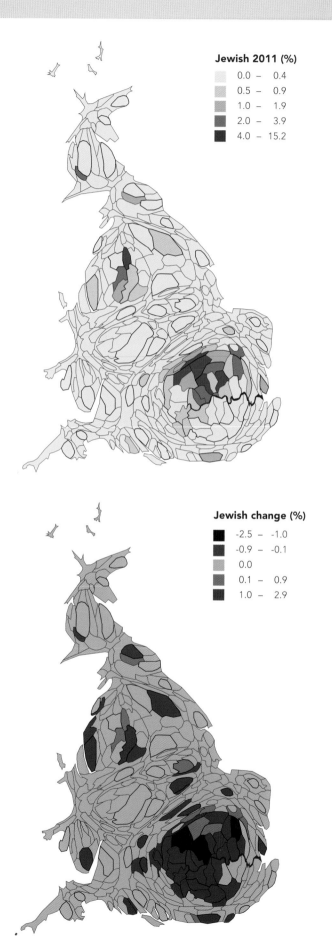

Jewish 2011 (%)

	0.0 – 0.4
	0.5 – 0.9
	1.0 – 1.9
	2.0 – 3.9
	4.0 – 15.2

Jewish change (%)

	-2.5 – -1.0
	-0.9 – -0.1
	0.0
	0.1 – 0.9
	1.0 – 2.9

People of Jewish religion by broad ethnic group, England and Wales 2011 %

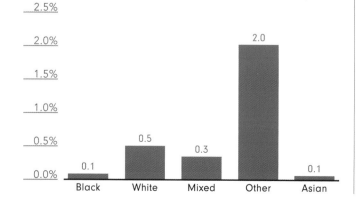
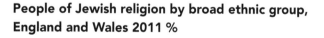

Black 0.1, White 0.5, Mixed 0.3, Other 2.0, Asian 0.1

BUDDHIST

By 2011 almost as many people said they were Buddhist (0.3 million) as Jewish, and the number will be higher by the time you read these words, as it is increasing quickly; it rose from 0.2 million in 2001. The highest proportion of Buddhists in any one area in 2011 was located in Rushmoor in Surrey (3.0%), where there are a small number of temples and monasteries. Buddhism is most common within London with more than 1% of the population being Buddhist in many London boroughs; Cambridge (1.3%); Reading (1.2%); Brighton & Hove (1.0%); Oxford (0.9%); and Surrey Heath (0.9%).

The greatest increase in Buddhism since 2001 has been in Rushmoor (+2.9%), where only 0.4% of the population were Buddhist in 2001. Hounslow (+0.7%) and Greenwich (+0.7%) were the next largest increases. The only decrease in numbers was found in Wellingborough (-0.1%). One in every 30 people of Asian ethnicity living in England and Wales in 2011 was of the Buddhist religion compared to one in every 600 people of White ethnicity, a rate some 20 times lower. Some religions are particularly closely connected to particular ethnicities, and the two then often get muddled.

We now turn to look at the distributions of ethnicities.

People of Buddist religion by broad ethnic group, England and Wales 2011 %

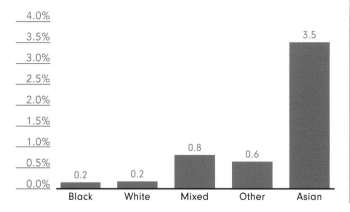

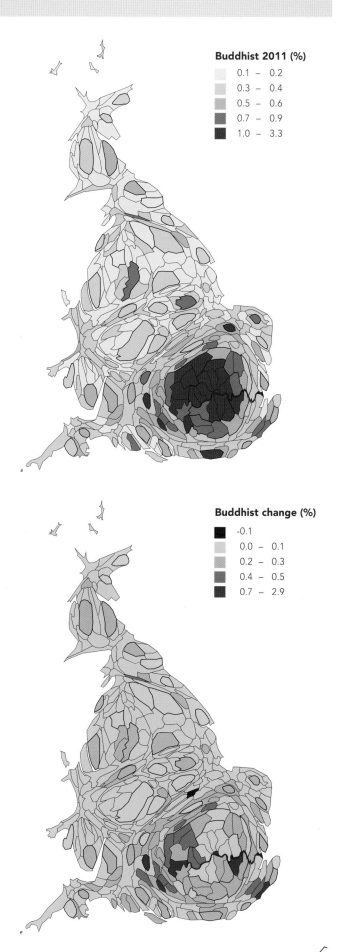

Buddhist 2011 (%)

	0.1 – 0.2
	0.3 – 0.4
	0.5 – 0.6
	0.7 – 0.9
	1.0 – 3.3

Buddhist change (%)

	-0.1
	0.0 – 0.1
	0.2 – 0.3
	0.4 – 0.5
	0.7 – 2.9

WHITE

Of the 63.2 million UK residents in 2011, 55.1 million (87.2%) described themselves as ethnically White. Much of the UK is an ethnic monoculture, hardly multicultural at all, and being monocultural does not make a place cohesive. The most White districts of the UK are some of the most ethnically/religiously divided – all are in Northern Ireland: Ballymoney (99.5%); Larne (99.4%); and Strabane (99.3%). The least White areas of the UK are all in London, headed by Newham (29.0%); Brent (36.3%); and Harrow (42.2%). The three areas with the largest decreases in the share of local populations being White were also all in London where, as opposed to nationally, the falls were substantial: Barking & Dagenham (-26.9%); Redbridge (-21.0%); and Hillingdon (-18.5%). In contrast, there is nowhere in the UK where the proportion of White people has risen, and nowhere has seen the arrival of a 'White flight'. This, in a European context, is remarkable, and demonstrates how false a huge amount of the rhetoric is. Such a false rhetoric was common in the 1990s – the suggestion that White families were avoiding moving to areas with many non-White people in favour of other areas. No evidence for this was found in either the 2001 or 2011 Censuses. Since 2011 the proportion of people describing themselves as White has continued to fall slowly. Data for 2011 is not included on the bar chart below (and in many of the other charts in this chapter) because it had not been re-weighted at its time of publication in line with the 2011 Census results (which were released later). The data for 2012–14 shown below has been adjusted by ONS given the new Census data.

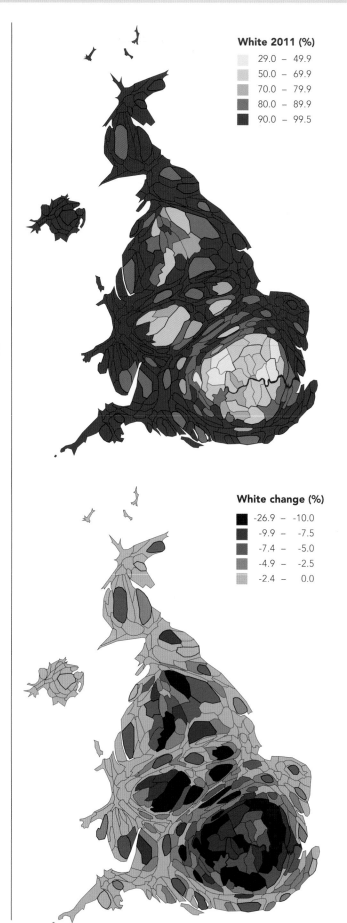

White 2011 (%)

	29.0 – 49.9
	50.0 – 69.9
	70.0 – 79.9
	80.0 – 89.9
	90.0 – 99.5

White change (%)

	-26.9 – -10.0
	-9.9 – -7.5
	-7.4 – -5.0
	-4.9 – -2.5
	-2.4 – 0.0

People of White ethnicity aged 16+, UK %

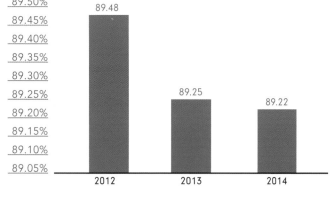

INDIAN

In 2011, 1.5 million people of Indian ethnicity lived in the UK, up from 1.1 million in 2001. The greatest proportion of the population being Indian is in Leicester (28.3%), followed by Harrow (26.4%) and Hounslow (19.0%). Elsewhere, and especially in London, the proportion of the population who are Indian is falling, by 2.3% in Ealing; 1.3% in Greenwich; and 0.8% in Barnet. The Indian ethnic group is one of the longer established minority ethnic groups of the UK and (seen as a group and on average) is both moving into the suburbs and becoming more settled in a series of cities and towns across the four nations.

Sometimes, because of high overall population increases, as in Barnet, the Indian share of the population fell despite the absolute number of people declaring themselves to be of Indian origin there rising from 27,130 to 27,920. The borough as a whole increased in population as it became more crowded. Where previously 314,600 people lived in 2001, 356,400 lived in 2011. An overcrowded and still overcrowding city borough becomes less attractive to a more established group. In contrast, there have been falls in numbers in parts of the North (such as Redcar & Cleveland and South Tyneside) where people of Indian origin are leaving a little faster than the population as a whole is declining. Since 2011 the proportion of the UK population who are Indian continued to rise. Again, no 2011 data is shown in the chart below because the annual population survey had still not been re-weighted to reflect the 2011 Census findings.

People of Indian ethnicity aged 16+, UK %

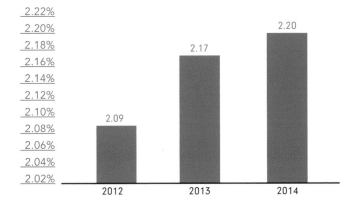

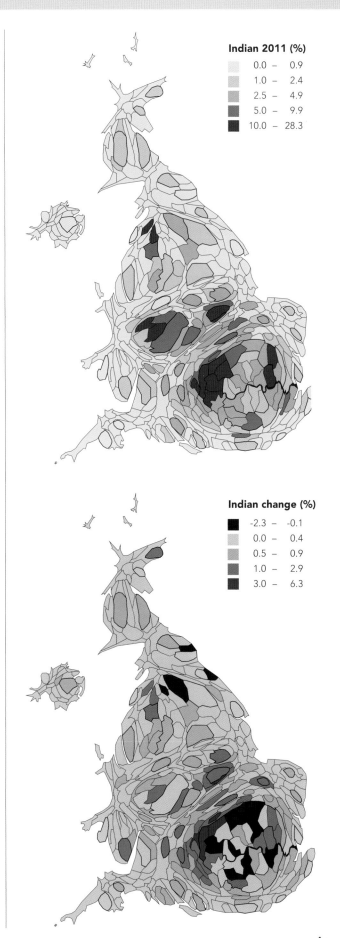

Indian 2011 (%)
- 0.0 – 0.9
- 1.0 – 2.4
- 2.5 – 4.9
- 5.0 – 9.9
- 10.0 – 28.3

Indian change (%)
- -2.3 – -0.1
- 0.0 – 0.4
- 0.5 – 0.9
- 1.0 – 2.9
- 3.0 – 6.3

MIXED

By 2011, 1.3 million people in the UK were describing their ethnicity as Mixed. It would be quite legitimate for the entire population to describe themselves in this way should they wish and if they knew enough of their own origins. Your ethnicity is simply where you feel or believe your origins to lie. Indeed, very few of us are unmixed if you look back just a few generations to all your direct ancestors. We are often more mixed than we know because paternal fidelity is easily faked and family histories are often edited.

The number who are Mixed in the UK has almost doubled since 2001. The district containing the most people who describe themselves as Mixed is Lambeth (7.6%), followed by Lewisham (7.4%) and Nottingham (6.6%). These are also some of the areas that saw the greatest increases in the proportions of people describing themselves as being of Mixed ethnicity. Part of the increase is because more people are mixing in these places and especially in London, which, since it took over Rome's mantle, has been the real 'Big Apple', the melting-pot that New York claimed to be. However, another part of the reason will be people in these areas embracing the fact that they are Mixed faster than others elsewhere. We are all mixing more, and a little mixing has always annoyed some people, at times and in some groups. Since 2011 the national proportion of people describing themselves as being of Mixed ethnicity has continued to both rise and accelerate. If this were to continue, in some areas a majority of the population would be of Mixed ethnicity in the future.

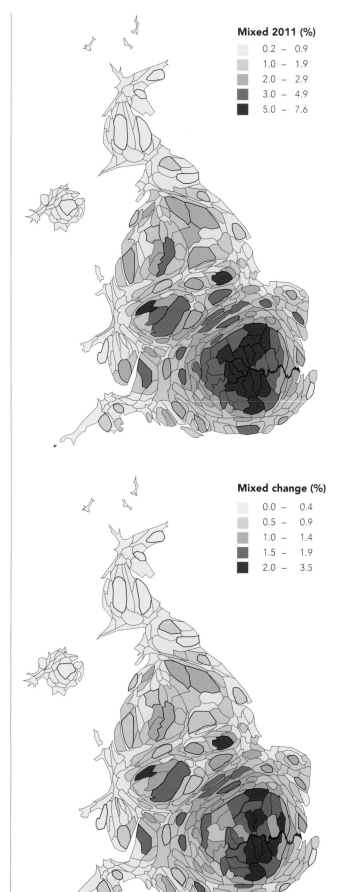

Mixed 2011 (%)

	0.2 – 0.9
	1.0 – 1.9
	2.0 – 2.9
	3.0 – 4.9
	5.0 – 7.6

Mixed change (%)

	0.0 – 0.4
	0.5 – 0.9
	1.0 – 1.4
	1.5 – 1.9
	2.0 – 3.5

People of Mixed ethnicity aged 16+, UK %

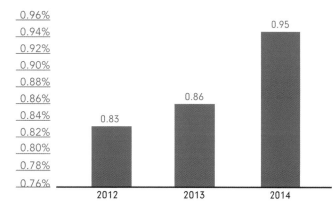

0.96%			
0.94%			0.95
0.92%			
0.90%			
0.88%			
0.86%		0.86	
0.84%			
0.82%	0.83		
0.80%			
0.78%			
0.76%			
	2012	2013	2014

PAKISTANI

In 2011, 1.2 million UK residents were of Pakistani ethnic origin compared to 0.7 million in 2001. A small part of this rise might be more people choosing to describe themselves as Pakistani in 2011 compared to how they chose to describe themselves in 2001, or how their parents described them on the Census form. However, most of the rise will be because this is such a young group compared to the population as a whole, and many young Pakistanis, born in the UK in the 1970s and 1980s, have now had their own children. Immigration will only play a very minor role. This group is now a predominantly Northern English minority ethnic group, with the greatest proportions of local residents identifying as Pakistani in Bradford (20.4%); Slough (17.7%); Pendle (17.1%); Luton (14.4%); Birmingham (13.5%); and Blackburn with Darwen (12.1%). Of those areas, only Slough is in the South.

The greatest falls in the Pakistani population in any local areas have all been in London: Hackney (-0.3%); Haringey, Kensington & Chelsea and Hammersmith & Fulham (all -0.2%); and the City of London and Islington (both -0.1%). In 2001, 8,060 people of Pakistani origin lived in those boroughs. By 2011, that number had fallen to 7,315. Given that this is a relatively young group, a very high level of out-migration is required to achieve that. In the UK as a whole, the proportion of people who identify as Pakistani or Bangladeshi has been falling since 2011.

At this point it is worth pointing out that not only were the 2011 annual survey results not re-based by the 2011 Census until 2012, but also that from April 2011 onwards, the six ethnicity categories were changed as slightly different survey questions were asked, resulting in the ONS deciding not to publish estimates for the period April 2010-September 2011. From 2012 the Pakistani and Bangladeshi counts were combined in official publications.

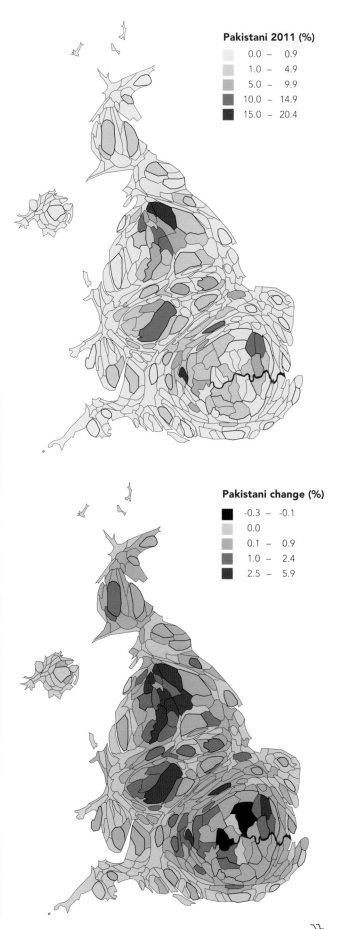

People of Pakistani or Bangladeshi ethnicity aged 16+, UK %

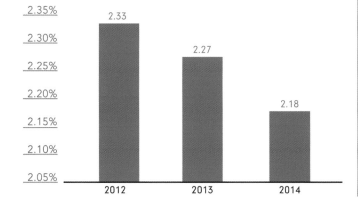

AFRICAN

In 2011, 1.0 million people described their ethnicity as African, a doubling from 0.5 million in 2001. Again, people having children and very low mortality rates among a relatively young group were key to explaining this increase, as well as decisions each individual makes about how to describe themselves and those for whom they fill the form in at each Census. Many people do change ethnicity over time as they see their identity differently from one decade to the next. Anyone who has watched the popular BBC programme *Who Do You Think You Are?* will know how we can each see our origins in a new light. Someone who adopts a very literal answer to 'Where did your ancestors originally come from?' might be tempted to tick 'Africa'. However, as yet, the vast majority ticking this box were more recent arrivals from that continent or their children.

The highest proportions of people identifying as African are found in Southwark (16.4%); Barking & Dagenham (15.4%); Greenwich (13.8%); Newham (12.3%); Lambeth and Lewisham (11.6%); and Hackney (11.4%). Of these areas the proportion since 2001 has fallen in the most central boroughs (Newham and Hackney) and risen further out (Greenwich +6.7% and Barking & Dagenham +11.0%). The next largest rises have been in Bexley (+5.0%) and Thurrock (+5.5%). People of African origin are being moved or choosing to move out of the centre and towards outer East London at a very fast rate.

The chart shows the number of people estimated to be living in the UK born in different countries in Africa. This is not the same as African ethnicity, but the totals are very similar, at around 1 million people, and the numbers are declining slightly over time in sharp contrast to the rise in ethnicity, which will include children who align with their parents' ethnicity but who were born in the UK. Particular countries occasionally see increases such as in those from Somalia in the UK in 2014. The largest increase in the intercensal years in Somalia-born was seen in Bristol, where an extra 1% of the population was born in Somalia in 2011 compared to 2001.

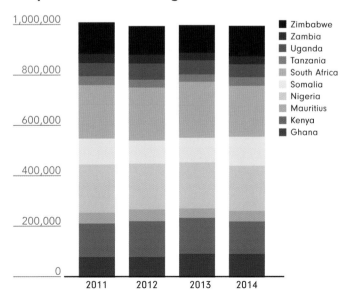

People born in Africa living in the UK

Legend:
- Zimbabwe
- Zambia
- Uganda
- Tanzania
- South Africa
- Somalia
- Nigeria
- Mauritius
- Kenya
- Ghana

Y-axis: 0, 200,000, 400,000, 600,000, 800,000, 1,000,000
X-axis: 2011, 2012, 2013, 2014

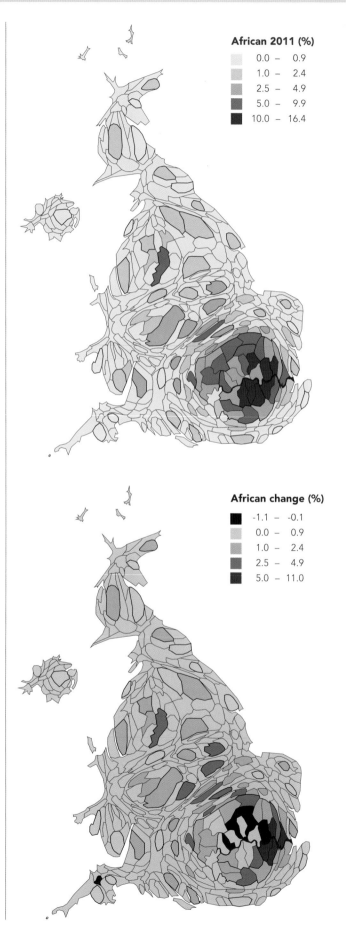

African 2011 (%)
- 0.0 – 0.9
- 1.0 – 2.4
- 2.5 – 4.9
- 5.0 – 9.9
- 10.0 – 16.4

African change (%)
- -1.1 – -0.1
- 0.0 – 0.9
- 1.0 – 2.4
- 2.5 – 4.9
- 5.0 – 11.0

OTHER ASIAN

Just under 0.9 million people in the UK described themselves as being Asian but not Chinese, from the Indian subcontinent, or Mixed. Asia is the world's most populous continent. Anyone describing him or herself as Sri Lankan, Japanese, Malay, Thai, Iranian or Arabic, among many other possible origin descriptions, will be in this group that also includes people who describe themselves as Kenyan Asian or Ugandan Asian. The definition of this group will also have changed slightly as wording on Census forms changes over time. The number who described themselves in this way in 2001 were over three times fewer than in 2011, just 0.25 million.

The greatest concentrations are in a set of boroughs that are contiguous (except for Richmond upon Thames not yet joining the group): Harrow (11.3%); Ealing (9.3%); Brent (9.2%); Hounslow (8.2%); Kingston upon Thames (8.1%); and Merton (7.9%). In all these areas the proportions of the local population who are Other Asian have roughly doubled since 2001, mostly as people start families and few are old enough to be dying.

There are some signs of spreading out geographically as numbers have risen by 7.1% in nearby Rushmoor and 4.6% in Hillingdon, which neighbours three of the areas of greatest current concentration. The graph shows numbers born in selected Other Asian countries and the total rising in 2013 due to an influx from Nepal consisting of former Ghurkhas and their families to Aldershot – continuing the rise seen between the last two Census years in the Rushmoor district.

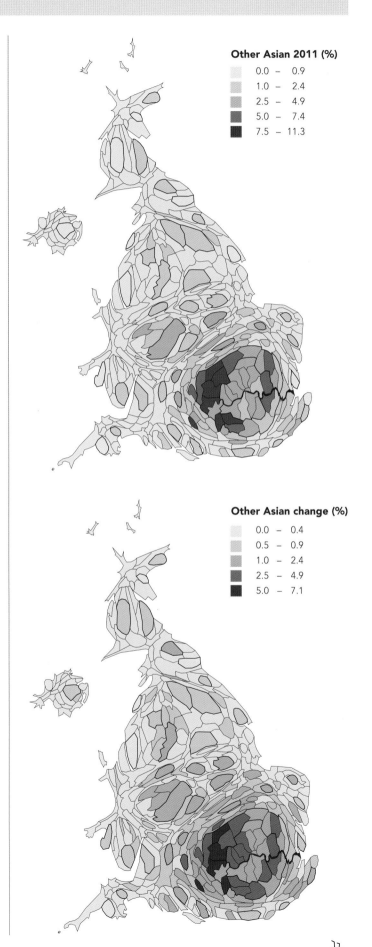

Other Asian 2011 (%)

	0.0 – 0.9
	1.0 – 2.4
	2.5 – 4.9
	5.0 – 7.4
	7.5 – 11.3

Other Asian change (%)

	0.0 – 0.4
	0.5 – 0.9
	1.0 – 2.4
	2.5 – 4.9
	5.0 – 7.1

People born in 'other Asia' living in the UK

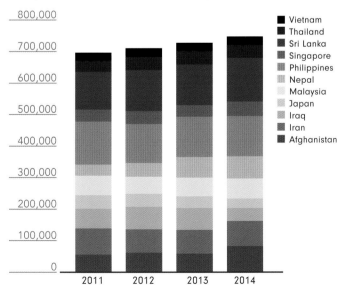

Legend:
- Vietnam
- Thailand
- Sri Lanka
- Singapore
- Philippines
- Nepal
- Malaysia
- Japan
- Iraq
- Iran
- Afghanistan

CARIBBEAN

In 2011, 0.6 million people were of Caribbean ethnicity in the UK. A decade earlier that proportion was very similar. However, there has been a great shift in *where* the population with this identity now live: a great suburbanisation has taken place. The only areas with concentrations of more than one person in every dozen being of this group are to be found in Lewisham (11.2%); Lambeth (9.5%); and Croydon (8.6%). In 2001, Brent, Hackney and Haringey fell into this group of areas, with more than one person in 12 having been born in the Caribbean, but these places are no longer part of the Caribbean centre in the UK. Caribbean identity is diluting, and in places becoming less distinctive.

There has been an exodus to the suburbs and further afield. Suburban Croydon was not in the original group of areas of higher concentration, but it is now. The greatest increase has been in Broxbourne, just North of London (+0.8%), and then Croydon (+0.7%), some way South of the centre of London. But these increases in concentration are smaller than the decreases recorded elsewhere, and since 2013 a reduction has been evident in those born in the most populous Caribbean island with British links – Jamaica.

The graph shows how few people now living in the UK were born in Jamaica, and how net numbers from there have fallen most recently, reflecting the stabilisation and then fall overall in the population from the islands. In just one year were there enough people from any other island for them to be shown here, and that year was 2013 for those from Trinidad and Tobago.

People born in the Caribbean living in the UK

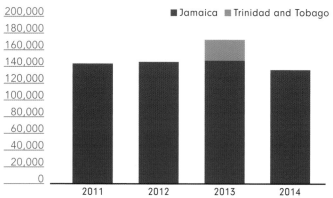

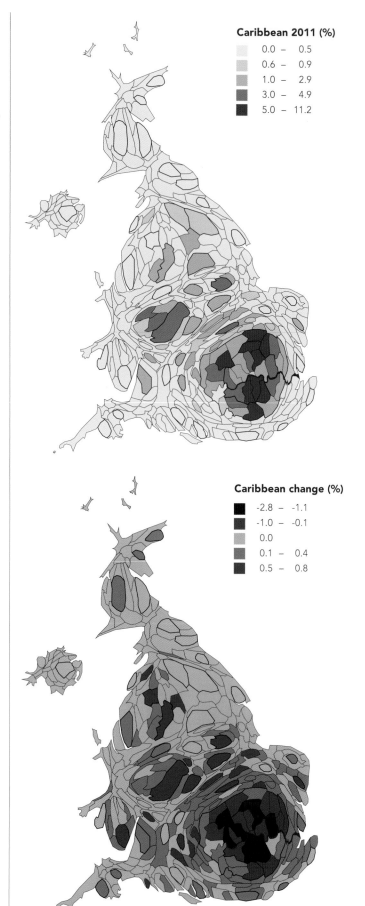

Caribbean 2011 (%)

0.0 – 0.5
0.6 – 0.9
1.0 – 2.9
3.0 – 4.9
5.0 – 11.2

Caribbean change (%)

-2.8 – -1.1
-1.0 – -0.1
0.0
0.1 – 0.4
0.5 – 0.8

OTHER ETHNICITY

In 2011, 0.6 million people were of another ethnicity, after rejecting White, Indian, Pakistani, Bangladeshi, Black, African or Caribbean, Chinese or other Asian, or Mixed. These people are something else entirely. They are found in their second greatest numbers in the most cosmopolitan borough of London, Kensington & Chelsea (7.2%), where a higher proportion of people are 'something else entirely' than are Mixed (5.7%), Other Asian (4.8%), African (3.5%), Chinese (2.5%), Caribbean (2.1%), Indian (1.6%), Pakistani (0.6%) or Bangladeshi (0.5%). In fact 'Other' is the most common minority ethnic group in Kensington & Chelsea. Over half the people who are labelled by the Census authorities as Other in that area actually ticked the 'Arab' box that was offered on the Census form. The same is found in the borough where 'Other' is most common overall, Westminster (11.1%), which has also seen the fastest rise by far (+7.0% in the decade). Nowhere else is it true that 'Other' is the most common group. This is also a rapidly growing group. In 2001, just 0.2 million people were of 'Other ethnicity'; there have been some declines, often in areas where the American armed forces have withdrawn.

Between 2011 and 2013 the number of people living in the UK born in Russia increased from 41,000 to 49,000, and the number from Saudi Arabia from 28,000 to 31,000. The number of Russia-born then fell by 9,000 in the year to 2014, while the number of Saudi-born returned to its 2012 maximum of 34,000. These estimates are based on a sample survey and so cannot be relied on to be that accurate. However, over time, once a trend becomes established, it can usually be seen in these UK totals.

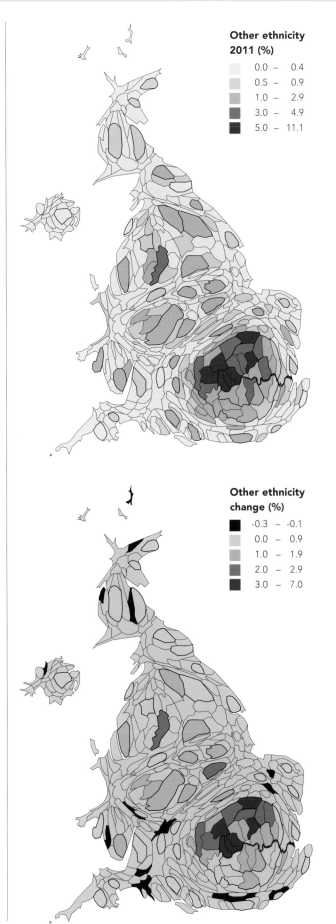

Other ethnicity
2011 (%)

- 0.0 – 0.4
- 0.5 – 0.9
- 1.0 – 2.9
- 3.0 – 4.9
- 5.0 – 11.1

Other ethnicity
change (%)

- -0.3 – -0.1
- 0.0 – 0.9
- 1.0 – 1.9
- 2.0 – 2.9
- 3.0 – 7.0

People born in Saudi Arabia and Russia living in the UK

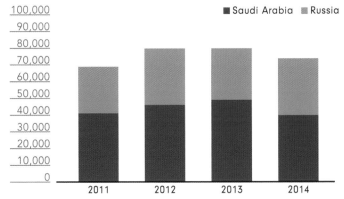

BANGLADESHI

By 2011 there were 0.5 million people of Bangladeshi heritage living in the UK, up from 0.3 million in 2001. The 9 districts with the largest proportions of their local populations being of Bangladeshi origin were Tower Hamlets (32.0%); Newham (12.1%); Oldham (7.3%); Luton (6.7%); Redbridge (5.7%); Camden (5.7%); Barking & Dagenham (4.1%); City of London (3.1%); and Birmingham (3.0%). Almost half of all Bangladeshis in the UK live in these 9 districts (some 48% of the total population); however, in 2001, the concentration was greater (51% of what was a smaller population).

There have been falls in the share of the local population who are Bangladeshi in Tower Hamlets (-1.4%); Camden (-0.7); City of London (-0.7%); Hackney (-0.4%); and Kensington & Chelsea (-0.2%). The largest local rises have been further out of London or even further afield: Redbridge (+4.0%); Barking & Dagenham (+3.7%); Newham (+3.3%); Oldham (+2.7%); Luton (+2.6%); Burnley (+1.2%); and Rossendale (+1.1%). Although some of these increases will be due to (mostly internal) migration, others will be due to births. In contrast, where there are falls, it is out-migration and deaths that will be mostly at play, not (international) emigration. The graph shows the effects of deaths being greater than net in-migration through to 2014.

People born in Bangladesh living in the UK

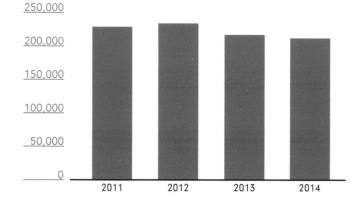

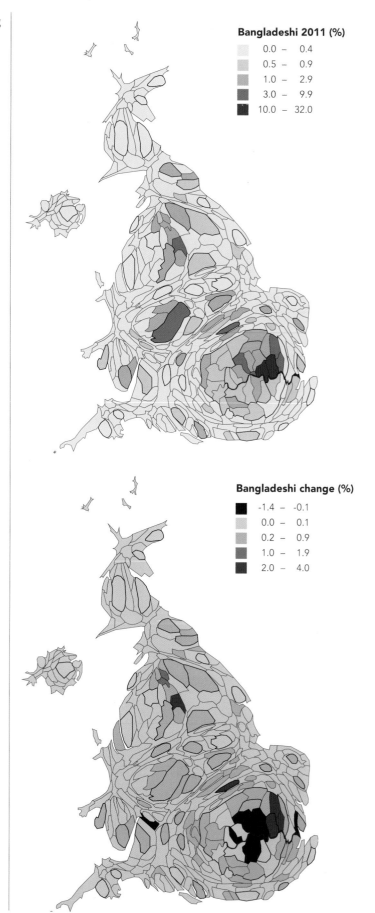

Bangladeshi 2011 (%)

0.0 – 0.4
0.5 – 0.9
1.0 – 2.9
3.0 – 9.9
10.0 – 32.0

Bangladeshi change (%)

-1.4 – -0.1
0.0 – 0.1
0.2 – 0.9
1.0 – 1.9
2.0 – 4.0

CHINESE

In 2011, 0.4 million people of Chinese ethnicity lived in the UK, up from 0.2 million in 2001. The 10 largest concentrations are in many cases associated with universities: Cambridge (3.6%); City of London (3.6%); Tower Hamlets (3.2%); Camden (2.9%); Southwark (2.8%); Westminster (2.7%); Manchester (2.7%); Kensington & Chelsea (2.5%); Oxford (2.3%); and Barnet (2.3%).

The following 10 Local Authority districts have seen the greatest proportional increases in Chinese ethnicity, in all cases more than doubling local populations within a decade. In the list that follows, local populations in 2011 are given: Newcastle upon Tyne (6,000), Exeter (2,000), Nottingham (6,000); Glasgow (11,000); Hammersmith & Fulham (3,000); Welwyn Hatfield (2,000); Sheffield (7,000); Edinburgh (8,000); York (2,000); and Norwich (2,000). In all these cases the proportion of the population who are of Chinese ethnicity has increased by around 1% or a little more in 10 years. Annual changes in the numbers of people living in the UK born in China are shown in the graph, and illustrate how volatile the proportions can be as cohorts of university students leave and arrive. The apparent stability of the last two years is perhaps a little misleading.

People born in China living in the UK

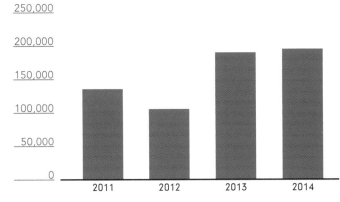

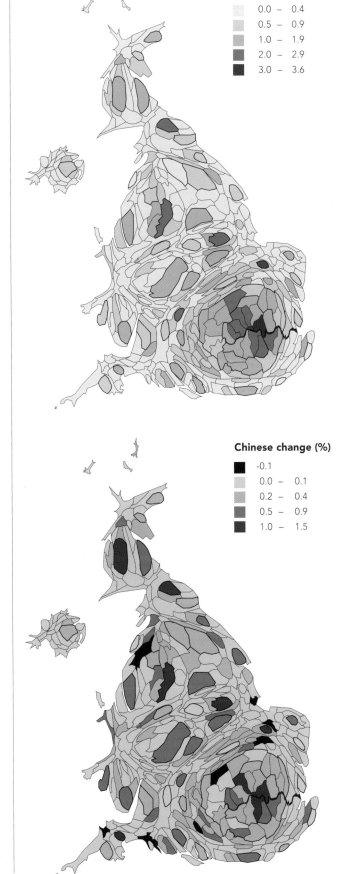

Chinese 2011 (%)

- 0.0 – 0.4
- 0.5 – 0.9
- 1.0 – 1.9
- 2.0 – 2.9
- 3.0 – 3.6

Chinese change (%)

- -0.1
- 0.0 – 0.1
- 0.2 – 0.4
- 0.5 – 0.9
- 1.0 – 1.5

OTHER BLACK

The Other Black ethnic group includes people who ticked 'Any other Black/African/Caribbean background' in preference to ticking simply 'Black African' or 'Black Caribbean'. This also includes people who wrote in more complex answers about their Black ethnicity in the space provided on the Census form. Many people in this group will have been born in the UK or elsewhere in Europe and some in Canada, the US or elsewhere. In 2011, 0.3 million people were of this ethnicity, up from 0.1 million in 2001. The local proportions are highest in 16 London boroughs (with proportions ranging from 4.8% to 1.8%) and then Birmingham (1.7%); Bristol and Manchester (both 1.6%). The largest increases in share of local population between 2001 and 2011 have all been in much the same places: Lambeth (+2.7%); Croydon (+2.5%); Southwark (+2.4%); Lewisham (+2.3%); Enfield, Brent and Islington (all +1.8%); Hackney (+1.6%); Harrow and Bristol (both +1.4%); Greenwich, Hillingdon, Barking & Dagenham, Haringey, Newham, Waltham Forest and Ealing (all +1.3%); Camden and Birmingham (both +1.2%); and Manchester (+1.1).

The graph shows how there were still twice as many Black people in England and Wales in 2011 who described themselves as Caribbean rather than Black British or Black Other, and as many Black people who described themselves as African as all other Black groups combined.

People of Black ethnicity by sub-ethnic group, England and Wales 2011

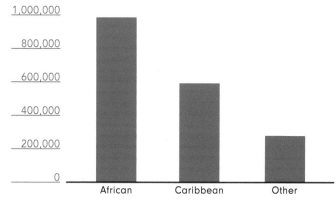

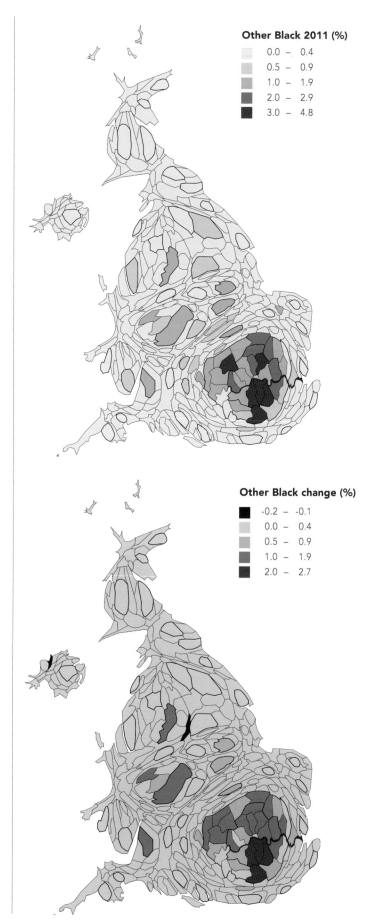

Other Black 2011 (%)

	0.0 – 0.4
	0.5 – 0.9
	1.0 – 1.9
	2.0 – 2.9
	3.0 – 4.8

Other Black change (%)

	-0.2 – -0.1
	0.0 – 0.4
	0.5 – 0.9
	1.0 – 1.9
	2.0 – 2.7

HOME COUNTRY NATIONAL IDENTITY/BRITISH NATIONAL IDENTITY

The 2011 Census was the first Census to ask people 'How would you describe your national identity?' The options that were offered were 'English', 'Welsh', 'Scottish', 'Northern Irish', 'British' or 'Other – write in'. Had 'World citizen' or 'European' been proffered the results might have been quite different. However, people could tick more than one box, and so were not forced to choose which identity label might best apply to them, even of the few that were offered. Here we plot the proportion that ticked a 'Home' category and the proportion that ticked 'British' and any other combination, including none. Thus 'Home' is any combination that includes English in England, Welsh in Wales, Scottish in Scotland and Northern Irish in Ireland; and British is any combination that includes British, with or without another category. In 2011 44.1 million people chose a home identity out of 63.2 million residents, 57.9 million of whom dutifully ticked they were 'British'. The most British place in the UK was in Scotland – East Ayrshire – closely followed by Redcar and Cleveland (both at 99.1% when rounded). Only a minority of the residents of both Newry & Mourne and Derry ticked 'British' (44.8% in both cases). The graph below shows how quickly identities can be diluted if the UK press tries to cast doubt, for example, on Scotland's ability to govern itself in the run-up to the Independence Referendum.

If forced to choose an identity would choose 'Scottish', people living in Sotland %

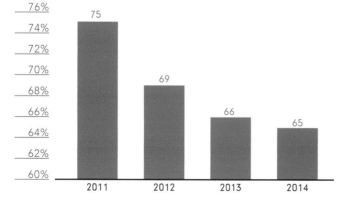

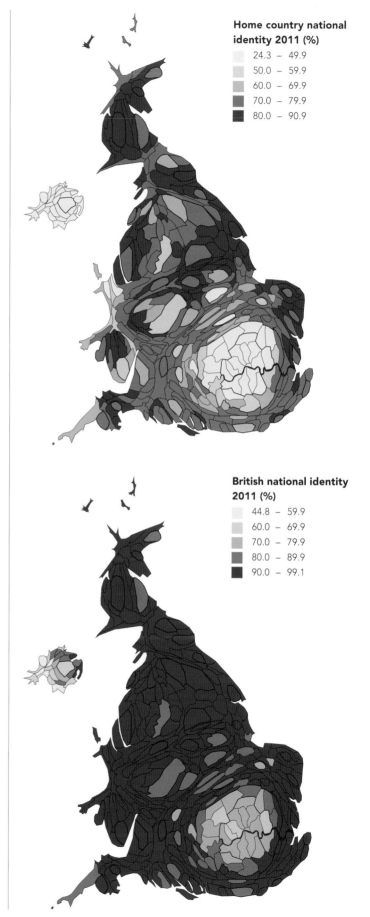

Home country national identity 2011 (%)
- 24.3 – 49.9
- 50.0 – 59.9
- 60.0 – 69.9
- 70.0 – 79.9
- 80.0 – 90.9

British national identity 2011 (%)
- 44.8 – 59.9
- 60.0 – 69.9
- 70.0 – 79.9
- 80.0 – 89.9
- 90.0 – 99.1

OTHER NATIONAL IDENTITY / IRISH NATIONAL IDENTITY

In 2011, 4.8 million people in the UK have a national identity other than British anywhere, English in England, Scottish in Scotland, Welsh in Wales and/or Irish (the latter is asked only if they live in Northern Ireland). Over a third of the residents of Kensington & Chelsea (34.0%) have a national identity as being British or English, whereas 37.8% identify *only* with a place outside of the UK (the question actually mapped above for all of the UK). This means that the remainder, 28.2%, have either two or more national identities or are Scottish, Welsh or Irish living in England. Identity is complex.

Some 25.4% of the residents of the City of London identify with a country outside of the UK. Outside of London it is Slough that is the most cosmopolitan in terms of the commonality of identities outside of the UK being mentioned as predominant (23.2%), then Cambridge (22.4%); Oxford (20.5%); Forest Heath, which has US military installations (20.3%); Luton (18.7%); Reading (17.8%); Leicester (17.2%); and Manchester (17.0%). Peterborough (14.6%); Boston (14.0%); and Bedford (11.3%) also rank highly.

In Northern Ireland almost exactly 0.5 million people explicitly stated that they had Irish identity and not Northern Irish identity, 34% of the Northern Irish population. In both Derry (54.6%) and Newry & Mourne (52.5%), a majority expressed this identity. In contrast, at the other extreme in Northern Ireland, was in Ards, where 91.7% stated their identity was British and in Carrickfergus, where 93.1% said they were British.

The graph shows answers in Scotland to what is probably currently the most important question on national identity to be asked within the UK, at least until those who will get a vote in the referendum are asked if they wish to remain in the European Union.

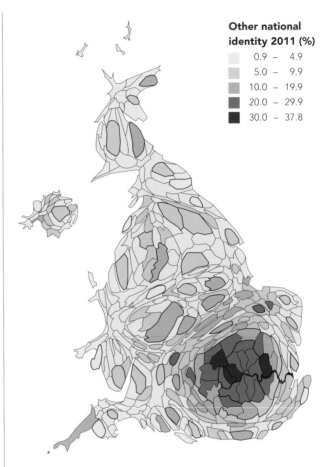

Other national identity 2011 (%)

- 0.9 – 4.9
- 5.0 – 9.9
- 10.0 – 19.9
- 20.0 – 29.9
- 30.0 – 37.8

Irish national identity 2011 (%)

- 5.2 – 9.9
- 10.0 – 19.9
- 20.0 – 29.9
- 30.0 – 39.9
- 40.0 – 54.6

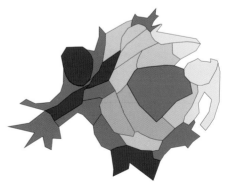

Intention if there was a vote tomorrow on independence in Scotland in 2015

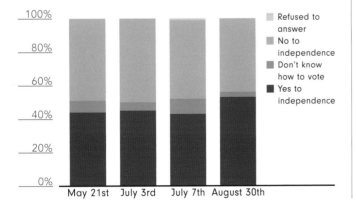

- Refused to answer
- No to independence
- Don't know how to vote
- Yes to independence

May 21st   July 3rd   July 7th   August 30th

ENGLISH PROFICIENCY

A decision was made to ask people in the UK whose main language is not English whether, in addition to their main language, they can also speak English 'very well', 'well', 'not well', or 'not at all'. In Scotland it is probable that a sizeable group in the population showed their contempt for the question by ticking that their main language was not English but Scots, and then saying that their English was simply passable. The only likely significant area of large amounts of long-established non-English-speaking is in a few parts of Wales. Interestingly in Wales, where the question appeared later in the form (personal question 19), there was little evidence of similar reactions as in Scotland.

No one who stated that English was their main language was asked if they could speak any other language, let alone 'well', or 'very well'. There is an extraordinariness in Britishness that currently involves not being interested in being able to speak other languages.

As the grading of spoken English is so subjective, there is little point quoting any particular statistics, save for listing the 11 areas of the country where people whose main language is not English are mostly like to say that they can speak English 'very well': East Dorset, Derbyshire Dales, South Staffordshire, South Hams, West Dorset, East Devon, North East Derbyshire, Castle Point, Purbeck, Staffordshire Moorlands and North Norfolk. In all cases more than 96.6% of English-as-a-second-language speakers living in these areas said their English was 'very good'. The graph below (on a log scale) shows how few children living in each country of the UK are bilingual; the highest proportion is in Wales. The data comes from the UK National Association for Language Development in the Curriculum (NALDIC).

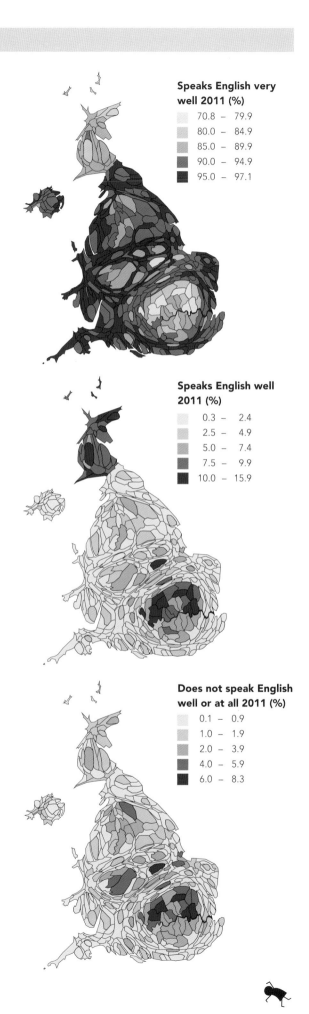

Speaks English very well 2011 (%)
- 70.8 – 79.9
- 80.0 – 84.9
- 85.0 – 89.9
- 90.0 – 94.9
- 95.0 – 97.1

Speaks English well 2011 (%)
- 0.3 – 2.4
- 2.5 – 4.9
- 5.0 – 7.4
- 7.5 – 9.9
- 10.0 – 15.9

Does not speak English well or at all 2011 (%)
- 0.1 – 0.9
- 1.0 – 1.9
- 2.0 – 3.9
- 4.0 – 5.9
- 6.0 – 8.3

Bilingual children aged 5–16 in UK schools by country of residence 2013

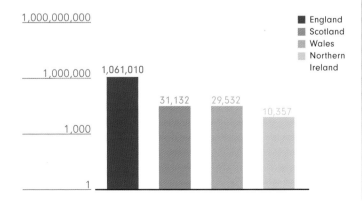

- England
- Scotland
- Wales
- Northern Ireland

1,000,000,000

1,000,000   1,061,010   31,132   29,532   10,357

1,000

1

MAIN LANGUAGE ENGLISH, WELSH, IRISH, GAELIC, SCOTS / FRENCH

The first map includes all those who gave Welsh, Irish, Gaelic or Scots as their first language, with the assumption that almost all are also virtually first-language English speakers. In England people are not asked if they speak any of the other options just listed. In the UK as a whole, more than 96% of the population speak English (or any 'home' language elsewhere) in the Derbyshire Dales, East Dorset, South Staffordshire, North East Derbyshire, Staffordshire Moorlands, Castle Point, South Hams and North Norfolk. Between 55% and 70% of the population speak one of these as their main language in Waltham Forest, Kensington & Chelsea, Leicester, Slough, Harrow, Hounslow, Haringey, Westminster, Ealing, Tower Hamlets, Brent and Newham. In contrast, only 150,000 people speak French as their main language in England and Wales, but more than 1% of the population do so in Kensington & Chelsea (4.7%); Hammersmith & Fulham (3.0%); Westminster (2.9%); City of London (2.1%); Camden (1.9%); Lambeth, Southwark, Islington, Lewisham, Wandsworth, Hackney, Tower Hamlets and Haringey (all at 1.1%). Less than 0.02% of the population are first-language French speakers in Barrow-in-Furness, Halton, Knowsley, Blaenau Gwent and Torfaen (0.01%). In understanding these figures it might help to consider the number of people living in the UK who were born in its nearest neighbour where English is not an official language: France.

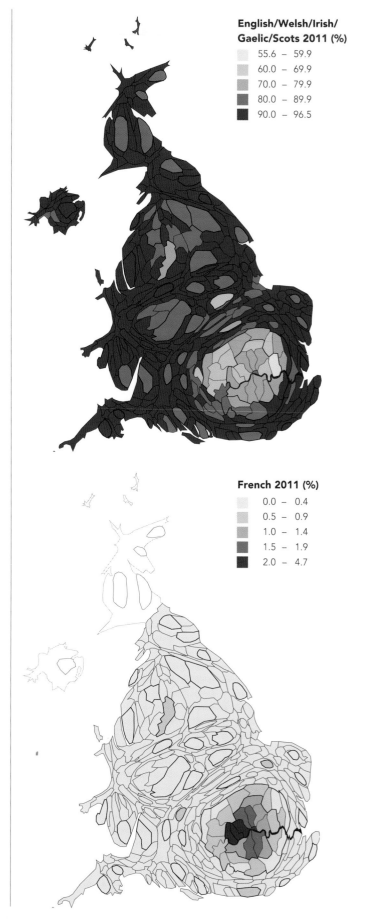

English/Welsh/Irish/Gaelic/Scots 2011 (%)

- 55.6 – 59.9
- 60.0 – 69.9
- 70.0 – 79.9
- 80.0 – 89.9
- 90.0 – 96.5

French 2011 (%)

- 0.0 – 0.4
- 0.5 – 0.9
- 1.0 – 1.4
- 1.5 – 1.9
- 2.0 – 4.7

People born in France living in the UK

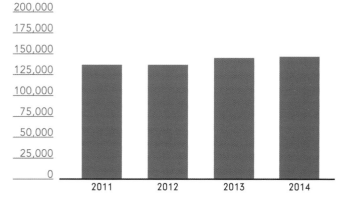

MAIN LANGUAGE PORTUGUESE AND SPANISH / POLISH

Just over 250,000 people living in England, Wales and Northern Ireland speak Spanish or Portuguese as their main language. People resident in Scotland were not asked if they did (or it was not reported, even if they did volunteer that information). Rates were highest in Kensington & Chelsea (3.9%); Westminster (3.8%); Southwark, Hammersmith & Fulham, Brent, Haringey, Hackney, Islington, City of London, Camden, Wandsworth, Newham, Tower Hamlets, Lewisham and Oxford (all at 1.6%); and Cambridge (1.5%). Rates were lowest in Moyle and Strabane, where in each district just two people had Spanish or Portuguese as their main language.

In contrast to the low numbers speaking Portuguese or Spanish, 600,000 people listed Polish as their main language in the UK. Rates were highest in Ealing (6.0%); Slough (5.9%); Boston (4.7%); Haringey (4.1%); Luton and Hounslow (both 3.9%); Peterborough and Corby (both 3.6%); Southampton (3.5%); Merton and Brent (3.3%); South Holland and Waltham Forest (3.1%); and Aberdeen (2.8%). Only in Castle Point in Essex are less than 0.1% of the population primarily Polish speakers. Even on the Isles of Scilly there are at least 16 Polish speakers. There are some Polish speakers everywhere in the UK, although a majority of the population of the UK live in areas where at least 99.2% of their fellow residents do not give Polish as their main language.

The graph shows how there appears to have been a small increase in the numbers of people coming to the UK from these three countries in 2013, which became a much larger increase in every case during 2014.

People born in Spain, Portugal and Poland living in the UK

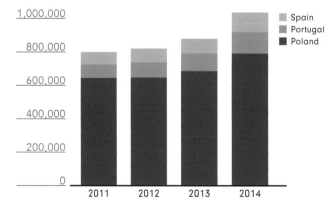

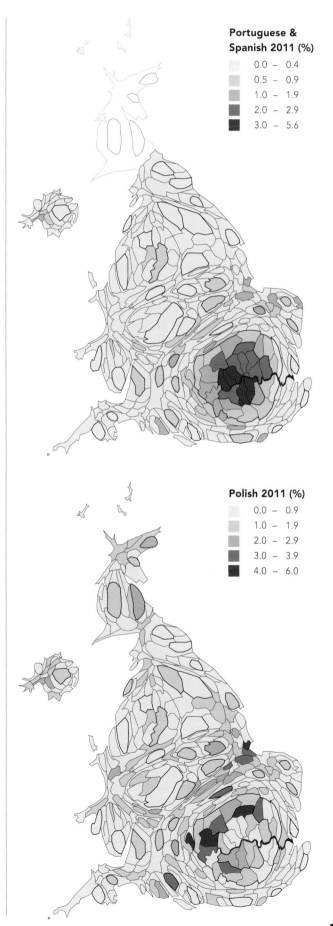

MAIN LANGUAGE: OTHER EU / NON-EU EUROPEAN

Some 0.7 million people speak a main language of an EU country that is not the UK, France, Portugal, Spain or Poland. Outside of London this group of languages are most often the main language of people who were living in 2011 in Boston (4.9%); Cambridge (4.8%); Peterborough (4.1%); Dungannon (3.6%); and Oxford (3.5%). A further 0.2 million people have their main language being a European language of a non-EU country. Of this group of languages the largest proportions of local residents giving them as their main language outside of London are found in Boston (1.2%); Corby, Cambridge, Broxbourne and Oxford (all at 1.1%). Some 41% of all the people living in the UK whose main language is another EU language live in London, while 59% of all those giving a non-EU European language also live in London.

The graph shows the 2011–14 increases in people from selected countries where some of these other European languages are spoken. The largest relative increase has been in arrivals from Hungary (+46% in the two years to 2013), then Romania (+38%), Latvia and Italy (both +15%) and Lithuania (+12%). Then in the one year to 2014, all but one of these five country-of-birth origins again saw rapid increases in net growth of UK residents by these birthplaces: Hungary (+13% in the one year to 2014), faster increases from Romania (+31%) and Latvia (+26%), but slowing from Italy (+6%), and a slight reversal in the numbers coming from Lithuania (-2%). Again, sampling size is not large, but the longer-term trends are becoming clearer.

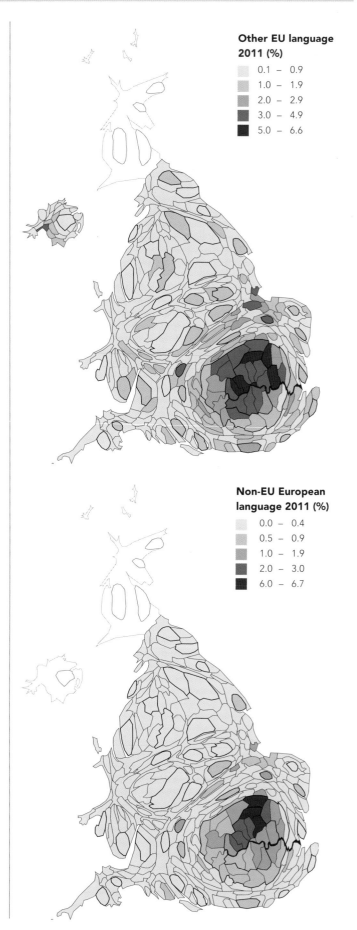

Other EU language 2011 (%)

- 0.1 – 0.9
- 1.0 – 1.9
- 2.0 – 2.9
- 3.0 – 4.9
- 5.0 – 6.6

Non-EU European language 2011 (%)

- 0.0 – 0.4
- 0.5 – 0.9
- 1.0 – 1.9
- 2.0 – 3.0
- 6.0 – 6.7

People born in selected EU countries living in the UK

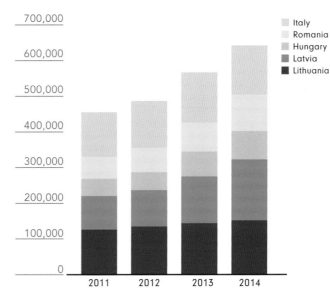

Legend:
- Italy
- Romania
- Hungary
- Latvia
- Lithuania

MAIN LANGUAGE SOUTH ASIAN / EAST ASIAN

Some 1.3 million people living in the UK speak one of many possible South Asian languages as their main language. Over a 20th of the population speaking a main language from South Asia are living in Newham (20.9%); Tower Hamlets (18.2%); Leicester (16.9%); Harrow (16.0%); Redbridge (15.2%); Brent (14.0%); Slough (13.3%); Hounslow (12.9%); Ealing (12.0%); Luton (10.7%); Blackburn with Darwen (9.9%); Bradford (9.1%); Hillingdon (9.0%); Birmingham (8.1%); Oldham (8.0%); Waltham Forest (7.2%); Sandwell (7.0%); Rushmoor and Merton (both 6.7%); Oadby & Wigston (6.2%); Pendle (6.0%); Barking & Dagenham (5.9%); Wolverhampton (5.8%); Kirklees (5.7%); Rochdale and Coventry (both 5.3%); Croydon and Preston (both 5.2%); and Watford (5.1%).

In contrast, just under 0.4 million people living in the UK spoke an East Asian language as a main language in 2011. Nowhere did more than a 20th of the population speak one of these languages, of which the most common may have been Chinese.

Outside of London the highest proportions of people speaking an East Asian or South Asian language are found in Kingston upon Thames and Cambridge (both 3.1%); Oxford (2.4%); and Manchester (2.2%). The continuing increase in people born in India and Pakistan living in the UK will contribute a little to a continued rise in speakers of these languages living in the UK. This is illustrated in the graph, which shows a continuing steady growth in the size of both groups, accelerating a little in 2014.

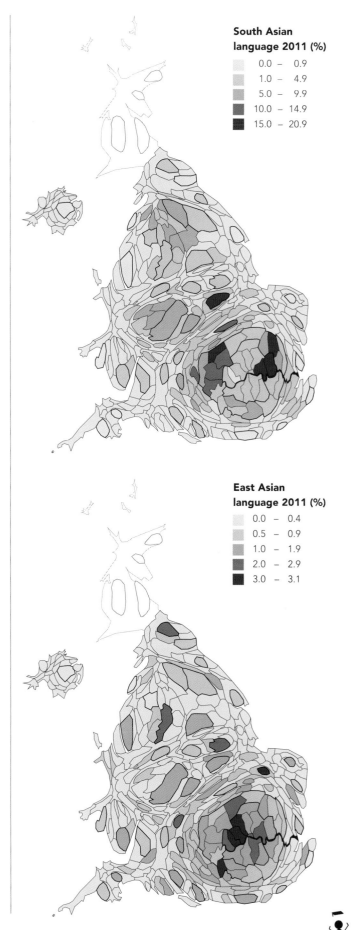

South Asian language 2011 (%)
0.0 – 0.9
1.0 – 4.9
5.0 – 9.9
10.0 – 14.9
15.0 – 20.9

East Asian language 2011 (%)
0.0 – 0.4
0.5 – 0.9
1.0 – 1.9
2.0 – 2.9
3.0 – 3.1

People born in India and Pakistan living in the UK

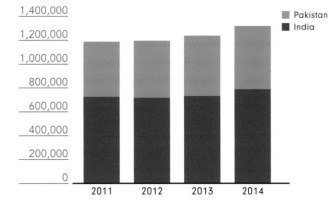

HOME LANGUAGE SKILLS

Welsh, Gaelic and Irish are referred to as 'home' languages. Some 0.9 million people living in Wales have some skill in their home language, or 28% of the Welsh population. People in Wales speaking Welsh make up the majority of the 1.4 million people living in the UK who have any skill in any of the home languages. However, almost everywhere in Wales the proportion that has any skill is falling. There has been a rise in Cardiff (0.1%) and Monmouthshire (1.1%) in the local proportions of people showing any ability in Welsh, which has been enough to offset the falls almost everywhere else in Wales. In great contrast there have been rapid increases in the proportions of people living in Scotland able to demonstrate any skill at all in Gaelic. The fastest increase has been an additional 3.9% of all people living in Aberdeenshire, an extra 10,000 people to the previous total of just under 2,000 in 2001. In contrast, the proportion able to speak Gaelic in Eilean Siar (formerly known as the Western Isles or Outer Hebrides) has fallen by 7.2% to just over 1,000 people. However, those 1,000 people, mostly very elderly, will have spoken Gaelic far better than the newcomers to the language in Aberdeenshire. In contrast again, in Northern Ireland there are many areas of home language decline and rise. In England no home language remains. The last was extinguished many centuries ago following wave after wave of invasion and conquest.

Finally, consider the proportion of children in Wales who can speak Welsh, as shown in the graph below. Many Welsh children may stop using Welsh in adulthood, but now so many are learning Welsh at school, despite their parents often being unable to speak it, it is likely that future Censuses may record a revival in the language, albeit slow and steady, and offset to an extent by (mainly) English immigrants who don't learn as easily as children.

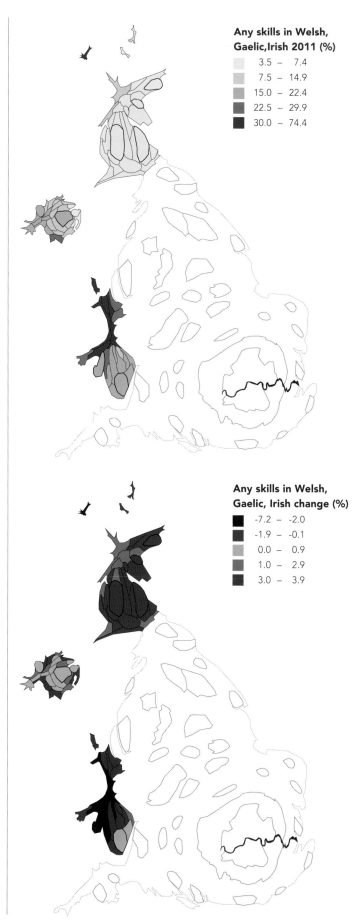

Any skills in Welsh, Gaelic,Irish 2011 (%)
- 3.5 – 7.4
- 7.5 – 14.9
- 15.0 – 22.4
- 22.5 – 29.9
- 30.0 – 74.4

Any skills in Welsh, Gaelic, Irish change (%)
- -7.2 – -2.0
- -1.9 – -0.1
- 0.0 – 0.9
- 1.0 – 2.9
- 3.0 – 3.9

People living in Wales who can speak Welsh by age 2011 %

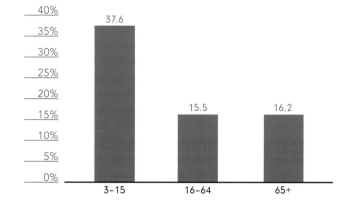

In June 2015 it was announced
that the UK population had
risen to 64,596,800.

64,596,800

POPULATION

Birthplace and Nationality

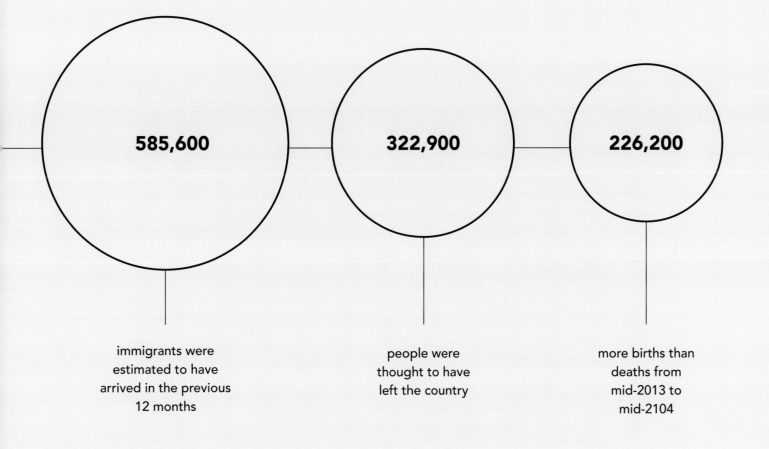

585,600

immigrants were
estimated to have
arrived in the previous
12 months

322,900

people were
thought to have
left the country

226,200

more births than
deaths from
mid-2013 to
mid-2104

Birthplace and Nationality

The Censuses provide a detailed snapshot of a rapidly changing picture. In June 2015 it was announced that the UK population had risen to 64,596,800 by mid-2014; 585,600 immigrants were estimated to have arrived in the previous 12 months, and 322,900 people were thought to have left the country. The figures had also been bolstered by 226,200 more births than deaths in those 12 months (from mid-2013 to mid-2014). This was a slowdown on the rise in births that had been recorded every year since the last Census had been taken in 2011. A quarter of these UK births were to mothers who had been born outside of the UK. As a result, 46% of the rise in population in the year to June 2014 was due to natural change (births and deaths), 53% to net migration, and 1% due to movements of members of the armed forces. Policy debate in the UK is often dominated by such figures, but they are rarely put in the very long-term context that a series of Censuses provide when it comes to understanding immigration.

The graph below was created by painstakingly collecting data from each British Census that asked about country of birth and amalgamating countries so that a consistent time series could be constructed. For 2011, where the Census data is insufficiently detailed, we have used estimates from the 2011 Annual Population Survey. The first Census to ask where people were born was held in 1841 and only differentiated between people born in Ireland (which was then part of the UK), the rest of the then British Empire, and the rest of the world. Back then just 2.9% of the population of the UK had been born outside of England, Wales and Scotland. However, for some this may have been a few too many: just as the first UK Census was taken in 1801 due partly to fears raised by Thomas Malthus over population growth due to fertility, so a question on birthplace of residents was added to the 1841 Census because of fears among those in power over who was entering the country and from where. At that time, the population of Britain was only 18.5 million, of whom 0.4 million, 2.2%, had been born in Ireland; 1,360 had been born elsewhere in the Empire – a tiny number; and 0.1 million elsewhere in the world. With the advent of famine in Ireland, that 2.2% would grow to 3.8% in 1851 and 4.3% in 1861 before falling back to reach a 100-year low of 2.8% in 1931. This was due to the high internal birth rate; there were by then 44.8 million people in Britain. Throughout all this time the UK was exporting far more people than it was importing, but those who got to choose what questions were asked worried more

People living in Britain born outside of the UK or in Ireland

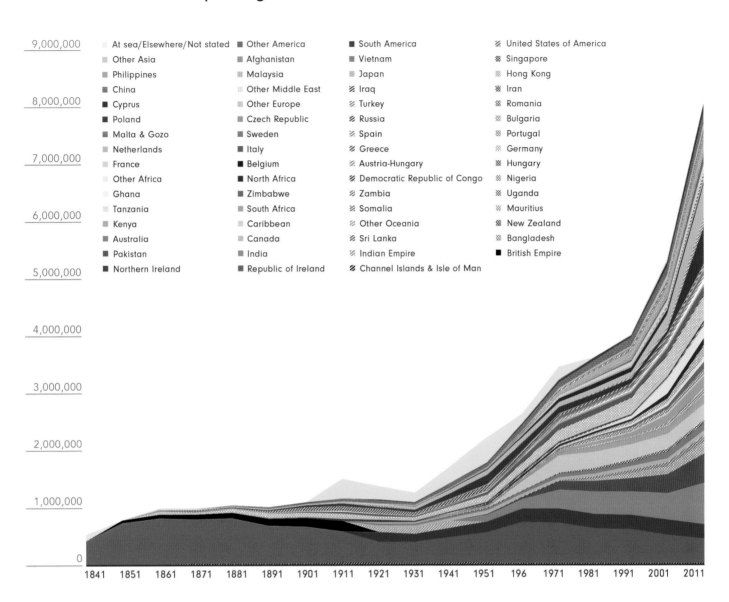

At sea/Elsewhere/Not stated	Other America	South America	United States of America
Other Asia	Afghanistan	Vietnam	Singapore
Philippines	Malaysia	Japan	Hong Kong
China	Other Middle East	Iraq	Iran
Cyprus	Other Europe	Turkey	Romania
Poland	Czech Republic	Russia	Bulgaria
Malta & Gozo	Sweden	Spain	Portugal
Netherlands	Italy	Greece	Germany
France	Belgium	Austria-Hungary	Hungary
Other Africa	North Africa	Democratic Republic of Congo	Nigeria
Ghana	Zimbabwe	Zambia	Uganda
Tanzania	South Africa	Somalia	Mauritius
Kenya	Caribbean	Other Oceania	New Zealand
Australia	Canada	Sri Lanka	Bangladesh
Pakistan	India	Indian Empire	British Empire
Northern Ireland	Republic of Ireland	Channel Islands & Isle of Man	

and more about who was coming in and from where, and so asked more and more detailed questions about country of birth as time progressed.

The graph above shows the absolute numbers of people born overseas living in Britain that rises over time along with the rest of the population. However, the overseas-born also become a progressively larger share of the UK population from 1931 onwards, as people again begin to move further and further distances around the world. The First World War had brought a temporary halt to much immigration or emigration.

After the First World War, and once the UK stopped having net emigration, immigration controls were brought in to try to reduce the numbers of people arriving from overseas. Such controls are never very effective – the overseas-born share of the British population rose to 3.7% in 1941 (estimated because there was no Census), 4.6% in 1951, 5.2% in 1961, 6.4% in 1971, 6.8% in 1981, 7.3% in 1991, 9.3% in 2001 and 13.1% in 2011. The fastest increases had been in the 1930s, 1960s,

1990s and the 2000s. More and more people born in the UK were also emigrating, especially in their retirement.

For the entire 1841–2011 period, the largest contributing overseas country of birth was Ireland, each year, until it was surpassed by India in 2011. After Ireland and India it had been Germany that provided the most immigrants from 1861 through to 1891, then Russia from 1901 to 1921 inclusive, various parts of Europe in 1931, Poland in 1941 and 1951, the Caribbean from 1961 to 1981, Pakistan in 2001, and Poland again in 2011. However, what really stands out when the graph is examined is how the range of countries in which people have been born has become wider and wider, so that no single place of origin in any way dominates any more.

There have always been a few people who have complained about immigrants. In 1901 it was the 6.3% of all overseas-born people who had been born in Russia, many of whom were Jewish. In 1951 it was the 7.3% of the overseas-born who had been born in Poland; in 1971 the National Front objected to the 8.2% of overseas-born from the Caribbean; in 2001 the British National Party (BNP) were angered by the 6.0% of overseas-born from Pakistan; in 2011 the UK Independence Party (UKIP) complained about the 7.9% of overseas-born people from Poland. There is always a place from which more people have recently come than any other place, which usually constitutes between a 20th and a 10th of all migrants. This group is often the largest because they are the most needy and there is subsequently, although sometimes only decades later, embarrassment about those who opposed their immigration because most of them will have left their homelands out of desperation, including to escape poverty or persecution: the Jews, the Poles, the West Indians.

To put this in context, the graph below shows the percentage of the population of Great Britain born within and outside the British Isles since 1841.

British Isles born and non-British Isles born people UK %

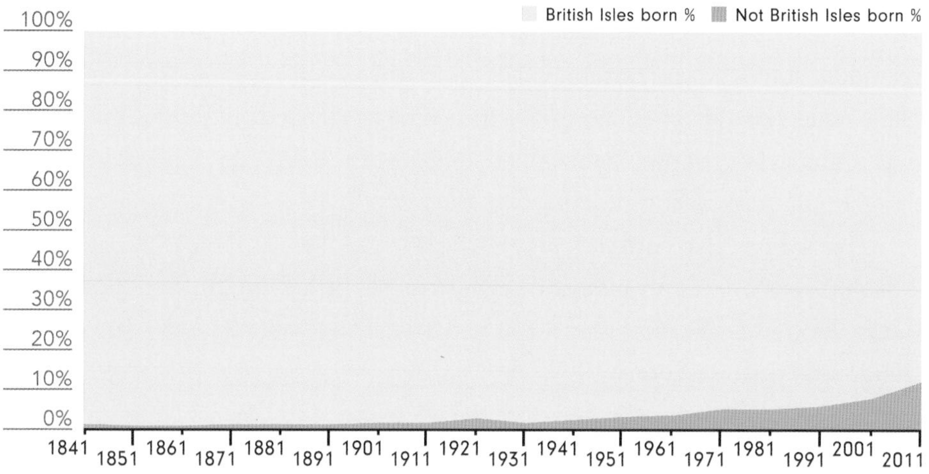

BORN IN ENGLAND

In 2001 there were 44.0 million people living in the UK who had been born in England. By 2011 that number had increased to 45.4 million, a rise of over 3.2%. However, the population as a whole increased from 58.8 to 63.3 million, or 7.7%, so the overall proportion of people living in the UK who had been born in England fell from 75% to 72%, even though the absolute number rose. More children were being born in England compared to the numbers of people who had been born in England who were dying or emigrating. The Second World War had begun some 72 years before the 2011 Census was taken. Birth rates in the UK were very low before and during that war, and so there were relatively few people likely to die or possibly retire overseas. In contrast, and partly thanks to immigration into England from abroad, a growing number of younger adults have become parents in recent years, even though fertility has fallen since 2011.

An increasing proportion of the England-born are the children of people who were not themselves born in England. And as they move around more, and as the older English travel further afield on retirement, the proportion of England-born living in Wales, Scotland and most of Northern Ireland rises. Mobility is increasing for everyone, including the England-born, a large proportion of whom will now be living overseas, especially in mainland Europe. Greater mobility does not mean that areas continue to see fewer and fewer people living there who were born locally.

Up to 2012 the proportion of people born in the UK living in London had been slowly rising as so many children had been born in London, often to mothers not born in the UK. Since 2012, births in London have reduced, and more people from the rest of the EU have arrived in London. Net, 929,000 EU but not UK-born people were living in London in 2014 compared to 788,000 in 2013, a rise from 9.9% to 11.0% of London's population.

Living in London, born in the UK %

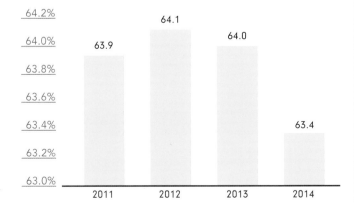

	2011	2012	2013	2014
	63.9	64.1	64.0	63.4

England 2011 (%)

- 2.1 – 39.9
- 40.0 – 69.9
- 70.0 – 79.9
- 80.0 – 89.9
- 90.0 – 96.4

England change (%)

- -18.8 – -10.1
- -10.0 – -5.1
- -5.0 – -2.6
- -2.5 – -0.1
- 0.0 – 4.1

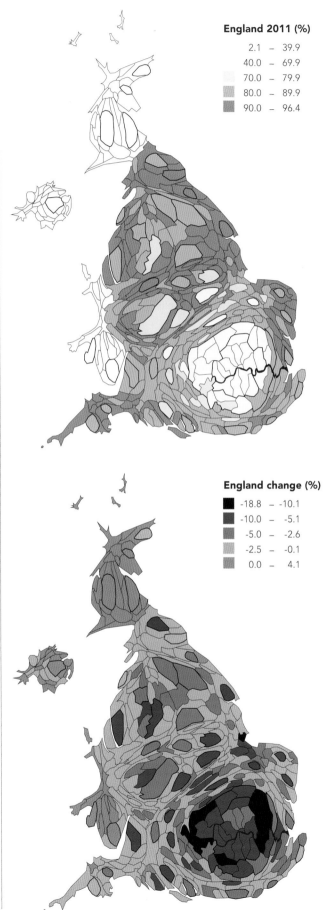

BORN IN SCOTLAND

In 2001 there were 5.2 million Scotland-born people living in the UK, 4.4 million of whom lived in Scotland. To the nearest tenth of a million those figures remained unchanged some 10 years later. However, the overall population of Scotland had increased, from 5.1 to 5.3 million people, so the share of people living in Scotland who were born in Scotland fell over the last decade, and fell slightly faster than it did across England. In contrast, the England-born living in Scotland rose from 0.4 million to 0.5 million. In Wales and Northern Ireland there was hardly any change in the very small numbers born in Scotland living in those countries. Since 2011 it is likely that the number of people born in Scotland moving to England has not increased as Scottish universities are free at the point of use for Scottish students, whereas if they travel to England, in most cases they would have to pay £9,000 a year in fees. Despite Scottish university funding rules retaining a high proportion of young Scotland-born people in Scotland after 2011, the overall proportion of people born in the UK living in Scotland, as a share of everyone living in Scotland, fell between 2011 and 2012. This was because there was an influx of people from outside the UK looking for work in many parts of the UK, including Scotland. That influx reduced a little in net effect in 2013, but returned again in 2014 to just 7.3% of the population of Scotland by 2014 having been born outside of the UK, mostly being from somewhere else in the EU. Just like London, Scotland is becoming more cosmopolitan, but not being a single city the change so far is to a lesser extent. Nevertheless, immigration from much further afield than England is altering Scotland rapidly, especially its major cities.

Scotland 2011 (%)

0.3	–	1.9
2.0	–	12.9
70.0	–	79.9
80.0	–	89.9
90.0	–	93.5

Scotland change (%)

-9.3	–	-6.1
-6.0	–	-3.1
-3.0	–	-1.1
-1.0	–	-0.1
0.0	–	0.2

Living in Scotland, born in the UK %

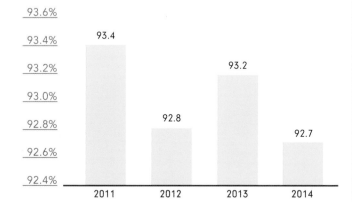

Year	%
2011	93.4
2012	92.8
2013	93.2
2014	92.7

BORN IN WALES

In 2011 there were 2.8 million Wales-born people living in the UK, 2.2 million in Wales itself. As in Scotland, these are statistics that were identical 10 years earlier. Again, the population of Wales as a whole had risen, from 2.9 million in 2001 to 3.1 million in 2011, and so the Wales-born living in Wales shrank as a proportion of the Welsh population. Again, the largest immigrant group was the England-born who rose from 590,000 to 636,000 residents of Wales by 2011, or by +1.6% of the population in Wales in 10 years. Many of this large influx of England-born people will be retirees with a high mortality rate among them, so many more than 46,000 will have had to come to create the net rise. However, in relative terms it is only fractionally greater than the increase in non-UK EU-born people living in London in 2014 compared to 2013, and that is a change that occurred in just one year, not 10.

Again, proportions of Wales-born rose slightly in those parts of the UK furthest from Wales as the overall mobility of the Wales-born, like all groups, rose, and so their numbers increased in Scotland and Northern Ireland. However, numbers also rose within a few parts of Wales and the nearby Forest of Dean in England. It is worth noting that although Welsh university students still had to pay fees after 2011, their fees were capped at £3,810, but this cap applied regardless of where they studied in the UK. It is possible that because the new arrangements in Wales allow Welsh students to leave Wales that the proportion of people living in Wales born in the UK fell after 2012 and continued to fall through to 2014.

Living in Wales, born in the UK %

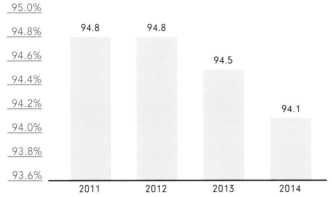

Wales 2011 (%)

0.1 – 0.9	
1.0 – 6.3	
49.0 – 59.9	
60.0 – 79.9	
80.0 – 90.3	

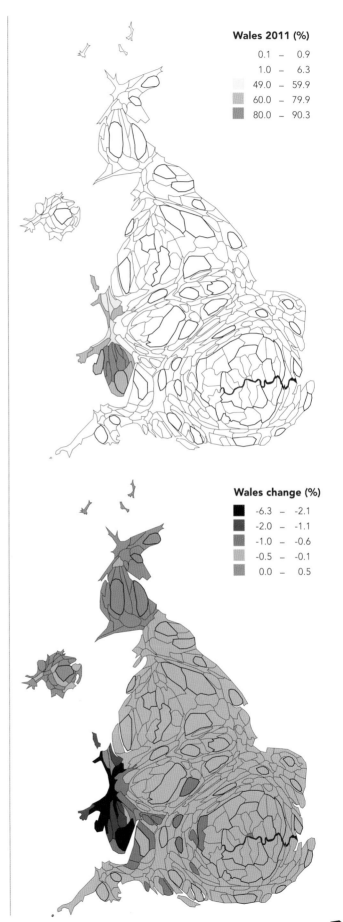

Wales change (%)

-6.3 – -2.1	
-2.0 – -1.1	
-1.0 – -0.6	
-0.5 – -0.1	
0.0 – 0.5	

BORN IN NORTHERN IRELAND

In 2011 there were 1.8 million people born in Northern Ireland living in the UK, 1.6 million in Northern Ireland itself (out of a total population of 1.8 million people living in the province). Thus the number of Northern Ireland-born people now living in other parts of the UK is equal to the number of people now in Northern Ireland who were not born there. This is similar to what we know for the UK as a whole, in that there are roughly as many people who were born in the UK but who now live abroad as there are people living in the UK who were born abroad.[5]

In 2001 the population of Northern Ireland was a little lower, at 1.7 million, 1.5 million of whom were born in the province, out of 1.8 million people born in Northern Ireland living in the UK in total. Although the number of people born in Northern Ireland living in Northern Ireland has increased, it has not increased quite as quickly as migration from other countries to Northern Ireland. For example, by 2011 there were 20,000 people living in Northern Ireland from Poland and Romania, compared to only 200 people being from those countries in 2001, a 100-fold rise in just 10 years.

Student financing in Northern Ireland is designed to encourage students to stay in Northern Ireland, and this may have had an influence on the numbers born in the province living in the province rising over time. If more people from overseas had come to Northern Ireland since 2012, the proportion would have fallen, but it has been stable since 2012, as the graph below shows. The changing pattern of the Northern Ireland-born population in the British mainland suggests a population that is now ageing and retiring and moving towards retirement areas in England, but especially Scotland.

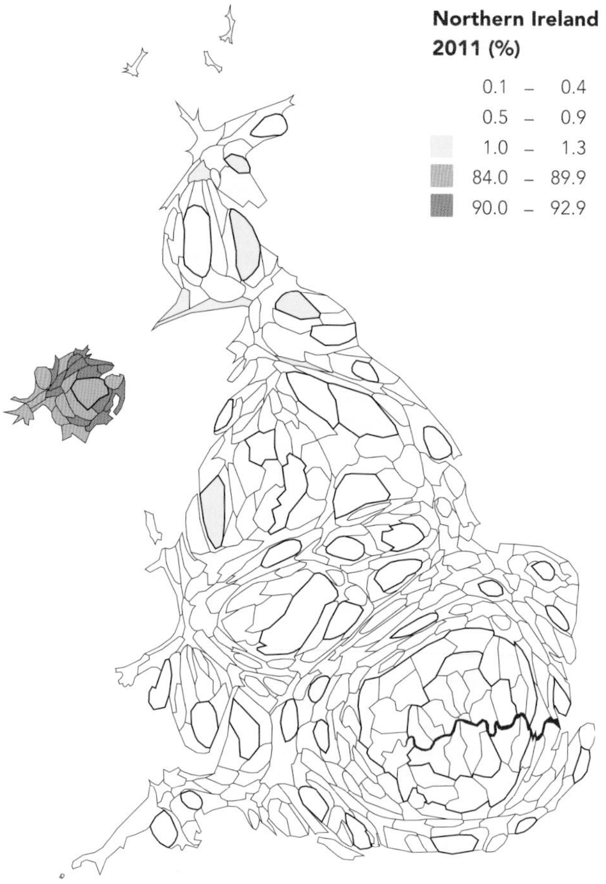

Northern Ireland 2011 (%)

0.1 – 0.4
0.5 – 0.9
1.0 – 1.3
84.0 – 89.9
90.0 – 92.9

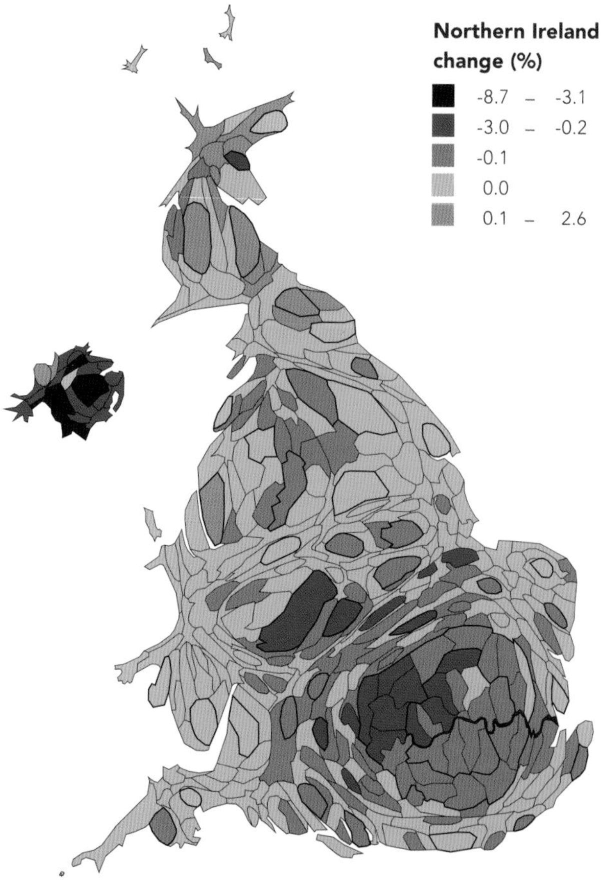

Northern Ireland change (%)

-8.7 – -3.1
-3.0 – -0.2
-0.1
0.0
0.1 – 2.6

Living in Northern Ireland, born in the UK %

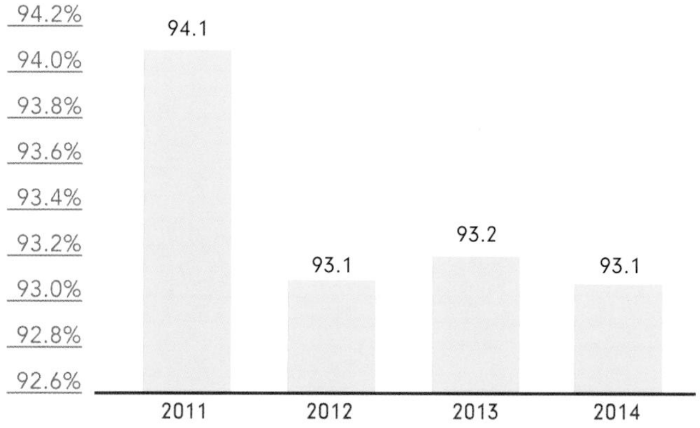

BORN IN SOUTH ASIA

In 2011, 1.7 million people living in the UK had been born in South Asia: India (0.7 million), Pakistan (0.5 million), Bangladesh (0.2 million) and other nearby South Asian countries (0.3 million). In 2001 the number of people born in these countries living in the UK was 1.0 million. Between 2% and 3% of the population of the UK were born in these countries depending on how many countries are included. The graph below uses a smaller set of countries and shows a continued increase in people born in these parts of the world. The greatest concentration of people born in South Asia living in the UK in 2001 was found in Tower Hamlets (19.3%, falling to 17.5% in 2011); Newham (15.5%, up to 23.2% by 2011); Slough (11.9%, up to 18.0% in 2011); Brent (11.4%, up to 16.0%); Hounslow (10.3%, up to 17.6%); Ealing (10.3%, up to 14.5%); and Leicester (10.0%, up to 13.7%). Ten years later, Redbridge joined this group (South Asia-born proportion rising from 9.9% to 18.5%); Harrow (9.8% to 17.1%); Luton (8.2% to 12.5%); and Hillingdon (5.1% to 11.3%). Migration, mostly from overseas, led to the rises; out-migration and mortality led to the falls. In general the South Asian population is moving away from Central London to the suburbs, and rising in other mostly urban areas, apart from Redcar & Cleveland on the North East coast. The influx in 2014 was part of the overall rapid rise in international immigration to the UK in that year.

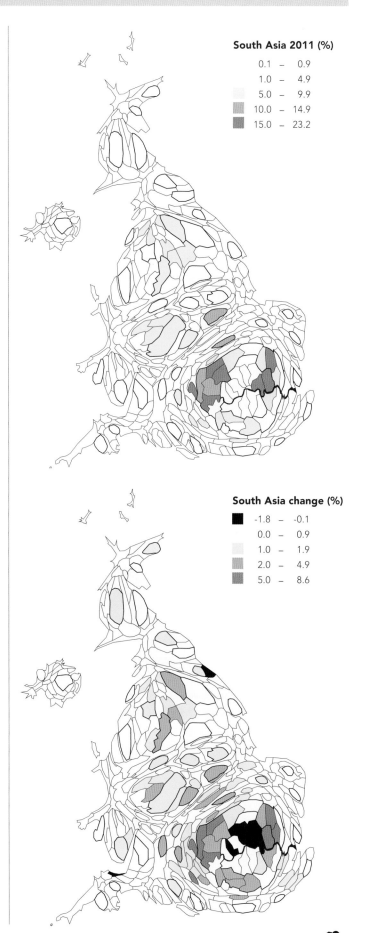

South Asia 2011 (%)

0.1	– 0.9
1.0	– 4.9
5.0	– 9.9
10.0	– 14.9
15.0	– 23.2

South Asia change (%)

-1.8	– -0.1
0.0	– 0.9
1.0	– 1.9
2.0	– 4.9
5.0	– 8.6

Living in the UK, born in South Asia (India, Pakistan, and Bangladesh) %

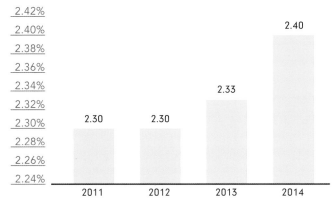

BORN IN OTHER EU COUNTRIES (NOT OTHERWISE LISTED)

In 2011 around 1.2 million people living in UK had been born in another EU country – not including Germany (0.3 million), Poland and Romania (0.7 million) or Ireland, which appear later in this chapter. The graph below shows the number of people living in the UK born in an EU country that is not the UK or the Republic of Ireland (0.5 million). These countries include the original EU-13, that is, Austria, Belgium, Denmark, Finland, France, Germany, Greece, Italy, Luxembourg, Netherlands, Portugal, Spain and Sweden, and the eight countries that joined the EU in 2004: Czech Republic, Estonia, Poland, Hungary, Latvia, Lithuania, Slovakia and Slovenia. When Ireland, Malta, Cyprus, Bulgaria and Romania are added, this makes 26, and Croatia joining in July 2013 makes 27.

In the graph below the 2.7 million people born in the rest of the EU made up just 4.3% of the population in 2013, but this jumped to 4.7% in 2014. In the maps, just under half that group of countries is shown. People from these countries are most concentrated in Kensington & Chelsea (14.1%) and Westminster (11.8%); and least commonly found in West Dunbartonshire (0.25%), Blaenau Gwent (0.26%) and Limavady (0.27%).

In 2001 people born in the same set of countries numbered 0.5 million, so have more than doubled in size as a group as people move further within the EU and more are permitted to move than before. The largest increases in share of local populations have been in Boston (+6.5%); Haringey (+5.7%); Newham (+5.3%); Enfield (2.2%); and Dungannon (+5.1%) in Northern Ireland, which, like Boston, has seen a recent influx of people working in agriculture, including meatpacking.

Living in the UK, born in the rest of the EU %

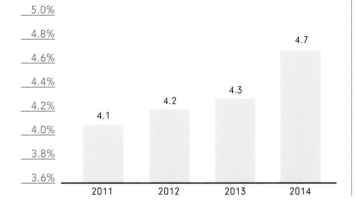

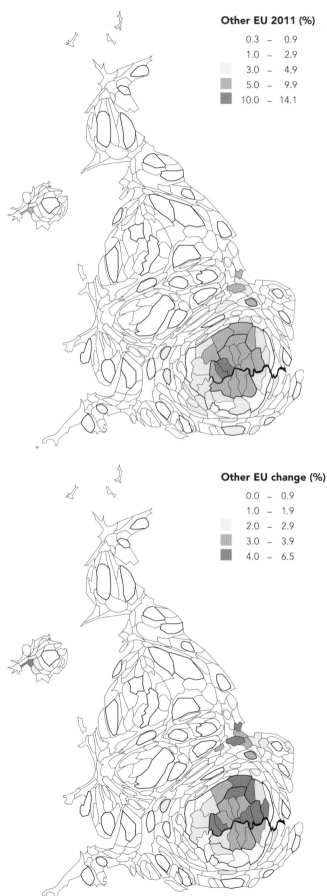

Other EU 2011 (%)

0.3 – 0.9
1.0 – 2.9
3.0 – 4.9
5.0 – 9.9
10.0 – 14.1

Other EU change (%)

0.0 – 0.9
1.0 – 1.9
2.0 – 2.9
3.0 – 3.9
4.0 – 6.5

BORN IN POLAND AND ROMANIA

There were 0.7 million people born in Poland and Romania living in all of the UK in 2011. It had only been 0.1 million in 2001. The maps of increase and of total numbers are so similar because most of the people born in these countries now living in the UK arrived between 2001 and 2011. The greatest share of local population born in these two countries now lives in Ealing (6.6%, from 1.3%); Slough (6.3%, from 0.5%); Brent (5.4%, from 0.7%); Haringey (5.2%, from 0.5%); Waltham Forest (4.8%, from 0.2%); and Boston (4.7%, from 0.1%). The least popular areas for people born in these two countries to live in (in all of the UK) were both in Essex: Castle Point (0.11%) and Rochford (0.13%). The smallest increases were in South Staffordshire (+0.06%); Castle Point (+0.07%); East Dunbartonshire (+0.08%); Torfaen (+0.09%); and Redcar & Cleveland (+0.10%). Migrants tend not to arrive in places where there is little work nearby or where there might be greater hostility to immigrants. They tend to arrive in areas where a few arrived a few years earlier and established shops, churches and other facilities that make migration and staying a little less daunting. The graph below shows the overall proportion of the population of the UK who were born in these two countries edging towards 1.3% in 2013, or just under a third of all non-UK EU-born residents in the UK. In 2014 that proportion jumped to just over 1.5%, in line with the overall increase from the rest of the EU that occurred that year.

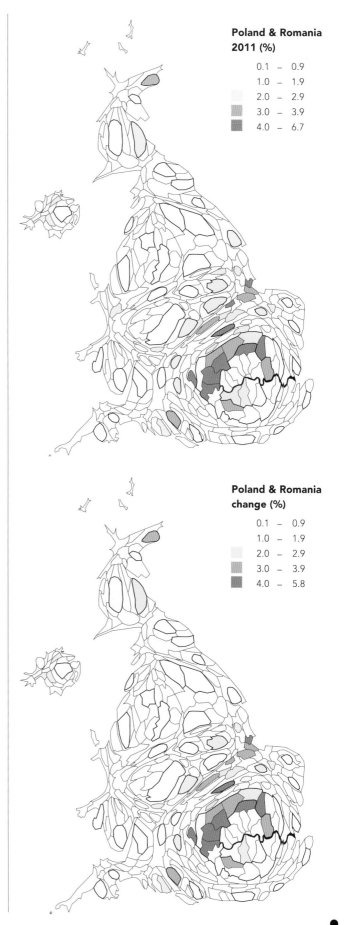

Poland & Romania
2011 (%)

0.1 – 0.9
1.0 – 1.9
2.0 – 2.9
3.0 – 3.9
4.0 – 6.7

Poland & Romania
change (%)

0.1 – 0.9
1.0 – 1.9
2.0 – 2.9
3.0 – 3.9
4.0 – 5.8

Living in the UK, born in Poland or Romania %

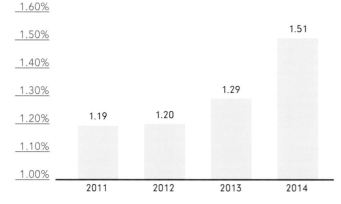

1.19	1.20	1.29	1.51
2011	2012	2013	2014

BORN IN THE REPUBLIC OF IRELAND

For most of the last two centuries the largest overseas-born migrant group living in the UK were born in what is now the Republic of Ireland. In 2011 just 0.47 million Irish Republic-born residents lived in the UK, down from 0.53 million a decade earlier, a 10% fall. Deaths are outweighing net immigration, as this is in part a rapidly ageing population. Unsurprisingly the largest proportions are found in districts bordering the Republic, but there are still more Irish Republic-born in Luton compared to Omagh, Dungannon or Belfast. The highest proportions are: Fermanagh (6.7%); Strabane (5.4%); Newry & Mourne (4.4%); Derry (4.1%); Armagh (3.0%); Brent (2.9%); Islington (2.8%); Hammersmith & Fulham (2.7%); Camden (2.4%); and Luton (2.3%). The only areas with increases are in Scotland, which might well be connected to the right that Irish citizens, and all other non-UK EU citizens, have to study for free at universities in Scotland. Between 2001 and 2011 the largest increases in the Irish Republic-born living in any part of the UK were the Shetland Islands (+0.5%); Edinburgh (+0.3%); Aberdeen (+0.3%); East Lothian (+0.2%); and Scottish Borders (+0.1%). In contrast, the greatest falls in local population shares are all in or near London: Brent (-2.1%); Islington, Ealing and Luton (all -1.1%); and Westminster, Hammersmith & Fulham and Manchester (all -1.0%). Some of these declines will be due to retirement migration, but others, especially along the South coast of England, to deaths. The drop in 2013 is within the margin of error of the ONS survey from which it is estimated, but also continues the 2001–2011 trend and was not reversed in 2014.

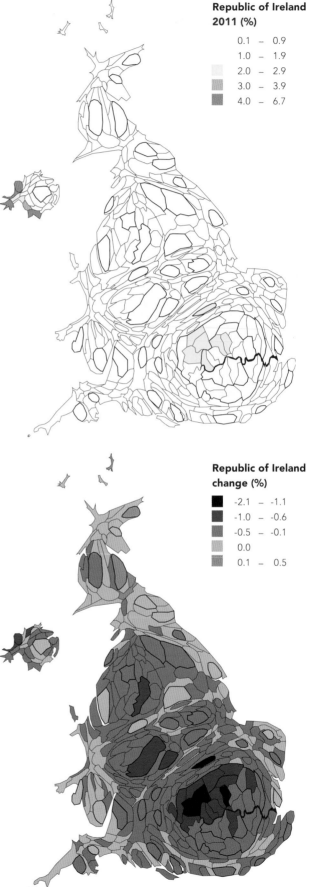

Republic of Ireland
2011 (%)

0.1	–	0.9
1.0	–	1.9
2.0	–	2.9
3.0	–	3.9
4.0	–	6.7

Republic of Ireland
change (%)

-2.1	–	-1.1
-1.0	–	-0.6
-0.5	–	-0.1
0.0		
0.1	–	0.5

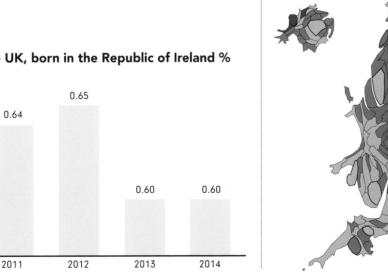

Living in the UK, born in the Republic of Ireland %

	2011	2012	2013	2014
	0.64	0.65	0.60	0.60

BORN IN SOUTH AFRICA AND ZIMBABWE

In 2011 there were 0.3 million people living in the UK who had been born in South Africa or Zimbabwe. In 2001 the combined populations of these two groups of UK residents was 0.2 million, and the greatest concentrations were in Wandsworth (2.1% of the resident population) and Merton (2.0%). By 2011, these two London boroughs were still home to the largest groups but had traded places – Merton (3.4%) and Wandsworth (2.4%) – and were joined by Elmbridge in Surrey (2.1%) as places where at least one in 50 people resident in 2011 had been born in either African country. The greatest increase anywhere in the UK was in Merton, the peak among a pattern of a general suburbanisation. In contrast, populations born in these two African countries (that were already not high) were falling fastest in areas of London that were more central: Brent (-0.4%); Hammersmith & Fulham (-0.3%); and Haringey (-0.2%). The proportion of the overall population of the UK born in these two countries is small, at just over 0.5% in total, and so the fluctuations shown in the trend since 2011 (below) could include the influence of sampling error in government surveys. However, numbers may well fluctuate significantly year on year for some groups who may move between countries when they have the right of residence in more than one, and when the overall size of the group is small. The drop shown here to 2012 is just one in 5,000 of the UK population, and the rise to 2013 is half that number again, but the further drop to 2014 suggests that the 2001–11 rise has now ended.

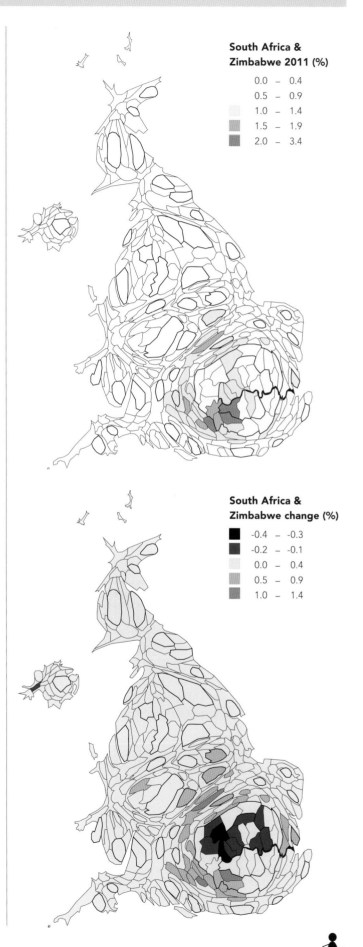

Living in the UK, born in South Africa or Zimbabwe %

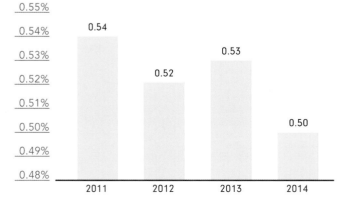

BORN IN THE MIDDLE EAST

In 2011 just over 0.3 million people living in the UK had been born in the countries of the Middle East, 0.49% of the total population of 63.2 million. Although this proportion is very small, just 10 years earlier almost exactly half as many people born in Middle Eastern countries lived in the UK. The greatest proportions of people born in Middle Eastern countries were found in Westminster (7.0%); Kensington & Chelsea (4.4%); Barnet (4.2%); Ealing (3.6%); Brent (3.1%); and Hammersmith & Fulham (2.6%). Thus, the proportion of people born in the Middle East in these few London boroughs varies from more than five times to just over 14 times the national average. But despite such high concentrations, only about one in five of all people born in the Middle East living in the UK live in these boroughs, with four-fifths living elsewhere in the UK.

In contrast to particular areas of London, the following six districts of the UK are home to almost no one born in the Middle East. Here the proportions are, for all sensible purposes, as near as 0% as the Census can record. In Northern Ireland: Strabane, Cookstown, Limavady and Ballymoney; in Wales: Blaenau Gwent; and in England: Bolsover. In contrast, every district in Scotland has at least a few people born in the Middle East (possibly due to oil connections). The greatest increases in the Middle East-born population, both in absolute and relative terms, has been in Westminster, where numbers and proportions have almost doubled. After that, the greatest relative rises have often been in cities with larger universities.

The graph below shows that since 2011 there has been a rise in the entire non-EU-born population living in the UK of about a tenth of 1% to 2013 and another tenth of 1% in the year to 2014. The Middle East-born population are just 6% of that non-EU-born total.

Living in the UK, born outside of the EU %

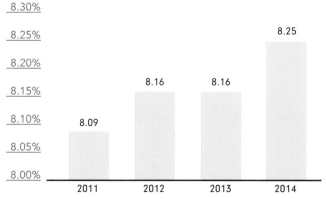

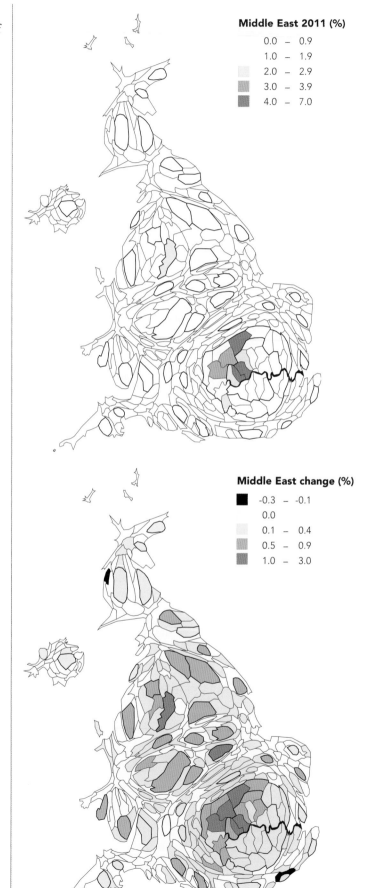

BORN IN GERMANY

In 2011 just under 0.3 million people living in the UK had been born in Germany, 0.47% of the UK population. Just as some people born in the Middle East will have been the children of UK-born expats who have since returned, perhaps from working in the oil industry, so a proportion of people born in Germany were born to UK-born parents, often those serving in the army of the Rhine in the 1970s and 1980s. The echoes of older times live on for as long as the offspring survive. Thus the place with the highest proportion of German-born residents in the UK in 2011 was Richmondshire in Yorkshire, home to the Catterick barracks. In that one district 2.1% of all people were born in Germany. But today the places with the next largest proportions of Germany-born are Kensington & Chelsea (1.7%); Cambridge and the City of London (both 1.6%); and Oxford and Westminster (both 1.4%). Students, financiers and entrepreneurs are now more numerous than the children of the UK's overseas armed forces.

There is nowhere in the UK with almost no Germany-born residents any more. The largest increases in local populations being born in Germany are in Tower Hamlets and the City of London (both +0.4%); and Wandsworth and Merton (both +0.3%). The national share of the UK population who were born in Germany has gone up and down slightly since 2011, but remains below half a per cent of the total population, and appears stable.

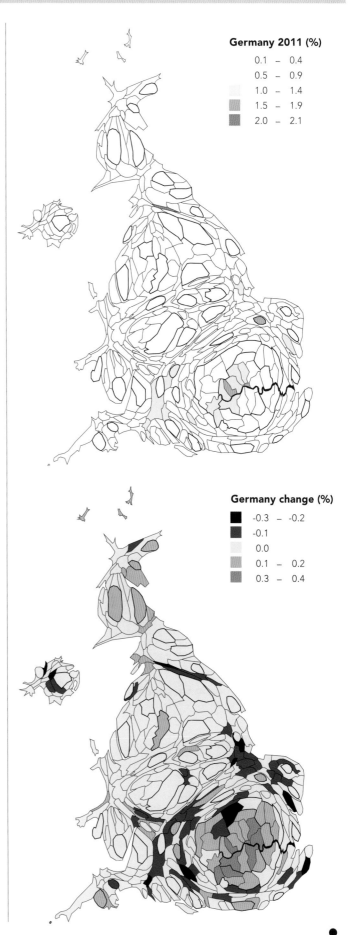

Germany 2011 (%)

0.1 – 0.4
0.5 – 0.9
1.0 – 1.4
1.5 – 1.9
2.0 – 2.1

Germany change (%)

-0.3 – -0.2
-0.1
0.0
0.1 – 0.2
0.3 – 0.4

Living in the UK, born in Germany %

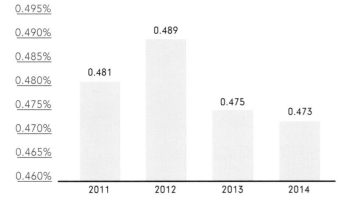

	2011	2012	2013	2014
	0.481	0.489	0.475	0.473

BORN IN CHINA AND HONG KONG

By 2011 there were 0.28 million Hong Kong and China-born people living in the UK, 0.45% of the total population, a proportion almost doubling from 0.15 million in 2001. The highest proportions in any one locality were found in Cambridge (2.4%); City of London (2.3%); Tower Hamlets (1.9%); Manchester and Oxford (both 1.7%); and 1.5% in each of Newcastle upon Tyne, Camden and Southwark. The greatest concentrations of increases during the 2000s had been in the City of London (+1.3%); Tower Hamlets and Exeter (both +1.2%); Cambridge, Newcastle upon Tyne and Nottingham (all +1.1%); and Manchester (+1.0%). University towns feature highly in this list of places that have enjoyed the greatest increases. In contrast, the greatest falls were all smaller, each of just 0.1% of the local population share, and found in Torridge, Boston, East Cambridgeshire, Purbeck, Wealden and West Dorset. This list of well-to-do largely retirement locations suggests that perhaps some of the children of the former Hong Kong colonial administration might well have found their way to such areas in the past, but have died within the last decade due to old age. Since 2011 there has been a small but persistent decline in the proportion of the national population born in Hong Kong and China, as recorded in the Annual Population Survey. That survey recorded 0.1% less than the Census as a *national* share in 2011, 0.35% against 0.45%, suggesting a considerable discrepancy between the different ways in which the national Census and other government surveys counted them. If many of them lived in student accommodation, they may not have been counted by household surveys. The graph below suggests that the recent fall in the number of China-born residents living in households in the UK possibly ended in 2014.

Living in the UK, born in China including Hong Kong %

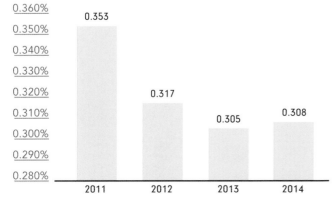

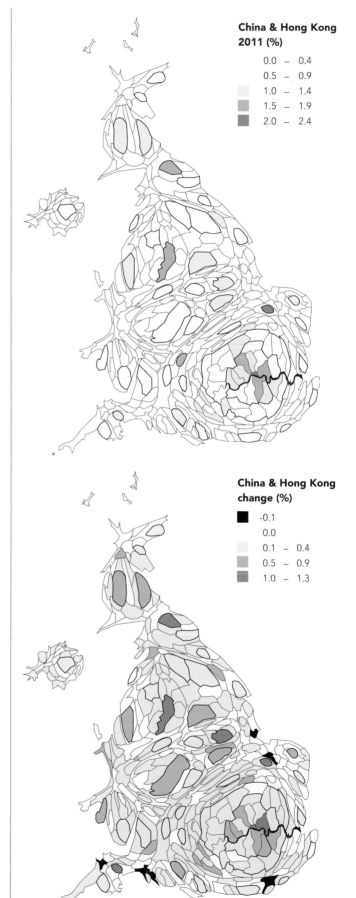

China & Hong Kong 2011 (%)

- 0.0 – 0.4
- 0.5 – 0.9
- 1.0 – 1.4
- 1.5 – 1.9
- 2.0 – 2.4

China & Hong Kong change (%)

- -0.1
- 0.0
- 0.1 – 0.4
- 0.5 – 0.9
- 1.0 – 1.3

BORN IN THE CARIBBEAN

In 2011, 2.7 million people living in the UK had been born on a Caribbean island, 0.42% of the total UK population, and up slightly from 2.5 million in 2001. All the Local Authority areas where more than one in 50 people were born in the Caribbean are in London: Lewisham (4.6%); Lambeth (4.0%); Hackney (3.7%); Brent (3.6%); Croydon (3.2%); Haringey (3.2%); Waltham Forest (3.0%); Southwark (2.7%); Enfield (2.3%); and Newham (2.1%). In all of these areas that proportion has been falling or has only risen by 0.1%, apart from in Croydon, where it rose by 0.6% between 2001 and 2011. There has been a clear and rapid suburbanisation of this birthplace group. The greatest increases have been in Croydon and then in Barking & Dagenham (+0.3%); and +0.2% in Bromley, Broxbourne and Rushmoor. The map of change clearly shows a movement away from areas of initial concentration – often concentration from a very long time ago. Over a quarter of all the people who were born in the Caribbean and lived in Hackney in 2001 are no longer living there. Some will have died, others moved outwards to outer London, or beyond, including a few returning to the Caribbean in old age. The graph below shows that the proportion of people living in the UK who were born in one of the largest Caribbean islands with strong British connections, Jamaica, had been rising steadily since 2011, but then fell in 2014. Some of the fall will be people retiring to Jamaica, possibly renting London property out to new incomers. Roughly half the UK Caribbean-born population were born in Jamaica.

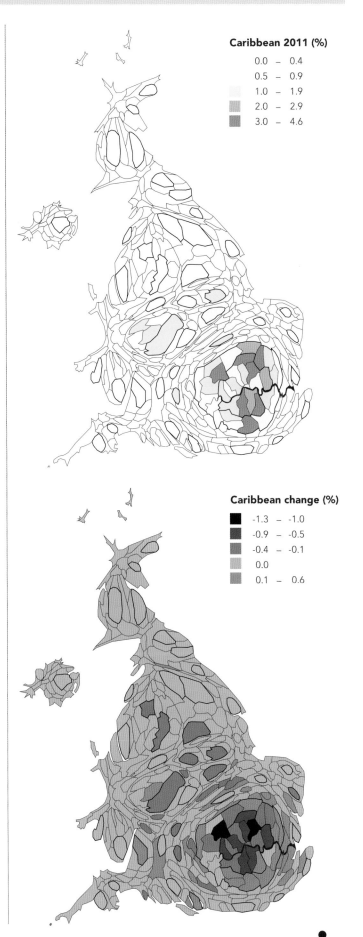

Caribbean 2011 (%)

- 0.0 – 0.4
- 0.5 – 0.9
- 1.0 – 1.9
- 2.0 – 2.9
- 3.0 – 4.6

Caribbean change (%)

- -1.3 – -1.0
- -0.9 – -0.5
- -0.4 – -0.1
- 0.0
- 0.1 – 0.6

Living in the UK, born in Jamaica %

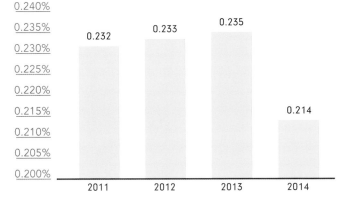

BORN IN AUSTRALASIA

In 2011, 0.20 million people born (mostly) in Australia or New Zealand were living in the UK, 0.31% of the population, up from 0.17 million in 2001. This population is rapidly changing its geographical loci in the UK. The largest increases in local shares of the population who are Australasia-born have been in London and an eclectic mix of other areas: Wandsworth (+0.9%); Isles of Scilly and Lambeth (both +0.7%); Hackney (+0.6%); Hammersmith & Fulham (+0.5%); Richmondshire in Yorkshire, Southwark and Islington (+0.4%); and +0.2% in Lewisham, Richmond upon Thames, Camden and Cotswold. All but one of the areas with a decline in excess of -0.1% were in London: Brent (-0.7%); Kensington & Chelsea (-0.4%); Ealing (-0.3%); Limavady in Northern Ireland (-0.3%); Barnet (-0.3%); and Waltham Forest (-0.2%). As a result of all these changes, the areas of the UK where Australians and New Zealanders are most commonly found are still all in London, but in some of these areas there are now more and more of them and in others they are rapidly disappearing. In 2011 the snapshot proportions in the most common locations were: Hammersmith & Fulham (3.8%); Wandsworth and the City of London (both 3.0%); Westminster (2.7%); Camden (2.4%); Kensington & Chelsea (2.2%); and Islington and Lambeth (both 2.1%). Since 2012 there has been a noticeable rise in the numbers from these countries living in the UK, which accelerated during 2014.

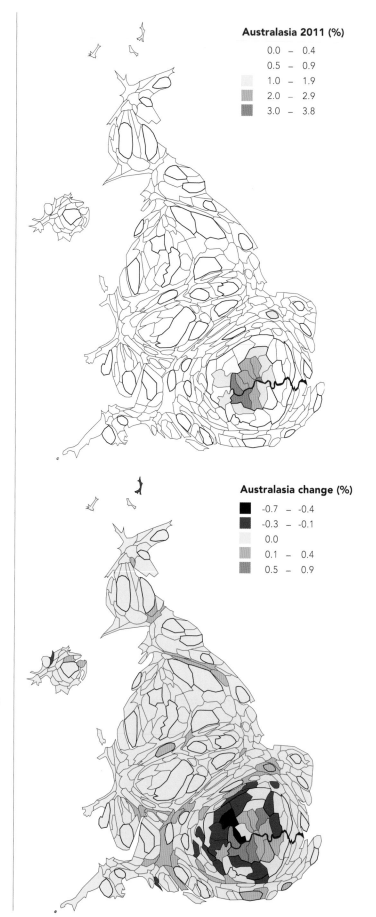

Australasia 2011 (%)

	0.0 – 0.4
	0.5 – 0.9
	1.0 – 1.9
	2.0 – 2.9
	3.0 – 3.8

Australasia change (%)

	-0.7 – -0.4
	-0.3 – -0.1
	0.0
	0.1 – 0.4
	0.5 – 0.9

Living in the UK, born in Australia or New Zealand %

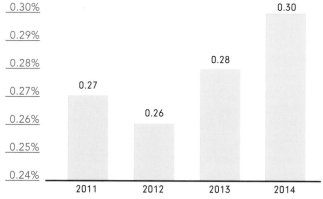

	2011	2012	2013	2014
	0.27	0.26	0.28	0.30

BORN IN THE USA

By 2011, 0.20 million people who were born in the USA lived in the UK – 0.31% of the UK population, and a fraction less than the proportion born in Australasia. In 2001 the USA-born numbered 0.16 million, so their numbers have risen, slightly faster than for the Australasians. 'Over here, overpaid and oversexed' was a common retort a lifetime ago when so many of the US military were stationed in the UK during the Second World War. US military bases and in some cases their disappearance or persistence will affect the patterns shown here. The Local Authority district with the most US citizens, Forest Heath, contains a large military base, while the secret listening stations located in Harrogate presumably contribute to the 2,799 USA-born residents of that area (down from 2,851 in 2001). Secret underground military bases cannot operate without employees who live above ground. Centres for the financial and other highly paid occupations also attract a great many USA-born people. The most USA-born residents are now found in Forest Heath (13.0%); Kensington & Chelsea (5.0%); Westminster (3.6%); Camden and the City of London (both 2.8%); East Cambridgeshire (2.0%); Cambridge and Harrogate (both 1.8%); Oxford and Elmbridge (both 1.7%); Hammersmith & Fulham (1.6%); and Islington and Huntingdonshire (both 1.5%). The largest falls have mostly been in areas of military interest: Forest Heath (-4.3%); Breckland (-0.7%); South Bucks (-0.5%); Elmbridge (-0.5%); and East Cambridgeshire (-0.4%). The largest rises have mostly been in areas of financial interest: City of London (+0.9%); Camden (+0.7%); Islington (+0.7%); Hackney (+0.5%); and +0.4% in each of Tower Hamlets, Hammersmith & Fulham, Cambridge and Southwark. Since 2012 there have been falls as both the banking and military industries have been in a state of some flux and as other parts of the world may be of increasing interest to people born in the USA.

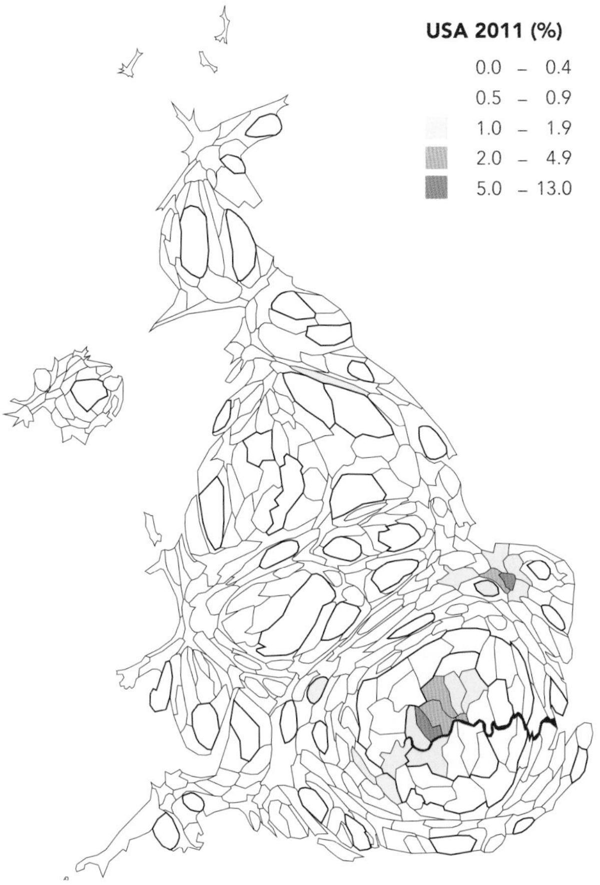

USA 2011 (%)

- 0.0 – 0.4
- 0.5 – 0.9
- 1.0 – 1.9
- 2.0 – 4.9
- 5.0 – 13.0

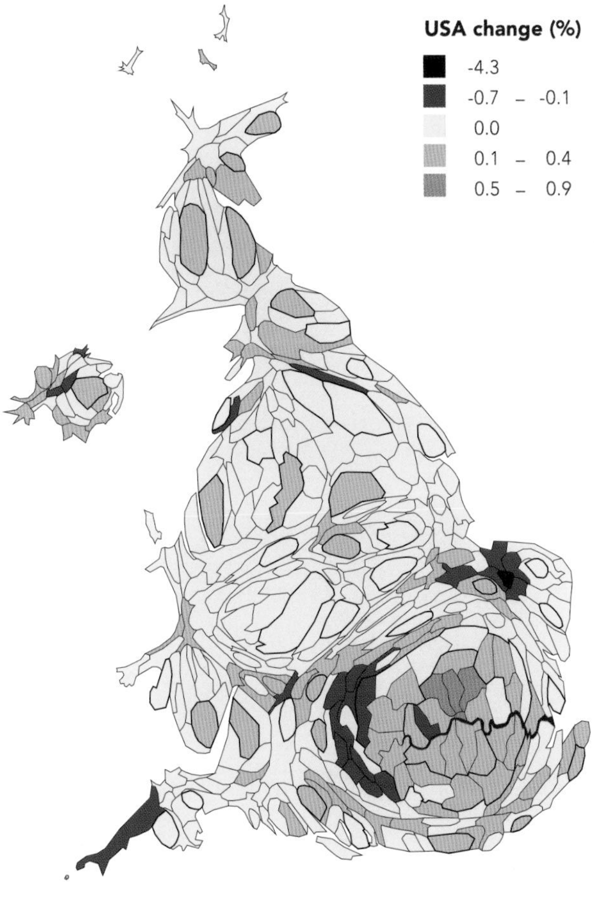

USA change (%)

- -4.3
- -0.7 – -0.1
- 0.0
- 0.1 – 0.4
- 0.5 – 0.9

Living in the UK, born in the USA %

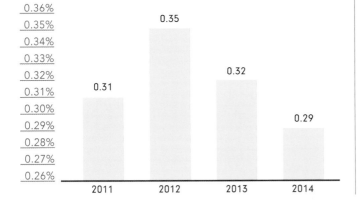

	2011	2012	2013	2014
	0.31	0.35	0.32	0.29

BORN IN EUROPE

For detailed country of birth statistics for many other countries, comparable data over time is only available for England and Wales for the latest Census. In 2011 the highest proportion of Ireland-born in England and Wales were living in Brent (2.85%); in Kensington & Chelsea were found the highest proportions of France-born (4.20%), Italy-born (2.72%), Spain-born (1.70%) and people born in all other 'old' EU countries combined (3.30%); Germany-born were most numerous in Richmondshire (2.12%); Portugal-born in Lambeth (2.31%); Poland-born in Ealing (6.35%); Romania-born in Harrow (2.00%); Turkey-born and Other Europe-born in Enfield (4.47% and 6.45%) respectively.

Within England and Wales, the greatest increase in overseas-born groups from the rest of Europe have been of those born in the Republic of Ireland in Norwich (+0.04%); France-born in the City of London (+1.30%); Germany-born in Tower Hamlets (+0.40%); Italy-born in Tower Hamlets (+0.83%); Portugal-born in Great Yarmouth (+1.05%); Spain-born in Tower Hamlets (+0.58%); Other 'old' EU countries-born in the City of London (+0.81%); Poland-born in Slough (+5.54%); Romania-born in Harrow (+1.96%); Turkey-born in Enfield (+2.21%); and Other Europe-born in Boston (+5.88%, and the largest rise of any single birth place group in any place in England and Wales).

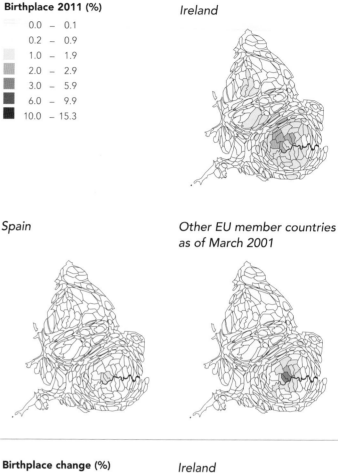

Birthplace 2011 (%)

	0.0 – 0.1
	0.2 – 0.9
	1.0 – 1.9
	2.0 – 2.9
	3.0 – 5.9
	6.0 – 9.9
	10.0 – 15.3

Ireland

Spain

Other EU member countries as of March 2001

Birthplace change (%)

	-4.3 – -1.0
	-0.9 – -0.1
	0.0 – 0.1
	0.2 – 0.9
	1.0 – 1.9
	2.0 – 3.9
	4.0 – 5.9

Ireland

Spain

Other EU member countries as of March 2001

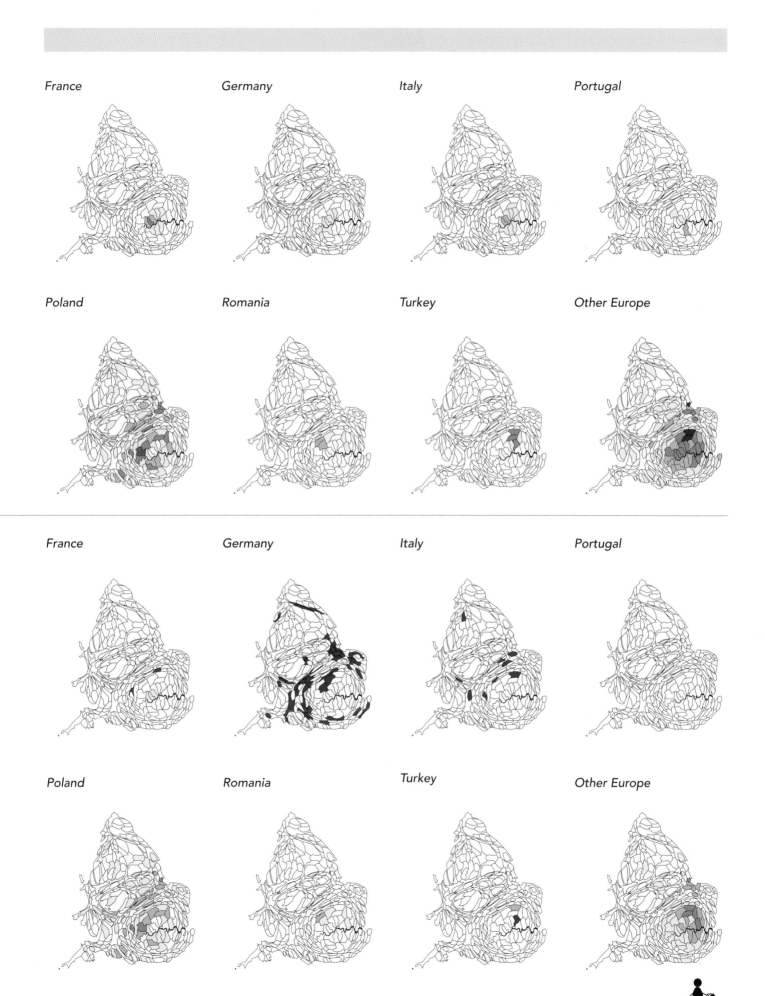

France

Germany

Italy

Portugal

Poland

Romania

Turkey

Other Europe

France

Germany

Italy

Portugal

Poland

Romania

Turkey

Other Europe

BORN IN AFRICA AND THE MIDDLE EAST

Among the Local Authority districts of England and Wales the highest proportions of Africa and Middle East-born local residents in 2011 were as follows: North Africa-born in Westminster (2.60%), Nigeria-born in Greenwich (5.11%); people born in all other Central and Western Africa countries in Southwark (4.33%); Kenya-born in Harrow (4.90%); Somalia-born in Brent (2.20%); South Africa-born in Merton (2.83%); Zimbabwe-born in Leicester (1.02%); people born in other South and Eastern Africa countries in Leicester (3.76%); Iran-born in Barnet (2.03%) and Other Middle East-born in Westminster (5.62%).

An extra one in every 100 people living in Bristol were born in Somalia by 2011 compared to 2001. The greatest local increases in each African and Middle Eastern country birthplace group between 2001 and 2011 in England and Wales were as follows: North Africa-born in Westminster (+0.78%); Nigeria-born in Barking & Dagenham (3.78%); Other Central and Western Africa-born also in Barking & Dagenham (+1.98%); Kenya-born in Oadby & Wigston (+0.32%); Somalia-born in Bristol (+1.00%); South Africa-born in Merton (+1.22%); Zimbabwe-born in Leicester (+0.70%); Other South and Eastern Africa country-born in Crawley (+1.12%); Iran-born in Barnet (+1.07%); and Other Middle East-born in Westminster (+2.22%).

Birthplace 2011 (%)

	0.0 – 0.1
	0.2 – 0.9
	1.0 – 1.9
	2.0 – 2.9
	3.0 – 5.9
	6.0 – 9.9
	10.0 – 15.3

North Africa

South Africa

Birthplace change (%)

	-4.3 – -1.0
	-0.9 – -0.1
	0.0 – 0.1
	0.2 – 0.9
	1.0 – 1.9
	2.0 – 3.9
	4.0 – 5.9

North Africa

South Africa

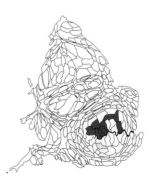

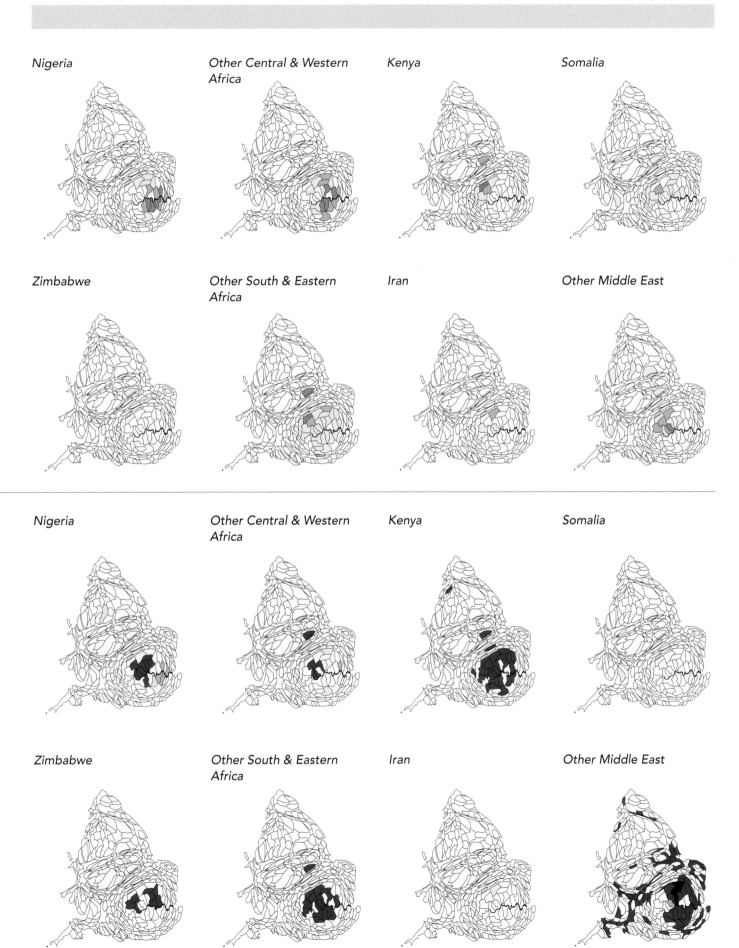

Nigeria

Other Central & Western Africa

Kenya

Somalia

Zimbabwe

Other South & Eastern Africa

Iran

Other Middle East

Nigeria

Other Central & Western Africa

Kenya

Somalia

Zimbabwe

Other South & Eastern Africa

Iran

Other Middle East

BORN IN ASIA

The Censuses distinguish people born in Hong Kong from those born in China and, of course, it is possible for people to have been born in parts of India that are now Pakistan or Bangladesh. Of people born in various countries in Asia and living in England and Wales, the greatest concentrations in 2011 found were of China-born in Cambridge (1.86%); Hong Kong-born in Rushmoor (1.06%); Other Eastern and South East Asia-born in Kensington & Chelsea (4.35%); Bangladesh-born in Tower Hamlets (15.30%); India-born in Leicester (11.29%); Pakistan-born in Slough (8.03%); Sri Lanka-born in Harrow (4.35%); and Other Southern Asia-born in Rushmoor (5.23%), the district that contains Aldershot where many people born in Nepal who had been Gurkhas now live.

In the decade to 2011 in England and Wales the greatest increases in China-born residents was recorded in the City of London (+1.13%); Hong Kong-born residents rose in number the most in Rushmoor (+0.67%); Other Eastern and South East Asia-born were found to have increased in number the most in Hammersmith & Fulham (+1.46%); Bangladesh-born in Newham (+1.99%); India-born in Hounslow (+3.50%); Pakistan-born in Redbridge (+2.70%); Sri Lanka-born in Harrow (+1.81%); and Other Southern Asia-born in Rushmoor (+4.98%). The previous total of 0.25% means that 95% of those people living in Rushmoor arrived there sin ce 2001. This is the largest increase found anywhere except for the slightly larger rise in Poland-born in Slough and Other European country-born in Boston.

Birthplace 2011 (%)

	0.0 – 0.1
	0.2 – 0.9
	1.0 – 1.9
	2.0 – 2.9
	3.0 – 5.9
	6.0 – 9.9
	10.0 – 15.3

China

Pakistan

Birthplace change (%)

	-4.3 – -1.0
	-0.9 – -0.1
	0.0 – 0.1
	0.2 – 0.9
	1.0 – 1.9
	2.0 – 3.9
	4.0 – 5.9

China

Pakistan

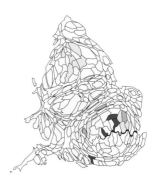

Hong Kong

Other Eastern & South
East Asia

Bangladesh

India

Sri Lanka

Other Southern Asia

Hong Kong

Other Eastern & South
East Asia

Bangladesh

India

Sri Lanka

Other Southern Asia

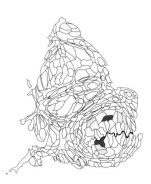

BORN IN AMERICA OR AUSTRALASIA

Of people living in England and Wales born in the Americas or Australasia, the highest concentrations were recorded in 2011 of USA-born in Forest Heath (12.96%); Other North America-born in the City of London (0.89%); Central America-born in Kensington & Chelsea (0.28%); South America-born in Lambeth (2.98%); Caribbean-born in Lewisham (4.64%); Australia-born in Hammersmith & Fulham (2.52%); along with Other Australasia-born also found at their greatest concentration in that borough (1.29%); and Other Oceania-born being most concentrated, despite being in such small numbers, in Richmondshire (0.44%), possibly as a result of its military establishments.

The greatest increases in people born in each separately identified country or group of countries in the Americas and Australasia between 2001 and 2011 was a rise in USA-born in the City of London (of +0.86%); an increase in Other North America-born in Islington (of 0.18%); an increase in South America-born people living in London that was greatest in Southwark (+1.64%); and of Caribbean-born increasing most in Croydon (+0.59%); while the numbers of Australia-born rose most abruptly in Lambeth (+0.49%); and Other Australasia-born in Wandsworth (+0.35%); with Other Oceania-born residents increasing in concentration the most in Richmondshire (+0.38%).

Birthplace 2011 (%)

0.0	0.1
0.2	0.9
1.0	1.9
2.0	2.9
3.0	5.9
6.0	9.9
10.0	15.3

United States

Other Australasia

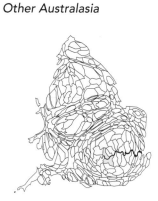

Birthplace change (%)

-4.3	-1.0
-0.9	-0.1
0.0	0.1
0.2	0.9
1.0	1.9
2.0	3.9
4.0	5.9

United States

Other Australasia

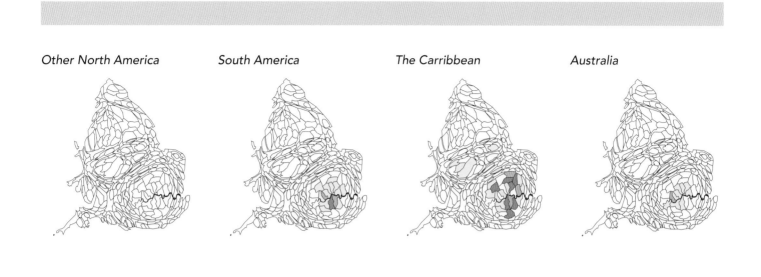

Other North America *South America* *The Carribbean* *Australia*

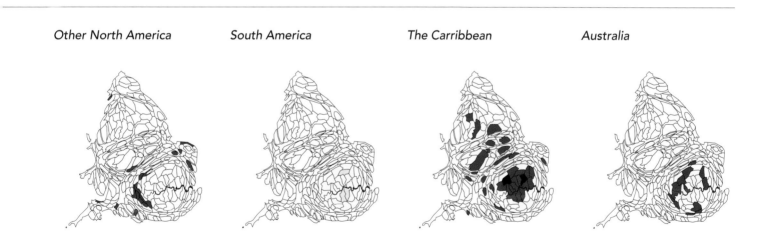

Other North America *South America* *The Carribbean* *Australia*

INTERNATIONAL MIGRATION

The number of people in an area who were living in another country outside of the UK a year before Census day is a measure of annual international migration. In 2011, just over 0.6 million people living in England, Wales and Northern Ireland were such international migrants. Data for Scotland was not available at the time we drew this map. Ten years earlier, in 2001, only 0.4 million recent overseas migrants lived in these countries. The increase has been rapid as more and more people move around the world, and it is particularly within Europe that they have also been able to do so with greater freedom over this period. The greatest concentrations of recent international migrants in 2011 were found in Westminster and the City of London combined (6.4%); Kensington & Chelsea (5.5%); Camden, Cambridge and Forest Heath (all 4.6%); Oxford and Hammersmith & Fulham (both 4.4%); Tower Hamlets (4.1%); Islington (3.6%); Newham (3.2%); and Wandsworth (3.0%). These contrast with the places where the least international migrants are found, the places to which people from outside the UK are least likely to come: Caerphilly, Torfaen, South Staffordshire, Neath Port Talbot, Knowsley and Redcar & Cleveland (all 0.2%). The most rapid increases in international migrants have been recorded in Tower Hamlets (+2.2%); Newham (+1.8%); and Islington (+1.5%). The graph below shows the reasons why they had migrated given by a sample of the 4.9 million non-British international migrants living in the UK in 2014; for most it was to work or to join someone working.

Overseas-born non-British residents by reason to migrate, UK 2014

Formal study
767,000

Other
811,000

Accompany/join
1,561,000

Work-related
1,790,000

| 0 | 500,000 | 1,000,000 | 1,500,000 | 2,000,000 |

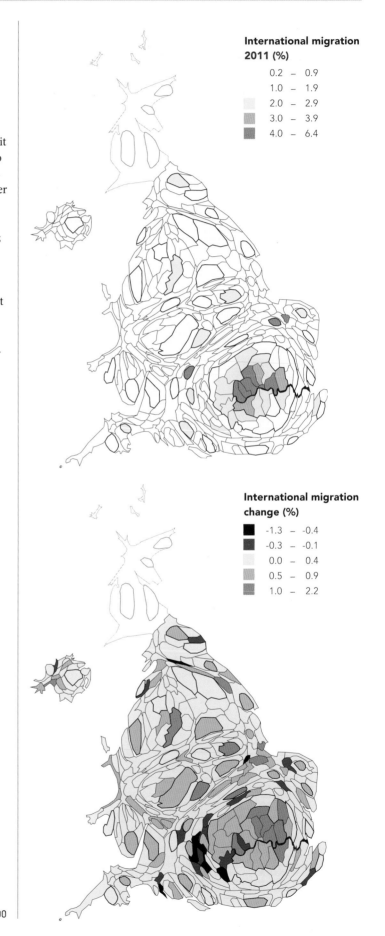

International migration 2011 (%)

0.2	– 0.9
1.0	– 1.9
2.0	– 2.9
3.0	– 3.9
4.0	– 6.4

International migration change (%)

-1.3	– -0.4
-0.3	– -0.1
0.0	– 0.4
0.5	– 0.9
1.0	– 2.2

NO PASSPORT/UK PASSPORT

In contrast to people who have migrated to the UK from abroad are people living in the UK who cannot travel abroad because they have no passport. Because the UK is not part of the Schengen Agreement it is not possible to leave the country easily without a passport. While the Census in Scotland did not enquire about the passports that people held, 9.8 million people living in the UK, outside of Scotland, had no passport in 2011. The areas of the country where people were most likely not to have a passport were: Blaenau Gwent (30.0%); Great Yarmouth and the Isle of Anglesey (both 28.9%); East Lindsey (28.8%); Gwynedd (27.8%); North Norfolk, Bolsover and Moyle (27.4%); Stoke-on-Trent (27.3%); and Pembrokeshire and Boston (both 27.2%). It is intriguing that so many people in Boston cannot travel overseas while so many people from overseas work there. As might be expected, almost everyone has a passport who lives in Kensington & Chelsea and City of London (only 3.2% do not in both) and Westminster (3.6% do not). Interestingly people are least likely to hold a UK passport if they live in Derry (36.9%) or Newry & Mourne (38.5%), as in those two districts more people hold Republic of Ireland passports (43.7% and 40.9% respectively). UK passports are most frequently held in Hart in Hampshire (86.2%) and Brentwood in Essex (85.9%). The graph below shows the most common nationality of people living in the UK who are not British and who were born abroad.

Overseas-born non-British residents by country of nationality, UK 2014

USA	114,000
Lithuania	134,000
France	117,000
Italy	124,000
Portugal	117,000
Romania	154,000
Pakistan	185,000
Republic of Ireland	313,000
India	329,000
Poland	756,000

0   100,000   200,000   300,000   400,000   500,000   600,000   700,000   800,000

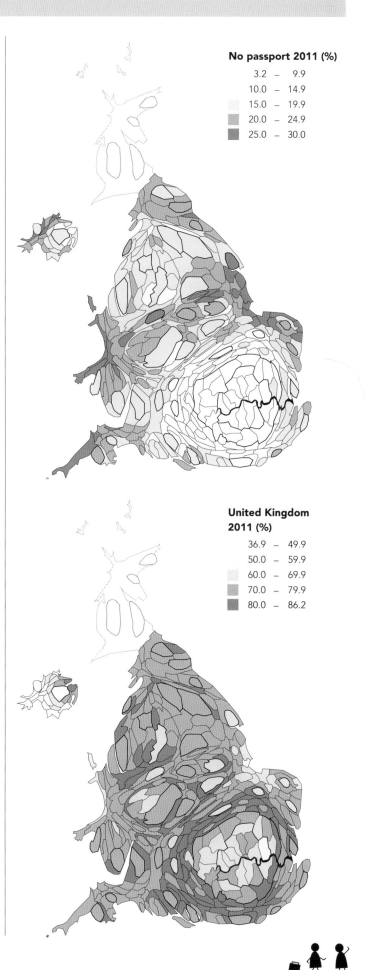

No passport 2011 (%)

3.2 – 9.9
10.0 – 14.9
15.0 – 19.9
20.0 – 24.9
25.0 – 30.0

United Kingdom 2011 (%)

36.9 – 49.9
50.0 – 59.9
60.0 – 69.9
70.0 – 79.9
80.0 – 86.2

REPUBLIC OF IRELAND PASSPORT / OTHER EU COUNTRY PASSPORT

The final pair of maps in this chapter shows the distribution of the 0.8 million people living in the UK (apart from Scotland, where the question was not asked) who held a Republic of Ireland passport in 2011 and the 2.0 million who held a passport from another EU country other than the UK and the Republic of Ireland. Within Northern Ireland the two districts where holding an Irish passport is most common have already been mentioned (see above). The two where such passports were most rare in 2011 were Ards (6.4%) and Carrickfergus (4.8%). In England they are most common in Brent (3.4%); Islington (3.3%); Hammersmith & Fulham (3.2%); Camden (2.8%); Ealing and Harrow (both 2.6%); and Luton (2.5%). Irish passports are least commonly held in areas where there have not been many job opportunities for many years: South Tyneside, Blaenau Gwent, Hartlepool, Kingston upon Hull, Ashfield and Barrow-in-Furness (all 0.1%). A similar but different set of high unemployment areas are home to the least people with other EU passports: Torfaen (0.3%); Redcar & Cleveland, Knowsley and South Staffordshire (all 0.4%); North East Derbyshire and Neath Port Talbot (both 0.5%). Other EU passports are most commonly held in a set of places in England that overlap a little with where Irish passports are also most common in England: Kensington & Chelsea (19.9%), Westminster (16.7%); Haringey (14.9%); Brent (14.0%); Hammersmith & Fulham (13.9%); and Ealing (13.3%).

The graph below shows the five countries of birth for which it is most common for people living in the UK not to have British nationality and a UK passport. These are all in the EU. The graph also shows the five countries of birth where, for those living in the UK, it is most common to have a British passport and nationality. All but one of those countries is in Africa.

Living in the UK with British nationality by selected countries of birth 2014 %

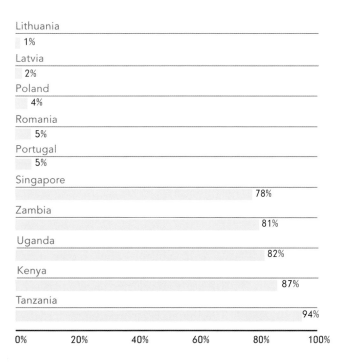

Lithuania	1%
Latvia	2%
Poland	4%
Romania	5%
Portugal	5%
Singapore	78%
Zambia	81%
Uganda	82%
Kenya	87%
Tanzania	94%

0%   20%   40%   60%   80%   100%

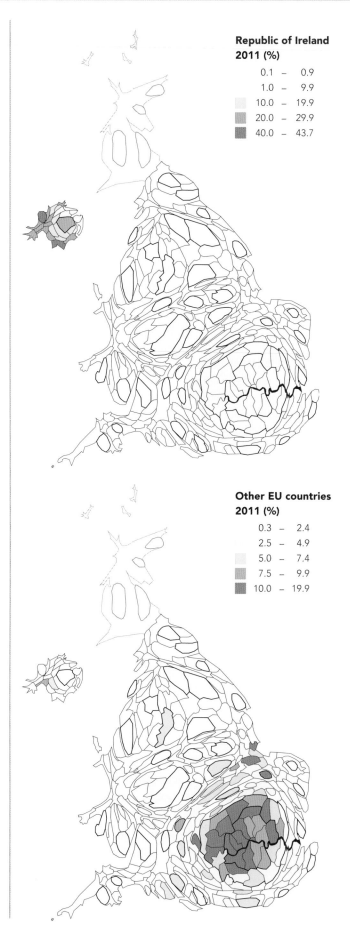

Republic of Ireland 2011 (%)

0.1 – 0.9	
1.0 – 9.9	
10.0 – 19.9	
20.0 – 29.9	
40.0 – 43.7	

Other EU countries 2011 (%)

0.3 – 2.4	
2.5 – 4.9	
5.0 – 7.4	
7.5 – 9.9	
10.0 – 19.9	

Of all the qualification groups in the UK, the most common qualification is now Level 4 (a university degree or its equivalent).

2011

Just under a quarter (24.2%) of the population aged 16 to 64, held this qualification

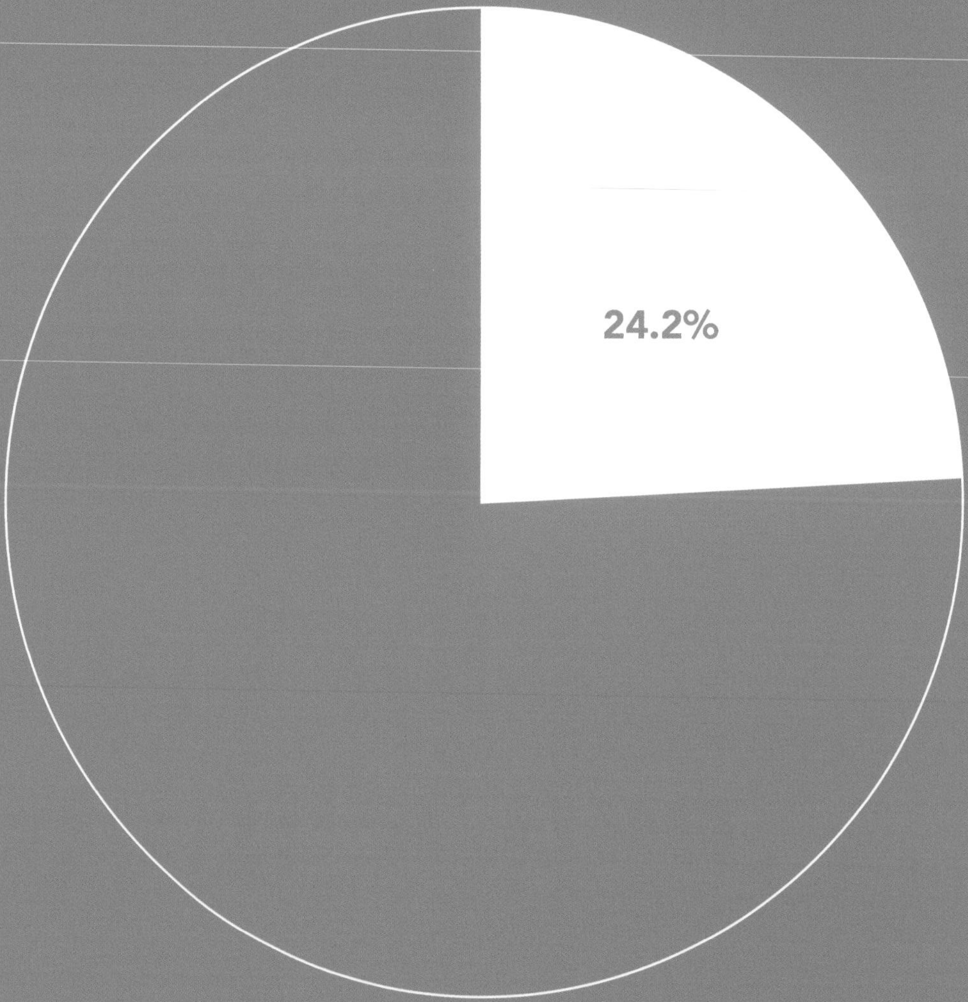

24.2%

Qualifications and Employment

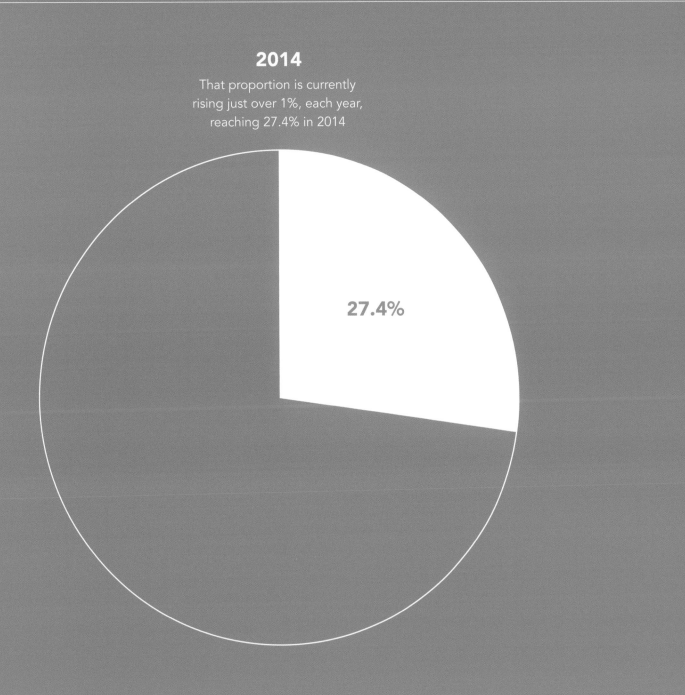

2014

That proportion is currently rising just over 1%, each year, reaching 27.4% in 2014

27.4%

Qualifications and Employment

People in the UK now possess a huge range of qualifications, including many gained overseas, that can be difficult to categorise. The 2011 Census asked about this bewildering array of certificates, diplomas and degrees that are currently used to classify people and to deem how employable they might be – and which, in theory, channel them into suitable areas of employment. This chapter begins by mapping employment before mapping qualifications, but it can be useful to appreciate the overall picture and temporal trends first. Here is the Census question on qualifications, showing how they are grouped. It is a very long and wordy Census question:

'Which of these qualifications do you have? Tick every box that applies if you have any of the qualifications listed. If your UK qualification is not listed, tick the box that contains its nearest equivalent. If you have qualifications gained outside the UK, tick the 'Foreign qualifications' box and the nearest UK equivalents (if known)'.

The seven groups of educational qualification recognised by the UK Censuses

Level 1	• 1–4 O levels/CSEs/GCSEs (any grades), Entry Level, Foundation Diploma • NVQ Level 1, Foundation GNVQ, Basic Skills
Level 2	• 5+ O levels (passes)/CSEs (grade 1)/GCSEs (grades A*–C), School Certificate, 1 A level/2–3 AS levels/VCEs, Higher Diploma • NVQ Level 2, Intermediate GNVQ, City and Guilds Craft, BTEC First/General Diploma, RSA Diploma
Apprenticeship	• Apprenticeship
Level 3	• 2+ A levels/VCEs, 4+ AS levels, Higher School Certificate, Progression/Advanced Diploma • NVQ Level 3, Advanced GNVQ, City and Guilds Advanced Craft, ONC, OND, BTEC National, RSA Advanced Diploma
Level 4+	• Degree (eg, BA, BSc), Higher Degree (eg, MA, PhD, PGCE) • NVQ Level 4–5, HNC, HND, RSA Higher Diploma, BTEC Higher Level • Professional qualifications (eg, teaching, nursing, accountancy)
Other	• Other vocational/work-related qualifications • Foreign qualifications
None	• No qualifications

People aged 16–64 who are economically active by highest level of their academic qualifications, UK%

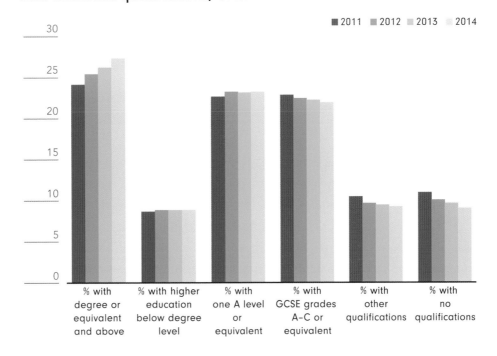

Of all the qualification groups in the UK, the largest and most common qualification is now Level 4, a university degree or its equivalent. In 2011, just a quarter of the population aged 16–64 (24.2%), held this qualification. That proportion is currently rising by just over 1% a year, each year, and reached 27.4% in 2014. This group of the most highly qualified people increases rapidly in size as more people are awarded university degrees with every year that passes, and as more graduates migrate into the UK with similar degrees.

"Everything in this atlas is related to everything else, but not as many might presume."

The most rapidly declining qualification group are those with no qualifications. This decline is mainly due to people turning 65, as well as early deaths among poorer older people who often die before age 65. With similar effect, the early overseas retirement of the elderly also tends to reduce the proportions of people living in the UK with low or no qualifications.

Everything in this atlas is related to everything else, but not as many might presume. Take ethnicity, mapped in the *Religion and Ethnicity* chapter. There are high correlations between ethnicity and qualifications gained that are related to many other things, not least the average age of each ethnic group in the UK, because younger groups tend to be better qualified.

By ethnicity the highest proportion of people within any ethnic group who hold no qualifications and who are living in the UK are those who tick 'White Gypsy and Irish Traveller' (this group also happens to be those least likely to have gone to school). All other minority ethnic groups (of which the Census identified another 13 groupings in 2011) tend to be less likely to have no qualifications than the White majority groups. The minority ethnic group least likely to tick no qualifications is Black Africans, some 40% of whom hold a university degree or higher.

The only ethnic group in the UK more likely to hold a university degree than Black Africans are the Chinese (43%). Mixed White and Asian, White and Black African, Other Mixed and Arab are all next most likely not to be lacking qualifications in the UK. The Indian group is the generally next best-qualified minority ethnic group.

Despite the overall connectedness between high qualifications and well-remunerated employment, none of the correlations just described mean that these minority ethnic groups are likely to be well paid compared to other groups. The same is true whether we define groups by ethnicity, birthplace, immigration status, being male or female, ill, Northern, moneyed, or whatever. This is because gaining well-paid work, or just full-time low-paid work, is not simply related to the qualifications you hold. What also matters is who you know, where you live, the prejudice of others and the advantages of age. The Census can help us to see this – showing that good qualifications do not simply equate to high later remuneration, or at least employment in occupations within which such pay is possible. So this chapter begins by looking at age before turning to how many or how few hours a week people in different places work.

People in each ethnic group by highest level of qualification, UK % (ordered by % with none)

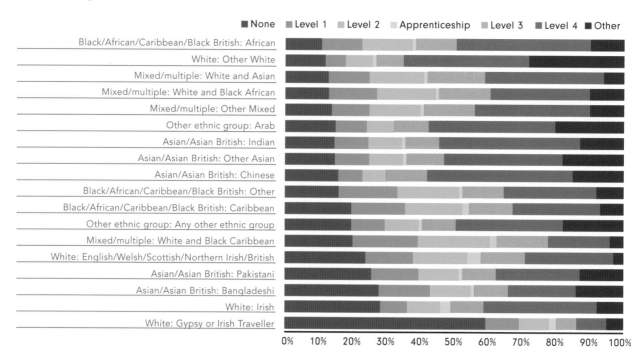

YOUNG CHILDREN AND OLDER PENSIONERS (PEOPLE NOT AGED 16–74)

To begin to understand the changing geography of qualifications and employment it helps to start by looking at those who are not expected to be in employment and who will also have no or very few qualifications. Children aged under 16 almost never have qualifications, and only a few are in very limited employment, including working in their parents' shop after school. People aged 75 or over also tend to have few qualifications because most of this group will have left school at (or before) the age of 15, many without even a school certificate.

The school leaving age was not raised to 16 until 1972. A majority of children did not gain recognised qualifications until 1973 with CSEs (replaced, along with O levels in 1988, by GCSEs). People aged 75 or over are also as unlikely as children aged under 16 to be in paid work. In 2011 there were 16.8 million people who were not of 'extended working age', 16–74. This age group were most concentrated in Christchurch (31.6%) and Barking & Dagenham (31.4%), areas of especially elderly and young populations respectively. They are least commonly found in the City of London (14.5%) and Islington (19.9%). More than four out of every five people who reside in all of Islington, and much of the rest of Inner London, are of working age.

The largest fall in those aged 0–15 or 75+ has been in Newham (-4.5%). The largest rises have been in places such as Chiltern (+1.6%) and St Albans (+1.5%), where affluent London families have often moved. There is a very distinct ring of areas coloured green in the change map shown here. Nationally the proportion who are aged 16 or over and who are working or seeking work has been rising by about 0.2% a year since 2011. Between 2001 and 2011 the size of this age group rose by 1.1%, or roughly 0.1% a year, so in recent years there has been acceleration in the proportion of people who are of working age, until 2014, when so many more people retired than turned 16. The graph below excludes children but not the retired.

Working or seeking work aged 16+, UK %

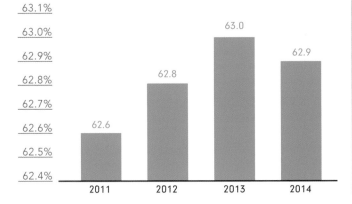

Not aged 16–74 2011 (%)

- 14.5 – 23.9
- 24.0 – 25.9
- 26.0 – 27.9
- 28.0 – 29.9
- 30.0 – 31.6

Not aged 16–74 change (%)

- -4.5 – -2.1
- -2.0 – -1.1
- -1.0 – -0.1
- 0.0 – 0.9
- 1.0 – 1.6

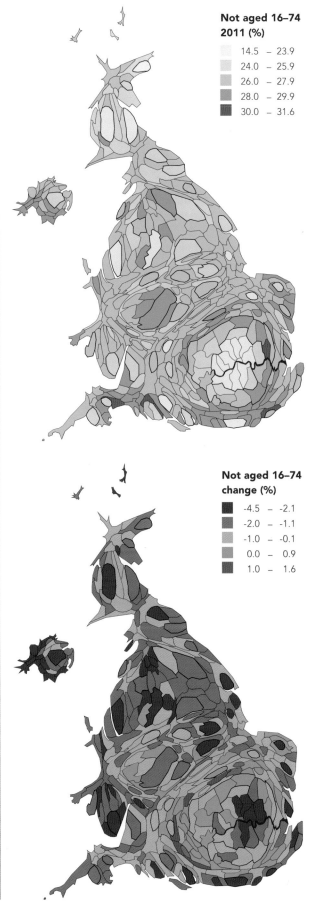

WORKING PART-TIME

Of the 63.2 million people who were living in the UK in 2011, 6.3 million, or around 10.0%, were working part-time – less than 31 hours a week. The graph below shows that this equated to just over a quarter of everyone in work in 2011, a proportion that rose in the year to 2012, but which then fell back again in 2013 and 2014. One reason for these fluctuations were changes in the rules over how many hours you had to work to be able to claim various forms of tax credit (government subsidies for low-paid work). Another reason was that many formerly full-time employees had to reduce their hours to become part-time workers by 2012 if they were to keep their jobs in one of the worst years of the Great Recession, the year when incomes had fallen the most since 2008.

Women undertake most part-time work. In 2001, 5.0 million jobs were part-time, and so the number is, in general, rising more quickly than the overall population available to work. Working part-time is most common in some of the UK's most isolated areas: in the Shetland Islands (12.9% of all people); Weymouth & Portland (12.5%); Carlisle (12.4%); and the Orkney Islands (12.3%). Working part-time is least common in the least isolated areas: City of London (4.9%); Kensington & Chelsea (5.4%); Westminster (5.7%); and Hammersmith & Fulham (6.1%). The greatest increases in the share of local populations working part-time between 2001 and 2011 have mainly been in Northern Ireland: Derry (+3.3%); Newham (+3.2%); Cookstown (+3.1%); and Moyle (+3.0%). The smallest increases have tended to be in more affluent areas where surviving on part-time pay is harder, and where there are more full-time jobs: Isles of Scilly (+0.2%); South Bucks (+0.4%); Oxford (+0.7%); and Aberdeen (+0.7%).

In the graph below, all people in employment are in part- or full-time work or registered as self-employed, but those temporarily off work due to sickness are not included. The fall is partly because the numbers in full-time work have been rising since 2012, and because more people are now self-employed.

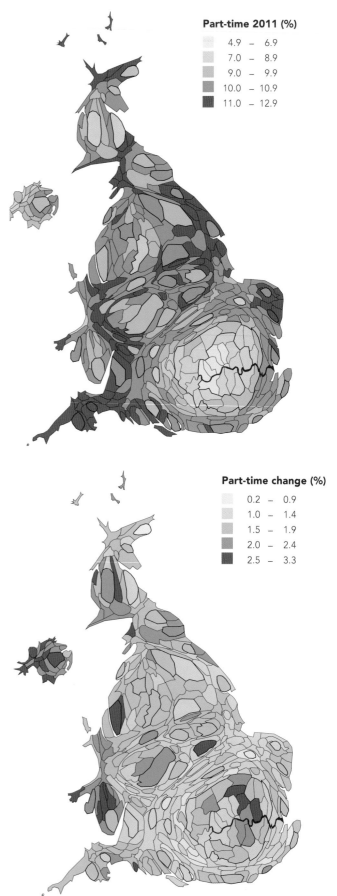

Part-time 2011 (%)

- 4.9 – 6.9
- 7.0 – 8.9
- 9.0 – 9.9
- 10.0 – 10.9
- 11.0 – 12.9

Part-time change (%)

- 0.2 – 0.9
- 1.0 – 1.4
- 1.5 – 1.9
- 2.0 – 2.4
- 2.5 – 3.3

Working part-time, % of all people aged 16–64 in employment, UK

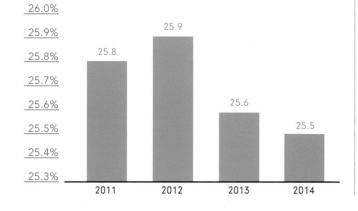

WORKING FULL-TIME

There were 17.9 million people in full-time work in the UK in 2011, up from 17.2 million in 2001. Thus 28.7% of the population of the UK were full-time workers, equal to 35.3% of all those aged 16 or older, or 56.4% of all those working in paid jobs or stating that they were seeking to work in such jobs. The areas of the country where it was most common for people to be working full-time were the City of London (44.0%), followed by areas with progressively lower proportions: Wandsworth, Rushmoor, Hammersmith & Fulham, Lambeth, Bracknell Forest, Aberdeen, Basingstoke & Deane, Shetland Islands, Forest Heath, Swindon, Crawley, Corby, Spelthorne, Islington, Milton Keynes, Watford, Reading and Huntingdonshire (which records 33.3%).

The lowest proportions of the population working full-time were found in Ceredigion (20.0%), Pembrokeshire (22.2%) and Gwynedd (22.8%) in Wales; Rother (20.4%), West Somerset (21.0%) and Tendring (21.3%) in England; Strabane (20.5%), Moyle (21.0%) and Derry (21.4%) in Northern Ireland; and Dumfries & Galloway (25.4%), South Ayrshire (26.0%) and Dundee (26.2%) in Scotland. In Scotland there are always an extra one in 20 people in full-time work compared to similar areas in the UK.

Between 2001 and 2011 the greatest increases in full-time work have been in Tower Hamlets (+4.4%); Shetland Islands (+2.9%); Islington (+2.8%); Eilean Siar (+2.8%); Merthyr Tydfil (+2.6%); Hackney (+2.6%); Glasgow (+2.2%); Dungannon (+2.2%); Orkney Islands (+2.1%); Southwark (+2.1%); and Liverpool (+2.0%). However, as the graph below shows, the number of people who are in work but temporarily sick has been rising since 2012. Labelled as not working, the temporarily sick are shown as a proportion of all the 'economically inactive' (adults aged 16–64 not working or looking for work and all people over 65 who are not working, even if they are looking for work).

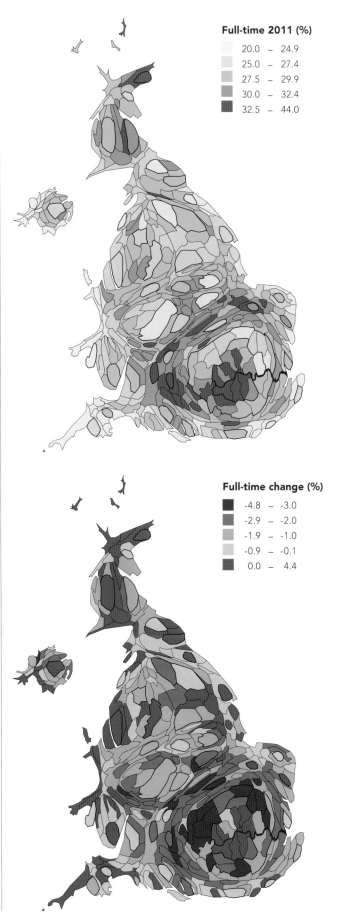

Full-time 2011 (%)

- 20.0 – 24.9
- 25.0 – 27.4
- 27.5 – 29.9
- 30.0 – 32.4
- 32.5 – 44.0

Full-time change (%)

- -4.8 – -3.0
- -2.9 – -2.0
- -1.9 – -1.0
- -0.9 – -0.1
- 0.0 – 4.4

Temporarily sick, % of all people aged 16+ who are not working, UK

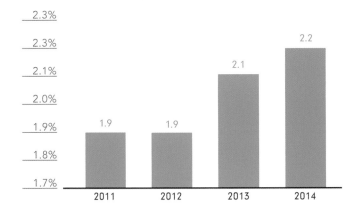

SELF-EMPLOYED

In 2001, 3.5 million people described themselves as self-employed. By 2011 that number had risen to 4.4 million. The rise in self-employment is dominated by the largest increases being within London. All but one of the areas with the greatest 2001–11 increase were within London: Waltham Forest and Haringey (both +3.8%); Newham (+3.6%); Hackney (+3.5%); Ealing (+3.1%); Brent (+2.8%); Merton (+2.5%); Barnet and Wandsworth (both +2.4%); Hounslow and Lewisham (both +2.3%); Lambeth, Brighton & Hove and Barking & Dagenham (all +2.2%); Southwark, Greenwich and Harrow (all +2.1%); and Tower Hamlets (+2.0%). A rapidly increasing number of people are declaring that they are self-employed. Some will be completely self-employed and earning all their income this way; others will be partly self-employed and using that income to supplement employment income, allowing them to afford to live and stay in London. Others will have been unemployed but now claim to be trying to run a business that might earn less than the minimum wage but that makes them eligible for tax credits and other benefits, and removes them from the unemployment register. There are also high rates of self-employment in parts of Devon and Cornwall, mid-Wales and rural Northern England associated with many small farms and similar businesses with few employees.

Self-employment rates fell in a few areas between 2001 and 2011, probably as authorities clamped down on employers making employees pretend to be self-employed, and crofting declined even further in the Isles of Scilly (-1.1%); Shetland Islands (-0.9%); Orkney Islands (-0.5%); and Magherafelt (-0.1%). There was no increase in Boston, and rises of just 0.1% in Blackpool, Richmondshire, South Holland and East Lindsey, where gang labour was often used in the recent past, and employees could be forced to pretend to be self-employed. Nationally self-employment continues to rise rapidly, and may be becoming more and more of a misnomer. The graph below shows the rising self-employed group as a percentage of all people in paid work.

Self-employed, % of all people aged 16+ who are working, UK

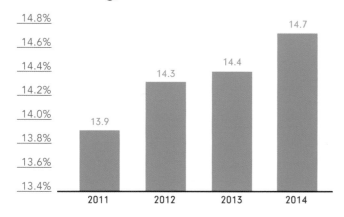

Year	%
2011	13.9
2012	14.3
2013	14.4
2014	14.7

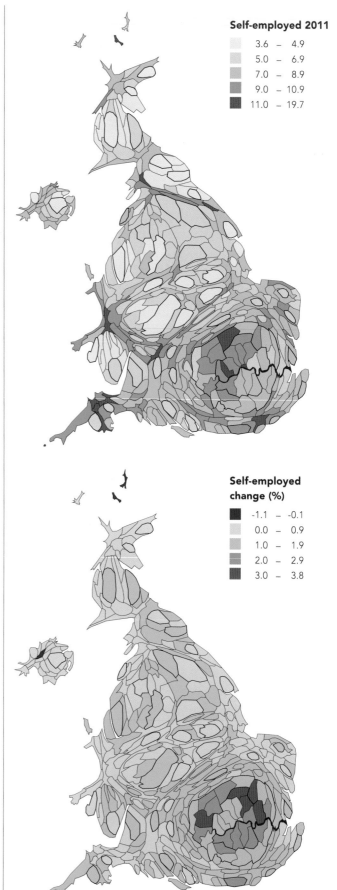

Self-employed 2011

- 3.6 – 4.9
- 5.0 – 6.9
- 7.0 – 8.9
- 9.0 – 10.9
- 11.0 – 19.7

Self-employed change (%)

- -1.1 – -0.1
- 0.0 – 0.9
- 1.0 – 1.9
- 2.0 – 2.9
- 3.0 – 3.8

UNEMPLOYED

Many people who are unemployed or not working for money would like to be in paid employment. Only a relatively small proportion of this group now qualify as unemployed, however, as they have to prove they are actively seeking work and able to start a job immediately. The Census question in 2011 asked if people were actively looking for work in the last four weeks and able to start a job within two weeks; if not, they were not counted as unemployed. Neither is anyone out of work who will be soon starting a job. Many have been put off registering themselves as unemployed by a benefits system that does not make them eligible for unemployment benefit if they live with family members who have incomes or who left their previous job 'voluntarily'. Despite these pressures, 2.1 million people said they were unemployed in 2011, up from 1.4 million in 2001. The rise was almost entirely due to the Great Recession of 2008–14.

By 2011 the 10 areas with the highest unemployment rates were Kingston upon Hull (6.0%); Wolverhampton (5.7%); Hartlepool (5.6%); Middlesbrough (5.5%); Derry (5.5%); Hackney (5.4%); Tower Hamlets (5.2%); Sandwell (5.2%); Liverpool (5.1%); and Newham (5.1%). The lowest rates were in rural areas including the district containing the Prime Minister's constituency, West Oxfordshire (1.7%); nearby Cotswold (1.8%); Vale of White Horse (1.8%); South Oxfordshire (1.8%); and Cherwell (2.1%). In a city such as Oxford (which these districts surround), the rate was just 2.5% of the population being unemployed in 2011. The five largest increases in the decade to 2011 had been in Barking & Dagenham (+1.9%); Wolverhampton (+1.9%); Blaenau Gwent (+1.8%); Hartlepool (+1.7%); and Walsall (+1.7%). Since 2011 the official unemployment rate has fallen, but this has partly been due to people increasingly being discouraged from describing themselves as unemployed. More people over retirement age (when officially you cannot be unemployed) getting paid work also reduces the rate.

Official unemployment rate, % of all those working and seeking work, UK

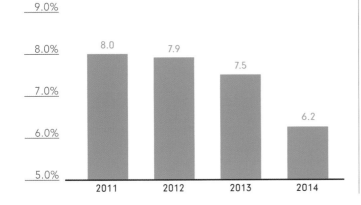

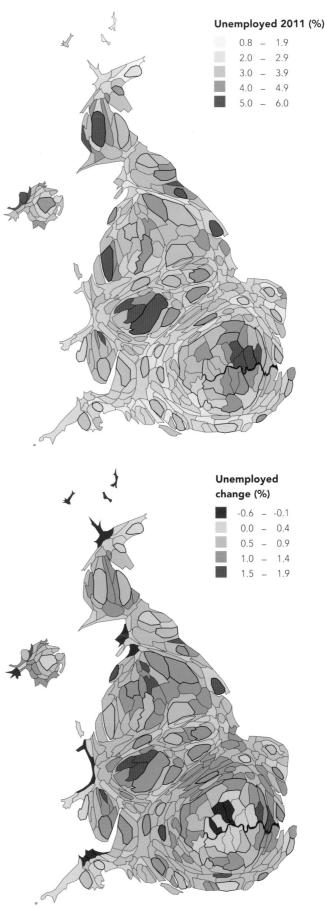

Unemployed 2011 (%)

	0.8 – 1.9
	2.0 – 2.9
	3.0 – 3.9
	4.0 – 4.9
	5.0 – 6.0

Unemployed change (%)

	-0.6 – -0.1
	0.0 – 0.4
	0.5 – 0.9
	1.0 – 1.4
	1.5 – 1.9

STUDENTS

By 2011 there were 4.3 million people who were students aged 16 and over in the UK, up from 3.1 million in 2001. In 2011, 1.6 million of these students also had a job on the side (or were studying while also doing a full-time job), whereas in 2001, only 1.1 million students were also working. There has therefore been an increase in the student population of 1.2 million, of which 0.5 million (net) are also working their way through college or university. A large number of these students will also be 16- and 17-year-olds at school, most of whom will not also be employed or self-employed.

The 10 greatest concentrations of students in the UK are found in Oxford and Cambridge (both 21.9%); Nottingham (17.1%); Manchester (16.1%); Newcastle upon Tyne (15.6%); Ceredigion (15.0%, home to Aberystwyth University); Canterbury (14.5%); Newham (14.3%); Exeter (14.0%); and Southampton (13.7%). The largest increases in students between Census years were found in Newcastle upon Tyne (+5.4%); Welwyn Hatfield (+5.3%); Nottingham (+5.2%); Lincoln (+4.9%); Newham and Canterbury (both +4.8%); Portsmouth (+4.4%); Manchester (+4.0%); Sheffield (+3.8%) and Hillingdon (+3.7%). The lowest proportions of students are found in places such as North Norfolk (3.2%) and South Holland (3.5%).

Numbers of students are given as a proportion of the 'economically inactive' (2.47 out of 9.27 million in 2011) in the graph below. The proportion rose rapidly from below 25% in 2011 to nearly 27% by 2014. Without much good work on offer for young adults, studying becomes more attractive, and ever growing student debts can be forgotten, for a while at least.

Student 2011 (%)

	0.9 – 4.9
	5.0 – 7.4
	7.5 – 9.9
	10.0 – 14.9
	15.0 – 21.9

Student change (%)

	-0.3 – -0.1
	0.0 – 0.9
	1.0 – 1.9
	2.0 – 2.9
	3.0 – 5.4

Students, % of all people aged 16+ who are not working, UK

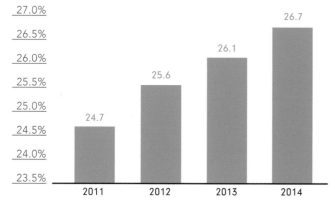

Year	Value
2011	24.7
2012	25.6
2013	26.1
2014	26.7

RETIRED

You might think that the largest group of people aged over 15 and not working would be those who are retired, but there were only 6.4 million people who were retired and not working for pay in 2011, a small rise on the 5.8 million in 2001. Students and carers (people looking after others for no pay) were a far larger combined group, but were found concentrated in very different places. The 10 areas with the highest proportions of pensioners in 2011 were East Lindsey (17.6%); North Norfolk (17.0%); West Somerset (16.6%); Tendring (16.2%); Christchurch (15.7%); East Devon (15.7%); Rother (15.6%); East Dorset (15.5%); Wyre (15.3%); and West Dorset (15.0%).

The graph below shows the proportion of 'economically inactive' people who are over 65 and unemployed but who would like to have work. They are never counted as officially unemployed, just retired. These rates, when converted into numbers of people, also fell, from 1.6 million in 2011 to 1.5 million in 2012, 1.4 million in 2013 and 1.3 million in 2014. Fewer and fewer people are able to retire early comfortably, or to survive well on their pension, but many also know that the jobs that they might have done in retirement are becoming harder to secure as younger people so desperately compete for work. Despite this, more and more people who are retired are also working. The proportion of people who are retired living in any local area has fallen the most in Barking & Dagenham (-2.3%); Tower Hamlets (-2.0%); Welwyn Hatfield (-1.9%); Crawley (-17%); Nottingham, Manchester and Slough (all -1.6%); Southwark (-1.5%); Bournemouth (-1.4%); and Brighton & Hove (-1.3%). The greatest increases in pensioners are found in some of the most remote areas, with the largest two being in Northern Ireland: Ards (+3.6%) and Limavady (+3.2%).

Retired 2011 (%)

	3.6 – 7.9
	8.0 – 9.9
	10.0 – 11.9
	12.0 – 13.9
	14.0 – 17.6

Retired change (%)

	-2.3 – -1.0
	-0.9 – -0.1
	0.0 – 0.9
	1.0 – 1.9
	2.0 – 3.6

Retired and wants work, % of all people aged 16+ who are not working, UK

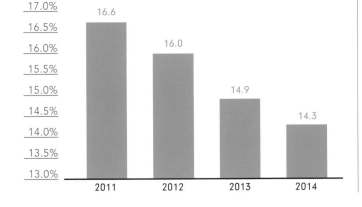

LOOKING AFTER HOME OR FAMILY

In 2011, only 2.0 million people not in paid employment described their main occupation as looking after the home or family. In 2001 this group was made up of 2.7 million. The reductions have been shocking and rapid. There are millions more young children below school age than the number of home carers, and there are far more disabled and ill adults needing care than there are people now able to care for them full-time in their families. Care has been privatised – parents do less care of their children, and children care less for their parents than older generations did when there were more children per family to share the load, and when people lived nearer their aged parents. More very young children are placed in nurseries, older children in afterschool clubs and older adults in old age care homes. In all the areas where being cared for by a family member is still most common, it is falling: Tower Hamlets (-2.1% to 5.4%); Newham (-1.9% to 5.4%); Barking & Dagenham (-1.5% to 5.1%); Kensington & Chelsea (-1.5% to 4.9%); Blackburn with Darwen (-1.2% to 4.8%); Luton (-0.7% to 4.8%); Redbridge (-0.4% to 4.7%); Bradford (-0.7% to 4.7%); Slough (-0.4% to 4.7%); and Leicester (-0.8% to 4.6%). The smallest reduction was in Slough (-0.4%) and the largest reduction in the Isle of Anglesey (-2.6%).

The graph below shows how the proportion of the 'economically inactive' who care for home and family has fluctuated since 2011 to remain just above a quarter of all those not in paid work. Some will be ineligible for some benefits that are aimed at preventing groups who cannot work or seek work living in abject poverty because they have to care for others. The change in the most recent year (2013–14) suggests that the economic pressure not to care for others is growing again, and so the frequency with which we care is again falling.

Homemakers, % of all people aged 16+ who are not in paid work, UK

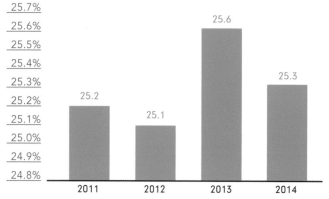

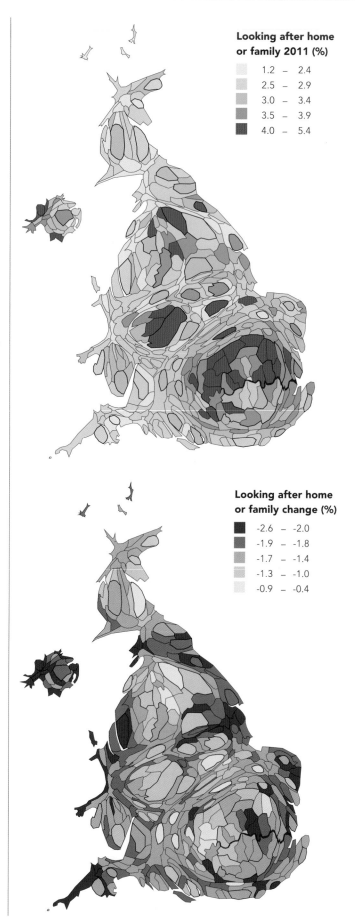

Looking after home or family 2011 (%)

- 1.2 – 2.4
- 2.5 – 2.9
- 3.0 – 3.4
- 3.5 – 3.9
- 4.0 – 5.4

Looking after home or family change (%)

- -2.6 – -2.0
- -1.9 – -1.8
- -1.7 – -1.4
- -1.3 – -1.0
- -0.9 – -0.4

LONG-TERM SICK OR DISABLED

By 2011 there were 2.0 million people who were long-term sick or disabled living in the UK, down from 2.5 million in 2001. Just as self-employment did not increase because more of the population became self-employed, and caring did not fall because fewer people wanted or needed to care, so being sick or disabled did not decrease simply because the population over time became healthier and/or less disabled.

Physical health did improve in the UK, not least because fewer people were now alive who had worked in the most health-damaging of industries in the past, such as coal-mining, but there was also a very large rise in people aged just under 65 by 2011 who had been born in the post-Second World War baby boom, so the population aged. However, the disincentives to declare yourself as being sick and disabled also increased. You often did better if you claimed to be self-employed, even if your business was not viable.

By 2011 the highest rates of long-term sickness and disability were confined to the furthest reaches of the UK: Derry (7.8%); Strabane (7.6%); Blaenau Gwent (7.2%); Belfast (7.1%); Neath Port Talbot and Merthyr Tydfil (both 7.0%); Inverclyde (6.7%); and Glasgow 6.5%). Contrast those rates with the lowest proportions: Isles of Scilly (0.6%); Hart (1.0%); Wokingham (1.1%); South Northamptonshire, Surrey Heath and Rutland (all 1.2%); Elmbridge, Uttlesford, Windsor & Maidenhead, South Bucks, Chiltern, West Oxfordshire and South Oxfordshire (all 1.3%); and Vale of White Horse (1.4%). After 2011, rates continued to fall as concerns over the deaths of people recently reassessed as fit for work rose.

Long-term sick or disabled 2011 (%)

- 0.6 – 1.9
- 2.0 – 2.9
- 3.0 – 3.9
- 4.0 – 4.9
- 5.0 – 7.8

Long-term sick or disabled change (%)

- -4.3 – -2.0
- -1.9 – -1.0
- -0.9 – -0.5
- -0.4 – -0.1
- 0.0 – 0.1

Long-term sick, % of all people aged 16+ who are not in paid work, UK

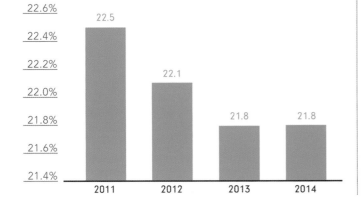

Year	%
2011	22.5
2012	22.1
2013	21.8
2014	21.8

NOT WORKING

More and more people in the UK are saying they are working as paid labour or have become self-employed. Some may have gained jobs that they enjoy doing. In other cases one long-term full-time job has become several temporary part-time short-term posts, and so it appears that the number of paid jobs has increased greatly, whereas what has actually risen is job insecurity and low pay. However, this is not the case everywhere, as the map of change indicates. In Surrey, to the West of London, and in some more affluent areas around Birmingham and in the outer commuting belts to London, there has been an increase in the proportion of people not in work. The reason may be that some families with high-income earners have been able to afford for one partner in the relationship not to be in paid work, or for grown-up children returning from university not to work.

In 2011 there were 33.0 million people not in paid work in the UK and 30.2 million in paid work. Ten years earlier those numbers were 32.1 million and 26.7 million respectively. Thus an extra 3.5 million people are in work whereas only an additional 0.9 million net are living in the UK and are not in work. The areas with the most rapid increases in people working are Tower Hamlets (+10.4%); Hackney (+9.2%); Newham (+8.5%); Liverpool (+7.6%); Southwark and Merthyr Tydfil (both +7.4%); Glasgow (+7.2%); Manchester (+7.1%); Islington (+6.7%); Knowsley (+6.5%); and Belfast (+6.3%). The three areas that now have the highest proportion of the population of all ages not working are Strabane (61.9%); Derry (61.5%); and Limavady (60.1%).

In 2001 there were 38 areas, not three, as in 2011, where just over 60% of the population were not working – where they were children, retired, unemployed, looking after family or otherwise engaged. Increasingly financial pressures cause both parents to go to work, the retired to get a job, and the disabled and elderly infirm to go into residential care rather than being looked after by relatives, because the relatives have to take paid employment. Since 2011 a rapidly growing proportion of the population who are not working tick the 'Other' box on official surveys and forms when asked what they are doing – perhaps 'keeping house' or doing voluntary work, supported by family or by unearned or undeclared income.

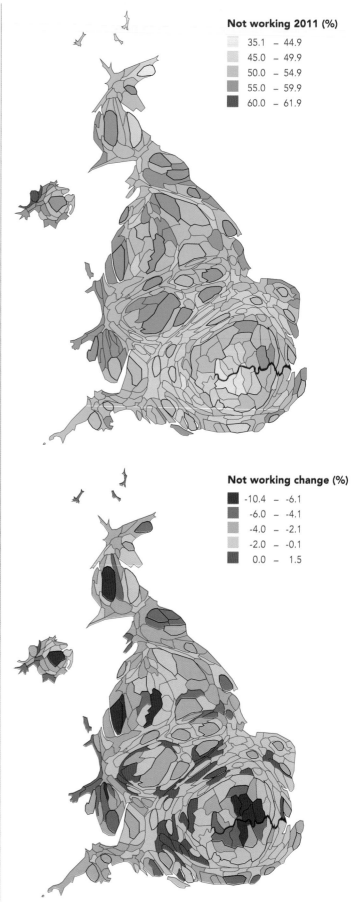

Not working 2011 (%)
- 35.1 – 44.9
- 45.0 – 49.9
- 50.0 – 54.9
- 55.0 – 59.9
- 60.0 – 61.9

Not working change (%)
- -10.4 – -6.1
- -6.0 – -4.1
- -4.0 – -2.1
- -2.0 – -0.1
- 0.0 – 1.5

Otherwise occupied, % of all people aged 16+ who are not in paid work, UK

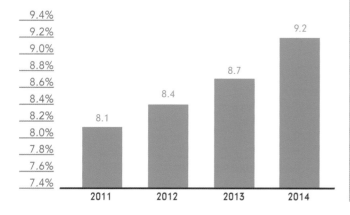

	2011	2012	2013	2014
	8.1	8.4	8.7	9.2

WORKING UNDER 16 HOURS

Of the 30.2 million people in paid work in the UK in 2011, 2.8 million were working under 16 hours a week, up from 2.2 million in 2001. Some 0.6 million, or a fifth, of the net 3.5 million increase in people working between 2001 and 2011 was in people working very few hours. Low-hours part-time work is most common in some generally very affluent places: Winchester (6.3%); Bath & North East Somerset (6.2%); Mid Suffolk, Cotswold and Guildford (all 6.0%); Canterbury, Suffolk Coastal, Uttlesford, Chichester, Chiltern and Derbyshire Dales (all 5.9%).

A person working less than 16 hours a week is not usually eligible for tax credits and other in-work benefits, so to be able to work so few hours a week often requires a partner who is earning much more. The lowest proportions of people working these few hours are found in a few parts of Scotland (in North Lanarkshire, 2.5%); Northern Ireland (in Strabane, 3.0%); and Wales (in Blaenau Gwent, 3.1%).

The five largest increases in people working under 16 hours a week often coincide with areas where there have also been increases in students: Newham (+2.5%); Tower Hamlets (1.8%); Manchester (1.6%); Ceredigion (1.5%); and Hackney (1.4%). The largest decreases have been in Scotland and the Isles of Scilly (-0.7%).

Nationally the numbers working even fewer than 10 hours a week have fallen since 2011 to just 3.6% of all those in employment in the UK by 2014. It is hard to work out why rates have fallen in the more rural areas of Scotland. It is possible that more young people from these areas have travelled to university than before, while others who might have taken a part-time job when they returned home have gone elsewhere in the UK in greater numbers than in 2001. Since 2011 there has been a national fall in the number of people working very low hours a week linked to changes in the benefits system, making such employees ineligible for certain in-work benefits.

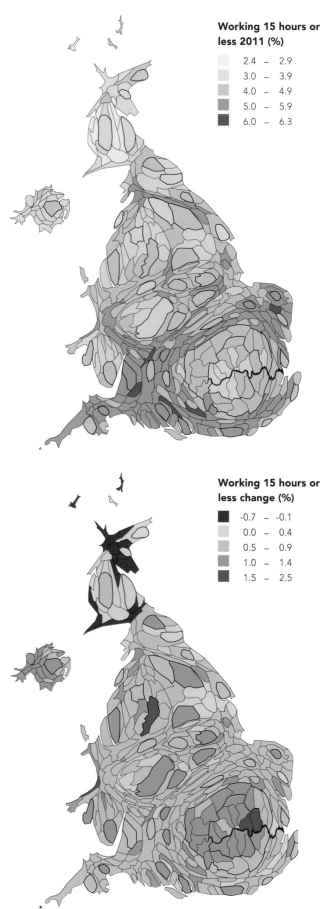

Working 15 hours or less 2011 (%)

- 2.4 – 2.9
- 3.0 – 3.9
- 4.0 – 4.9
- 5.0 – 5.9
- 6.0 – 6.3

Working 15 hours or less change (%)

- -0.7 – -0.1
- 0.0 – 0.4
- 0.5 – 0.9
- 1.0 – 1.4
- 1.5 – 2.5

All in employment who work under 10 hours a week, UK %

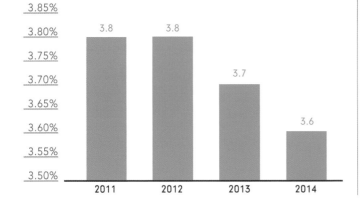

WORKING 16–30 HOURS

In 2011, 5.9 million people worked between 16 and 30 hours (inclusive) a week in paid work, up 1.5 million from 4.4 million in 2001 and, along with the 0.6 million rise in those working even fewer hours, accounting for the large majority (2.1 million) of the 3.5 million increase in jobs between 2001 and 2011. The greatest increases in part-time working (of 16+ hours a week) were found in a disparate set of areas, but none were very affluent places: Newham (+4.3%); Derry (+3.7%); Haringey (+3.1); North Lanarkshire and Cookstown (both +3.0%); Rhondda Cynon Taf, Glasgow, Knowsley, Allerdale, Hackney, Belfast, Antrim and the Orkney Islands (all +2.9%); Inverclyde, Brent, Liverpool, South Ayrshire, Moyle, Merthyr Tydfil and Barrow-in-Furness (all +2.8%).

The rise in part-time working in the UK was not a choice being made in more affluent areas. More people were taking more work there but usually only for a few hours a week, not for up to 30 hours. It is also very likely that the nature of the jobs is very different. Working behind a till at a supermarket for 30 hours a week is very different to working for five hours a week as a complementary or alternative therapist (and partner of a well remunerated spouse). To cement this point, the smallest increases in part-time work, all under 1.0%, were in South Bucks (+0.6%); Windsor & Maidenhead, Oxford, Kensington & Chelsea, Welwyn Hatfield and Hart (all +0.8%); Winchester, Camden, Guildford, Wokingham and Warwick (all +0.9%).

Nationally, since 2012, the proportion of people working part-time has been falling as a share of all those in work. Recent falls in part-time working may largely be due to people who want or need to work longer hours managing to get a few more hours of paid work a week, or people becoming self-employed and working at many very short-hours jobs a week that all then count as one longer-hours self-employed job.

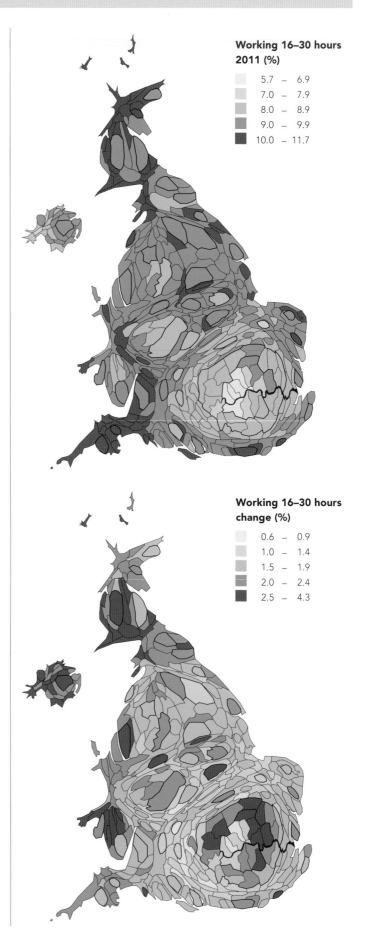

Working 16–30 hours 2011 (%)

- 5.7 – 6.9
- 7.0 – 7.9
- 8.0 – 8.9
- 9.0 – 9.9
- 10.0 – 11.7

Working 16–30 hours change (%)

- 0.6 – 0.9
- 1.0 – 1.4
- 1.5 – 1.9
- 2.0 – 2.4
- 2.5 – 4.3

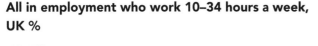

All in employment who work 10–34 hours a week, UK %

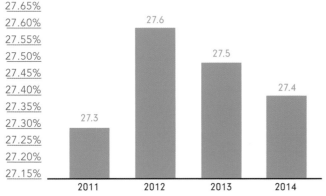

	2011	2012	2013	2014
	27.3	27.6	27.5	27.4

WORKING 31–48 HOURS

The number of people working full-time (31–48 hours a week) only rose from 15.8 million people in 2001 to 17.3 million by 2011, or by 1.5 million in 10 years. This was a far smaller absolute and relative increase in full-time work compared to that seen for part-time work. Furthermore, full-time work became more rare in many parts of the UK. The greatest decreases were in Enfield (-2.4%); Slough (-2.0%); Westminster (-1.9%); Luton and Limavady (-1.7%); Hart, Redbridge and Wyre Forest (-1.6%); Ealing (-1.5%); Ards, Harrow and Hillingdon (-1.4%); Carrickfergus, Croydon and the City of London (-1.3%). Only very rarely are those latter three administrative areas found in the same short list.

There are many reasons as to why full-time work has become less common in all these places. Similarly, the places with the greatest increases are also an eclectic bunch: Isles of Scilly (+4.7%); Shetland Islands (+3.9%); Merthyr Tydfil (+3.6%); Glasgow and Tower Hamlets (both +3.4%); Hackney (+3.3%); Boston, Barrow-in-Furness and Aberdeen (+3.2%); Knowsley (+3.1%); Mansfield (+3.0%); Bolsover (+2.9%); Liverpool, Dungannon, Eilean Siar and Aberdeenshire (+2.8%); Manchester and Bassetlaw (+2.7%).

Since 2011 the proportion of people working normal full-time hours has fallen from 44.8% of all those employed and self-employed to 44.2%, a surprising decline considering employment is alleged to be rising. However, the largest decline was in the year to 2012 at the very depth of the Great Recession. It is possible that the 0.5% fall in normal hours full-time employment then was due to a few people starting to work more than 44 hours a week to keep their jobs and their businesses afloat, while others will have had to have started working fewer than 35 hours a week, and, of course, many become unemployed every year as many others also gain work. There is now a very rapid turnover in employment in the UK, and many jobs are precarious.

Working 31–48 hours 2011 (%)

- 21.0 – 23.9
- 24.0 – 25.9
- 26.0 – 27.9
- 28.0 – 29.9
- 30.0 – 34.8

Working 31–48 hours change (%)

- -2.4 – -1.1
- -1.0 – -0.1
- 0.0 – 0.9
- 1.0 – 1.9
- 2.0 – 4.7

All in employment who work 35–44 hours a week, UK %

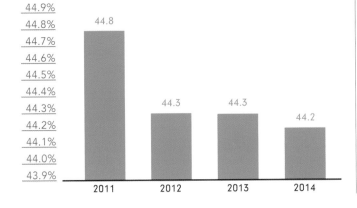

Year	%
2011	44.8
2012	44.3
2013	44.3
2014	44.2

WORKING OVER 48 HOURS

Overworking had been declining. In 2011, 3.9 million people worked 49 hours or more a week, down from 4.2 million in 2001. The greatest 'offenders' remain a core group of Local Authorities that stretch from the centre of London to its South-Western periphery. The self-employed are not paid to work any specific hours, and many others accept overtime (or work at two or more jobs) because they now need the money to afford to live where they live. Over a tenth of everybody living in the following areas works over 48 hours a week: City of London (24.6%); Kensington & Chelsea (18.0%); Westminster (15.8%); Richmondshire (14.2%); Wandsworth (12.8%); Hammersmith & Fulham (12.7%); Camden and Richmond upon Thames (both 11.4%); Islington and the Isles of Scilly (both 11.1%); Eden (10.7%); and Elmbridge (10.3%). This list includes a couple of affluent farming areas. And if you work near where you live, it is easier to increase your working hours because you spend less time commuting.

The proportion of the population working excessive hours has fallen everywhere save for a central cluster of Inner London boroughs, a North Yorkshire agricultural and military district, and one area of Wales, where only 3.5% of people overworked to begin with, and that has risen to 3.6%. The greatest rises have been in the City of London (+3.9%); Kensington & Chelsea (+2.2%); Tower Hamlets (+2.1%); Islington (+1.9%); Richmondshire (+1.7%); Southwark (+1.5%); Hackney (+1.4%); Westminster (+1.3%); Lambeth and Camden (both +0.5%); Wandsworth (+0.4%); and Blaenau Gwent (+0.1%).

Since 2011 the proportion of all those overworking as a share of everyone in paid work has risen relentlessly again; 2011 may have been a temporary hiatus in the long-term increase in working hours, most probably within the Central London financial heart, as the finance sector bounced back.

All in employment who work 45 or more hours a week, UK %

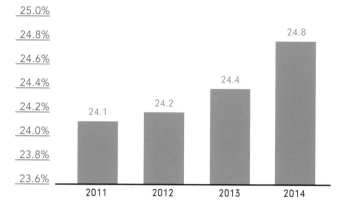

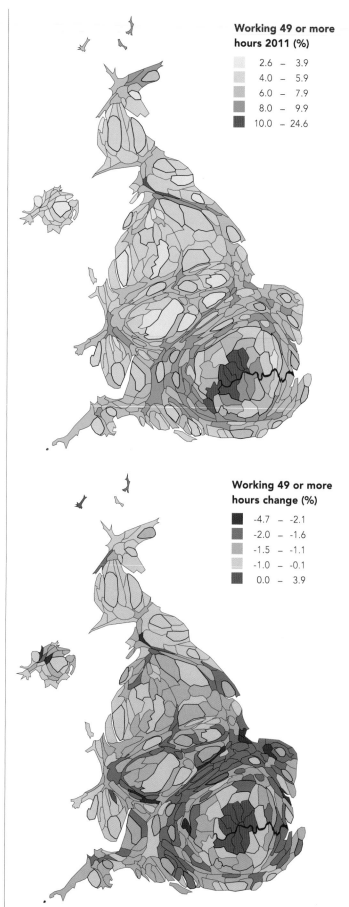

Working 49 or more hours 2011 (%)

- 2.6 – 3.9
- 4.0 – 5.9
- 6.0 – 7.9
- 8.0 – 9.9
- 10.0 – 24.6

Working 49 or more hours change (%)

- -4.7 – -2.1
- -2.0 – -1.6
- -1.5 – -1.1
- -1.0 – -0.1
- 0.0 – 3.9

LEVEL 1

Level 1 qualifications are the most basic and limited set of certificates someone might have – equating to fewer than five GCSE passes of any grade. In the UK in 2011, of those aged between 16 and 64 (inclusive), 6.6 million people's highest qualification was at Level 1. This is a rapid decrease from 7.7 million in 2001. The only districts where the proportion has risen is where the share with no qualifications has fallen rapidly, such as in Glasgow and Merthyr Tydfil. The areas where the lowest proportions of this age group have such low qualifications are the City of London (3.4%); Kensington & Chelsea (4.2%); Westminster and Wandsworth (both 5.0%); Richmond upon Thames (5.1%); Camden (5.2%); Hammersmith & Fulham and Cambridge (both 5.4%); Islington (6.4%); and Oxford (6.5%).

With every year that passes the population of the UK becomes more skilled. It is mostly people with few formal skills who are most likely to die or retire. And hardly anyone leaves school now without at least Level 1 qualifications. To cover the whole age range, Level 1 in England, Wales and Northern Ireland equates to 1–4 O levels/CSEs/GCSEs (any grades), Entry Level, Foundation Diploma, NVQ Level 1, Foundation GNVQ, Basic/Essential Skills. In Scotland this translates to O Grade, Standard Grade, Access 3 Cluster, Intermediate 1 or 2, GCSE, CSE, Senior Certificate or equivalent; GSVQ Foundation or Intermediate, SVQ Level 1 or 2, SCOTVEC Module, City and Guilds Craft or equivalent; and other school qualifications not already mentioned (including foreign qualifications). The wider choice of qualifications in Scotland is part of the reason for more people attaining Level 1 rather than no level at all there. The proportion continued to fall after 2011.

Level 1 2011 (%)

	3.4 – 7.9
	8.0 – 9.9
	10.0 – 11.9
	12.0 – 13.9
	14.0 – 20.6

Level 1 change (%)

	-5.2 – -3.1
	-3.0 – -2.1
	-2.0 – -1.1
	-1.0 – -0.1
	0.0 – 0.8

People aged 16–64 with NVQ1, UK %

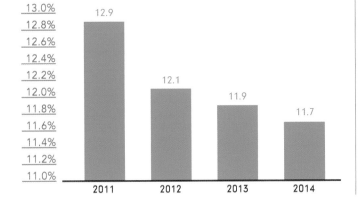

2011	2012	2013	2014
12.9	12.1	11.9	11.7

LEVEL 2

Around 7.0 million people aged 16–64 achieved qualifications at Level 2 in 2001, the equivalent of 5 GCSEs of grade C or above. This is down from 7.6 million in 2001 as more people gain higher qualifications compared to those who gain Level 2. The largest decreases have been in the Isles of Scilly (-7.2%); Hart (-5.2%); Harrow and Wokingham (both -4.8%); Mid Sussex (-4.7%); Windsor & Maidenhead (-4.6%); Chiltern, Surrey Heath, Slough and Woking (all -4.4%). The largest increase was in Dumfries in Galloway (+0.8%) and the largest proportion of the population holding qualifications at this level is found in Halton (14.0%). The 2001 Census asked for the qualification of all those people aged 16–74 and the 2011 Census of all those aged 16 and over. The 16–64 group is the only group we can reliably compare between Censuses because of how the data is released.

The exact definition of Level 2 in England, Wales and Northern Ireland is to gain at least: 5+ O levels (passes)/CSEs (grade 1)/GCSEs (grades A*–C), or a School Certificate, or 1 A level or 2–3 AS levels/VCEs, Higher Diploma, or one Welsh Baccalaureate Intermediate Diploma, NVQ Level 2, Intermediate GNVQ, City and Guilds Craft, BTEC First/General Diploma, RSA Diploma. In Scotland Level 2 requires at least one SCE Higher Grade, Higher, Advanced Higher, CSYS, A level, AS level, Advanced Senior Certificate or equivalent; GSVQ Advanced, SVQ Level 3, ONC, OND, SCOTVEC National Diploma, or City and Guilds Advanced Craft or equivalent.

Since 2011 the UK proportion of people with Level 2 qualifications as their highest level has fallen. The graph below only includes non-vocational qualifications and discounts vocational Level 2 qualifications, so it is not strictly comparable to the Census data.

People aged 16–64 with NVQ2, UK %

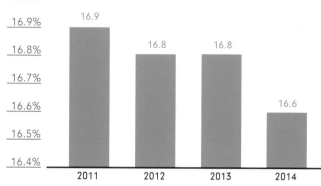

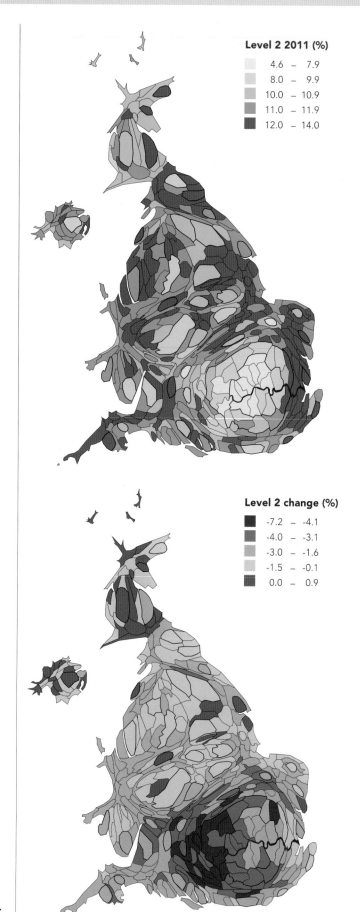

Level 2 2011 (%)

4.6 – 7.9
8.0 – 9.9
10.0 – 10.9
11.0 – 11.9
12.0 – 14.0

Level 2 change (%)

-7.2 – -4.1
-4.0 – -3.1
-3.0 – -1.6
-1.5 – -0.1
0.0 – 0.9

LEVEL 3

Level 3 qualifications are two or more A levels or equivalent. In 2011, 5.8 million people aged 16–64 held these as their highest qualifications, a rapid rise from 3.4 million in that same age group just 10 years earlier. There is a particular clustering for people with these qualifications as their highest in university towns and cities, boosted by university students who have not yet taken their first degrees. Thus the greatest concentrations are found in Ceredigion (15.6%); Lincoln and Nottingham (both 14.9%); Exeter (14.7%); Oxford (14.5%); Portsmouth (14.2%); and Cambridge (14.0%).

Across most of the country there are increasing proportions of people holding these qualifications as their highest level. The exceptions are in London where it is becoming normal to have even higher qualifications than these. The three areas with the greatest falls in the proportions with Level 3 qualifications are the City of London (-2.8%); Westminster (-2.3%); and Kensington & Chelsea (-2.1%).

In England, Wales and Northern Ireland the precise definition of Level 3 is: 2+ A levels/VCEs, or 4+ AS levels, or a Higher School Certificate, a Progression/Advanced Diploma, a Welsh Baccalaureate Advanced Diploma, NVQ Level 3; Advanced GNVQ, City and Guilds Advanced Craft, ONC, OND, BTEC National, RSA Advanced Diploma. In Scotland the equivalents are HNC, HND, SVQ Level 4 or equivalent; or other post-school but pre-Higher Education qualifications not already mentioned (including foreign qualifications).

Since 2011 the proportion of the UK population holding these qualifications has risen, but it now appears stable. This halt in any improvement could well be connected to the dramatic cuts in the funding of further education colleges after 2011.

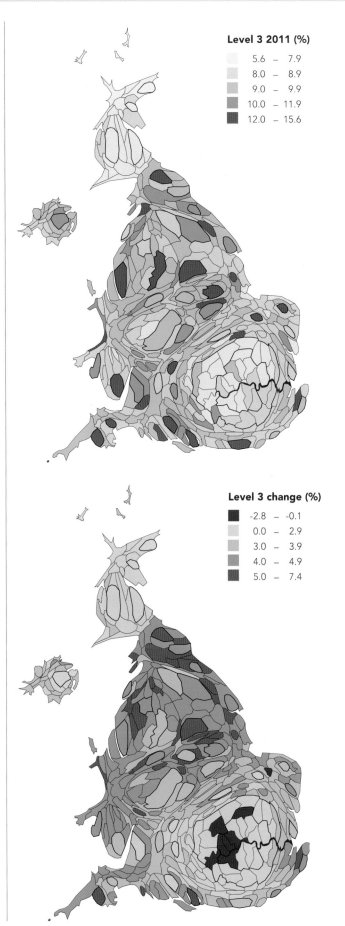

Level 3 2011 (%)

	5.6 – 7.9
	8.0 – 8.9
	9.0 – 9.9
	10.0 – 11.9
	12.0 – 15.6

Level 3 change (%)

	-2.8 – -0.1
	0.0 – 2.9
	3.0 – 3.9
	4.0 – 4.9
	5.0 – 7.4

People aged 16–64 with NVQ3, UK %

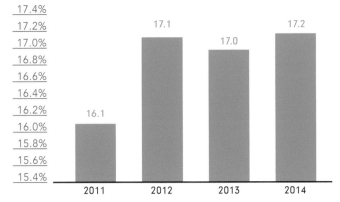

LEVEL 4 AND ABOVE

Level 4 qualifications are a university degree or equivalent. By 2011 there were a remarkable 12.0 million people aged 16–64 holding Level 4 qualifications living in the UK, up from 7.7 million in 2001. Most of the increase, of just under half a million new degree holders a year, is due to more and more young people going to university in the UK and there being very few older people holding degrees when they turn 65. However, the rise is also due to more people holding degrees coming to the UK as migrants than there have been people with degrees leaving the UK since 2001.

More than a third of the population aged 16–64 in the following areas have Level 4 qualifications: City of London (55.5%); Wandsworth (42.5%); Kensington & Chelsea (40.2%); Hammersmith & Fulham and Westminster (both 39.4%); Islington (38.6%); Camden (38.5%); Richmond upon Thames (37.9%); Cambridge (36.7%); Lambeth (36.6%); and Southwark (33.7%). Level 4 is a Degree (eg, BA, BSc), a Higher Degree (eg, MA, PhD, PGCE), NVQ Level 4–5, HNC, HND, RSA Higher Diploma, BTEC Higher Level, Foundation degree (NI), professional qualifications (eg, teaching, nursing, accountancy). In Scotland the equivalents are SVQ Level 5 or equivalent; professional qualifications (eg, teaching, nursing, accountancy); and other higher education qualifications not already mentioned (including foreign qualifications).

The area of the UK with the lowest proportion of people holding these qualifications is Great Yarmouth (9.6%). The areas with the greatest increase since 2001 are the areas of most gentrification: Tower Hamlets (+11.0%); Hackney (+8.7%); and Islington (+8.6%). There is no sign of any slowdown in the rise in the proportion of the population with Level 4 or above since 2011; it is increasing by about 1% a year.

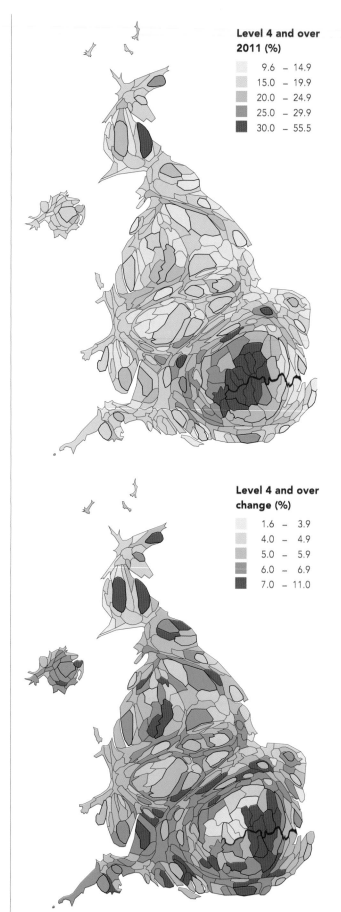

Level 4 and over 2011 (%)

	9.6 – 14.9
	15.0 – 19.9
	20.0 – 24.9
	25.0 – 29.9
	30.0 – 55.5

Level 4 and over change (%)

	1.6 – 3.9
	4.0 – 4.9
	5.0 – 5.9
	6.0 – 6.9
	7.0 – 11.0

People aged 16–64 with NVQ4+, UK %

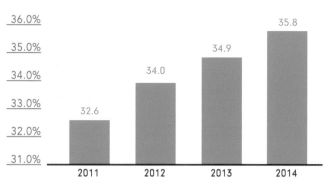

	2011	2012	2013	2014
	32.6	34.0	34.9	35.8

NO OR OTHER QUALIFICATIONS

In 2011, 8.4 million people aged 16–64 had no qualifications equivalent to one GCSE of any grade, or the qualifications they did have were purely vocational or work-related, including gaining a driving licence, or were qualifications gained outside the UK where the nature of the qualification was not stated or its UK equivalent level was not known to the person. Those filling in the Census are presented with such a complicated list of possibilities (many of which most people born in the UK know little about) that many international migrants with qualifications below Level 4 will be baffled. Only 'a degree' is an international term.

In 2001, 11.7 million people aged 16–64 had been in this same situation. The rapid fall is due to almost everyone leaving school in the UK in the last 10 years gaining some qualifications, and so many people of older ages having gained no qualifications, especially if they left school at the age of 15 before 1973. There has been a dramatic improvement in education for the majority of children, albeit perhaps now with far too much emphasis on gaining too many qualifications for the majority rather than far too few.

More than 21% of the population aged 16–64 in the following areas still have no formal qualifications: Strabane (25.3%); Limavady (23.4%); Newham (22.9%); Dungannon (22.7%); Cookstown (22.5%); Leicester (21.6%); Derry (21.4%); Newry & Mourne (21.3%); Boston (21.3%); and Ballymoney and Omagh (both 21.1%). It is worth noting that through to this day Northern Ireland retains the 11+ examination, and so the majority of children there have to attend secondary modern schools. The three areas of England with the highest proportions with no qualifications have had high rates of immigration of very unskilled migrants in recent years. The fastest decrease in people with no qualifications has been in Staffordshire Moorlands (-11.2%).

The proportion with no qualifications continued to decline rapidly after 2011 by about half a percentage point a year.

People aged 16–64 with no or other qualifications, UK %

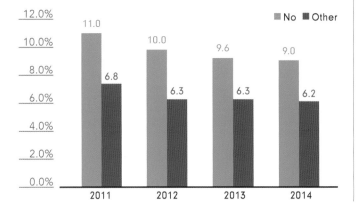

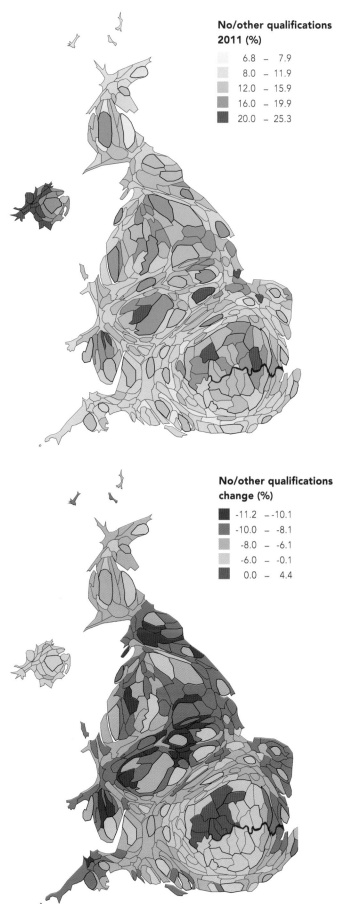

No/other qualifications 2011 (%)

	6.8 – 7.9
	8.0 – 11.9
	12.0 – 15.9
	16.0 – 19.9
	20.0 – 25.3

No/other qualifications change (%)

	-11.2 – -10.1
	-10.0 – -8.1
	-8.0 – -6.1
	-6.0 – -0.1
	0.0 – 4.4

APPRENTICESHIPS

The 2011 Census in England and Wales was the first modern Census to ask people if they were apprentices; 1.1 million said they were. The highest proportions were found in areas traditionally associated with industry or agriculture: Barrow-in-Furness (5.3%); Copeland (3.6%); South Tyneside (3.4%); Eastleigh (3.2%); Blaby, Redcar & Cleveland, Neath Port Talbot, South Ribble and Erewash (all 3.1%); Hyndburn, Selby, Hartlepool, Allerdale and South Somerset (all 3.0%); and Stockton-on-Tees (2.9%). In contrast, all the areas with the fewest apprenticeships were in London, and the list is so remarkable it is worth at least including a version of it with the same number of areas as above to illustrate this point, and to bring this chapter to an end: City of London (0.4%); Kensington & Chelsea, Westminster and Camden (all 0.5%); Haringey, Wandsworth, Tower Hamlets and Hackney (all 0.6%); Newham, Islington, Lambeth, Barnet and Southwark (all 0.7%); Brent and Hammersmith & Fulham (both 0.8%).

Since 2012 the proportion of people holding trade apprenticeships has been falling. Although the government says it supports apprenticeships, in practice these often involve basic office work, not much training, and allow employers to pay people far less per hour than they would otherwise be permitted to do. The UK qualifications sector is now a market, not the result of an education service designed with the interests of young people at heart.

The Censuses allow us to see all this in a much longer-term perspective (until they and other surveys are cut).[6] Fewer people with very good qualifications will find employment in highly ranked occupations and productive industries in future – the subject of the next chapter. This is because there are simply not enough such highly ranked jobs. There cannot be, because to rank highly requires others to be ranked below you. Similarly, so much education and training that is currently underway does not concern the most productive industries, but is channelled towards marketing and finance, not making and caring. And you cannot all advertise, account for and sell each other things you have not made while not valuing work that is not seen as quick money.

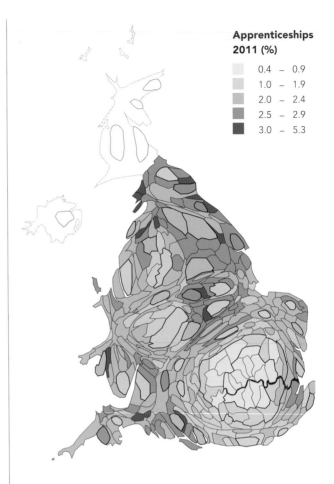

Apprenticeships 2011 (%)

- 0.4 – 0.9
- 1.0 – 1.9
- 2.0 – 2.4
- 2.5 – 2.9
- 3.0 – 5.3

People aged 16–64 with trade apprenticeships, UK %

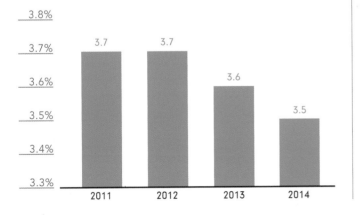

The proportion of jobs labelled as *Professional* has continued to increase, by a further 0.5% in total in just the three years from 2011 to 2014. *Managers & Directors, Associate professionals* and those in *Caring, Leisure and other services* have increased their share of the pie by just 0.2% and all other occupations by less, or they have fallen in proportion.

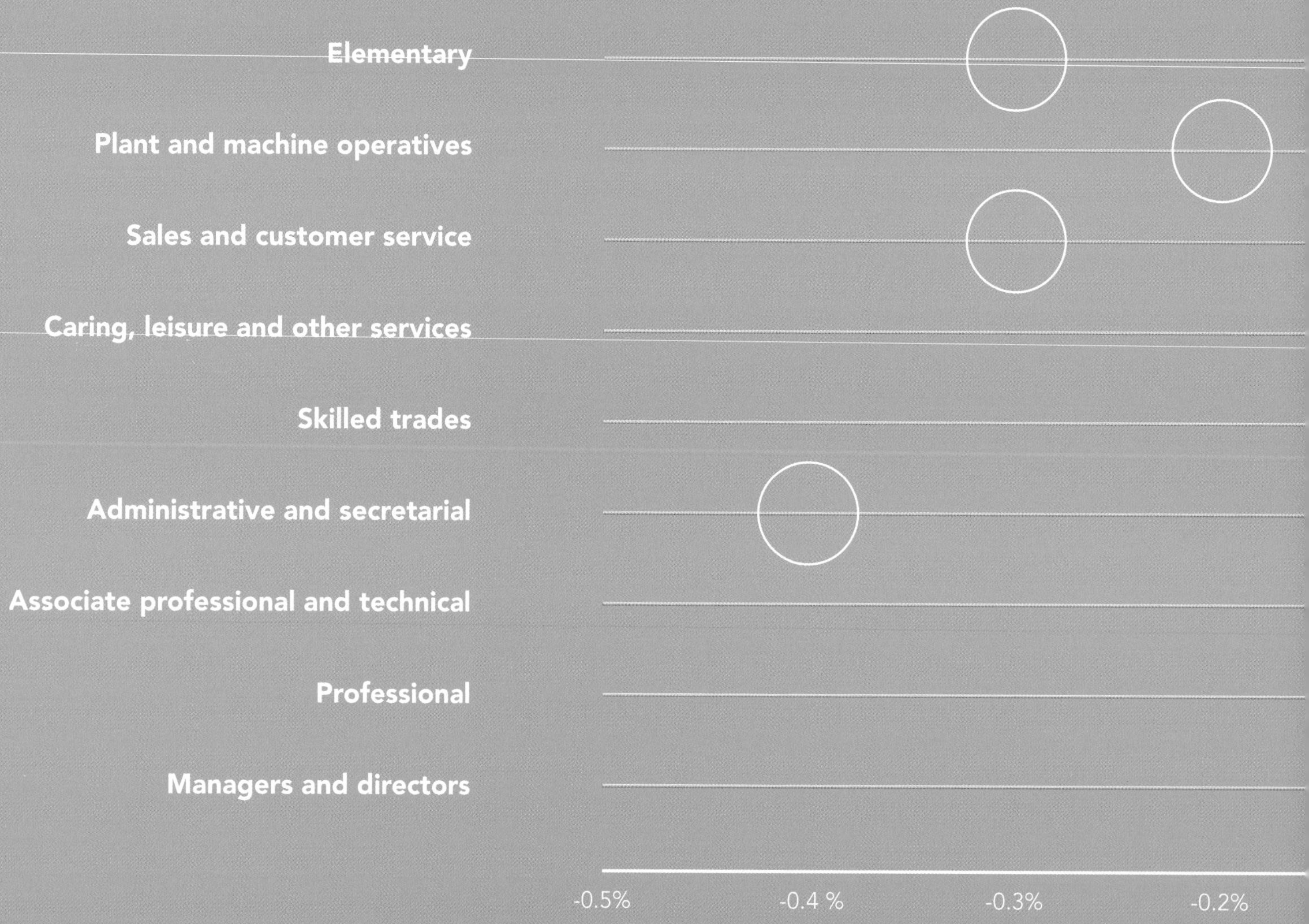

Elementary

Plant and machine operatives

Sales and customer service

Caring, leisure and other services

Skilled trades

Administrative and secretarial

Associate professional and technical

Professional

Managers and directors

| | -0.5% | -0.4 % | -0.3% | -0.2% |

Occupation and Industry

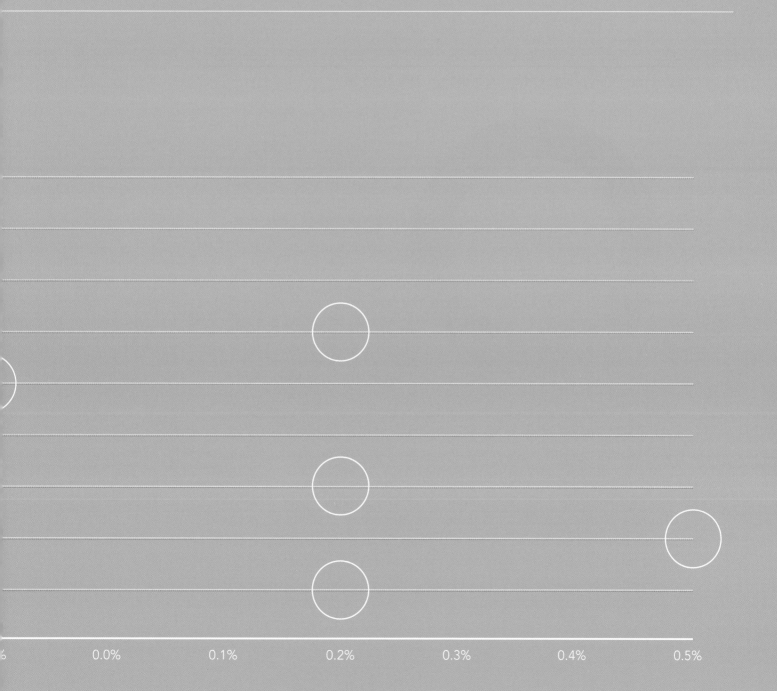

0.0%   0.1%   0.2%   0.3%   0.4%   0.5%

Occupation and Industry

For decades the Census has divided people in work by the nature of the occupation they work in and the industry that employs them. A century ago, in 1911, the Registrar General introduced social classes based on these occupations as well as three industrial classes (for those working in mining, textiles or agriculture). In addition to the three industrial classes, the five Registrar General's social classes were labelled *Professional, managerial and technical, Skilled, Partly-skilled* and *Unskilled.*

People in employment by occupation, UK 2011 %

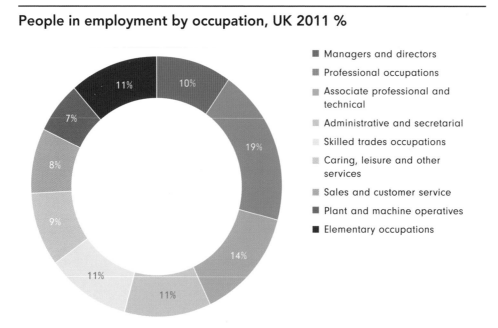

- Managers and directors
- Professional occupations
- Associate professional and technical
- Administrative and secretarial
- Skilled trades occupations
- Caring, leisure and other services
- Sales and customer service
- Plant and machine operatives
- Elementary occupations

Although there have been many changes since 1911, the labels first used just over a century ago to describe branches of work in the UK have tended to stick – except that the 2010 Standard Occupational Classification places *Managers and directors* first, before the demoted second occupational class, which is labelled *Professional.*[7] The chart above shows how that *Professional occupations* group has become the largest single occupational class in the intervening century, constituting 19% of all jobs by 2011. Only a tiny proportion, perhaps less than a tenth of that number, could have labelled themselves as *Professional* in 1911. The bar chart below shows how much 'professionalisation' there has been since just 2011. More and more jobs have come to gain this label over time.

Change in proportion of people working in different occupations, UK 2011–2014 %

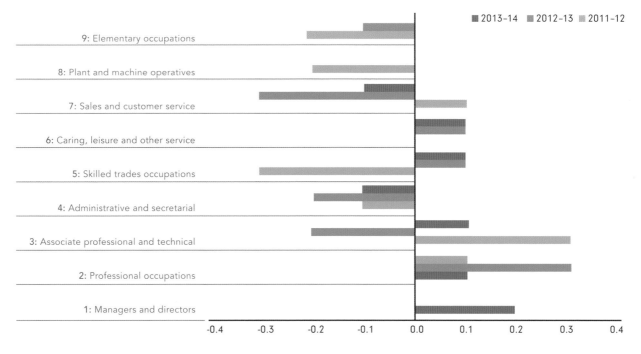

The proportion of jobs labelled as *Professional* has continued to increase, by a further 0.5% in total in just the three years from 2011 to 2014. *Managers and directors, Associate Professionals* and those in *Caring, Leisure and other services* have increased their share of the pie by just 0.2% and all other occupations by less, or they have fallen in proportion. These are very fast shifts in the space of very few years, and suggest a continual 'grade inflation' as more jobs are given fancier and fancier titles each year compared to those jobs that have, in effect, had their job labels downgraded by not being given a more 'fancy' title. It is not that so many jobs are all becoming more skilled. There will be more 'servants' working nowadays compared to a few years ago, but they may now be called 'professional educator and child hygienist' rather than 'nanny'. Similarly, someone in charge of a few other people may today be called a manager, whereas in the past you had to manage more people to be titled a manager.

The jobs market is changing shape. In the 1990s the second greatest growth in any occupational sector was found in *Elementary* occupations – over 1 million extra jobs in this lowest paid sector were created during 1991–2001. In contrast, the number of jobs in the UK in all the *Elementary* occupations combined only rose slightly, from 3.2 to 3.3 million, in the 2000s. The graph above shows that there was a collective fall of 0.3% in the share of these jobs among all occupations in the UK between 2011 and 2014. This is partly due to the nature of industrial change in the UK, and is also due to more people working in *Elementary* jobs in London for very long hours rather than having two people working part-time there.

The largest industries in 2011 were *Public administration, education and health* (30% of all jobs), followed by a series of mainly private sector industries, beginning

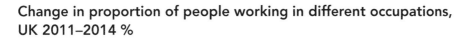

with people working in *Distribution, hotels and restaurants* (19%), and followed by a greatly swelled *Banking, finance and insurance* sector (16%) – one that is much larger in 2011 than it was in 2001 or 1991. The graph below shows half of all people (51%) in work in the UK now work in moving money about (Banking, finance and insurance, 16%), moving things about (Transport and communications, 9%), selling things, rooms or food (Distribution, hotels and restaurants, 19%), or building (Construction, 7%). A narrow minority (49% in total) are paid to provide care, teach or heal (Public administration, education and health, 30%), to undertake other similar services (6%), farm or fish (Agriculture and fishing, 1%), provide us with energy or water (2%), or make anything (Manufacturing, 10%).

Proportion of people working in different industries, UK 2011 %

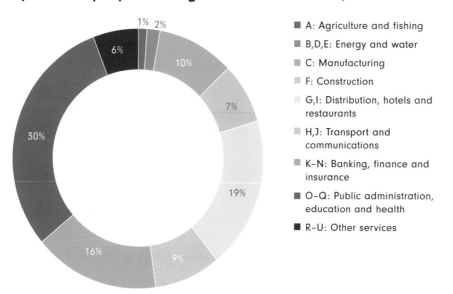

- A: Agriculture and fishing
- B,D,E: Energy and water
- C: Manufacturing
- F: Construction
- G,I: Distribution, hotels and restaurants
- H,J: Transport and communications
- K–N: Banking, finance and insurance
- O–Q: Public administration, education and health
- R–U: Other services

Since 2011 the *Banking, finance and insurance* sector has continued to grow in terms of its share of all UK jobs and, as an industry, increasing by 0.1% net to 2014, whereas jobs in *Distribution, hotels and restaurants* fell by 0.2% net over the same period. There are a large number of jobs where the occupation is labelled 'Elementary' in *Distribution, hotels and restaurants*.

Any sustained acceleration in the trend post-2011 and post-2001 would result in *Banking, finance and insurance* becoming the largest private sector of British industry by 2021, despite the financial crash of 2008 and the short-lived job loses of that year, the losses in 2009 and the further job loses in 2010 in such employment. However, the sector that was shrinking most strongly between 2011 and 2014 was *Public administration, education and health* (-0.2% + -0.2% = -0.4%). This is despite the budgets of the latter two (mostly public) sectors having been supposedly protected between 2011 and 2014.

Increasing numbers of people working in private healthcare and private education would slightly mitigate the overall job loses in the *Public administration, education and health* sector at that time. The next largest falls were in *Construction*, but these are half those experienced in *Public administration, education and health*.

After the spectacular rise in *Banking, finance and insurance* the largest growth sector since 2011 has been *Transport and communications* (+0.2%), which now includes the growing storage industry. This is the industry where you pay people to store things you own that you cannot fit in your own home. So, we borrow more money, we buy more stuff, we store more stuff, and we teach and heal and build less.

Although the rates of change in the graph below might look small, its net change statistic hides much greater gross turnover rates in jobs. In this graph change is measured in annual percentage point shifts in the share of jobs between sectors. Thus someone moving jobs or employer but staying in the same sector is not seen as a change, and someone retiring but their post being replaced by a new recruit is also not shown as a change. Change means change in overall share, not individual experience.

Change in proportion of people working in different industries, UK 2011–2014 %

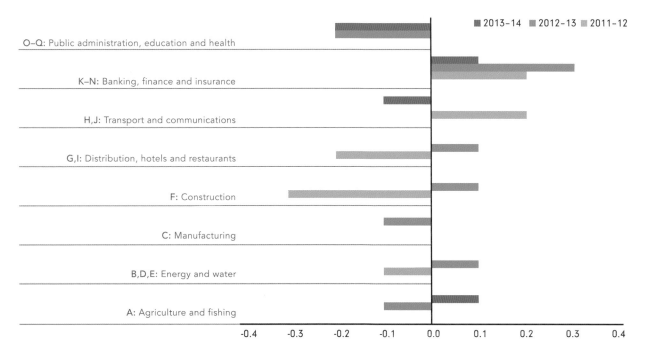

MANAGERS, DIRECTORS AND SENIOR OFFICIALS

The changing occupational groupings from the Standard Occupational classification of 2000 (SOC2000) to SOC2010 will have had the effect of slightly reducing the number of people labelled managers as a few occupations have been reassigned to other groups. However, this effect may well be smaller than grade inflation in other aspects of job titling. In 2011, 3.1 million people described their occupations as being involved in managing others, directing businesses and services, or in some other way being a senior official as part of their occupation. This is a reduction on the 3.9 million so employed in 2001, a number that had remained static since rising to that level in 1991. In the 1990s there was a great increase in people working in these jobs in London (especially to the South-East of the centre of London) and a smaller rise almost everywhere else. In contrast, in the 2000s there was a fall in the proportions of people working in jobs with these labels everywhere, and the falls were greatest around London.

By 2011 the highest concentrations of people in these occupations were found in Kensington & Chelsea (11.9%); Isles of Scilly (11.8%); City of London (11.5%); Westminster (10.1%); South Bucks and Richmond upon Thames (both 9.3%); Elmbridge (9.2%); Chiltern, Windsor & Maidenhead and Wandsworth (all 8.4%); Hart, Surrey Heath and South Northamptonshire (all 8.1%); and Hammersmith & Fulham (8.0%). The largest reductions had been in some of the areas where this group were most concentrated in the past. There was a loss of jobs at the top when the global recession struck in 2008. The places seeing the greatest reductions were Wokingham (-4.6%); Surrey Heath (-4.3%); Richmond upon Thames (-4.1%); Hart (-3.9%); St Albans (-3.9%); Windsor & Maidenhead and Kingston upon Thames (both -3.8%); Bracknell Forest and Woking (both -3.7%); West Berkshire, Chiltern and Wandsworth (all -3.6%); and Hammersmith & Fulham (-3.5%).

After 2011 there was an increase again in people in this group of occupations, but only of 0.2%, and the proportion has remained static since 2012.

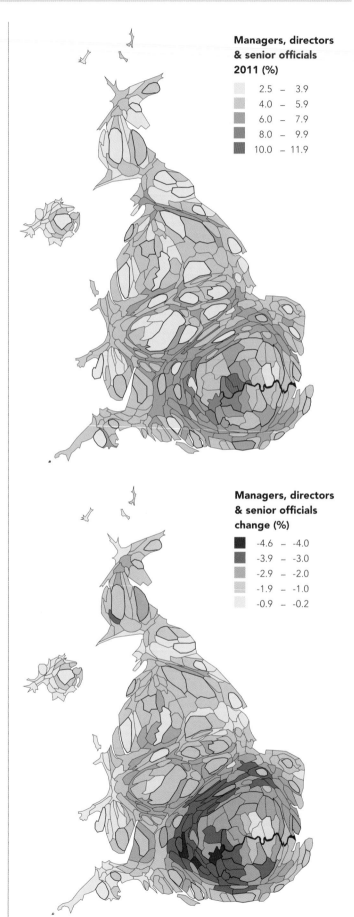

Managers, directors & senior officials 2011 (%)

	2.5 – 3.9
	4.0 – 5.9
	6.0 – 7.9
	8.0 – 9.9
	10.0 – 11.9

Managers, directors & senior officials change (%)

	-4.6 – -4.0
	-3.9 – -3.0
	-2.9 – -2.0
	-1.9 – -1.0
	-0.9 – -0.2

Managers and directors, UK % all jobs

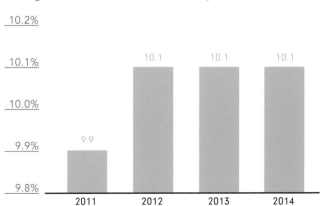

	2011	2012	2013	2014
	9.9	10.1	10.1	10.1

PROFESSIONAL OCCUPATIONS

In 2011 there were 5.2 million people employed in occupations that had been given the professional categorisation in the UK. This was a huge rise compared to the 3 million people whose jobs were labelled in this way in 2001. A small part of the rise may be due to the reclassification of certain occupations which nowadays requires a degree or equivalent qualification for admittance, and hence now being labelled as professional due to these changes (as well as some managerial jobs being reclassified as professional between the Censuses). However, the continued and very sustained and substantial increases in the national share of all jobs being in this sector since 2011, as illustrated in the graph below, suggests that professionalisation is a continuing and long-term trend. The most rapid increases shown in the map of change, within London, in Oxford and in and around Cambridge, suggests that there is a continuation of the widening divide seen when earlier Censuses were compared. A few places are experiencing the effects of the employment of more and more people in jobs labelled as 'professional'. Not all of these jobs will be that well paid, but when pay is relatively low in a profession, gentrification of poorer areas in the locality is accelerated as professionals have to find somewhere to live and then displace others who can no longer afford to live nearby.

By 2011 by place of residence, the highest proportions of people employed in these occupations were found in the City of London (25.7%); Cambridge (18.3%); Wandsworth (16.9%); Islington (16.2%); Camden (15.8%); Richmond upon Thames (15.7%); and Oxford (15.5%). Three to six times fewer professionals per resident were found in 2011 living in Great Yarmouth and Tendring (both 4.3%); Fenland and Blaenau Gwent (both 4.4%); Blackpool, Corby, Kingston upon Hull and Stoke-on-Trent (all 4.5%). The most rapid increase in the local proportion of professionals was in Islington (+7.3%) and the slowest was in Fenland (+1.4%). But nowhere was there a fall in the local share of people whose jobs are labelled in this way, and every year there is a national rise.

Professional occupations, UK % all jobs

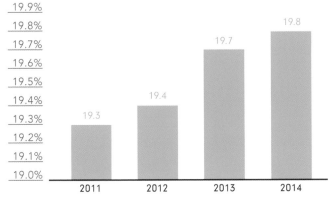

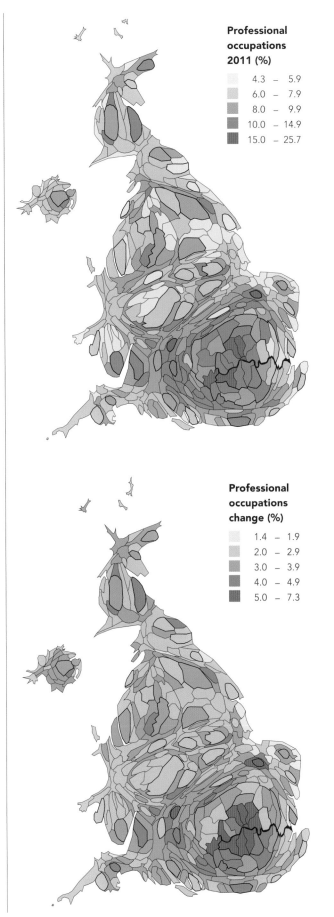

ASSOCIATE PROFESSIONAL AND TECHNICAL OCCUPATIONS

Around 3.8 million people in work in 2011 were in jobs labelled as either being 'associate professional' or in some way 'technical', often requiring a high-level vocational qualification. Police officers, fire officers and paramedics, for example, fall in this category, as do some marketing and cultural occupations. Some jobs are now labelled with phrases such as 'associate professional database administrator'. In 2001 the number of people working in these occupations had been just a fraction lower, at 3.7 million jobs. It is quite possible that many occupations that were previously classified as associate professional have had their job titles 'upgraded', resulting in them being classified as professional, and at the same time, jobs that were given a lower status have themselves been renamed to apparently be this level. It is thus hard to know whether most of what is being shown here is real change or re-branding. However, the changing geographical distribution of these jobs suggests that a complicated change is under way, with more such posts being created in Northern cities, an ex-urban belt ringing London, and a particularly rapid increase within specific parts of London (with very large decreases elsewhere in London of people working in these occupations).

The greatest increases over the course of the last decade were in Tower Hamlets (+2.3%); Hackney (+2.1%); Kensington & Chelsea (+1.8%); and the City of London (1.6%). All but one of the greatest decreases in the local share of jobs in these relatively skilled occupations was in Northern Ireland: Antrim (-3.3%); Limavady (-2.6%); Omagh (-2.2%); Down, Lisburn and North Down (all -1.9%); Castlereagh (-1.8%); and Oxford (-1.7%). In the last of these eight there was a 5.0% increase in professional jobs. Since 2011 the national proportion of people in associate professional and technical jobs has fluctuated.

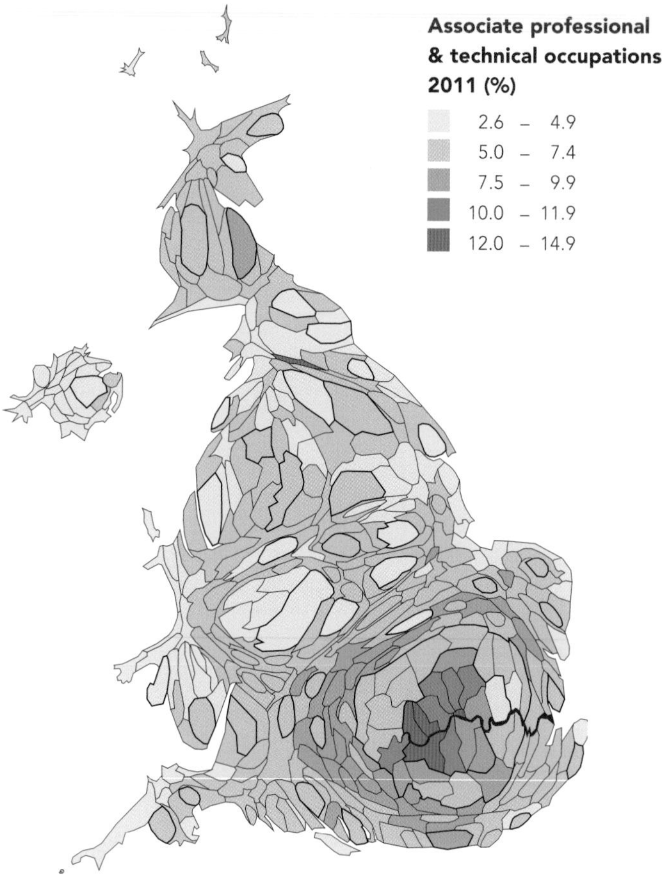

Associate professional & technical occupations, UK % all jobs

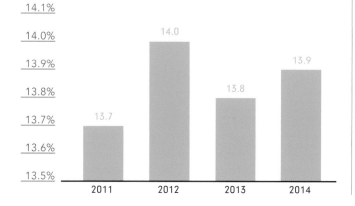

Associate professional & technical occupations 2011 (%)

- 2.6 – 4.9
- 5.0 – 7.4
- 7.5 – 9.9
- 10.0 – 11.9
- 12.0 – 14.9

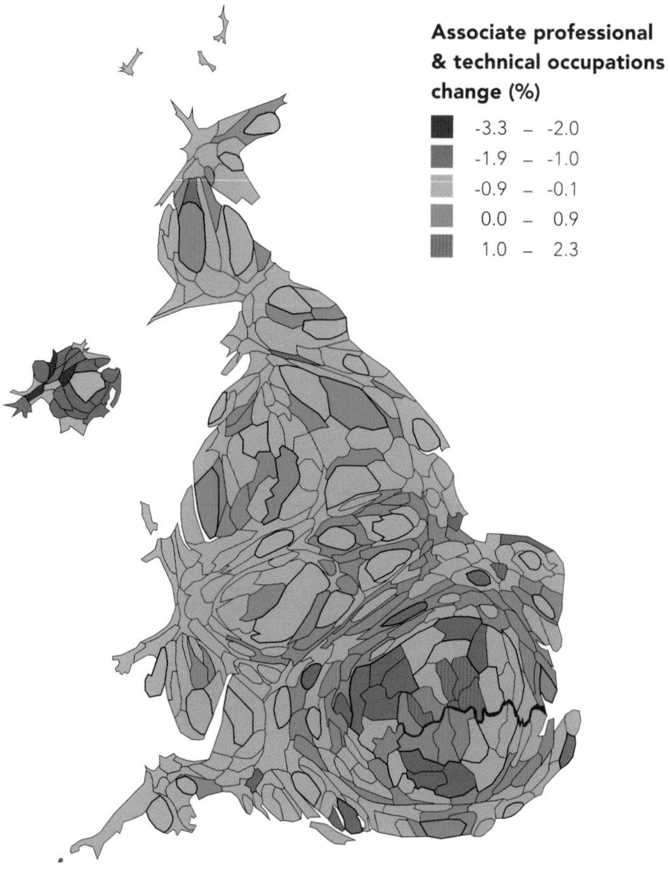

Associate professional & technical occupations change (%)

- -3.3 – -2.0
- -1.9 – -1.0
- -0.9 – -0.1
- 0.0 – 0.9
- 1.0 – 2.3

ADMINISTRATIVE AND SECRETARIAL OCCUPATIONS

There has been a slight reduction in UK employment in secretarial and administrative work. In 2001 there were 3.5 million people working in jobs with these labels, but by 2011 that number had fallen to 3.4 million, so the fall in these posts in net national terms was almost identical to the rise in associate professional and technical jobs documented in the pages immediately above. It is worth noting that because the overall number of jobs has risen between the Censuses, a slight absolute fall looks like a much larger relative set of falls when spread over the map of change shown. There have been relatively small falls in the proportions of people working in these occupations across all of the South of England, not least because people paid these wages cannot often be recruited when young as they cannot afford to live in many of the places that older people in administrative and secretarial occupations now live in.

The largest local concentrations of the residences of people working in administration and secretarial posts remain in far outer London and outer Belfast: North Down (8.5%), Havering (8.4%) and Bexley (8.3%). The lowest proportions are only just under half these magnitudes and are found in Cambridge and West Somerset (both 3.7%) and Oxford (3.8%). Nowhere in the UK can function without a certain minimum of administrators, and there is nowhere in the UK that requires much more than twice this proportion.

However, the national proportion of the population working in these posts is now falling steadily, as the graph below illustrates for 2011–14. The largest falls in office employment of these types have been in Slough (-2.4%); Barking & Dagenham (-2.2%); Reading (-2.2%); Redbridge (-2.1%); and Harrow (-2.0%). In contrast, there have been rises in Northern Ireland (highest in Larne, at +0.7%); Wales (highest in Neath Port Talbot, at +0.6% and Merthyr Tydfil, at +0.3%); and Northern England (Knowsley +0.5% and South Tyneside +0.4%).

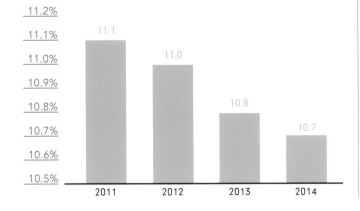

Administrative and secretarial occupations, UK % all jobs

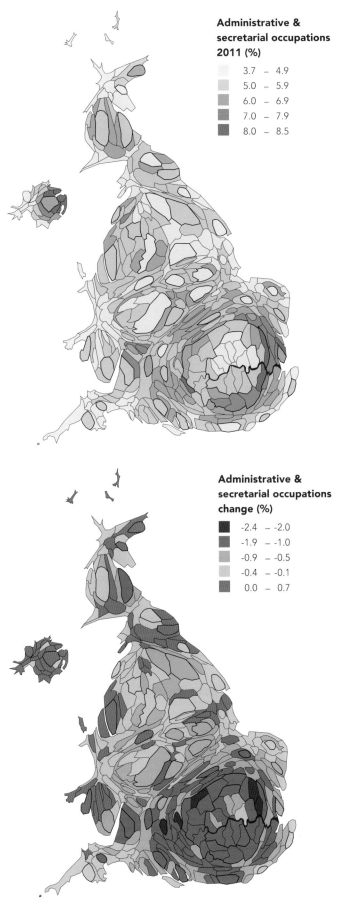

Administrative & secretarial occupations 2011 (%)

- 3.7 – 4.9
- 5.0 – 5.9
- 6.0 – 6.9
- 7.0 – 7.9
- 8.0 – 8.5

Administrative & secretarial occupations change (%)

- -2.4 – -2.0
- -1.9 – -1.0
- -0.9 – -0.5
- -0.4 – -0.1
- 0.0 – 0.7

SKILLED TRADES OCCUPATIONS

In 2011, 3.5 million people worked in what were labelled as skilled trades, up from 3.1 million in 2001. The official description of work in this area is that it includes occupations that involve the performance of complex physical duties that normally require a degree of initiative, manual dexterity and other practical skills. The main tasks of these occupations require experience with, and understanding of, machinery. That machinery can include computers and computer servers, which might explain part of the rapid rise in people employed in these occupations in parts of London including around the so-called 'Silicon Roundabout' near Old Street. Typical jobs might be electricians and plumbers, although similarly skilled jobs are also found in agriculture, textiles, printing, building and metal work.

The greatest concentrations of skilled tradespeople are now found in the Orkney Islands (11.9%); Isles of Scilly (11.7%); Shetland Islands (10.9%); Eden, Magherafelt and Powys (10.2%); and Torridge (10.0%). Skilled tradespeople are hardest to find in the City of London (1.5%); Kensington & Chelsea (1.8%); Westminster (1.9%); Camden (2.1%); Islington (2.6%); Richmond upon Thames (2.8%); Tower Hamlets (2.9%); Hammersmith & Fulham and Wandsworth (both 3.0%); Hackney (3.1%); Cambridge, Manchester and Oxford (all 3.2%); and perhaps a little surprisingly, given its industrial heritage, Belfast (3.3%).

The largest rises between 2001 and 2011 have been in Ealing (+1.4%); Newham and the Shetland Islands (both +1.2%); Waltham Forest (+1.1%); and Brent (+1.0%). The greatest decreases have been in Stoke-on-Trent (-1.6%); Banbridge and Ards in Northern Ireland (-0.9% and -0.8% respectively); Nuneaton & Bedworth (-0.8%); and Walsall, Luton and Redditch (all -0.7%). The West Midlands and several other formerly more industrial areas have clearly suffered in the years up to 2011 as the map of change demonstrates. Most industry had already gone from Wales, Scotland and Northern Ireland before 2001.

The number of people working as skilled tradespeople fell rapidly after 2011 but has been rising again since then.

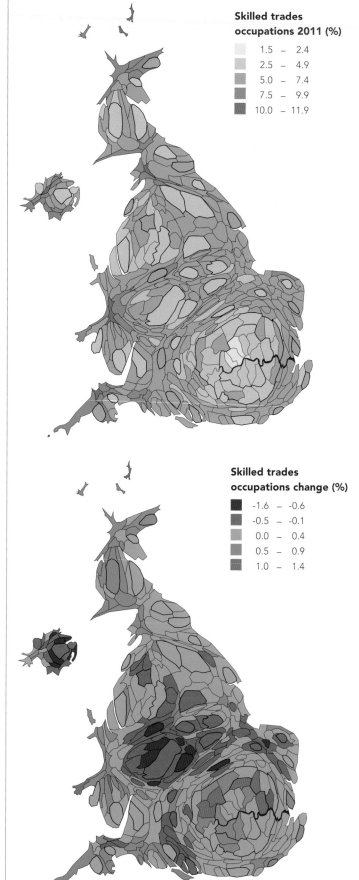

Skilled trades occupations 2011 (%)

- 1.5 – 2.4
- 2.5 – 4.9
- 5.0 – 7.4
- 7.5 – 9.9
- 10.0 – 11.9

Skilled trades occupations change (%)

- -1.6 – -0.6
- -0.5 – -0.1
- 0.0 – 0.4
- 0.5 – 0.9
- 1.0 – 1.4

Skilled trades occupations, UK % all jobs

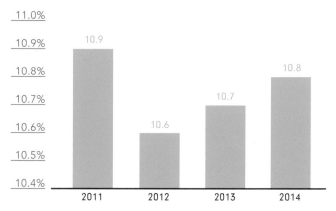

	2011	2012	2013	2014
	10.9	10.6	10.7	10.8

CARING, LEISURE AND OTHER SERVICE OCCUPATIONS

One rapidly growing area of employment, apparently impervious to recession, is work in the caring, leisure and other personal service occupations that employed 2.8 million in people in 2011, up from 1.8 million in 2001. A small part of the increase in this occupation group will be due to a few more occupations being included (eg, senior care workers) under the latest categorisation, but carer, hairdresser, personal trainer, lifeguard, bingo caller, tourist guide, and a whole host of less flamboyant but ever more popular occupations will all, in aggregate, be growing and have continued to grow in popularity since 2011. Some of the largest rises, such as in the Welsh Valleys, will have been associated with the fall in unemployment there and more people gaining work in industrial sectors associated with these occupations rather than a shift from other work. In other places, and especially around and near the coast, the demands of an ageing population relocating to retirement areas and downsizing from the cities has created more demand for jobs of this kind. The map of change shows the effect of a large amalgamation of different forces at play. As the graph below shows, since 2012 these jobs have been growing in popularity and/or necessity. Part of the increase will be growing numbers of childminders and qualified nursery nurses now looking after children who used to be looked after by their parents. As care is increasingly marketised, more jobs are created in the caring industries.

Personal services feature highly on islands, with the highest proportions of people working in these trades living in the Shetland Islands (7.3%); the Isles of Scilly (6.5%); Crawley and Forest Heath (both 6.3%); Hastings (6.0%); Denbighshire, Dover and Eilean Siar (all 5.8%); Midlothian and the Orkney Islands (both 5.7%). Personal services are hardest to locate (or at least the home addresses of those providing them) in the City of London (1.7%); Westminster, Camden and Tower Hamlets (all 2.8%); Islington (3.0%); and Kensington & Chelsea (3.1%). The most rapid rises of people working in these occupations have been seen in the Shetland Islands (+3.1%); Blaenau Gwent (+2.4%); Merthyr Tydfil, East Ayrshire, Rhondda Cynon Taf, West Dunbartonshire, Gloucester and Inverclyde (all +2.1%); Torfaen, Barrow-in-Furness, Forest Heath and Isles of Scilly (all + 2.0%); and Hastings (+1.9%).

Caring, leisure and other service occupations, UK % all jobs

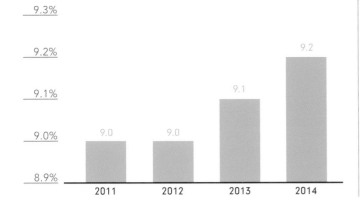

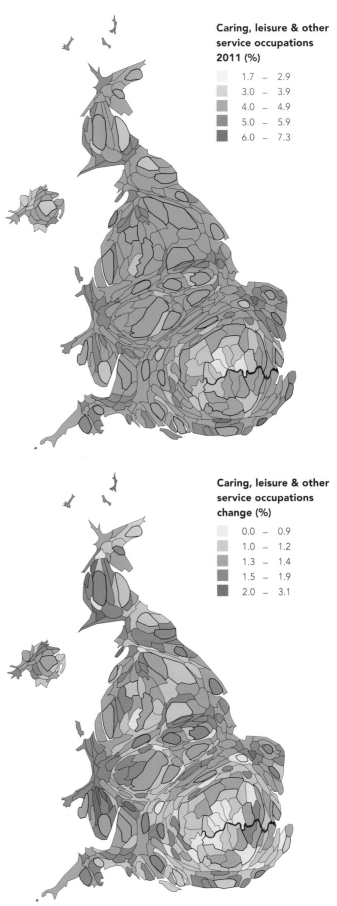

Caring, leisure & other service occupations 2011 (%)

- 1.7 – 2.9
- 3.0 – 3.9
- 4.0 – 4.9
- 5.0 – 5.9
- 6.0 – 7.3

Caring, leisure & other service occupations change (%)

- 0.0 – 0.9
- 1.0 – 1.2
- 1.3 – 1.4
- 1.5 – 1.9
- 2.0 – 3.1

SALES AND CUSTOMER SERVICE OCCUPATIONS

Another set of occupations that are growing in popularity are people working in sales and customer service jobs, including call centre phone operators. In 2011, 2.6 million people worked in these jobs where the principal aim was to encourage others to consume more. This is a rapid rise from 2.1 million in 2001, and has occurred at a time when there has been a slowdown in the rise in overall consumption, partly because wages and salaries have not risen greatly in recent years. It is possible that since 2012 the trend has turned (as the graph below suggests), and soon fewer and fewer people will be employed in these groups, but on the basis of trends over the course of the last few decades, this is unlikely.

The greatest concentration of people working in sales and customer service in 2011 was found in Lincoln (5.7%); Halton (5.6%); and Crawley (5.5%). Such jobs were most rare in the City of London (1.5%); Kensington & Chelsea (2.2%); and Richmond upon Thames (2.4%). However, there is a distinctive cluster within London in Tower Hamlets, where 3.7% of the population now work in jobs of this type, a rise of 1.3% since 2011. Nearby Newham has seen an even greater rise of an extra 2.3% of all people working in these occupations since 2001, bringing the proportion of people employed in these occupation there up to 5.5%, a 72% increase in employment in that type of work in this area if measured as a relative increase. In the past people working in shops and other areas of sales in London would have been more spread around London in terms of their home addresses.

The greatest increases in people living locally who work in these occupations have almost all been in Northern Ireland: Derry (+2.6%); Newham (in London, +2.1%); Fermanagh and Belfast (both +1.8%); Newry & Mourne and Cookstown (both +1.7%); Strabane and Manchester (both +1.6%). The greatest decreases have been in the Isles of Scilly, Waverley and Three Rivers (all -0.2%); and Thurrock, Elmbridge, Mid Sussex, Spelthorne, Plymouth and South Hams (all -0.1%). In general it is only in the South of England where there have been actual falls, and mostly in the North of England, Wales, Scotland and Northern Ireland where there have been rises.

Sales and customer service occupations, UK % all jobs

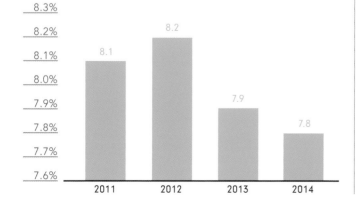

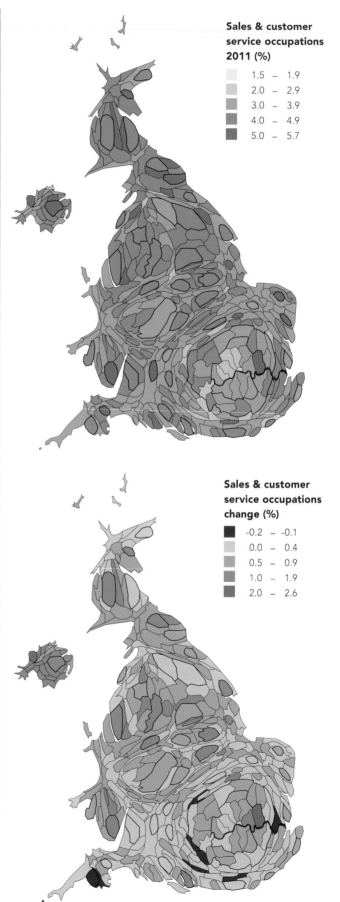

Sales & customer service occupations 2011 (%)

	1.5 – 1.9
	2.0 – 2.9
	3.0 – 3.9
	4.0 – 4.9
	5.0 – 5.7

Sales & customer service occupations change (%)

	-0.2 – -0.1
	0.0 – 0.4
	0.5 – 0.9
	1.0 – 1.9
	2.0 – 2.6

PROCESS, PLANT AND MACHINE OPERATIVES

A set of occupations that are becoming less common includes working on production line processes and operating industrial machinery more generally (including moving machinery and other work in transport). In 2011, 2.2 million people were working in such jobs, down from 2.3 million in 2001, which is a more rapid fall than it at first appears due to overall population rises. The general description of jobs in these areas includes jobs where you have to assemble products from component parts according to strict rules and procedures and then to subject assembled parts to routine tests; also included are jobs in which you are required to drive and assist in the operation of various transport vehicles and other mobile machinery, including agricultural machinery.

After 2011 there was a fall in the proportion of the workforce working in these jobs, but numbers have remained static since 2012. The most common places in the country for people to be working in these occupations in 2011 were Corby (8.1%); Boston (8.0%); South Holland (7.1%); Fenland (6.7%); North East Lincolnshire (6.6%); Dungannon (6.0%); North Lincolnshire (6.0%); Carlisle (5.9%); Craigavon (5.8%); and Wrexham (5.7%). Unremarkably, the lowest proportions are found in the City of London (0.7%); Kensington & Chelsea (0.9%); and Westminster (1.0%).

The only large increases in local populations working in these occupations in the decade to 2011 were recorded in Boston (+1.3%); Dungannon (+0.9%); Peterborough (+0.7%); and Brent and Fenland (+0.5%). Incidentally, these are mostly areas that have experienced rapid immigration from abroad. However, there have been many smaller increases, especially within London. The rise in new technology and the need to have more people who can fix computers in the office and ensure that printers and photocopiers work is likely to have led to part of this facet of the changing landscape of employment in the UK. Jobs with similar titles and pay can denote people doing very different things than were associated with such work in the past. The work computer terminal has taken over from the looms of past factories, but machines always break down and need tending.

Plant and machine operative occupations, UK % all jobs

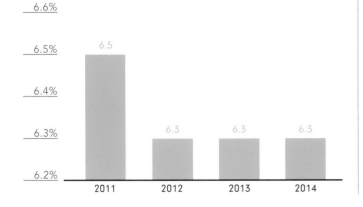

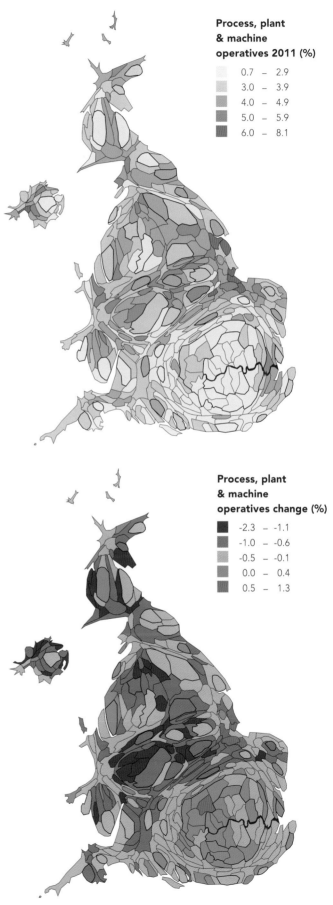

Process, plant & machine operatives 2011 (%)

- 0.7 – 2.9
- 3.0 – 3.9
- 4.0 – 4.9
- 5.0 – 5.9
- 6.0 – 8.1

Process, plant & machine operatives change (%)

- -2.3 – -1.1
- -1.0 – -0.6
- -0.5 – -0.1
- 0.0 – 0.4
- 0.5 – 1.3

ELEMENTARY OCCUPATIONS

In 2011, 3.3 million people worked in what are termed elementary occupations, a very modest rise from 3.2 million in 2001. The official language used to describe these jobs claims that this '… major group covers occupations which require the knowledge and experience necessary to perform mostly routine tasks, often involving the use of simple hand-held tools and, in some cases, requiring a degree of physical effort. Most occupations in this major group do not require formal educational qualifications but will usually have an associated short period of formal experience-related training.' In fact, many of the jobs are exhausting and hard to do well; they are also often essential to the efficient operation of our institutions and communities, from cleaning through to food preparation.

The areas of the UK with the highest proportions of people employed in these occupations are Corby (10.6%); Boston (9.1%); Newham (8.0%); Isles of Scilly (7.9%); and Peterborough (7.8%). The lowest proportions of residents having so-called elementary occupations are found in the City of London (2.3%); Richmond upon Thames (2.4%); Kensington & Chelsea and Elmbridge (both 2.6%); St Albans (2.9%); and East Renfrewshire (in Scotland, 3.1%). Pay is usually lowest in these occupations so very few people working in jobs of this kind are found in the more expensive districts and boroughs. However, this is changing in ways that only the Census can reveal.

The largest increases in people working in elementary occupations as a share of local residents between 2001 and 2011 have been in Newham (+2.7%); Haringey (+1.9%); Brent (+1.6%); Waltham Forest (+1.5%); Peterborough, Slough and Luton (all +1.3%); Ealing and Lambeth (both +1.0%). The most rapid declines have been in the Isles of Scilly (-3.1%); Shetland Islands (-1.3%); Worcester (-1.2%); North Kesteven (-1.1%); and King's Lynn & West Norfolk (-1.1%).

Nationally a gradual decline has been underway since 2011 in the total volume of people working in these areas, partly as a result of local government cutbacks, partly from automation, and partly for reasons that may not yet be clear.

Elementary occupations, UK % all jobs

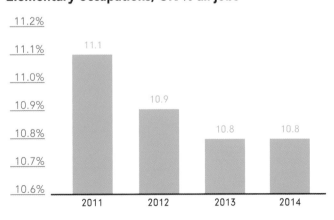

Elementary occupations 2011 (%)

	2.3 – 3.9
	4.0 – 4.9
	5.0 – 5.9
	6.0 – 6.9
	7.0 – 10.6

Elementary occupations change (%)

	-3.1 – -1.1
	-1.0 – -0.6
	-0.5 – -0.1
	0.0 – 0.9
	1.0 – 2.7

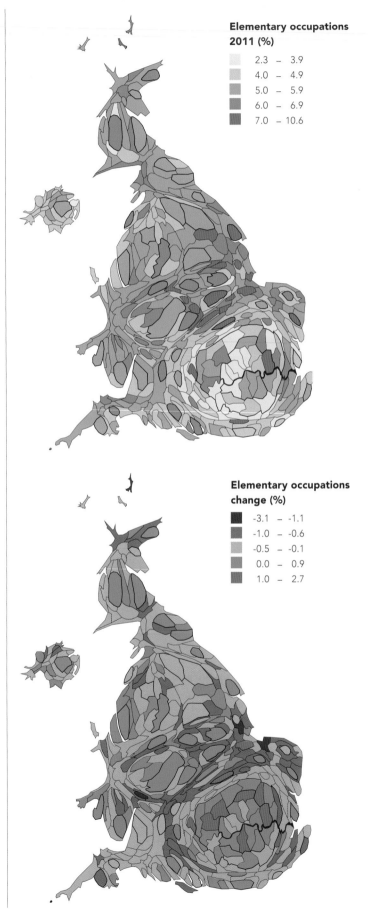

HUMAN HEALTH AND SOCIAL WORK ACTIVITIES

We now turn to look at the distribution of the industries in which people work.

By 2011 there were 3.8 million people working in health and social work in the UK. This is the first of the industrial classifications mapped in this atlas and is about the industry people work in, but mapped by where they sleep. This group can include people who have, for example, cleaning, managerial or secretarial jobs in this line of work, not just doctors, nurses and social workers. A hospital would not operate for long very well without cleaners, people to file the notes and a few managers.

In 2001 there were 2.9 million people working in these industries. The rapid increase is partly due to an ageing population and more care homes being needed, but also due to the population expecting more and better care (and to a small part due to the classifications of both industries and workers in them altering slightly between Censuses). The only falls have been in the City of London (-1.4%) and Westminster (-0.1%), most probably as the local – often on or near site dormitory – accommodation for nurses who work in hospitals such as 'St Barts' (in the City) has been reduced during the last decade.

There has been no increase in the number of people working in this industry who also live in Kensington & Chelsea, and only very small rises in Haringey (+0.1%); Brent and Hackney (both +0.2%); and St Albans (+0.3%). In contrast, the largest increases have all been in Scotland in West Dunbartonshire (+2.4%); East Ayrshire (+2.6%); and the Shetland Islands (+2.7%). By 2011 the largest concentrations of people found working in these industries were in the Shetland Islands (8.9%), Taunton (8.6%) and, outside of Scotland and England, in Antrim (7.9%) and Conwy (7.3%).

The graph below shows the overall proportion of jobs in all service industries combined rising from 79.2% in 2011 to 79.4% in 2014; a large part of this increase is due to more of these jobs becoming part-time, often splitting one job into two.

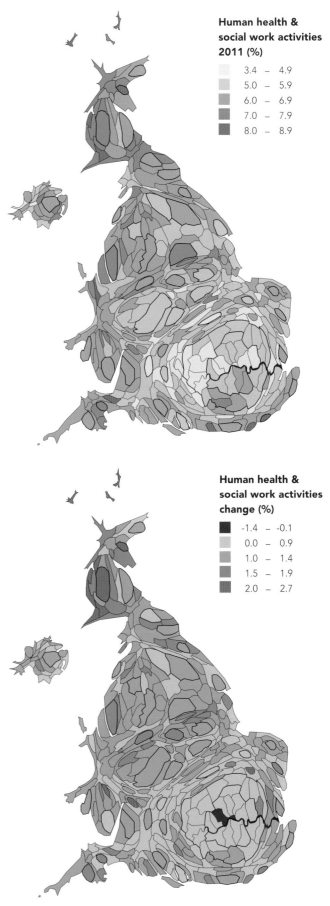

Human health & social work activities 2011 (%)

- 3.4 – 4.9
- 5.0 – 5.9
- 6.0 – 6.9
- 7.0 – 7.9
- 8.0 – 8.9

Human health & social work activities change (%)

- -1.4 – -0.1
- 0.0 – 0.9
- 1.0 – 1.4
- 1.5 – 1.9
- 2.0 – 2.7

Services industries (combined), UK % all jobs

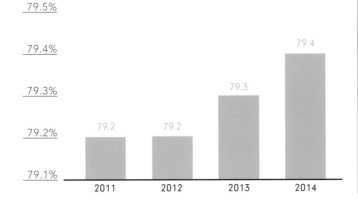

	79.2	79.2	79.3	79.4
	2011	2012	2013	2014

EDUCATION

In 2011, 2.9 million people worked in the education industry, the same number as had worked in health in 2001. In contrast, 2.1 million people worked in the education industry in 2001, so the increase of 0.8 million jobs was slightly less than the 0.9 million new jobs in health, but much higher as a proportion of the numbers working in education a decade ago. There has been a 38% increase in jobs in education over the last decade compared to a 31% increase in jobs in health. Again, definitions change between Censuses, and so these statistics will not be exactly comparing like with like. Most importantly, the rise in part-time work means that the number of jobs can appear to increase very quickly while the number of people working in these industries at any one time does not. Someone who teaches a few hours a week about health in a university and who also has two part-time jobs in local health services can count as having three jobs in two industries, whereas a decade ago they may just have had one, but have been working more predictable and probably longer hours.

In 2011 the greatest concentrations of work in education were found in Cambridge (11.0%); Oxford (10.8%); South Cambridgeshire (8.1%); Vale of White Horse (7.2%); and Rushcliffe (7.1%). These areas were also among those experiencing the largest increases in the last decade: Oxford (+2.0%); South Cambridgeshire and Cambridge (both +1.9%); East Cambridgeshire and West Oxfordshire (both +1.7%); similarly large increases were also recorded in Lancaster (+1.9%); Hammersmith & Fulham, Brighton & Hove and Ceredigion (all +1.7%); and Warwick (+1.6%).

In contrast to the general rise in the proportion of people working in services in 2011, there has been a fall in the proportions of those working in education, health and public administration (the only comparable grouping) since 2011. This has come about as state sector jobs have been cut.

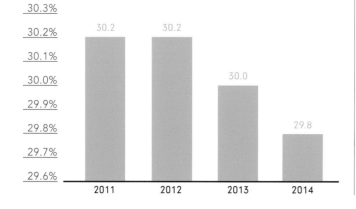

Public administration, education and health service sectors, UK % all jobs

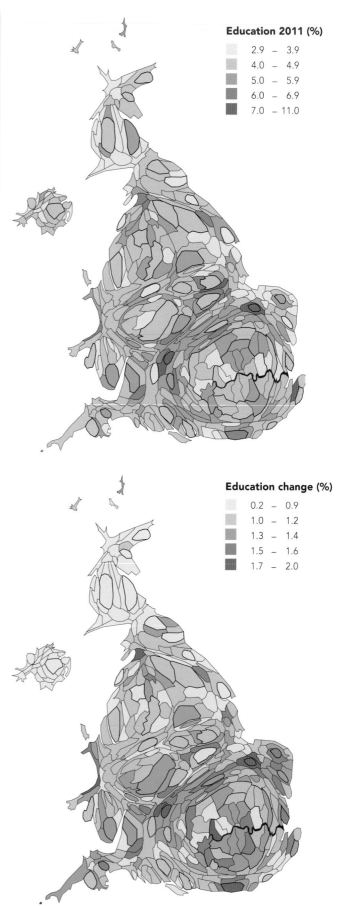

Education 2011 (%)
- 2.9 – 3.9
- 4.0 – 4.9
- 5.0 – 5.9
- 6.0 – 6.9
- 7.0 – 11.0

Education change (%)
- 0.2 – 0.9
- 1.0 – 1.2
- 1.3 – 1.4
- 1.5 – 1.6
- 1.7 – 2.0

MANUFACTURING

In contrast to health and education, industries that were expanding until 2011 and have then declined in terms of total numbers of employees, manufacturing has seen a continuous fall in the numbers of people it employs in the UK since long before 2001, and continuing through to at least 2014. In 2001, 3.9 million people were working in manufacturing; by 2011 it was 2.6 million, a fall of a third in just a decade and one that has continued since (as the graph below illustrates).

The largest falls have all been in the Midlands and North of England: Stoke-on-Trent (-5.5%); Tamworth (-5.2%); Wyre Forest and Hinckley & Bosworth (both -5.1%); Walsall (-5.0%); Dudley (-4.8%); Nuneaton & Bedworth (-4.7%); Burnley (-4.6%); East Northamptonshire (-4.5%); and Staffordshire Moorlands (also -4.5%). The only increases have been in a few small areas of Northern Ireland and Boston in East Anglia. By 2011 there was only one place where more than a tenth of the workforce made things (manufactured), and the 10 areas with the greatest concentrations of people working in manufacturing industries were Corby (11.9%); Redditch (9.7%); Barrow-in-Furness (9.5%); Copeland and Pendle (both 9.3%); Flintshire and Amber Valley (both 9.2%); North Lincolnshire (9.1%); Melton and South Derbyshire (both 8.7%).

In 2001 there were 26 districts where a higher proportion of people worked in manufacturing than in such occupations anywhere in 2011. By 2011 the two areas with the fewest people working in the manufacturing industry in any capacity were Camden and the City of London (both 0.9%). All the other areas with the lowest proportions were in London, apart from Edinburgh (1.7%). Even Oxford, with its car factory, only saw 2.3% of its residents working in manufacturing by the 2011 Census. That car factory, which manufactures Minis, produced 1% of all the UK's physical exports by price, despite employing so few people.

Manufacturing, UK % all jobs

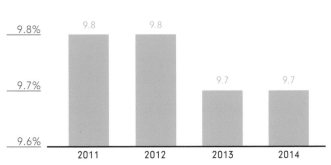

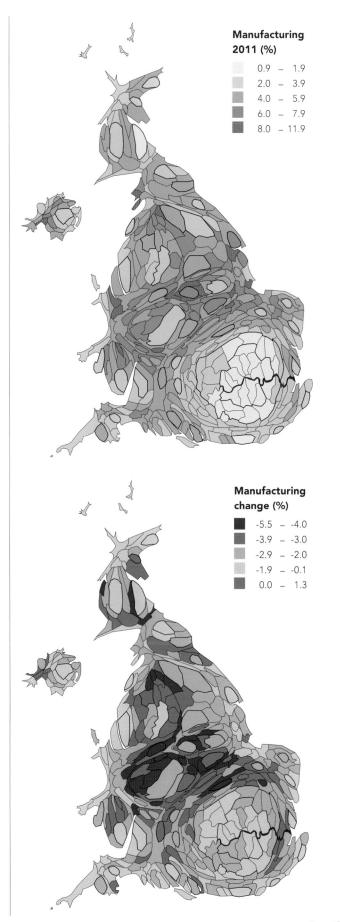

CONSTRUCTION

In contrast to manufacturing, work in the construction industry boomed between 2001 and 2011. Some 1.8 million jobs recorded in 2001 rose to become 2.3 million by 2011, a rise of 28% in just 10 years, but again the caveat about how full-time, stable or well-paid these new jobs might have been remains. It is very easy for there to be a large rise, but for the total of people employed to actually be being paid less for what they are doing because so many new jobs are so short-term and part-time.

A few areas saw falls in employment over this period. These were most pronounced in Northern Ireland: Moyle (-1.0%); Ballymoney (-0.7%); Banbridge (-0.6%); Down (-0.5%); Ards (-0.4%); and Coleraine (-0.3%), but also found in England where earlier construction projects had not been replaced by new ones leading to falls in construction employment in Reading (-0.2%); and Cambridge, Oxford and Norwich (all -0.1%). Similarly the largest increases will have been in places where there was little construction activity in 2001 but several major projects underway by 2011. This list of places is headed by areas affected by building work for the 2012 Olympics: Waltham Forest (+1.8%); Newham and Ealing (both +1.7%); Haringey (+1.5%); Brent (+1.4%); and Barnet (+1.3%).

By 2011 the places with the largest proportions of people employed in construction in the UK were Magherafelt (7.8%); Shetland Islands (6.2%); Broxbourne and Castle Point (both 5.9%); Orkney Islands (5.8%); and Maldon (5.7%). The 10 areas with the lowest proportions of local residents employed in construction in 2011 were the City of London (1.1%); Camden (1.4%); Westminster, Tower Hamlets and Kensington & Chelsea (all 1.5%); Cambridge (1.7%); Belfast, Hackney and Islington (1.8%); and Oxford (1.9%). Nationally employment in the construction industry by 2014 was down on 2011.

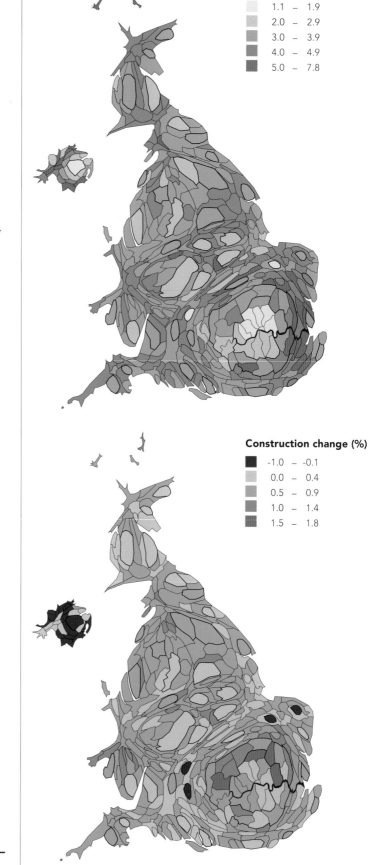

Construction 2011 (%)

- 1.1 – 1.9
- 2.0 – 2.9
- 3.0 – 3.9
- 4.0 – 4.9
- 5.0 – 7.8

Construction change (%)

- -1.0 – -0.1
- 0.0 – 0.4
- 0.5 – 0.9
- 1.0 – 1.4
- 1.5 – 1.8

Construction, UK % all jobs

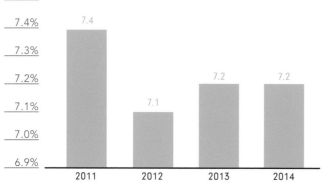

ACCOMMODATION AND FOOD SERVICE ACTIVITIES

Around 1.7 million people were employed to feed, wash up after and make the beds of others in 2011, or to manage and organise those that do. These are the hoteliers and hotel workers, the guesthouse managers, the restaurant washer-uppers and the café cooks. In 2001 there had been 'just' 1.3 million people working in the hotel and catering sector. Again, the definition of which particular jobs fit within which industries has changed a little, and again – and much more importantly – many more people are doing more part-time work in this sector including hundreds of thousands of university students who work part-time waiting on tables or mopping out bars in the early hours. Thus the rise of 31% in jobs of this type does not necessarily mean an increase of that amount in work of this type.

This has long been a precarious industry for many employed in it. However, only four areas have seen a fall in employment in this industry amounting to at least one person in every 1,000: Isles of Scilly (-3.1%); and Blackpool, Isle of Wight and Chorley (all -0.1%). The 15 largest increases in this industry taking a larger share of local jobs have all been in London or in three large Northern cities with growing student populations and each famous for their nightlife: Newham (+2.5%); Haringey (+1.8%); Tower Hamlets (+1.7%); Southwark and Waltham Forest (+1.5% each); Lambeth and Lewisham (both +1.4%); Greenwich, Brent and Hounslow (all +1.3%); Liverpool, Hackney, Hammersmith & Fulham, Newcastle upon Tyne and Manchester (+1.2% apiece).

The seven places where at least one in 20 of the local population is employed in this industry are: Isles of Scilly (14.2%); West Somerset (6.4%); South Lakeland and Eden (both 5.9%); Scarborough (5.3%); Blackpool (5.2%); and Newham (5.1%). Many people who keep the hotels and cafes of central London working at night, during the day sleep in East London. The graph below shows that since 2011, this industry, when combined with the distribution sector (transporting goods), has fluctuated only slightly in size.

Distribution, hotels and restaurants, UK % all jobs

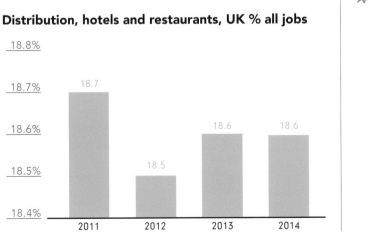

Accommodation & food service activities 2011 (%)

	1.6 – 1.9
	2.0 – 2.9
	3.0 – 3.9
	4.0 – 4.9
	5.0 – 14.2

Accommodation & food service activities change (%)

	-3.1 – -0.1
	0.0 – 0.4
	0.5 – 0.9
	1.0 – 1.4
	1.5 – 2.5

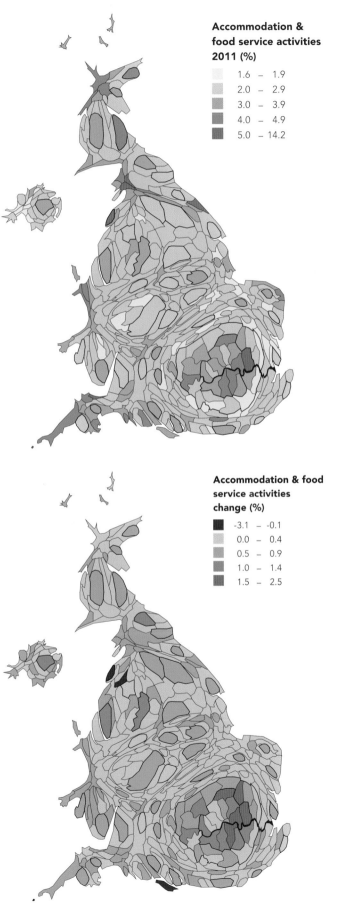

FINANCIAL AND INSURANCE ACTIVITIES

Finance and insurance (including banking) was a growth industry over the entire 2001–11 time period despite the meltdown and subsequent financial crisis of 2008, 2009, 2010 and onwards. The previous boom and then the banking bailout was so large and so effective that by 2011 there were 1.3 million people working in this industry, up from 1.2 million in 2001, although in between there will have been some great fluctuations and the total will almost certainly have been both higher (just before 2008) and lower (about a year after the financial catastrophe).

There are some places where financiers lived that did experience many lay-offs that have either not been reversed or people have moved to live elsewhere. The six places that are now home to fewer bankers having seen larger falls than were experienced anywhere else are Worthing (-1.4%); Broxbourne (-1.2%); Barking & Dagenham, Castle Point and Horsham (-1.1%); and Reading (-1.0%). These are not the most expensive of Southern addresses and so perhaps indicative that, in the longer term, it was not the highest paid of financiers who were most likely to lose their employment. In contrast, the six largest increases in bankers were experienced in the City of London (+3.9%); Kensington & Chelsea (+2.9%); Westminster (+2.5%); Tower Hamlets (2.2%); Southwark (1.1%); and Islington (1.0%).

With concentrations now greater than in almost any manufacturing district, the six most densely settled banking districts in the UK are now the City of London (14.5%); Kensington & Chelsea (11.0%); Westminster (8.6%); Tower Hamlets (7.1%); Brentwood (6.5%); and Wandsworth (6.3%). Since 2011 employment in the industry has continued to grow at a rapid rate year on year. Edinburgh retains its distinct banking and financial sector, as can be seen in the 2011 map, but it has not grown since 2001.

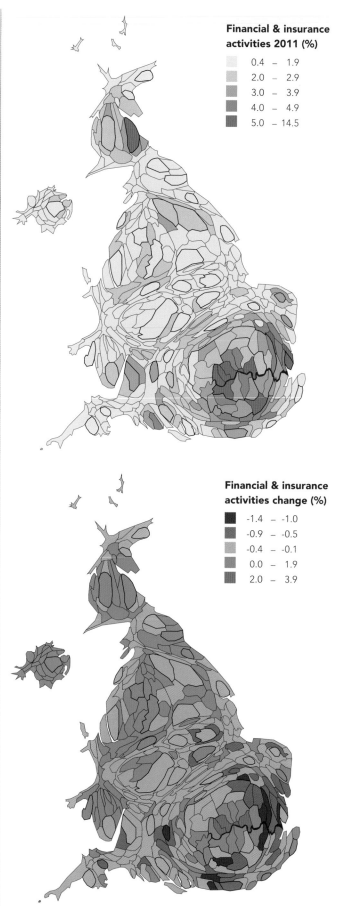

Financial & insurance activities 2011 (%)

- 0.4 – 1.9
- 2.0 – 2.9
- 3.0 – 3.9
- 4.0 – 4.9
- 5.0 – 14.5

Financial & insurance activities change (%)

- -1.4 – -1.0
- -0.9 – -0.5
- -0.4 – -0.1
- 0.0 – 1.9
- 2.0 – 3.9

Banking, finance and insurance, UK % all jobs

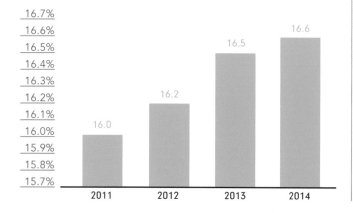

Year	Value
2011	16.0
2012	16.2
2013	16.5
2014	16.6

REAL ESTATE ACTIVITIES

In great contrast to finance and insurance, the fate of real estate during the aggregate of the 2000s was the very opposite of successful employment as an industry – at least as far as most of the employees were concerned. We do not have very comparable statistics for this group, but what we do have is telling. In 2011 the places of residence of the highest numbers of people working in estate agency were Kensington & Chelsea (1.7%); Hammersmith & Fulham (1.6%); Westminster (1.5%); Wandsworth (1.4%); Hertsmere, Barnet and the Isles of Scilly (all 1.3%); Richmond upon Thames (1.2%); Epping Forest, Lambeth, Mole Valley, Elmbridge and Enfield (all 1.1%); Camden, Chiltern, Hackney, Bromley, South Bucks, Cotswold, Sevenoaks, Christchurch, Redbridge, Haringey, Merton and Chichester (1.0%). Not one of this long list of areas is outside South East England.

The map of change may be a little misleading because in 2001 people working in businesses that rented machinery and equipment were also included in this industrial category, and so it was much larger. However, a significant part of the reason for the fall in numbers everywhere will not be reclassification but the huge declines in jobs in this industry that occurred after the housing market slumped in 2008.

When the volume of home sales falls drastically – by well over half year on year in the late 2000s – many estate agent workers have to be laid off. Their numbers fell from 3.4 million in 2001 to 0.4 million in 2011. However, note that the 2001 figure also includes some people working in related industries so the fall will not have been quite as dramatic. In between they will have spiked higher in 2007 and may have fallen even lower by early 2010. Estate agency is just part of 'other services'. The graph below shows the national fall in numbers in 'other services' continuing through to 2013 and then a rapid rise, coincident with the next housing bubble.

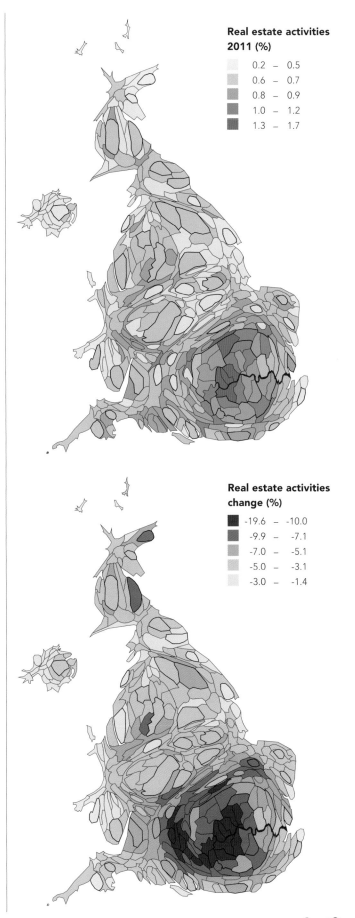

Real estate activities 2011 (%)

- 0.2 – 0.5
- 0.6 – 0.7
- 0.8 – 0.9
- 1.0 – 1.2
- 1.3 – 1.7

Real estate activities change (%)

- -19.6 – -10.0
- -9.9 – -7.1
- -7.0 – -5.1
- -5.0 – -3.1
- -3.0 – -1.4

Other services, UK % all jobs

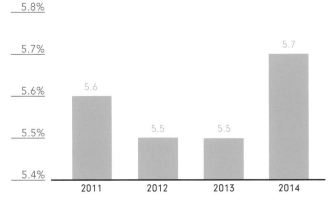

5.8%			
5.7%			5.7
5.6%	5.6		
5.5%	5.5	5.5	
5.4%			
	2011	2012 2013	2014

AGRICULTURE, FORESTRY AND FISHING

Just under 0.3 million people worked in the combined industries of farming, forestry and fishing in 2011, fewer than were estate agents even under the strictest definition of 'estate agency'. In 2001 there were well over 0.4 million people working in these primary industries. The relative fall in numbers in 10 years has been over 25%! The largest falls were in the Orkney Islands (-1.4%); South Holland, Ryedale and Mid Suffolk (all -1.0%); East Lindsey, Hambleton Chichester, King's Lynn & West Norfolk, Selby and Eilean Siar (all -0.9%). As a result of these falls the proportions working in these primary industries in these rural districts now varies between just 1.0% of the local population (in Chichester, nearest to London) and only at its very highest 5.4% (in Orkney, furthest away from London). However, there are some tiny signs of agricultural revival in just two places: Scottish Borders (+0.3%) and Falkirk (+0.2%).

By 2011 the 10 areas of the UK with the highest proportions of people working in agriculture were the Orkney Islands (5.4%); Eden (4.3%); Powys (4.1%); Scottish Borders and Dumfries & Galloway (both 4.0%); Ryedale and the Shetland Islands (both 3.6%); Torridge and the Isles of Scilly (both 3.4%); and Ceredigion (3.1%). Agriculture, forestry and fishing are a set of declining industries when it comes to employment, and the declines are generally greatest where agriculture is still an important part of local economies.

The graph below suggests that since 2011 the national proportion of people working in two of these three industries has remained mostly stable, but it is now such a small group that sampling error could be disguising further falls in the now very low employment levels in these industries. Farms still occupy almost as much land as ever. Apart from on organic farms, there has been a massive increase in productivity per person, decade after decade, over the course of the last century.

Agriculture and fishing, UK % all jobs

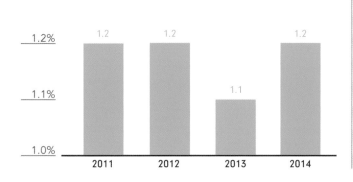

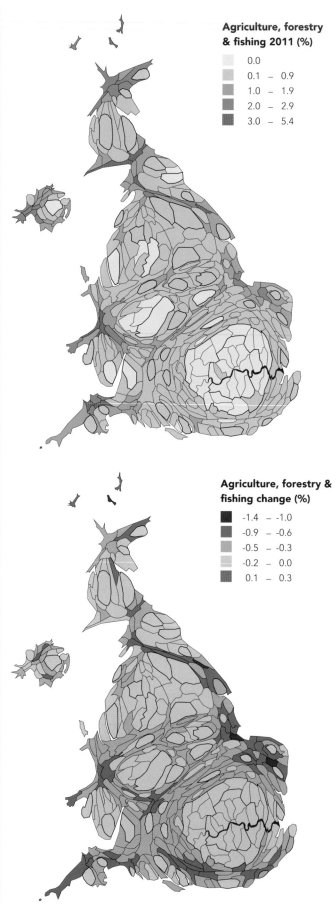

Agriculture, forestry & fishing 2011 (%)
- 0.0
- 0.1 – 0.9
- 1.0 – 1.9
- 2.0 – 2.9
- 3.0 – 5.4

Agriculture, forestry & fishing change (%)
- -1.4 – -1.0
- -0.9 – -0.6
- -0.5 – -0.3
- -0.2 – 0.0
- 0.1 – 0.3

TRANSPORT AND STORAGE / INFORMATION AND COMMUNICATION

The industries that involve transportation and storage and information and communication were counted separately in 2011, but were combined in 2001, so here we show them separately but without maps of change. In 2011, 1.5 million worked in transport and storage (more physical) and 1.1 million in the information and communication industry (more electronic). Combined, these 2.6 million workers are more concentrated in the South than the North, and are almost certainly all in growing industries.

When it comes to transport and storage, the greatest concentrations of people found to be working in these industries are in Crawley (8.1%, near Gatwick); Spelthorne (7.9%, near Heathrow); Slough (6.0%); Isles of Scilly (5.9%); Hounslow (5.8%); Shetland Islands (5.7%); Hillingdon (5.2%); Thurrock (4.9%); Orkney Islands (4.8%); and Suffolk Coastal (4.5%). In contrast to those 10 areas, the 10 districts with the highest proportions of people residing who during the day are working in the communications industry are Wokingham (6.7%); Richmond upon Thames (6.0%); Reading (5.7%); West Berkshire (5.6%); Hart (5.5%); Bracknell Forest (5.5%); Windsor & Maidenhead (5.4%); Wandsworth and Hammersmith & Fulham (5.3%); and Islington (5.2%). The eleventh district with the most people working in this industry is the City of London (5.1%).

Since 2011, these two industries combined have grown again, although falling back slightly in 2014 in size. The concentrations of people working near major airports and ports are clear to see on the maps. The rise in employment in these industries being concentrated in London would not be well known without a Census, and may well be associated with the information and communication side of these industries. London has tended to lead the way in many new trends. It might be doing so again in this industrial sector that is partly metamorphosing with the advent of ever more new information and communication technologies.

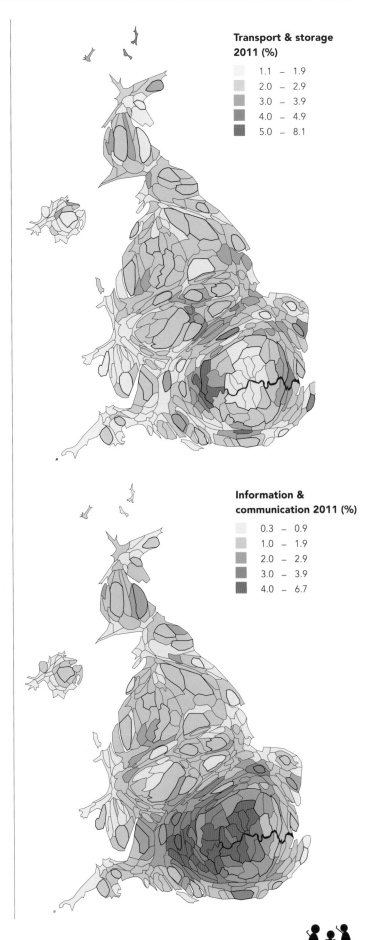

Transport & storage 2011 (%)

- 1.1 – 1.9
- 2.0 – 2.9
- 3.0 – 3.9
- 4.0 – 4.9
- 5.0 – 8.1

Information & communication 2011 (%)

- 0.3 – 0.9
- 1.0 – 1.9
- 2.0 – 2.9
- 3.0 – 3.9
- 4.0 – 6.7

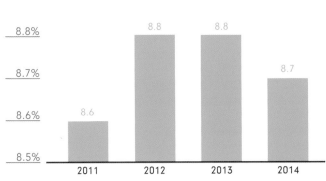

Transport & communications, UK % all jobs

2011: 8.6
2012: 8.8
2013: 8.8
2014: 8.7

WATER / POWER

Another pair of industries that have been separated out in 2011 and that were combined as a general utility in one group in 2001 are water supply, sewerage, waste and pollution management activities ('water' for short), and electricity, gas, steam and air conditioning supply ('power' for short). There were only just over 0.2 million people working in the water industries by 2011 across all of the UK and just under that number working in power. These are relatively small numbers of people to keep basic infrastructure operating, and those working in these industries were far from evenly spread about the country by 2011.

No more than one in 1,000 of the population living in the following 17 districts has any role to play in supplying water to those districts (or any other place): Camden, Kensington & Chelsea, City of London, Westminster, Wandsworth, Hammersmith & Fulham, Tower Hamlets, Lambeth, Redbridge, Hackney, Islington, Richmond upon Thames, Haringey, Southwark, Oxford, Barnet and Brent. The highest proportions are, unsurprisingly, found where the largest reservoirs or water company offices are: Copeland (1.5%); Warrington (0.9%); Halton, Allerdale, Worthing, Cannock Chase and Highland (all 0.7%).

When it comes to power, there are a staggering 93 areas where only one person in every 1,000 works in supplying power. In contrast, the highest proportions are found near power stations, especially nuclear ones, in Copeland (1.8%, surrounding Sellafield); Perth & Kinross and Isle of Anglesey (both 1.3%); Lancaster and Hinckley & Bosworth (1.2%); and Selby (1.0%). Since 2011 employment in the water and power industries, combined, has been largely stable, at just under 2% of the UK total workforce, dipping slightly in 2012.

Energy and water, UK % all jobs

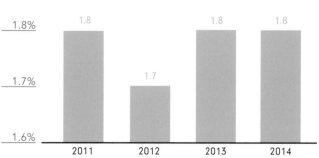

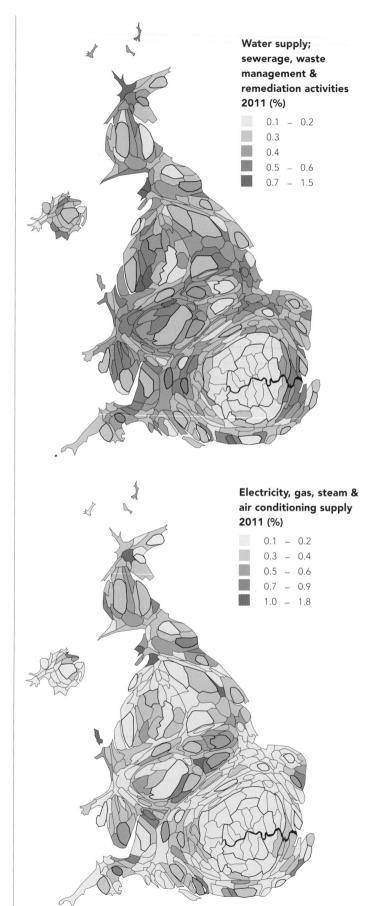

Water supply; sewerage, waste management & remediation activities 2011 (%)

- 0.1 – 0.2
- 0.3
- 0.4
- 0.5 – 0.6
- 0.7 – 1.5

Electricity, gas, steam & air conditioning supply 2011 (%)

- 0.1 – 0.2
- 0.3 – 0.4
- 0.5 – 0.6
- 0.7 – 0.9
- 1.0 – 1.8

If the experience is counted from the viewpoint of people rather than households then a very different picture emerges.

Families, Caring and Health

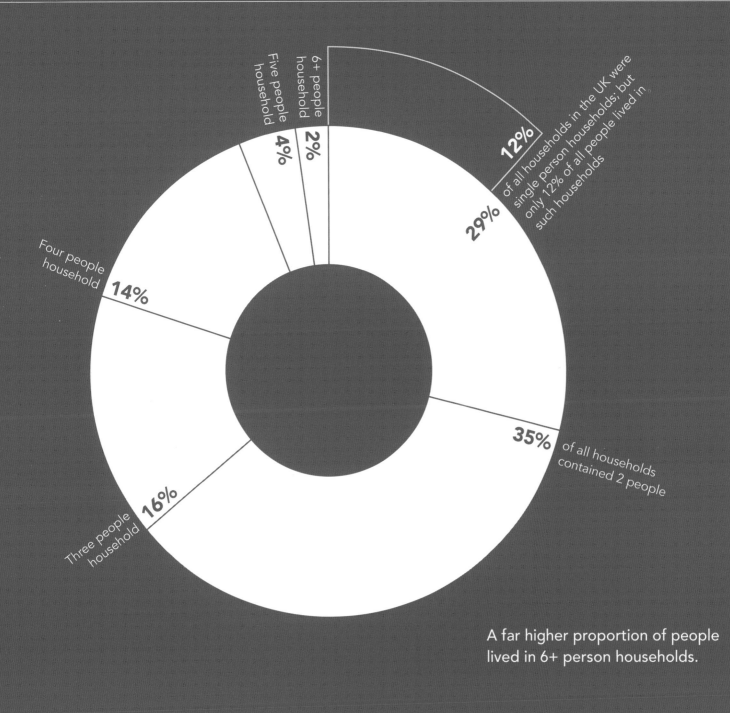

6+ people household

Five people household

2%

4%

12% of all households in the UK were single person households; but only 12% of all people lived in, such households

29%

Four people household

14%

35% of all households contained 2 people

Three people household

16%

A far higher proportion of people lived in 6+ person households.

Families, Caring and Health

For many decades the Census has collected data on the types of families that people live in, whether they have children, their marital relationships, if they are a lone parent, (more recently) if any couples are cohabiting and very recently, if they are in a same-sex civil partnership. Census questions tend to lag behind societal changes, but they do catch up eventually. However, there is always a catch-all category of 'other family types' that often includes those that will in future come to have their own labels and be disaggregated. For example, we may in future identify some families that live in the same household but where the children are cousins and two sisters are the adults. All new family types appear 'odd' before they become 'normal'.

By 2011 just under a quarter of people in the UK were living in households consisting of a couple (either married, cohabiting or joined legally together by a civil ceremony) but had *no children* living with them. Just over a quarter were similar couples but *with children*, and only just under 8% of people were part of a family with a mum and dad and three or more children. That latter category was the norm not many Censuses ago; today half the population live in households without children.

People by family type, UK 2011 %

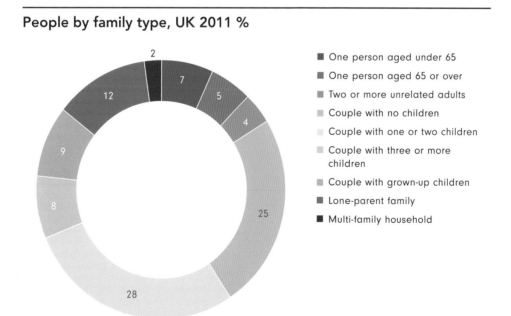

- One person aged under 65
- One person aged 65 or over
- Two or more unrelated adults
- Couple with no children
- Couple with one or two children
- Couple with three or more children
- Couple with grown-up children
- Lone-parent family
- Multi-family household

Between 2011 and 2014 only three types of family became more common, in terms of the kinds of household people live in across the UK. The largest rise was of people living in multi-family households, which was still the smallest group in 2011. These are families who share a home and kitchen with at least one other family. By 2014 compared to 2011, one extra person in every 200 lived in these kinds of households, which had been very common in the Victorian slums. The next largest rise was in families with grown-up children living with their parents. Both these groups grow in size when there are affordable housing shortages. Third, families with one or two dependent children also grew in size slightly – today's 'traditional' family, which would have been considered as small in our grandparents' day. In contrast, the largest falls were in people living on their own under the age of 65; again, housing shortages make it harder to live alone today.

People living in each type of household, UK 2011–2014 % change

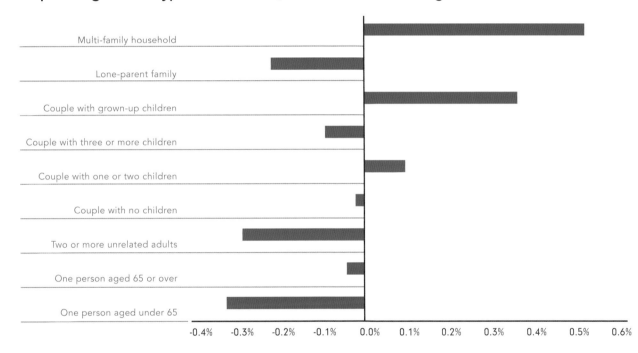

By 2011, 29% of all households in the UK were single-person households, but only 12% of all people lived in such households. Some 35% of all households contained two people and only 2% of households contained six or more people. However, a far higher proportion of people lived in six or more person households. If the experience is counted from the viewpoint of people rather than households, then a very different picture emerges. The graphs below illustrate both this and the way in which one-person households fell fastest during the most recent years for which we have data (2013–14), with four-, five- and six-person households all becoming a little more common again by 2014. Thus the structure of both households and families keeps changing rapidly in the UK, which is why the Census needs to be taken every 10 years.

Households by size, UK 2011 %

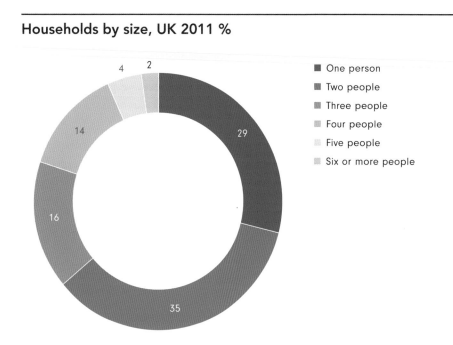

- One person
- Two people
- Three people
- Four people
- Five people
- Six or more people

Households by size, UK 2001–14 annual % point change

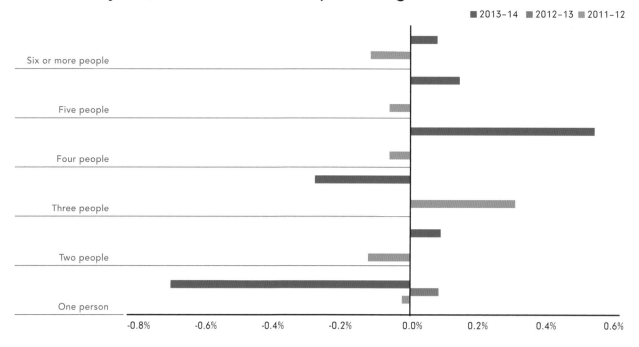

■ 2013–14 ■ 2012–13 ■ 2011–12

The changing family structure of the UK is partly caused by ageing and changing fertility rates as well as the provision of housing and of how well, or increasingly how poorly, housing is shared out. In this chapter, after mapping how different types of family are distributed and how that has changed since 2001, we show how there has been a huge increase in the number of rooms in houses and flats available for people to live in since 2001 – an extra 13 million or an additional 10% on the number recorded in 2001! However, households that already have a great deal of space are getting many of the additional rooms. As the population ages we are not necessarily altering how we house ourselves as quickly.

Communal establishments for the over-65s are considered next: there has been an absolute fall in the numbers of people living in these since 2001 and, proportionately (for the share of the population so housed) a far more rapid fall. Elderly people are staying in family homes for longer. To begin to understand this we next look at who cares for those who are ill, disabled and elderly in the community on a voluntary basis, often caring for family and friends, and we end the chapter by looking at the changing nature and distribution of good and poor health, and how that limits many people's abilities to look after themselves.

We begin by considering single pensioner households, how many there are, where they are, how this has been changing, and how it appears to be changing across the countries of the UK.

SINGLE PENSIONER HOUSEHOLDS

In 2011 there were 3.3 million pensioners living alone as a single-person household in the UK, a fall from 3.5 million in 2001. This fall was due to the number of more elderly pensioners falling from 5.9 million to 4.4 million over this same period. Very elderly pensioners are those most likely to be living on their own because they are the group who most frequently suffer the loss of a spouse or partner due to death. Their numbers fell because of the low and falling birth rate between 1922 and 1936, and so we see fewer single pensioners living alone by 2011. Unless there is large-scale increased emigration of the elderly, this trend is very unlikely to continue as the birth rate rose rapidly in 1946, nine months after most troops returned from the Second World War. The babies born that year were aged 65 in 2011, and the years after were also high birth rate years. The graph below shows a rapid rise in people of pensionable age living on their own since 2011, although with a fall in 2014, this could have been partly due to the very high death rate among elderly women that year.[8]

In 2011 the highest proportions of local people being pensioners living alone were found in Christchurch (9.1%); Rother (8.9%); West Somerset (8.8%); Tendring (8.4%); Arun and East Devon (both 8.2%). The greatest falls between 2001 and 2011 were in Manchester (-2.5%); Greenwich (-2.4%); Kensington & Chelsea and Barking & Dagenham (both -2.3%); and Eastbourne (-2.2%). The areas with the greatest increases were the Isles of Scilly (+1.1%); South Staffordshire (+0.5%); and East Dunbartonshire, Hambleton and Blaby (all +0.4%). Single pensioners living on their own are least likely to be found in Newham (2.3%); Tower Hamlets (2.4%); Brent (2.8%); Slough (2.9%); Hackney and Lambeth (both 3.0%); Southwark and Haringey (both 3.1%); and then least commonly found in Magherafelt and Limavady (both 3.2%).

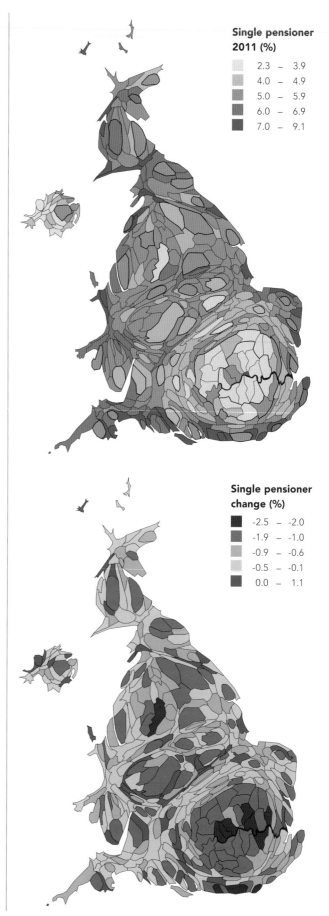

Single pensioner 2011 (%)

- 2.3 – 3.9
- 4.0 – 4.9
- 5.0 – 5.9
- 6.0 – 6.9
- 7.0 – 9.1

Single pensioner change (%)

- -2.5 – -2.0
- -1.9 – -1.0
- -0.9 – -0.6
- -0.5 – -0.1
- 0.0 – 1.1

People living alone aged 65 or over, UK %

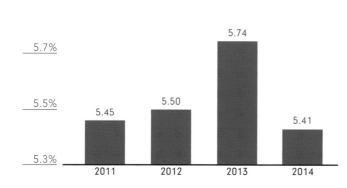

	2011	2012	2013	2014
	5.45	5.50	5.74	5.41

5.9%
5.7%
5.5%
5.3%

SINGLE NON-PENSIONER HOUSEHOLDS

By 2011, 4.8 million people who were not pensioners were living on their own in a single-person household, up from 3.9 million in 2001. Part of the reason for this rise was the growing number of older but not yet pensioner people in the age distribution; another reason was the continued effect of divorce and separation on people who had before been in a couple; but this growth in single-person households is also something of a universal trend in affluent countries, when and where it can be afforded. As the map of change shows, living alone became much less affordable in London and a few surrounding areas over the course of the 2000s, and so the only falls in the proportion of people living alone and not of an elderly age are found there. However, as the graph below shows, there has been a sudden and rapid fall in the overall UK share of the population living alone since 2012. Housing benefit changes reducing the amount of rent that can be claimed by single, and particularly single young, people has partly brought this about, but there has also been such a high increase in rents in recent years that a fall in younger people living alone could also be caused by that, and by a few more baby boomers turning 65 after 2012.

The nature of local housing stock and availability of bedsits and one-bed flats influences the geographical distribution of this type of household, and there are still many extremely affluent people who can afford to live alone and who may have other property elsewhere. The highest proportions of people below pensionable age living alone are found in the City of London (26.4%); Kensington & Chelsea (17.8%); Westminster (16.8%); Glasgow (14.6%); Islington (13.9%); Camden (13.4%); Edinburgh (12.8%); Hammersmith & Fulham (12.7%); Aberdeen (12.4%); and Dundee (12.3%).

People living alone aged under 65, UK %

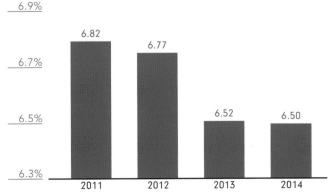

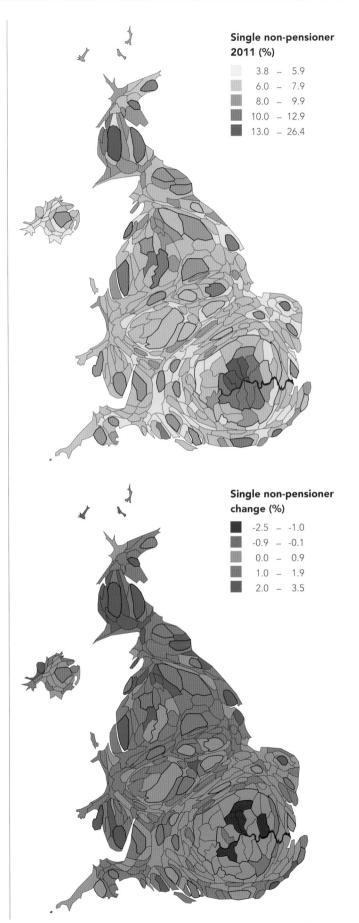

Single non-pensioner 2011 (%)

	3.8 – 5.9
	6.0 – 7.9
	8.0 – 9.9
	10.0 – 12.9
	13.0 – 26.4

Single non-pensioner change (%)

	-2.5 – -1.0
	-0.9 – -0.1
	0.0 – 0.9
	1.0 – 1.9
	2.0 – 3.5

MARRIED WITHOUT CHILDREN

In 2001 there were 6.3 million people in married couples living without anyone else in their family; by 2011 that had increased slightly to 6.4 million (or 3.2 million couples). Many of these will be couples who have had children who have all left home, others will have chosen or not been able to have children, and others may have children soon. The first group of older married couples dominates, and this is reflected in the more rural nature of where the greatest concentrations are. Couples who are both pensioners are not included here but are mapped later in this section as 'pensioner families', and so no married pensioner couples are mapped here. The greatest concentrations of married couples without children are found in the Isles of Scilly (15.8%); East Lindsey (15.5%); Ryedale (15.2%); West Lindsey (15.1%); and North Kesteven (15.0%). It is worth noting that Lincolnshire has a remarkably high number of such families and may be seeing an increased in-migration of older couples moving towards areas of cheaper property after their children leave home, but there may also be more newly arrived married migrant couples there, and numerous other factors at play.

The map of change shows increases all around the coasts, suggesting early or partial retirement moves, but it also shows increases within the centre of London which are more likely to result from a rising number of younger married couples waiting later to have children, or not having them at all in greater numbers than before. The largest increases in this family type in the 2000s were recorded in Kensington & Chelsea (+2.1%); City of London (+1.8%); Eilean Siar (+1.7%); and Argyll & Bute (+0.9%). Since 2011 the share of this group has fallen and then risen again.

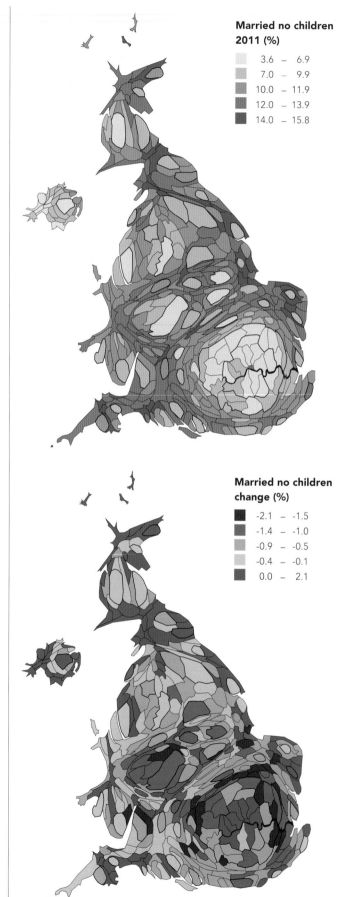

Married no children 2011 (%)

	3.6 – 6.9
	7.0 – 9.9
	10.0 – 11.9
	12.0 – 13.9
	14.0 – 15.8

Married no children change (%)

	-2.1 – -1.5
	-1.4 – -1.0
	-0.9 – -0.5
	-0.4 – -0.1
	0.0 – 2.1

People in a married couple family living without children, UK %

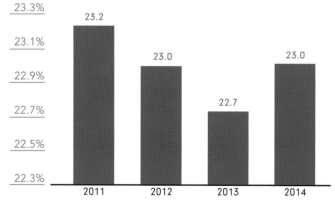

MARRIED WITH CHILDREN

In 2011 there were three times as many people in households classified as married couples living *with* children than there were people in non-pensioner married couple households who were living *without* children. By 2011 there were 21.2 million people, including the children, in these (often thought of as 'traditional') families. This means that there has been a fall from 22.5 million in 2001. People who are married are waiting longer until they have children; this results in final family sizes being slightly smaller than they were a decade earlier. The only parts of the UK that have seen a rise in the local proportions of families of this type have been in or near London, the complete list being: Westminster and City of London (both +2.0%); Richmond upon Thames (+1.7%); Wandsworth (+1.3%); Kensington & Chelsea and Hammersmith & Fulham (both +1.2%); Elmbridge (+0.7%); and Camden (+0.7%). All these areas saw falls in the number of single-person households of between 1.3% and 3.4%. Traditional married families may well be squeezing into smaller homes that were occupied by single people in 2001 in these areas. Finally, St Albans also saw a +0.7% rise in people living in this type of household and a commensurate -0.7% fall in single pensioner households.

The 12 areas with the most people in these types of household are all found in Northern Ireland, which contains the only places where a majority of the population live in such households. The nine areas with the least are all in London, other than Norwich (22.3%). Since 2011 there has been a continued gradual decline in the proportion of people living in households of this type, except for an aberration in 2013.

People in a married couple family living with dependent children, UK %

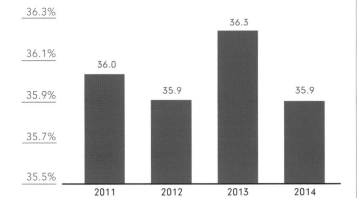

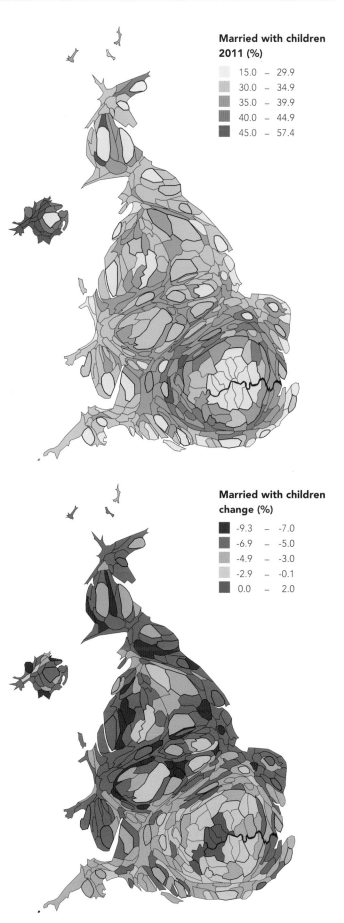

Married with children 2011 (%)

15.0	– 29.9
30.0	– 34.9
35.0	– 39.9
40.0	– 44.9
45.0	– 57.4

Married with children change (%)

-9.3	– -7.0
-6.9	– -5.0
-4.9	– -3.0
-2.9	– -0.1
0.0	– 2.0

CIVIL PARTNERSHIPS / PENSIONER FAMILIES

Civil partnerships did not exist in 2001. The Act that created them was passed into law in 2004, allowing same-sex couples to, in effect, marry, with all the same rights as are granted to people who have a civil wedding, other than being able to call themselves 'married'. If there is a Census in 2021, it may have to try to differentiate between people of the same sex who have been married following the Marriage (same-sex couples) Act 2013. The 2001 Census was the first to record same-sex cohabiting couples, but this is a much larger category (and a much looser relationship) than those who chose to have a civil partnership, and so change over time cannot be shown before 2011, although, strictly speaking, the 2011 map is also the 2001–11 change as all the counts in each district were zero in 2001. Since 2013 there has been a slight decline in the numbers of people in civil partnerships, possibly because same-sex marriage is now possible, but also possibly because sampling errors when a still small group of people are being estimated each year can be high.

In 2011 there were just 75,000 people living in civil partnership families in the UK. The largest proportions were found in the City of London (1.3%); Brighton & Hove (0.7%); Islington and Westminster (both 0.5%); and Southwark, Kensington & Chelsea, Camden, Lambeth and Wandsworth (all 0.4%). Contrast the map with that showing where most of the UK's 4.3 million pensioner families live, the highest concentrations being in East Dorset (14.6%); Christchurch (14.4%); North Norfolk (13.8%); East Devon (13.5%); and West Somerset (13.2%) – all places with only between 0.1% and 0.2% of local residents being in civil partnerships. There is currently no count of pensioners in civil partnerships. There will be one day.

Same-sex civil partnership 2011 (%)

- 0.0
- 0.1
- 0.2
- 0.3 – 0.4
- 0.5 – 1.3

Pensioner family 2011 (%)

- 1.0 – 2.4
- 2.5 – 4.9
- 5.0 – 7.4
- 7.5 – 9.9
- 10.0 – 14.6

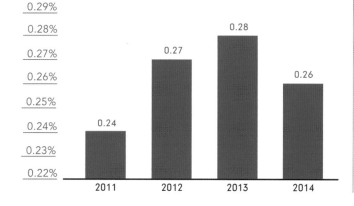

People in same sex civil partnership, UK %

Year	%
2011	0.24
2012	0.27
2013	0.28
2014	0.26

COHABITING WITHOUT CHILDREN

In 2011, 2.7 million adults lived as a cohabiting couple (not married or in a civil partnership) with no children, a rapid rise from 2.2 million in 2001. Thus by 2011, for every eight people living with children in a traditional married family, there was one in a cohabiting couple family without children. In 2001 that ratio had been 10:1. It was most common for people to be living in this kind of family in 2011 in the following areas: City of London (9.5%); Islington (8.2%); Wandsworth (8.1%); Brighton & Hove (7.3%); Norwich (7.0%); Camden, Edinburgh and Lambeth (all 6.6%); Aberdeen (6.5%); Westminster, Hammersmith & Fulham and Bristol (6.4%); Kensington & Chelsea (6.3%); Cheltenham and Lincoln (6.2%); Southwark (6.1%); Richmond upon Thames, Hackney and Tower Hamlets (all 6.0%). Apart from in Harrow (1.8%) all the lowest rates were in Northern Ireland. The fastest increase in people living in families of this type has been in Islington, Glasgow, Gateshead and Salford (all +1.7%); Corby and Barnsley (both +1.6%); and the Isles of Scilly (+1.5%). The areas with the largest decreases have been Slough (-2.4%); Ealing (-1.2%); Waltham Forest and Barking & Dagenham (both -1.0%). It is not that fewer people who are cohabiting want to live in these areas, but that a cohabiting couple can now be out-bid by three unrelated adults willing to share the same flat and possibly share bedrooms despite not being couples; or couples now having lodgers and are no longer simply a couple; or two pairs of cohabiting couples share one home that 10 years ago just held one couple. Nationally the proportion fell to 2013 and then rose in 2014 in an almost identical way to the trend seen for married couples without children, as fewer people had children in 2014 compared to 2013.

People in opposite-sex cohabiting couple families living without children, UK %

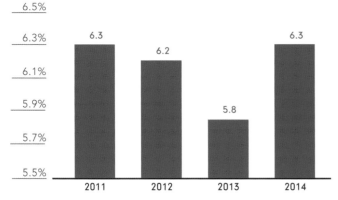

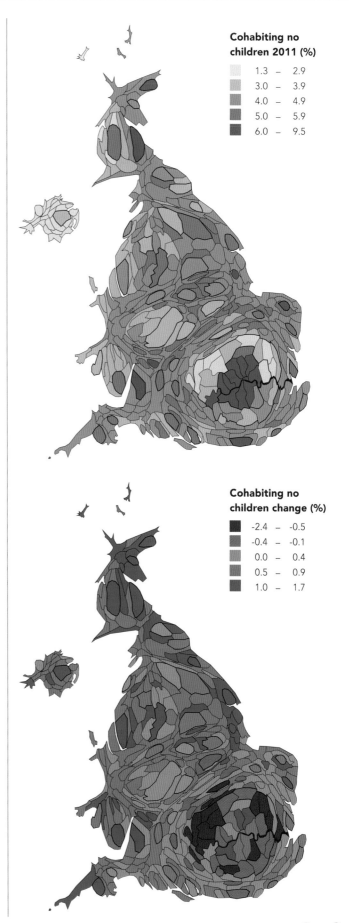

Cohabiting no children 2011 (%)

- 1.3 – 2.9
- 3.0 – 3.9
- 4.0 – 4.9
- 5.0 – 5.9
- 6.0 – 9.5

Cohabiting no children change (%)

- -2.4 – -0.5
- -0.4 – -0.1
- 0.0 – 0.4
- 0.5 – 0.9
- 1.0 – 1.7

COHABITING WITH CHILDREN

A total of 4.4 million people, including children, lived in families where their parents were living together but were neither married nor in a civil partnership in 2011, a rapid rise from 3.7 million in 2001. Thus, by 2011, for every five people living with children in a traditional married family there was one in a cohabiting couple family with children. In 2001 that ratio had been 6:1. It was most common for people to be living in this kind of family in 2011 in the following areas: Kingston upon Hull (11.3%); Great Yarmouth (10.5%); Corby, Barnsley, North East Lincolnshire and Tameside (all 10.3%); Doncaster (10.2%); Cannock Chase, Rossendale, Blaenau Gwent and Caerphilly (all 10.1%); and Ashfield, Mansfield and Wigan (all 10.0%). The areas where the smallest proportions of the local population are in these families are Westminster (2.3%); Kensington & Chelsea and Harrow (2.7%); Omagh (2.8%); Magherafelt and Armagh (both 2.9%); Tower Hamlets and Strabane (both 3.0%). The largest percentage point increases in people living in these families in the 2000s were recorded in Merthyr Tydfil (+4.0%); Blaenau Gwent (+3.6%); Isles of Scilly (+3.4%); North Lanarkshire (+3.2%); Midlothian, Blackpool, Caerphilly, Mansfield, North Lincolnshire and Halton (all 3.1%); Barnsley, King's Lynn & West Norfolk, Neath Port Talbot and Doncaster (all + 3.0%). The only decreases have been in or near London, led by Hackney (-0.6%). Since 2012 this type of family has continued to become more common nationally, if not quite everywhere.

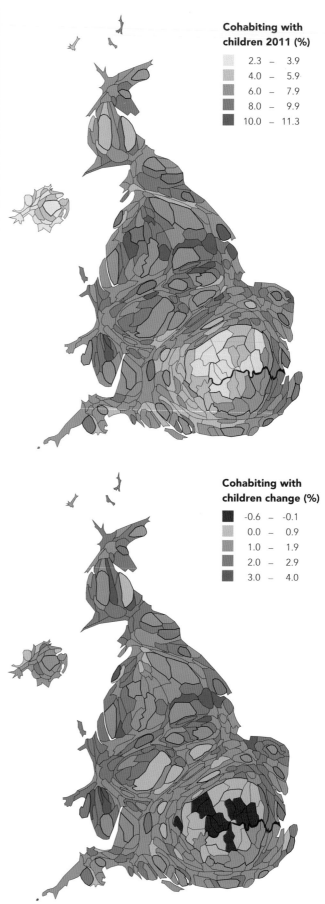

Cohabiting with children 2011 (%)

2.3 – 3.9
4.0 – 5.9
6.0 – 7.9
8.0 – 9.9
10.0 – 11.3

Cohabiting with children change (%)

-0.6 – -0.1
0.0 – 0.9
1.0 – 1.9
2.0 – 2.9
3.0 – 4.0

People in opposite-sex cohabiting couple families living with children, UK %

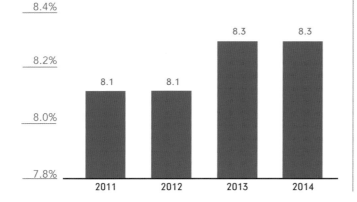

2011	2012	2013	2014
8.1	8.1	8.3	8.3

LONE-PARENT FAMILIES

There were 7.4 million people, a majority of them being children, living in lone-parent families in 2011. Of these, the very large majority, those with dependent children, 92.3%, were lone-mother families in 2011. That proportion dropped slightly to 92.0% in 2014. Thus for every three people living in a traditional married couple with children there is one person in a lone-parent family. The proportion of children living in lone-parent families is higher than that, because (by definition) there is only one adult in a lone-parent family.

There were 8.6 million dependent children living in married family households by 2014, 2.0 million such children living in cohabiting couple families, and 3.1 million dependent children living in lone-parent families that year, 23% of all dependent children in the UK. In 2001 there were 9.0 million dependent children in married couple families, 1.3 million in cohabiting couple families, and 2.9 million children in lone-parent families, or 22% of all dependent children in the UK. The biggest drop in these 13 years has been of children in married couple families (-0.4 million), with rises in children living with cohabiting parents (+0.7 million) and just one parent (+0.2 million).

The highest proportions of people living in lone-parent families in 2011 were living in Derry (21.0%); Belfast (20.2%); Knowsley (19.8%); Barking & Dagenham (19.6%); Lewisham (18.0%); West Dunbartonshire (17.9%); Liverpool (17.8%); Glasgow and Enfield (both 17.6%); and Lambeth (17.2%). The smallest proportions were in the Isles of Scilly (3.9%); City of London (4.7%); Cambridge, Winchester and Hart (all 6.7%); East Cambridgeshire and South Cambridgeshire (both 7.0%); Guildford (7.1%); and Waverley and Cotswold (both 7.0%). The largest rises have been in Enfield (+5.6%) and Slough (+4.2%). The largest falls, possibly migrating to Outer London, have been in Newham (-3.0%) and the City of London (-2.8%). Since 2013 national statistics have suggested that lone-parent family numbers have been stable at a fraction below their 2011 proportions, at around one-seventh of the UK population. The 2012 peak was also the overall birth year peak in the UK in recent years.

People in lone parent families, UK %

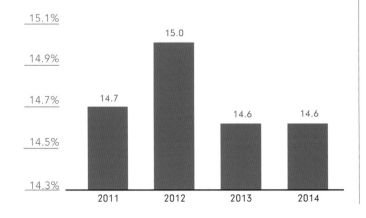

Lone parent 2011 (%)

3.9 – 7.4
7.5 – 9.9
10.0 – 12.4
12.5 – 14.9
15.0 – 21.0

Lone parent change (%)

-3.0 – -0.1
0.0 – 0.9
1.0 – 1.9
2.0 – 2.9
3.0 – 5.6

OTHER HOUSEHOLD TYPES

There are many other types of households in the UK that are not included in the above categorisations and in total these were home to 7.4 million people in the UK in 2011, up greatly from 5.7 million in 2001. A large number of these households are unrelated adults living together, such as students and young adults sharing a home, estimated to be 2.4 million in 2011, falling to 2.3 million by 2014. Another large group are people living in multi-family households that rose from 1.4 million in 2011 to 1.7 million in 2014. These households can be two separate families, possibly both with children, sharing one house or flat. However, there are also sets of more complex households, households with a lodger, or where a daughter also has a son, or where an uncle is staying, or a grandparent or even two sets of grandparents.

All combined, these other types of household are home to the largest proportions of people in Newham (37.0%) and Brent (31.9%). They are extremely common, if not the dominant household type, in all other London boroughs and Slough (22.4%); Oxford (22.1%); Manchester (22.1%); Leicester (21.5%); Luton (21.4%); Nottingham (19.7%); and Cambridge (19.2%). Since 2001 the largest increases have mostly been in London, led by Newham (+13.4%); but also in Boston (+7.4%); Luton (+6.4%); and Leicester (+5.5%). As private renting increases in all these places, landlords may be letting more and more properties to more unconventional families or, often illegally, to several families (one per room). Between 2011 and 2014 the number of people living in multi-family households in the UK increased from 2.2% to 2.7%. This is a huge increase in such a small number of years.

**Other households
2011 (%)**

	4.5 – 9.9
	10.0 – 14.9
	15.0 – 19.9
	20.0 – 24.9
	25.0 – 37.0

**Other households
change (%)**

	-3.1 – -0.1
	0.0 – 1.9
	2.0 – 3.9
	4.0 – 5.9
	6.0 – 13.4

People in families where more than one family share a home, UK households %

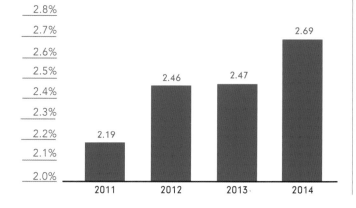

ROOMS PER PERSON

This pair of maps shows the availability of rooms in people's homes as expressed in rooms per resident, and so gives an indication of the housing conditions in which people are living, and how cramped or spacious those are. It also provides a good measure of latent housing demand and how stressed some areas are becoming due to lack of housing or the inefficient use of much existing housing in the area.

The 2011 Census recorded a remarkable 140 million rooms in houses and flats in the UK (not counting bathrooms, toilets, halls, landings and large storage cupboards). Thus, apart from kitchens and living rooms, all these rooms could be bedrooms. In 2001 there were 127 million rooms. In the 10 years after that, an extra 13 million were added, some through house building but often by adding extensions or putting rooms in the attics of existing properties. The places with the most rooms per person in 2011 were Cotswold and Powys (both 2.60 per person); North Norfolk and Eden (both 2.59); West Lindsey, Malvern Hills and Hambleton (all 2.58); and Fylde and Stratford-upon-Avon (both 2.57). The fewest rooms per person were all in London, with the least of all being in Newham (1.44 per person); Tower Hamlets (1.54); Brent (1.61); and Hackney (1.67). The greatest reductions have also been in London, again led by Newham (-0.19), and then in Waltham Forest, Greenwich and Barking & Dagenham (all -0.18). The largest increases between 2001 and 2011 were recorded where there is more space to expand into, in Strabane (+0.29); Limavady (+0.28); Eilean Siar (+0.27); Omagh and Argyll & Bute (both +0.26); South Lanarkshire (+0.25); and the Orkney Islands and Armagh (both +0.24 rooms per person). The graph below shows how many households were overcrowded in 2011 or had many spare bedrooms. Each couple should have their own bedroom by this standard, and unrelated people over the age of 10 should not have to share bedrooms if they are of the opposite sex. The 4.5% of households that have too few bedrooms will represent a much larger proportion of people in the UK and an even larger proportion of children. Almost all properties with many spare rooms are in the owner-occupied housing sector.

Households by occupancy standard, UK 2011 %

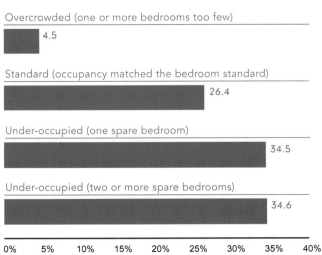

Overcrowded (one or more bedrooms too few)
4.5

Standard (occupancy matched the bedroom standard)
26.4

Under-occupied (one spare bedroom)
34.5

Under-occupied (two or more spare bedrooms)
34.6

0% 5% 10% 15% 20% 25% 30% 35% 40%

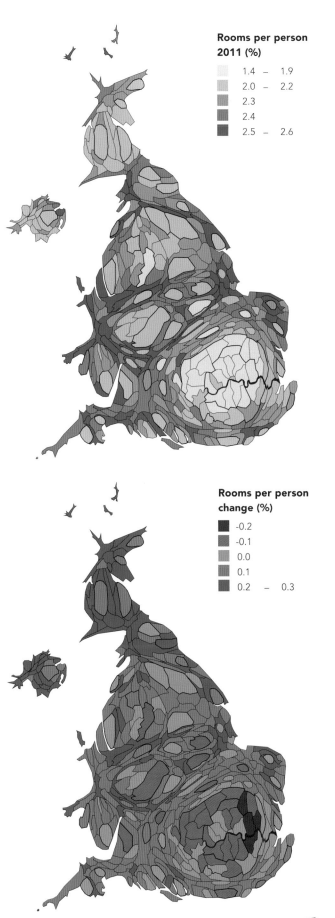

Rooms per person
2011 (%)

1.4 – 1.9
2.0 – 2.2
2.3
2.4
2.5 – 2.6

Rooms per person
change (%)

-0.2
-0.1
0.0
0.1
0.2 – 0.3

COMMUNAL ESTABLISHMENT RESIDENTS AGED 65 AND OVER

Many people in the UK do not live in conventional households. Of these, the largest group, and just under half of the total of 850,000 people not living in households, are those aged 65 and over. Of the elderly, 0.4 million lived in a communal establishment in 2011 (3.9% of that age group), a slightly lower number than in 2001, and a much lower proportion (which was 4.6% of everyone aged 65 or over). Part of the reason that the number of elderly people living in communal establishments has not risen greatly is that the numbers of very old people living in the UK have fallen because so many of those born in the post-First World War baby boom of 1919 died between the two Censuses. They died while in their eighties or very early nineties. So we might expect a boom in the care home industry in the years ahead as demand should soon rise again.

The greatest concentrations of elderly people living in communal establishments are found in Rother (1.5%); Conwy, Worthing, Isle of Wight, Arun, Eastbourne and Torbay (all 1.3%); Fylde, Hastings, East Devon, Teignbridge and the Malvern Hills (all 1.2%). The lowest proportions are all in or near London led by the City of London (none) and Hackney and Tower Hamlets (both 0.1%). The greatest increases have been in Epping Forest, North Warwickshire, Basildon and Oadby & Wigston (all +0.2%); followed by East Dorset, Windsor & Maidenhead, Maldon, Strabane, West Oxfordshire, Chelmsford, Barrow-in-Furness and the Vale of White Horse (all +0.1%). The greatest falls over the decade have been larger, led by Denbighshire and Worthing (-0.7%); Eastbourne, Bournemouth and the Isles of Scilly (all -0.6%); and Hastings, Torbay and Rother (all -0.5%). This pattern may well have begun to change after 2011 as the national proportions of people living in all kinds of communal establishments has started to rise steeply, up to 950,000 by 2014, although that number includes student halls of residence, prisons and homeless hostels and care homes for younger people.

People living in communal establishments, UK %

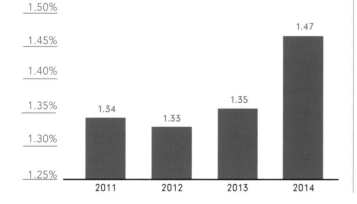

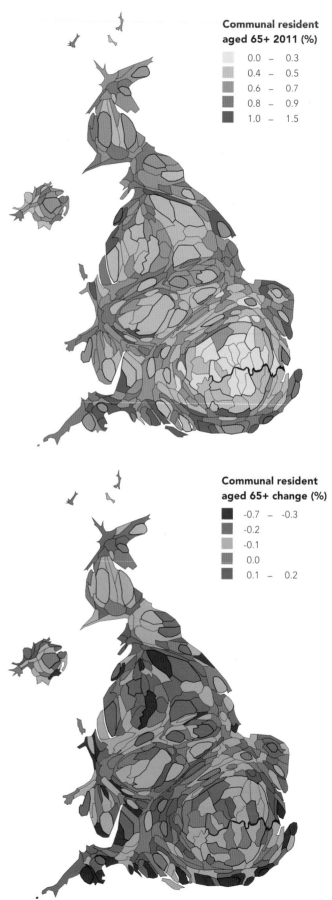

Communal resident aged 65+ 2011 (%)

	0.0 – 0.3
	0.4 – 0.5
	0.6 – 0.7
	0.8 – 0.9
	1.0 – 1.5

Communal resident aged 65+ change (%)

	-0.7 – -0.3
	-0.2
	-0.1
	0.0
	0.1 – 0.2

UNPAID CARE: NO CARE

Most people living in the UK do not have to provide unpaid care, giving help or support to family members, friends, neighbours or others because of either their long-term physical or mental ill health/disability or because of problems related to old age. Childcare is not included in this definition of unpaid care unless the child is long-term ill or disabled. However, 6.5 million do provide such unpaid care (5.9 million did in 2001), and we look at their distribution in the next few pages and how it is changing. Here we show the distribution of the 56.7 million who don't have such responsibilities (they numbered 52.9 million in 2001).

Since 2001 the population as a whole has risen, but the proportion providing unpaid care has risen even faster, so in general this group of non-carers is declining in proportion. Non-carers are found in greatest concentrations in London, but also in university cities with a great many young people and fewer older residents. The four boroughs with the most non-carers in the UK are Wandsworth (93.5%); Lambeth and Hammersmith & Fulham (both 93.2%); and Kensington & Chelsea (93.1%). But even here a significant proportion of the population are carers. The least non-carers are found in Neath Port Talbot (85.4%) and Ards (86.4%). The largest increases in people not caring were recorded in Eilean Siar and Barking & Dagenham (both +1.0%); Tower Hamlets, Aberdeen, Newcastle upon Tyne and Clackmannanshire (all +0.9%); and in Edinburgh, Glasgow and Dundee (all +0.8%). These proportions may well be rising because in these places a falling proportion of the population need such care. A surprisingly high proportion of children are carers (often for a parent), and more than 10% of those aged under 16 in England and Wales, as the graph below makes clear.

Unpaid care: no care 2011 (%)

- 85.4 – 87.9
- 88.0 – 89.9
- 90.0 – 90.9
- 91.0 – 91.9
- 92.0 – 93.5

Unpaid care: no care change (%)

- -2.0 – -1.0
- -0.9 – -0.5
- -0.4 – -0.1
- 0.0 – 0.4
- 0.5 – 1.0

People providing no unpaid care by age, England and Wales 2011 %

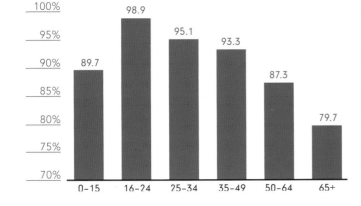

Age	%
0–15	89.7
16–24	98.9
25–34	95.1
35–49	93.3
50–64	87.3
65+	79.7

UNPAID CARE: 1–19 HOURS A WEEK

In 2011, 4.1 million people were providing 1–19 hours of unpaid care, just a few more than the 4.0 million who did so in 2001. This rise was small because of the great increases there have been in people having to provide more than 20 hours of care a week for others, unpaid, in recent years. Cuts to social services provision and home visits had begun before 2011 but have continued to occur more rapidly since then. Labour, the Coalition and then Conservative governments all said that the cuts had to be made because tax receipts had fallen since the 2008 financial crash and government debt was rising. When people provide care for free it doesn't appear as if it is being provided as far as government accounts are concerned.

The areas in which the most unpaid care is now being provided of up to 19 hours a week per carer, according to the proportion of residents who were such carers in 2011, were not necessarily the poorest areas but those with many elderly people and fewer local services: Derbyshire Dales (9.2%); Malvern Hills (8.8%); Purbeck (8.7%); Craven, North Down and Staffordshire Moorlands (8.6%); East Dorset, South Hams, North East Derbyshire and South Staffordshire (8.5%); Castlereagh, West Somerset and West Dorset (8.4%). The largest increases have been in the Isles of Scilly (+1.0%); Eden (+0.9%); and Ballymoney, Purbeck and West Somerset (all +0.8%). Hardly anyone aged 16–24 provides this kind of care unpaid.

People providing 1–19 hours a week of unpaid care by age, England and Wales 2011 %

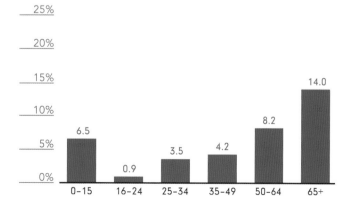

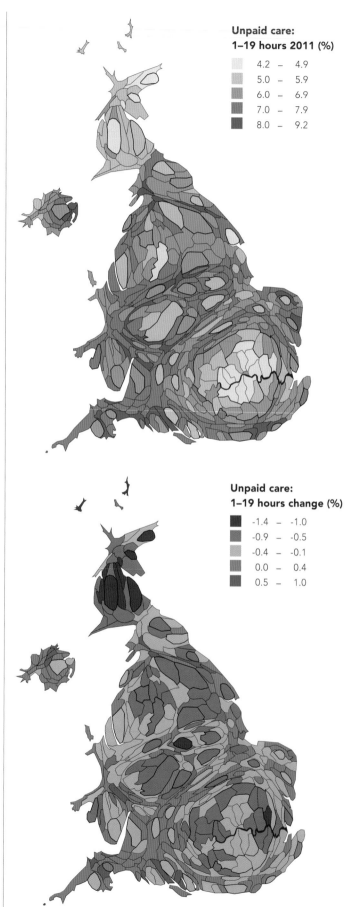

Unpaid care:
1–19 hours 2011 (%)

	4.2 – 4.9
	5.0 – 5.9
	6.0 – 6.9
	7.0 – 7.9
	8.0 – 9.2

Unpaid care:
1–19 hours change (%)

	-1.4 – -1.0
	-0.9 – -0.5
	-0.4 – -0.1
	0.0 – 0.4
	0.5 – 1.0

UNPAID CARE: 20–49 HOURS A WEEK

Providing unpaid care of between 20 and 49 hours a week is the equivalent time commitment to having a full-time job, and yet many of the people will be doing this on top of having a job, or even school, to go to. One large group providing such care are probably retired; these are the 0.2 million people aged 65 or over who provide unpaid care for this length of time on average each week, up to seven hours a day including weekends. However, this group is less than one-quarter of the 0.9 million people in the UK who provide this much care. In 2001, only 0.7 million people were providing this much care, unpaid.

There is not a single district in the UK in which this amount of care being given has not risen since 2001. The smallest rises have been in Newcastle upon Tyne and Hartlepool (both near to 0.0%), where there has been a decline in the numbers of the elderly population. The next smallest rise is in Tower Hamlets and the City of London (both +0.1%), almost certainly small for similar reasons. The largest rises have all been in Scotland, led by Argyll & Bute and West Dunbartonshire (both + 0.6%). The highest proportions of local populations giving such care are now found in Neath Port Talbot and Blaenau Gwent (both 2.3%); Strabane, Knowsley, Merthyr Tydfil and Belfast (all 2.2%); and North Lanarkshire and Derry (both 2.1%). The lowest proportions of carers providing 20–49 hours a week of unpaid care are now found in the City of London (0.7%); and Elmbridge and Cambridge (both 0.8%).

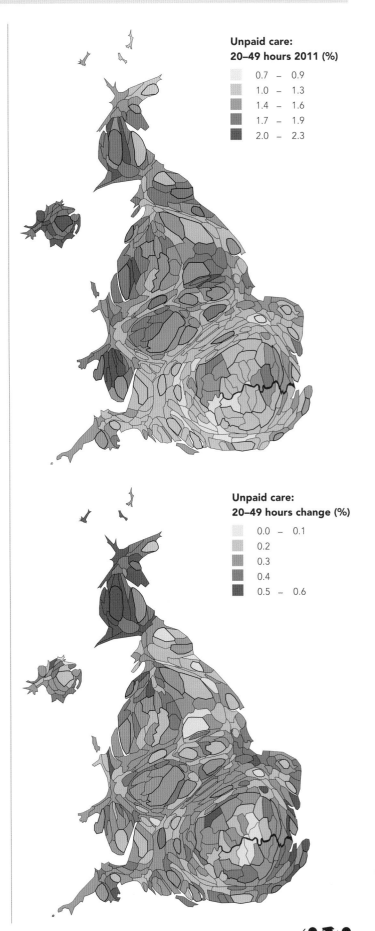

**Unpaid care:
20–49 hours 2011 (%)**

- 0.7 – 0.9
- 1.0 – 1.3
- 1.4 – 1.6
- 1.7 – 1.9
- 2.0 – 2.3

**Unpaid care:
20–49 hours change (%)**

- 0.0 – 0.1
- 0.2
- 0.3
- 0.4
- 0.5 – 0.6

People providing 20–49 hours a week of unpaid care by age, England and Wales 2011 %

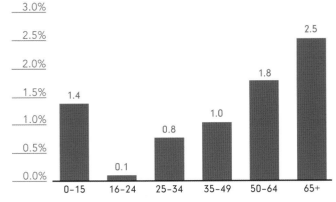

Age	%
0–15	1.4
16–24	0.1
25–34	0.8
35–49	1.0
50–64	1.8
65+	2.5

UNPAID CARE: 50 HOURS OR MORE A WEEK

A massive 1.5 million people are now providing unpaid care of over 50 hours a week to someone who is ill, disabled or unable to cope without that care due to old age. These are essentially full-time carers with little time free to work or study or even rest properly. In 2001 the number was 1.25 million. Half a million of these carers are aged 65 or older; a million are aged under 65, including some 10,000 children. The greatest concentrations of people providing this much care are found in Neath Port Talbot (4.8%); East Lindsey (4.1%); Knowsley, Blaenau Gwent, Merthyr Tydfil, Rhondda Cynon Taf and Bridgend (all 4.0%); Caerphilly and Carmarthenshire (both 3.9%); Torfaen (3.8%); St Helens (3.7%); and Halton, Denbighshire, Blackpool, Torbay and Swansea (all 3.6%). Such more-than-full-time unpaid carers are least often to be found living (and thus caring) in the City of London (0.9%); Kensington & Chelsea (1.2%); Richmond upon Thames, Cambridge and Wandsworth (all 1.3%); Oxford, Hammersmith & Fulham, Lambeth, Hart and Elmbridge (all 1.4%). The largest increases have been in East Lindsey (+0.9%); Rother, Waveney, Torbay, Tendring and King's Lynn & West Norfolk (all 0.8%).

Despite the huge national rise, there are also areas that have seen actual declines in the numbers of carers who can afford to live there unpaid. The largest of these falls have been in Tower Hamlets (-0.4%); Barking & Dagenham, City of London and Newham (all -0.2%). We have no idea what has happened since 2011 as no statistics on unpaid care have been published since the Census was taken.

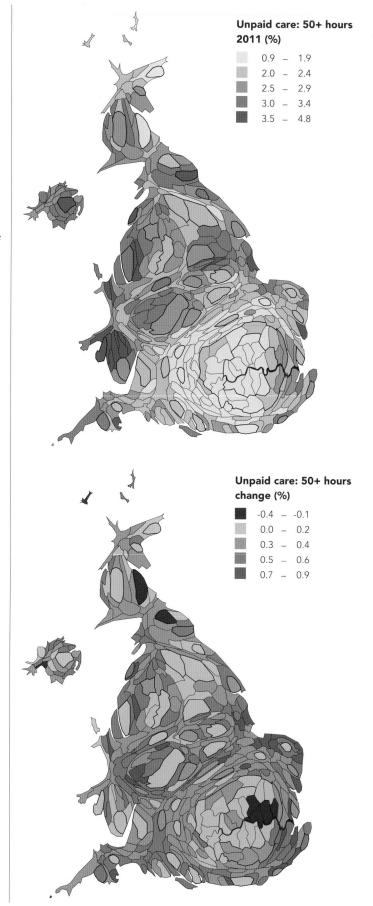

Unpaid care: 50+ hours 2011 (%)

	0.9 – 1.9
	2.0 – 2.4
	2.5 – 2.9
	3.0 – 3.4
	3.5 – 4.8

Unpaid care: 50+ hours change (%)

	-0.4 – -0.1
	0.0 – 0.2
	0.3 – 0.4
	0.5 – 0.6
	0.7 – 0.9

People providing 50+ hours a week of unpaid care by age, England and Wales 2011 %

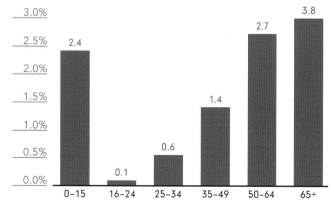

Age	%
0–15	2.4
16–24	0.1
25–34	0.6
35–49	1.4
50–64	2.7
65+	3.8

DAY-TO-DAY ACTIVITIES LIMITED A LOT OR A LITTLE

So for whom are all these carers caring? In 2011 there were 11.5 million people living in the UK whose day-to-day activities were limited by a health problem or disability that has lasted or is expected to last at least 12 months, including problems related to old age. However, the map of activities limited a lot very much reflects the old industrial and mining heartlands of the UK, which suggests that some elderly people who lived and worked in such places are far more likely to find their activities limited now than are others. Some 5.5 million said their activities were limited a lot and 6.0 million said they were limited a little. Of those who said there activities were limited a lot, the highest proportions were found in Neath Port Talbot (16.1%); Merthyr Tydfil (15.8%); Blaenau Gwent (15.7%); Strabane (14.8%); Belfast (14.7%); Rhondda Cynon Taf (14.5%); Knowsley (14.2%); Caerphilly (14.0%); Derry (13.7%); Carmarthenshire (13.6%); and Blackpool and Bridgend (both 13.5%). Of those who were limited a little by illness, disability or age, such limitations were most common among the populations living in a largely different set of areas: West Somerset (13.2%); East Lindsey (13.1%); Tendring and North Norfolk (both 13.0%); Rother (12.8%); Christchurch (12.7%); Isle of Wight (12.3%); Torbay and Conwy (both 12.2%); East Devon (12.1%); and Blackpool, Wyre and Scarborough (all 12.0%).

The maps show that having day-to-day activities limited by illness or disability is least common in London and the Home Counties, with very low rates of being greatly limited by illness, disability or age in the Western Home Counties and Surrey. However, there are people who are limited by illness everywhere: nowhere is the overall rate lower than 11.2%. Using a more generous official definition, almost 19% of the UK population aged 16–64 had a limiting disability between 2013 and 2014.

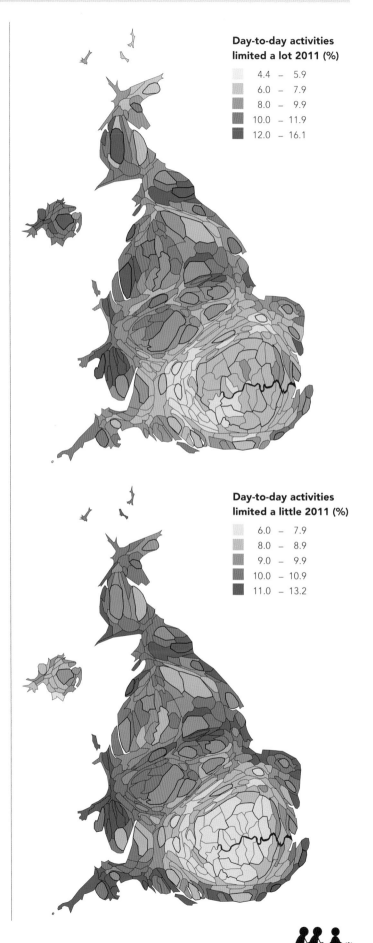

Day-to-day activities limited a lot 2011 (%)

4.4	– 5.9
6.0	– 7.9
8.0	– 9.9
10.0	– 11.9
12.0	– 16.1

Day-to-day activities limited a little 2011 (%)

6.0	– 7.9
8.0	– 8.9
9.0	– 9.9
10.0	– 10.9
11.0	– 13.2

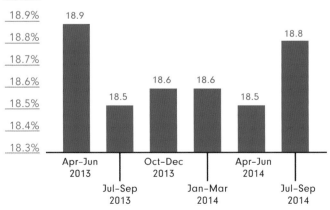

People aged 16–64 classified as Equality Act core disabled and/or work-limiting disabled, UK %

Apr–Jun 2013: 18.9
Jul–Sep 2013: 18.5
Oct–Dec 2013: 18.6
Jan–Mar 2014: 18.6
Apr–Jun 2014: 18.5
Jul–Sep 2014: 18.8

DAY-TO-DAY ACTIVITIES LIMITED

Measuring change in health over time between Censuses is difficult because the question changed after 2001 to differentiate between *a little* and *a lot*, which might have encouraged a few more people to answer that they did have a limitation even if they thought of it as minor. In 2001, 10.9 million people had a limiting long-term illness, and this increased to 11.5 million in 2011 despite there not being a great deal of ageing among the very elderly population (because of there being so few births in the 1920s and 1930s).

The greatest increases in people with a limiting illness or disability, including due to old age, were found in East Lindsey (+2.2%); Carrickfergus (+2.1%); Wyre Forest (+2.0%); Daventry, Castle Point, Maldon and Larne (all +1.9%); Ards and North Norfolk (both +1.8%); South Staffordshire and Limavady (both +1.7%). The 21 largest reductions were recorded in areas that were often attracting more younger people: Manchester (-3.8%); Tower Hamlets (-3.7%); Hackney (-3.6%); Barking & Dagenham and Newham (both -3.5%); Glasgow (-3.4%); Merthyr Tydfil (-3.2%); Newcastle upon Tyne (-2.8%); Greenwich (-2.3%); Islington, Liverpool and Wandsworth (all -2.2%); Salford, Hammersmith & Fulham, Southwark and Dungannon (all -2.1%); Nottingham and Waltham Forest (both -2.0%); Sheffield (-1.9%); Brighton & Hove and the City of London (both -1.8%). Nationally, reported poor health worsened greatly during 2011, although the jump is so high that increased anxiety due to the changing economic and political situation might have played a part in their general outlook. The coalition government cuts began in earnest in 2011 and 2012; welfare sanctions were also increased to dramatic levels by then, which became recognisably punitive by 2014.

People who are mostly disatisfied with their health, UK %

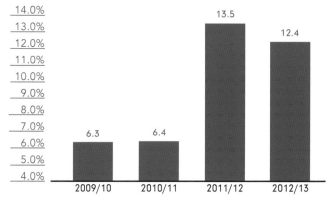

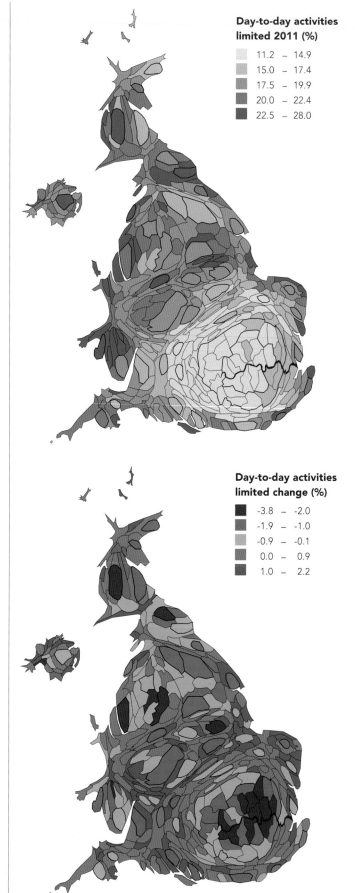

Day-to-day activities limited 2011 (%)
- 11.2 – 14.9
- 15.0 – 17.4
- 17.5 – 19.9
- 20.0 – 22.4
- 22.5 – 28.0

Day-to-day activities limited change (%)
- -3.8 – -2.0
- -1.9 – -1.0
- -0.9 – -0.1
- 0.0 – 0.9
- 1.0 – 2.2

HEALTH STATUS GOOD IN 2011

There remain a large number of people, even a majority in some areas, whose health is very good, and another group that is almost as large who say their health is good. In 2011, 30.1 million people defined their own health as very good. They were most likely to do this if they were living in East Renfrewshire (58.8%); Kensington & Chelsea (57.8%); Edinburgh (57.6%); Wandsworth (57.4%); Richmond upon Thames (57.3%); East Dunbartonshire (56.6%); Hammersmith & Fulham and Elmbridge (both 56.5%); Stirling and the City of London (both 55.8%); Aberdeenshire (55.4%); Oxford (55.2%); St Albans (55.1%); Hart (55.0%); Cambridge (54.7%); Perth & Kinross, the Shetland Islands and East Lothian (all 54.6%); Windsor & Maidenhead (54.5%); and Aberdeen (54.3%). Areas with younger than average populations feature in this list as well as more affluent areas and sometimes places that are both more affluent and younger than average. Traditionally Censuses in the UK have tended to show that people in Scotland have a tendency to be upbeat and describe their health in slightly better terms than it might be when objectively assessed.

Different adjectives can have particular regional meanings. For example, among the million people describing their health as good there is a remarkable geographical clustering in those areas where people are most likely to do this, almost all being in East Anglia: Fenland and North Norfolk (37.8%); South Holland (37.6%); Boston (37.5%); Peterborough and Breckland (37.3%); King's Lynn & West Norfolk (37.1%); and Wellingborough and Broadland (37.0%). Since 2009 the proportion of people declaring that they are completely satisfied with their health has been steadily falling. This will not simply be due to ageing but also to a culture shift in our understanding of complete satisfaction and what we have come to expect.

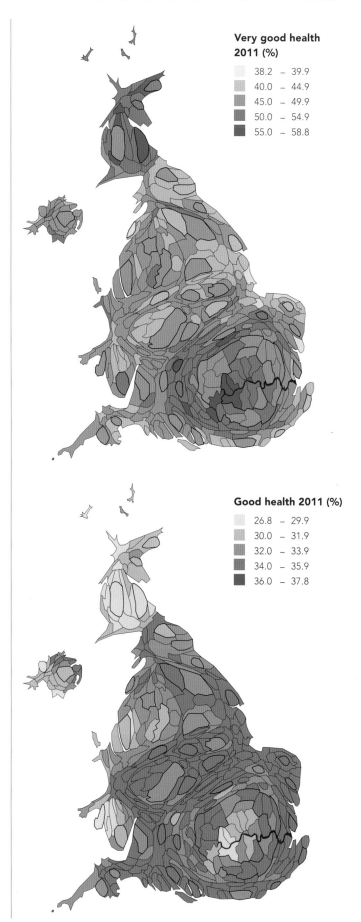

Very good health 2011 (%)

- 38.2 – 39.9
- 40.0 – 44.9
- 45.0 – 49.9
- 50.0 – 54.9
- 55.0 – 58.8

Good health 2011 (%)

- 26.8 – 29.9
- 30.0 – 31.9
- 32.0 – 33.9
- 34.0 – 35.9
- 36.0 – 37.8

People who are completely satisfied with their health, UK %

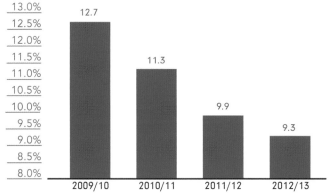

2009/10	2010/11	2011/12	2012/13
12.7	11.3	9.9	9.3

HEALTH STATUS BAD OR VERY BAD IN 2011

The 2011 Census also asked if people thought their health status was fair. We have not mapped this distribution. It is the four extremes we do map, and 8.3 million people chose 'fair' to describe their health in that year; the most common place to do this was again in East Anglia: East Lindsey (18.3%, which also features in the next list). A further 2.7 million people said their health was bad and another 0.8 million said it was very bad. Of those who said it was bad, the highest proportions were living in Merthyr Tydfil (8.3%); Blaenau Gwent (8.2%); Neath Port Talbot (7.9%); Rhondda Cynon Taf (7.4%); Knowsley and Blackpool (both 7.3%); Caerphilly (7.2%); Bridgend and Bolsover (both 6.8%); Liverpool (6.7%); Barnsley, Sunderland and Barrow-in-Furness (all 6.6%); Torfaen and St Helens (both 6.5%); Glasgow and East Lindsey (6.4%); County Durham, South Tyneside, Hartlepool and Belfast (all 6.3%). Again, as with those who were finding their day-to-day activities more limited, old industrial and mining areas dominate.

In previous Censuses it was noted that people recorded the worst levels of health in Wales, and that there may have been an opposite process to that occurring in Scotland. Wales still records the very worst levels, but now Glasgow joins it. Of those 0.8 million people reporting that their health is very bad, the most concentrated in 2011 were living in Merthyr Tydfil (2.8%); Neath Port Talbot (2.6%); Blaenau Gwent (2.5%); Glasgow (2.3%); Blackpool, Carmarthenshire, Knowsley and Rhondda Cynon Taf (2.2%); Caerphilly, Torfaen, Bridgend, Liverpool, Swansea and Sunderland (all 2.1%). Since 2011 there has been an abrupt increase in the national proportions of people who say they are completely dissatisfied with their health, rising to over 5% of the UK population.

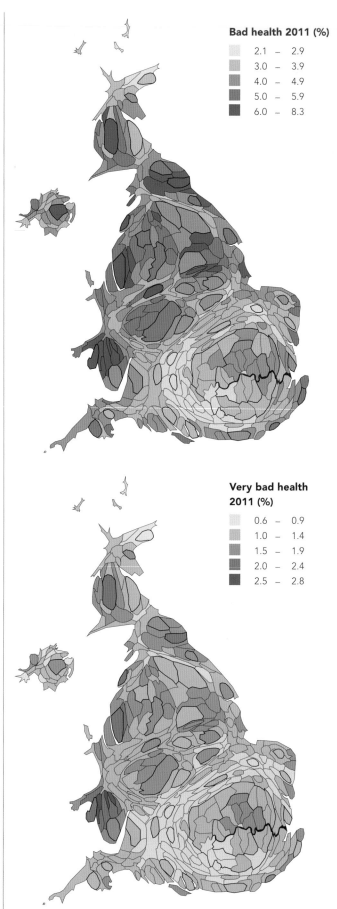

Bad health 2011 (%)

	2.1 – 2.9
	3.0 – 3.9
	4.0 – 4.9
	5.0 – 5.9
	6.0 – 8.3

Very bad health 2011 (%)

	0.6 – 0.9
	1.0 – 1.4
	1.5 – 1.9
	2.0 – 2.4
	2.5 – 2.8

People who are completely disatisfied with their health, UK %

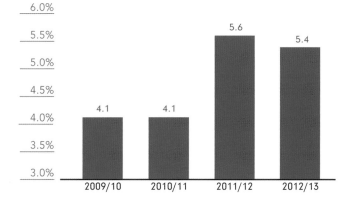

	2009/10	2010/11	2011/12	2012/13
	4.1	4.1	5.6	5.4

HEALTH IS GOOD, BROAD COMPARISON

Although the Census question has changed over time, it is still possible to make a broad comparison between the 2001 and 2011 Censuses. However, it was reported in 2009 that for the 2011 Census, the '...Adoption of the SILC [European] general health question will result in a significant reduction in the proportion of the population considered in "Good" health' (*Health Statistics Quarterly*, 41). This was because, by offering people the options to describe poorer health as *very bad*, *bad* or *fair* in 2011, compared to just *fairly good* and *not good* in 2001, more people might choose one of three boxes, rather than one of two, despite the more negative terms being used and even though a new *very good* option was also added on the 2011 Census form. Alternatively, health, including mental health, may have deteriorated.

In 2011, 51.3 million people described their health as good or very good compared to 53.3 million who said it was good or fairly good in 2001. One reason to believe that the deterioration may well not be entirely due to the changing question wording is that the graph below shows national levels of satisfaction with health falling year on year since 2011. Again, rising anxiety may matter.

The smallest falls in people reporting good health between 2001 and 2011 were in the City of London (-4.7%); Wandsworth (-5.5%); Edinburgh (-5.8%); Aberdeen (-5.9%); Hammersmith & Fulham (-6.1%); Kensington & Chelsea and Richmond upon Thames (both -6.2%); and Tower Hamlets, Aberdeenshire and Oxford (-6.4%). Many of these were places least affected by the 2008 economic crisis, or where financiers were most aided by the government bailout of 2008/09.

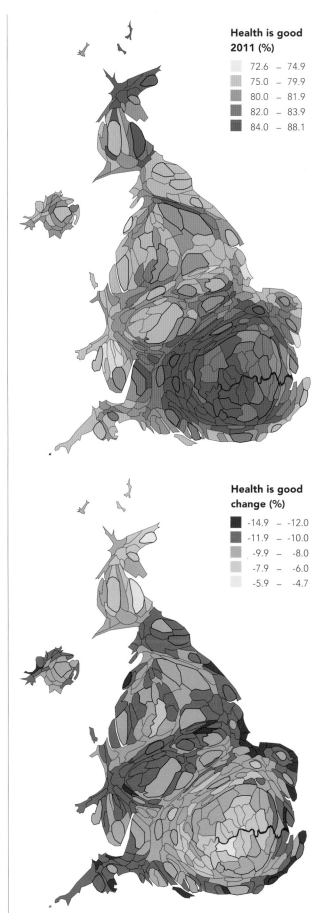

Health is good 2011 (%)

- 72.6 – 74.9
- 75.0 – 79.9
- 80.0 – 81.9
- 82.0 – 83.9
- 84.0 – 88.1

Health is good change (%)

- -14.9 – -12.0
- -11.9 – -10.0
- -9.9 – -8.0
- -7.9 – -6.0
- -5.9 – -4.7

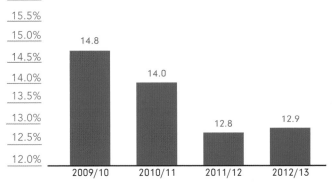

People who are somewhat satisfied with their health, UK %

Year	%
2009/10	14.8
2010/11	14.0
2011/12	12.8
2012/13	12.9

Driving to work or being driven as a passenger, being in a car pool or otherwise involved in shared-driving is the main means of travel to work for some 17.8 million commuters.

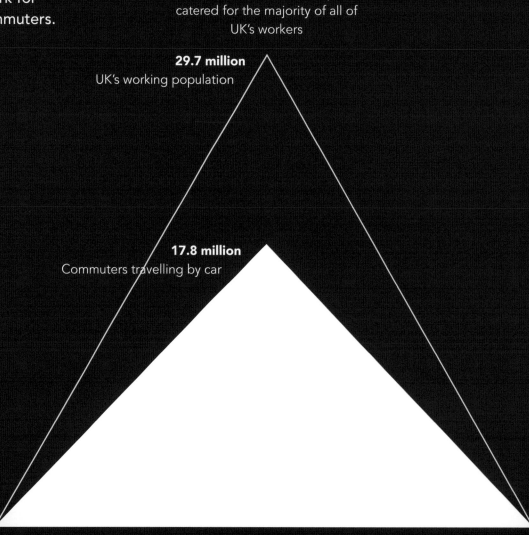

2011
This single mode of transport catered for the majority of all of UK's workers

29.7 million
UK's working population

17.8 million
Commuters travelling by car

Homes and Commuting

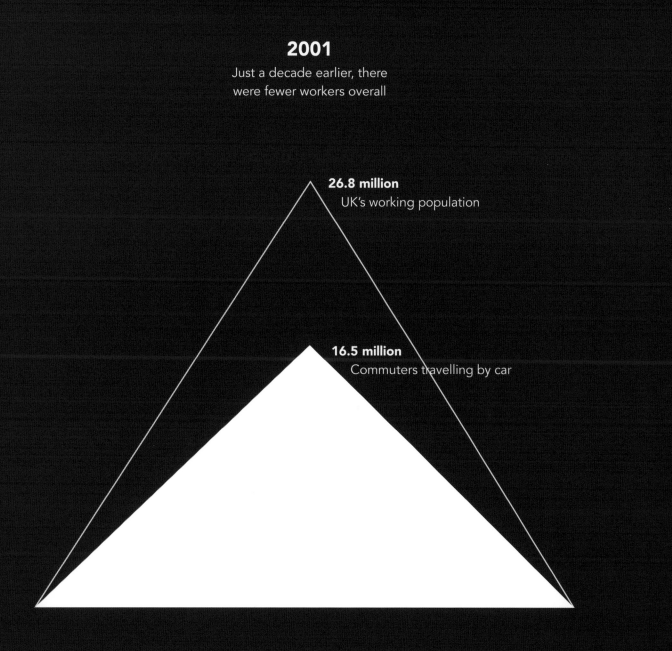

2001
Just a decade earlier, there
were fewer workers overall

26.8 million
UK's working population

16.5 million
Commuters travelling by car

Homes and Commuting

The Census is the main record of the UK housing stock. It also provides the most comprehensive survey of how people travel daily from that housing to places of work, of whether they own or rent where they live, including tying all that to what employment each might have. For example, in 2011 there were 413,000 households where the person who filled in the Census form and took responsibility for the household was a full-time student. Of those households, 238,000 were living in private rented accommodation, and these types of household constituted 1.0% of all households in England and Wales. The household reference person (HRP) is the first adult to be named in the Census form. The most common type of household by the job (or previous job, if retired) of the HRP and property tenure were the 2.3 million households living in mortgaged property where the HRP was also an administrator or in a lower managerial position. In 2011, 9.8% of all households in England and Wales were of this kind: they constitute the highest bar in the graph below.

This and subsequent graphs in this chapter use the National Statistics Socio-Economic Classification (NS-SeC).

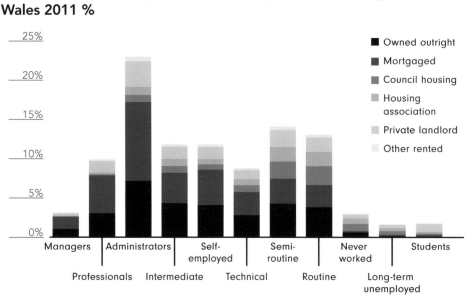

Households by housing tenure and job type (NS-SeC), England and Wales 2011 %

To be able to buy property, to pay a mortgage or pay the rent, several members of each household often now work. There has been a rapid reduction in households with only one earner, especially where house prices and rents have risen fastest. However, there are still people who have never worked who own property outright. In fact, as the graph above shows, there are more such people, possibly mostly elderly women who were housewives, than there are people who have never worked who rent privately! Of those who commute to work or study in England, a majority travel by car or van each day. Just over a seventh travel by public transport, a tenth of people now work from home most of the time and almost a fifth get to work by some other means, including walking, cycling, being a passenger in a vehicle or driving a motorbike.

The car availability statistics are for England and Wales because compatible data were not available for Scotland and Northern Ireland. Changes in definitions over time have to be considered, including how someone might choose to answer the same question differently 10 years later, for example, saying that the main part of their same daily commute is now walking because the need for regular exercise is emphasised more nowadays, rather than the train part of the journey.

All commuters, means of travel to work, England and Wales 2011

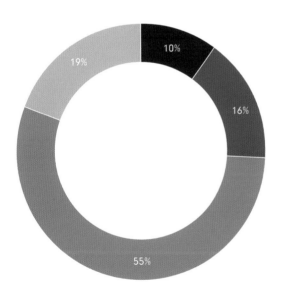

■ Work mainly at or from home

■ Train, underground, metro, light rail, tram, bus, minibus or coach

■ Driving a car or van

■ All other methods of travel to work

Means of travel to work by job type (NS-SeC), England and Wales 2011 %

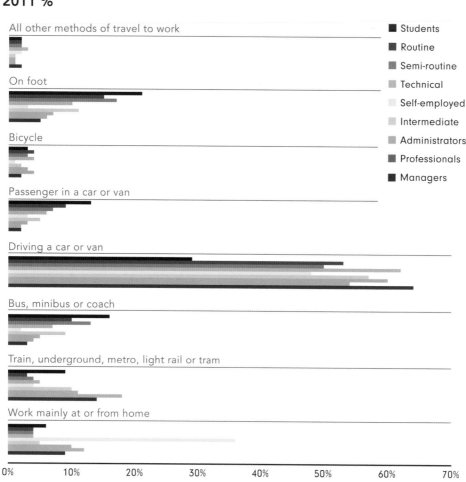

All other methods of travel to work

On foot

Bicycle

Passenger in a car or van

Driving a car or van

Bus, minibus or coach

Train, underground, metro, light rail or tram

Work mainly at or from home

■ Students
■ Routine
■ Semi-routine
■ Technical
□ Self-employed
■ Intermediate
▨ Administrators
■ Professionals
■ Managers

0%   10%   20%   30%   40%   50%   60%   70%

More people do appear to be walking to work or study than before, but fewer are cycling. In 2011 about 2.6 million people in England and Wales said that to get to work or study each day, they travelled on foot. The group most likely to do this were full-time students, although even for them only 21% walked (and only 3% cycled!). Some 29% of students in England and Wales get to school or university driving a car or van, and a further 13% commute as a passenger in a car or van. The Census will most likely record their mode of travel to work for the part-time job that most students now have, including many full-time students. The top line in each of the clusters of horizontal bars in the graph above reveals just how likely students were to use different modes of transport, and also emphasises how, for every other group (apart from the self-employed), a majority of people drive a car or van to work each day. For the self-employed, 48% still drive, but 36% work mainly or fully from home. This may be because if you are self-employed it is very likely that your home is your registered address of employment, and if you don't drive to work for (or with) others each day, you may well be a homeworker most of the time. The group least likely to work from home are people doing the lowest paid routine work (just 3.7% working from home).

The Census provides the most comprehensive picture of British society that any single statistical snapshot can achieve. It asks only a few dozen questions, but those questions, when combined, can paint the most complex of pictures. The Census is also vital in providing a denominator for many of the statistical series about what matters most in our lives. For example, it is only the Census that can reveal if working less and therefore driving less could have caused the sudden fall in road crash fatalities in the Great Recession years 2007–10. For some groups of commuters the Census allows us to know when this is a real fall in road crash fatalities. And the recorded fall may not be of crashes, but of the chances of dying in them as accident and emergency services improve. But the Census also tells us how many people work in each place in such services. Without a Census it is hard to see how everything is connected to everything else, and to then work out what questions need to be asked next. And the Census shows a few of the most crucial connections, especially about our geography, and how much where you live influences what you do, and what others do to you.

Road crash fatalities by mode of transport, Great Britain 2000–2013

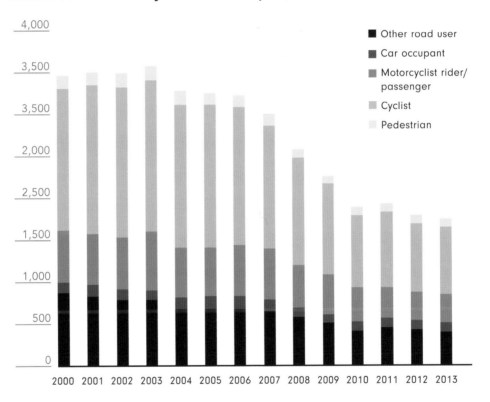

NO CAR

Despite travel to work and study by car being the commonest option in England and Wales, by 2011, 10.7 million people lived in households with no car or van available to any member of the household. This was an overall rise from 9.9 million people living in such households in 2001. The greatest increases in the proportion of people living in households with no access to a car were recorded in London, led by Hackney (+9.5%); and Southwark and Lambeth (both +8.1%). Outside of London the greatest increases were in the Isles of Scilly (+3.1%); Crawley (+2.6%); Cambridge (+2.3%); and Reading (+1.7%). These are all areas where the population is rising and the space to park cars is falling. The greatest decreases were in areas where money has been most tight and where gaining access to a car still relies on having enough money to buy and run a car, not on finding space to park it: South Tyneside (-5.6%); Gateshead (-5.3%); Blaenau Gwent (-4.7%); and North Tyneside and Knowsley (both -4.2%).

Nationally 12% of commuters in England and Wales who live in a household with no car and van still drive to work, possibly in a work vehicle or they get a lift with a friend or neighbour. They may also have ticked 'no car' despite driving a car because they were renting or borrowing one, a vehicle that no one in their household actually owned. The boroughs where a majority of households have no car or van are now in the City of London (62.5%); Hackney (56.3%); Islington (56.1%); Tower Hamlets (55.0%); Westminster (54.8%); Camden (51.6%); Southwark (51.1%); and Lambeth (50.7%). The lowest proportions of people living in carless households are found in Hart (4.7%); South Northamptonshire (5.3%); and Wokingham (5.4%).

No cars 2011 (%)

	4.7 – 9.9
	10.0 – 19.9
	20.0 – 29.9
	30.0 – 39.9
	40.0 – 62.5

No cars change (%)

	-5.6 – -2.1
	-2.0 – -1.1
	-1.0 – -0.1
	0.0 – 4.9
	5.0 – 9.5

Commuters with no cars or vans available to their household, means of travel to work, England and Wales 2011 %

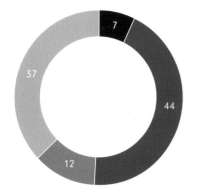

- ■ Work mainly at or from home
- ■ Train, underground, metro, light rail, tram, bus, minibus or coach
- ■ Driving a car or van
- ■ All other methods of travel to work

ONE CAR

Some 21.5 million people now live in households with access to a single car or van, but nowhere is this group in a local majority. Ownership of a single car per household is most common in Richmond upon Thames (48.3%); Merton (47.6%); Norwich (46.0%); Barrow-in-Furness (45.5%); Barking & Dagenham (44.7%); and Wandsworth, Gosport and Kingston upon Thames (all 44.5%). This group consisted of almost exactly the same number of people in 2001, 21.5 million, and so the overall proportion of people living in this group of households has fallen as the population has risen. More people have come to live in households with two or more cars than have come to find they are living in the new (mostly London-based) carless households. The greatest falls in one car ownership have been in Neath Port Talbot (-6.7%); Cornwall (-6.4%); and Pembrokeshire (-6.4), all areas where two-car ownership has risen by more than 8.0%.

Being a one car household has become more common in a small number of areas, but this is more often due to downsizing from being a two car household rather than upsizing. The largest rises were in the following areas: Richmond upon Thames (+1.9%); Elmbridge and Runnymede (both +1.0%); Kingston upon Thames (+0.7%); Epsom & Ewell and Sutton (both +0.5%); St Albans and Windsor & Maidenhead (both +0.3%); Barnet (+0.2%); and Chiltern (+0.1%). Being a one car household is now most rare in areas where around two-thirds of all households have two or more cars at their disposal. The lowest proportions having only one car or van are in Surrey Heath (26.1%); Hart (26.2%); South Bucks (26.7%); South Northamptonshire (27.0%); and Uttlesford (27.9%). Understandably only just under 50% of people in households across all of England and Wales with only one car or van use that vehicle to drive to work or study because for the other people in the household, there is no available car or van.

Commuters with one car or van available to their household, means of travel to work, England and Wales 2011 %

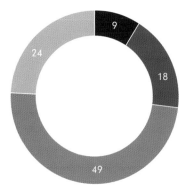

- Work mainly at or from home
- Train, underground, metro, light rail, tram, bus, minibus or coach
- Driving a car or van
- All other methods of travel to work

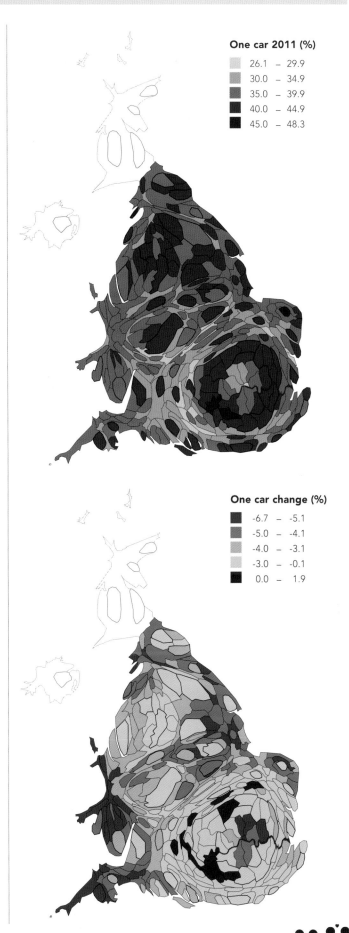

One car 2011 (%)

- 26.1 – 29.9
- 30.0 – 34.9
- 35.0 – 39.9
- 40.0 – 44.9
- 45.0 – 48.3

One car change (%)

- -6.7 – -5.1
- -5.0 – -4.1
- -4.0 – -3.1
- -3.0 – -0.1
- 0.0 – 1.9

TWO OR MORE CARS

In 2001 as many as 19.7 million people lived in households with access to two or more cars or vans per household. By 2011 that number had risen to 22.9 million, and at least 20 million vehicles. It is still almost certainly the case that all the spare cars and vans owned by households who have more cars than adults with driving licences, and hence more than they could drive at any time, would be enough to give every family with young children but without a car access to a car should they need one. This point was first reached in 2001. By 2011, the areas where two or more car ownership had become most common were in Hart (67.3%); South Northamptonshire (66.9%); South Bucks (65.8%); Surrey Heath (65.7%); Uttlesford (64.8%); Wokingham (64.6%); Chiltern (64.1%); East Hampshire (62.1%); and East Dorset and Harborough (both 62.0%). In contrast, fewer than 1 in 10 of all people living in the following areas had access to two or more cars by 2011: City of London (6.9%); Islington (7.0%); Hackney and Tower Hamlets (both 7.2%); Westminster (9.4%); Southwark (9.7%); and Camden (9.9%). All of these areas had seen a fall in two (plus) car ownership since 2001 except for the City of London, which remarkably, given the price of land there, recorded a 0.1% rise in such multi-car-owning households. However, this was of only eight more households having access to more than one car in their City of London residence in 2011 compared to 2001.

The largest rises were in some of England's, and especially Wales', poorer areas where two car ownership has, until very recently, been very rare: Neath Port Talbot (+10.2%); Blaenau Gwent (+10.1%); Caerphilly (+9.2%); Rhondda Cynon Taf (+9.1%); Pembrokeshire (+9.0%); Copeland (+8.7%); and Corby and Bridgend (both +8.4%). This may reflect cuts to public transport (especially bus) services, as well as publc transport price increases.

Commuters with two (or more) cars or vans available to their household, means of travel to work, England and Wales 2011 %

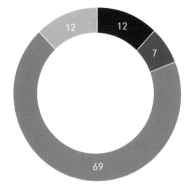

- Work mainly at or from home
- Train, underground, metro, light rail, tram, bus, minibus or coach
- Driving a car or van
- All other methods of travel to work

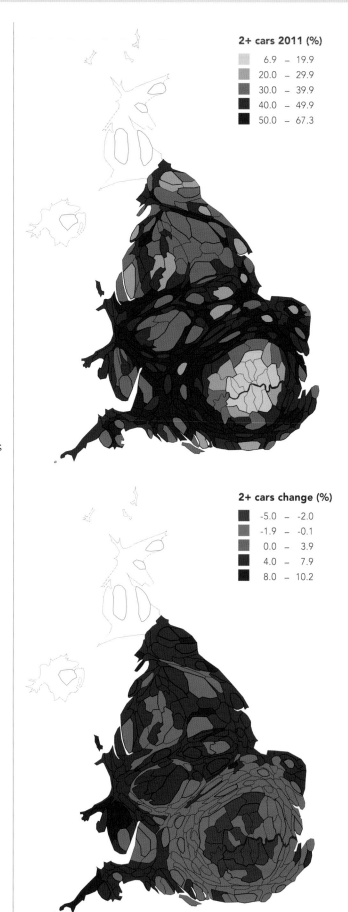

2+ cars 2011 (%)

- 6.9 – 19.9
- 20.0 – 29.9
- 30.0 – 39.9
- 40.0 – 49.9
- 50.0 – 67.3

2+ cars change (%)

- -5.0 – -2.0
- -1.9 – -0.1
- 0.0 – 3.9
- 4.0 – 7.9
- 8.0 – 10.2

COMMUTING BY CAR

Not all cars and vans are used for commuting, and so the number of cars available to households, even in just England and Wales, is far greater than the number of people who commute to work by car or van. Nevertheless, driving to work or being driven as a passenger, being in a car pool or otherwise involved in shared driving is the main means of travel to work for 17.8 million commuters. A further 0.8 million who mainly work from home use a car to travel for work purposes, but they are not included here. Thus this single mode of transport catered for the majority of all the UK's 29.7 million workers in 2011. Just a decade earlier, in 2001, there were fewer workers overall, 26.8 million, of whom around 16.5 million travelled by car. In a decade an extra 1.3 million people go to work by car, and it is likely that more of these involve just a single driver in each vehicle, as car ownership spreads in areas that had fewer vehicles in the past. This is an extra 1.3 million drivers a year, driving at least twice a day for at least five days a week, resulting in an additional 0.7 billion car journeys a year.

The greatest increases in commuting by car have been recorded in Merthyr Tydfil (+5.8%); Blaenau Gwent (+5.1%); Neath Port Talbot and Mansfield (both +4.9%); Bolsover (+4.7%); Copeland and Corby (both +4.5%); Carmarthenshire (+4.4%); Knowsley (+4.3%); and Barnsley (+4.2%). If those who mainly work at home but who use a car for work at other times are included, 'petrol-head central' by 2011 was South Northamptonshire (41.9%, 39.5% not including car-using home-based workers), followed by Bracknell Forest (40.9%); South Derbyshire (40.8%); Forest Heath (40.6%); Blaby and North Warwickshire (both 40.3%); Hinckley & Bosworth (40.2%); and Eastleigh (40.0%). In contrast, such commuting is most rare among those who live in the City of London (2.1%, 2.0% excluding mainly home-based workers); Islington (5.1%); Westminster (5.2%); and Camden (5.3%). The biggest comparable (excluding homeworker) reductions have been in Edinburgh (-4.5%); Richmond upon Thames (-4.2%); Ealing (-3.7%); and Kingston upon Thames and Hounslow (both -3.6%). Of all commuters by job type in England and Wales, managers are mostly likely to arrive at work in a car, but so, too, are a majority of those doing the most routine of jobs, such as cleaning the managers' offices.

Drives car or van to work by job type (NS-SeC), England and Wales 2011 %

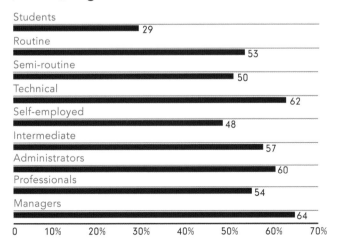

Job type	%
Students	29
Routine	53
Semi-routine	50
Technical	62
Self-employed	48
Intermediate	57
Administrators	60
Professionals	54
Managers	64

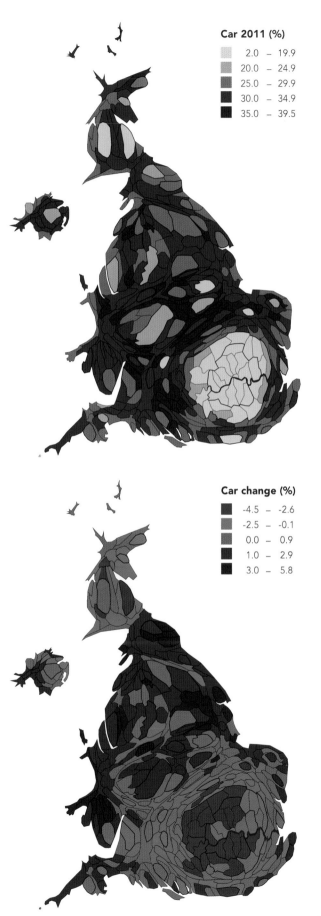

Car 2011 (%)
- 2.0 – 19.9
- 20.0 – 24.9
- 25.0 – 29.9
- 30.0 – 34.9
- 35.0 – 39.5

Car change (%)
- -4.5 – -2.6
- -2.5 – -0.1
- 0.0 – 0.9
- 1.0 – 2.9
- 3.0 – 5.8

HOMEWORKER

In 2001, 2.4 million people living in the UK said they mainly worked from home. By 2011, that number had increased greatly to 3.1 million, a rise of almost 30% in just a decade. Twenty years ago, between 1991 and 2001, one of the more remarkable changes in commuting was the rise in people working from home, a rise that was only just beginning to accelerate then. Before this time most people who worked from home were working on farms or in similar employment. Today we can see that this was just the start of a longer-term trend, although working from home still includes many farmers.

The 10 most popular places to be working from home in 2011 were, largely as a result of farming influences: Isles of Scilly (19.4%); West Somerset (11.2%); Eden (11.0%); Orkney Islands (10.8%); Powys (10.2%); Ryedale (9.9%); West Devon (9.8%); Cotswold (9.6%); and Richmondshire and South Hams (both 9.4%). In contrast, less than 1 in 35 of the residents of the following areas were working from home in 2011: Kingston upon Hull (2.2%); Blaenau Gwent, Middlesbrough and Knowsley (all 2.4%); Sandwell and Barking & Dagenham (both 2.5%); Liverpool and South Tyneside (both 2.6%); Hartlepool (2.7%); and Stoke-on-Trent, Sunderland, Belfast, Torfaen and Leicester (all 2.8%). Places with few farms and also few people in occupations that allow them to work from home, or demand that they do, will have the lowest rates.

Working from home increased the most in places where it is unlikely that university or school students had a great effect: Isles of Scilly (+5.7%); West Somerset (+3.7%); and the City of London and Argyll & Bute (both +3.3%). Where it declined it only fell slightly, by most in Ballymoney (-0.4%) and Banbridge (-0.3%). One key reason for the rise is that so many more people are now self-employed.

Works from home by job type (NS-SeC), England and Wales 2011 %

Job type	Value
Students	6
Routine	4
Semi-routine	4
Technical	4
Self-employed	36
Intermediate	5
Administrators	10
Professionals	12
Managers	9

Working at home 2011 (%)

- 2.2 – 3.9
- 4.0 – 5.9
- 6.0 – 7.9
- 8.0 – 9.9
- 10.0 – 19.4

Working at home change (%)

- -0.4 – -0.1
- 0.0 – 0.4
- 0.5 – 0.9
- 1.0 – 1.9
- 2.0 – 5.7

COMMUTING BY FOOT

Although the increase in commuter car journeys being undertaken in the UK is very large when expressed as billions of trips a year, and more people are working from home and so using no method of transport, there has also been an increase since 2001 in people who commute to work by walking. This does not include people who work from home and who may also walk out of their home as part of their work. It is possible that part of the reason for the increase is people who use more than one mode of transport by 2011, stressing the walking element that is now promoted as more valuable for our health. Nevertheless, in 2001, 2.8 million people walked to work, and by 2011, 2.9 million did so, a rise of 4% in a decade and a reversal of decade after decade in which walking to work became less and less commonly reported. A small part of the increase might be that more students are included in these statistics if they also have a job, but another important reason might be that it is often quicker to walk than to sit in traffic jams.

The greatest increases in the proportion of local populations walking to work were recorded in Tower Hamlets (+2.2%); Exeter (+2.0%); Lincoln (+1.9%); Brighton & Hove and Bristol (both +1.8%); Manchester (+1.7%); York (+1.6%); Southampton, Hackney and Ipswich (all +1.5%); Liverpool (+1.4%); and Salford, Barrow-in-Furness, Cardiff and Oxford (all +12%). More than a tenth of the population now walk to work in the City of London (29.5%); Isles of Scilly (15.5%); Norwich (10.8%); Exeter (10.7%); and Brighton & Hove (10.0%). The fewest walkers are found in East Renfrewshire (1.6%); Ballymoney and Limavady (both 1.8%); and Dungannon, East Dorset and Armagh (all 2.1%). Nationally it is students who are most likely to walk (although they may be walking to a part-time job), and it is the self-employed, especially those men (and a few women) who own white vans, who are least likely to do so.

Commutes on foot by job type (NS-SeC), England and Wales 2011 %

Students — 21
Routine — 15
Semi-routine — 17
Technical — 10
Self-employed — 3
Intermediate — 11
Administrators — 7
Professionals — 6
Managers — 5

0   5%   10%   15%   20%   25%

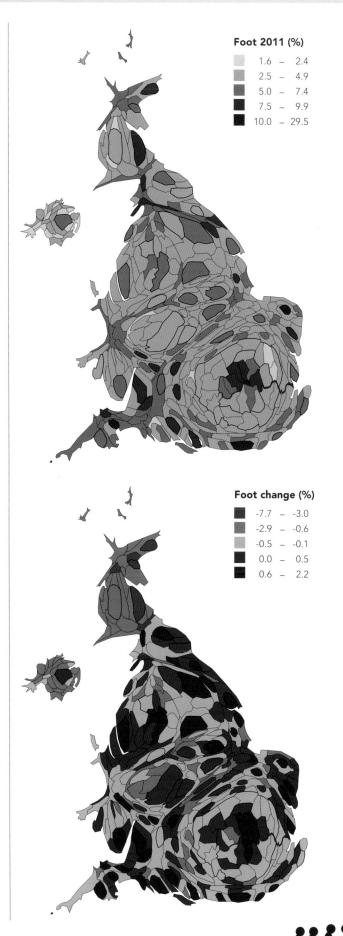

Foot 2011 (%)
- 1.6 – 2.4
- 2.5 – 4.9
- 5.0 – 7.4
- 7.5 – 9.9
- 10.0 – 29.5

Foot change (%)
- -7.7 – -3.0
- -2.9 – -0.6
- -0.5 – -0.1
- 0.0 – 0.5
- 0.6 – 2.2

COMMUTING BY BUS

In 2011 the third most popular method of getting to work or study in the UK was to go by bus or coach. This is still the case, although more people are now homeworkers than bus commuters for the first time in many decades. In 2011, 2.2 million people used this form of transport, or a minibus, to get to work, up just slightly from 2.1 million in 2001. In both 2001 and 2011 the Census question in Scotland included asking explicitly about the method of travel for those who were studying, including schoolchildren. Partly because the number of students studying in Scotland rose, deterred by university fees in England, and because more people began to mainly work at home, commuting by bus appeared to fall in popularity in Scotland, possibly by more than it really did.

If we include people who say they mainly work at home but who also use a bus for commuting, between 1 in 7 and 1 in 14 of the entire population of the following areas commute by bus to work most days: Southwark (13.6%, or 13.2% excluding homeworkers); Hackney (12.8%); Edinburgh (11.9%); Lambeth and Islington (both 10.8%); Manchester (9.5%); Brent (8.7%); Midlothian (8.6%); Haringey (8.5%); Lewisham (8.4%); Liverpool and Hounslow (both 8.3%); Nottingham (8.1%); Newcastle upon Tyne (7.9%); Wandsworth (7.7%); Hammersmith & Fulham (7.6%); Oxford, Greenwich and Westminster (all 7.5%); Camden and Glasgow (both 7.3%); Gateshead and Brighton & Hove (both 7.0%); Ealing and Croydon (both 6.9%); Birmingham (6.8%); and Leeds (6.7%). The place you would have found the fewest in 2011 was the Isles of Scilly (0.4%); followed by Cookstown in Northern Ireland (0.4%); Powys in Wales (0.5%); and Rutland in England (0.5%); with the Cotswolds (0.6%) and Chilterns (0.7%) not far behind. The largest increases in bus use have all been recorded in London, led by Southwark (+3.9%, or +3.4% excluding homeworkers); Lambeth (+3.6%); Brent (+2.9%); and Haringey (+2.8%). After students, those most likely to use the bus are in semi-routine, routine or intermediate work.

Commutes by bus/coach by job type (NS-SeC), England and Wales 2011 %

Job type	%
Students	16
Routine	10
Semi-routine	13
Technical	7
Self-employed	2
Intermediate	9
Administrators	5
Professionals	4
Managers	3

0   2%   4%   6%   8%   10%   12%   14%   16%   18%

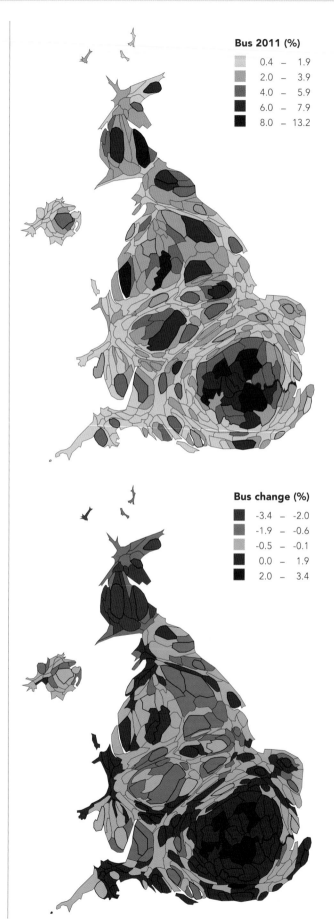

Bus 2011 (%)
0.4 – 1.9
2.0 – 3.9
4.0 – 5.9
6.0 – 7.9
8.0 – 13.2

Bus change (%)
-3.4 – -2.0
-1.9 – -0.6
-0.5 – -0.1
0.0 – 1.9
2.0 – 3.4

COMMUTING BY TRAIN

In 2011, 1.4 million people were commuting by train daily. A further 0.1 million people who mainly worked from home used the train when they did travel for work. Professionals and managers are the two occupational groups most likely to commute by train, which may well explain why this form of commuting is often given more prominence than travelling by bus, despite bus travel being far more common. However, in 2001 only 1.1 million people commuted to work by train, and so there is a huge increase in the popularity, or necessity, of this form of transport. The residential areas where the greatest concentrations of rail commuters lived in 2011, including here commuters who mostly work from home, were all in London, led by Bromley (15.1%, or 14.7% excluding those who work at home); Lewisham (13.9%); and Bexley (11.9%). Just outside of London the highest proportions of commuters are found in Brentwood (11.4%); Epsom & Ewell and Elmbridge (both 10.3%); Sevenoaks (9.7%); St Albans (9.6%); Tandridge (9.1%); Dartford (8.8%); Woking (8.2%); and Basildon (7.9%).

In a continuation of the trend seen since 1991, the greatest increases in rail commuting have been experienced all outside of Greater London by the nearby residents of Elmbridge and Tandridge (both +2.2%); Epsom & Ewell (+2.1%); Woking (+1.9%); and Reigate & Banstead and North Hertfordshire (both + 1.8%). In all these places the increase is between 0.2% and 0.4% if homeworkers who occasionally commute are included, but this assumes no such part-time commuters in 2001, so it is not a good comparison. The declines in train commuting include absolute declines in West Dunbartonshire (-1.4%) and East Renfrewshire (-0.8%), which will not simply be caused by definition change there or a growing number of local people studying at school or university. In England, the largest declines (even including homeworkers in 2011 who occasionally travel for work by train) have been in Castle Point (-0.2%); Sunderland, Oldham and Ashfield (all -0.1%); North East Lincolnshire (-0.02%); and East Lindsey, Great Yarmouth and Mansfield (all -0.01%).

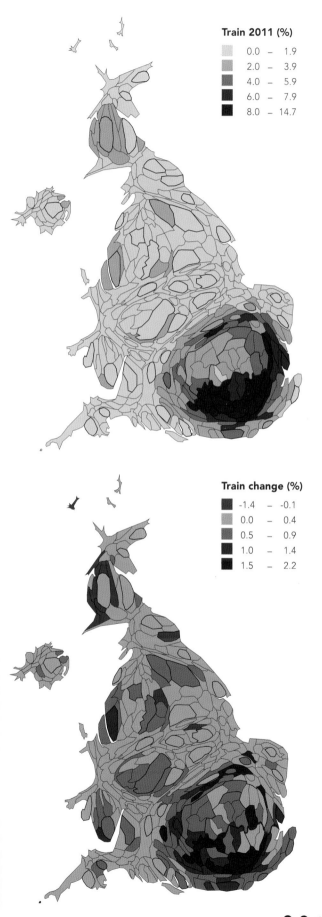

Train 2011 (%)

- 0.0 – 1.9
- 2.0 – 3.9
- 4.0 – 5.9
- 6.0 – 7.9
- 8.0 – 14.7

Train change (%)

- -1.4 – -0.1
- 0.0 – 0.4
- 0.5 – 0.9
- 1.0 – 1.4
- 1.5 – 2.2

Commutes by train, underground, tram or light rail, by job type (NS-SeC), England and Wales 2011 %

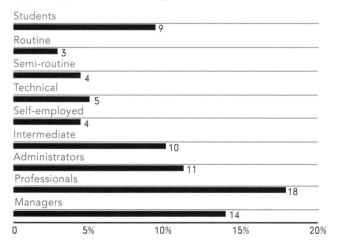

Job type	%
Students	9
Routine	3
Semi-routine	4
Technical	5
Self-employed	4
Intermediate	10
Administrators	11
Professionals	18
Managers	14

0   5%   10%   15%   20%

COMMUTING BY UNDERGROUND

By 2011, 1.0 million people in the UK were commuting each day by underground, metro, light rail or tram. In 2001 the numbers had been just 0.7 million and thus, proportionately (which is not far off a 50% increase), some of the greatest changes of all travel to work occurred in the 2000s for light rail and underground travellers. Almost everywhere became more crowded. The exceptions to this rule were in Glasgow, where the underground was being modernised during Census taking, with Hillhead station not being fully open again until 2012. As a result of such temporary set-backs (and more people walking in the very centre of London), the following areas saw overall falls in use between the 2001 and 2011 Censuses: City of London (-1.1%); Glasgow (-0.6%); Wyre (-0.2%); and Blackpool, Renfrewshire, East Renfrewshire, East Dunbartonshire and West Dunbartonshire (all -0.1%).

When those who work from home but who use this mode for work travel are included, the greatest concentrations of light rail and underground commuters lived in the following areas in 2011: Hammersmith & Fulham (21.4%, 20.7% with homeworkers); Kensington & Chelsea (18.7%); Tower Hamlets (18.6%); Haringey (17.8%); Newham (17.1%); Camden (16.9%); and Westminster and Lambeth (16.8%). Outside of London, use is greatest among those who live in nearby Epping Forest (9.5%) and Three Rivers (5.3%); and then further away where the Metro runs in North Tyneside (4.3%); South Tyneside (3.9%); Newcastle upon Tyne (2.3%); and Gateshead (2.2%). The next highest use is found where there are relatively new trams in Trafford (2.5%); Bury (2.3%); and Sheffield (1.5%). The largest increases in the 2000s were all in London led by Newham (+5.8%); Tower Hamlets (+4.0%); Greenwich (+3.6%); Lewisham (+ 3.0%); and Waltham Forest (+2.8%). Since 2011 the number of passengers travelling on the London underground has continued to steadily rise and rise, as has the distance they travel in total each year.

Passengers travelling by underground, Great Britain 2010–2014 billions of kilometres

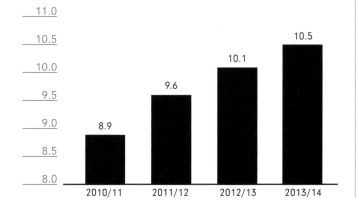

Year	Billions of kilometres
2010/11	8.9
2011/12	9.6
2012/13	10.1
2013/14	10.5

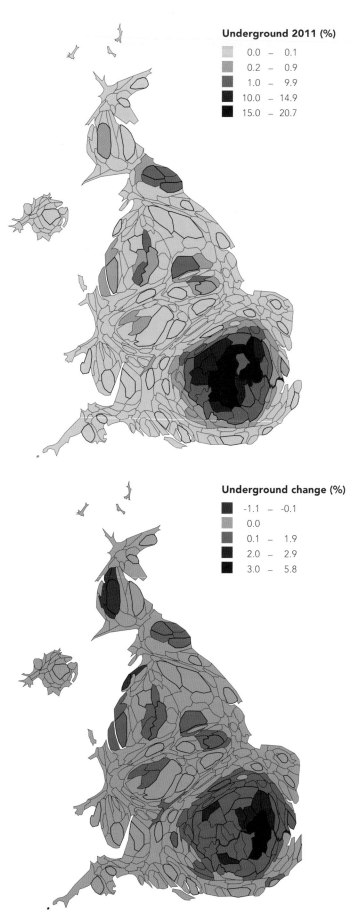

Underground 2011 (%)

- 0.0 – 0.1
- 0.2 – 0.9
- 1.0 – 9.9
- 10.0 – 14.9
- 15.0 – 20.7

Underground change (%)

- -1.1 – -0.1
- 0.0
- 0.1 – 1.9
- 2.0 – 2.9
- 3.0 – 5.8

COMMUTING BY BICYCLE

Commuting by bicycle is often portrayed as increasing, but in most places it is becoming more and more rare. However, because of increases in popularity in a few areas, the overall rate of cycling is increasing slightly, from 2.4% of workers' journeys in 2001 to 2.6% in 2011 (and by a further 0.1% if home-based workers who occasionally use a bike for work travel are included). In absolute numbers this rise was because in 2001, 0.7 million cycled to and from work everyday in the UK, and by 2011 that had increased to 0.8 million. Small falls in cycling are found in many places as fewer children learn to ride a bicycle and more adults gain access to a cheap car. The largest falls have been in Boston (-1.5%); Moray (-1.3%); Kingston upon Hull (-1.1%); Fenland, Peterborough and Waveney (all -0.9%); North Norfolk and North East Lincolnshire (both -0.8%); and North Lincolnshire, Rushmoor, North Kesteven, Rutland, South Holland, Sedgemoor and Breckland (all -0.7%).

The small but widespread falls outweighed the large rises in just 20 areas: Hackney (+4.6%, or 4.2% excluding home-based workers); Islington (+2.8%); Cambridge (+2.6%); Isles of Scilly, Lambeth and the City of London (all +2.4%); Wandsworth and Southwark (both +2.2%); Tower Hamlets (+2.1%); Hammersmith & Fulham and Bristol (both +1.7%); Camden (+1.5%); Oxford (+1.4%); Haringey (+1.3%); Brighton & Hove, Richmond upon Thames and Kensington & Chelsea (all +1.2%); Lewisham and Westminster (both +1.1%); and Exeter (+1.0%). In the next area of highest increase the rise is much less: South Cambridgeshire (+0.6%). The areas of the UK with the highest rates of cycling in 2011 were: Cambridge (14.3%, 3.9% excluding home-based workers); Isles of Scilly (9.5%); Oxford (8.1%); Hackney (7.0%); and York (5.7%). In Northern Ireland cycling is now most rare in Magherafelt (0.1%); in Scotland in Inverclyde (0.1%); in Wales in Merthyr Tydfil (0.1%); and in England in Barnsley (0.3%). In most places cycling is becoming less common; although 4.0% of workers in routine occupations across England and Wales still cycle to work, that proportion is falling, and may soon be overtaken by a higher proportion of professionals cycling.

Commutes by bicycle by job type (NS-SeC), England and Wales 2011 %

Students
3.4

Routine
4.0

Semi-routine
3.4

Technical
3.8

Self-employed
0.9

Intermediate
2.0

Administrators
2.6

Professionals
3.6

Managers
2.5

0%   1%   2%   3%   4%   5%

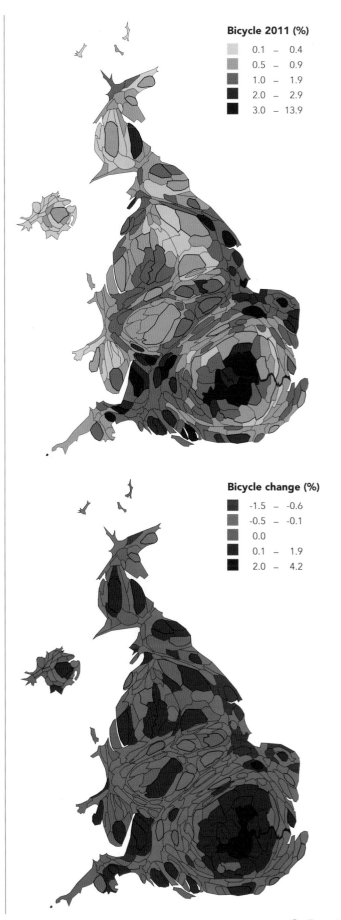

Bicycle 2011 (%)

	0.1 – 0.4
	0.5 – 0.9
	1.0 – 1.9
	2.0 – 2.9
	3.0 – 13.9

Bicycle change (%)

	-1.5 – -0.6
	-0.5 – -0.1
	0.0
	0.1 – 1.9
	2.0 – 4.2

COMMUTING BY MOTORCYCLE

Only 0.2 million people commuted to work by motorbike, moped or motor scooter in 2011, down from 0.3 million in 2001, and falling far quicker than cycling in most of the country while increasing in a few places where parking a car can be difficult. By 2011 the highest rates of motorbike use were recorded in the Isles of Scilly (1.7%, 1.5% excluding home-based workers); Wandsworth, Hammersmith & Fulham and Gosport (all 1.2%); Kensington & Chelsea (1.1%); Plymouth and Richmond upon Thames (both 0.9%); Barrow-in-Furness, Lambeth, Weymouth & Portland, Sutton and Spelthorne (all 0.8%); and Kingston upon Thames, Isle of Wight, South Gloucestershire, Poole, Dartford, Merton, Torbay, Epsom & Ewell, Broadland and Fareham (all 0.7%).

The five areas of the UK that had increases in people using this means of commuting to work in the 2000s are almost all in London: Kensington & Chelsea (+0.3%, +0.2% excluding home-based workers); Isles of Scilly (+0.2%); and Hammersmith & Fulham, Haringey and Brent (all +0.1%). Contrast these with the many more areas of large decreases in motorcycle and moped use: Swindon and York (-0.4%); Broxbourne, Bexley, Boston, Craigavon, Rushmoor, Barking & Dagenham, Taunton Deane, Lisburn, Fareham, Ards, South Holland, Castlereagh, South Somerset and North Down (all -0.3%), and a further 106 areas with a fall of 0.2% in the proportion of local residents using a motorbike to get to work.

It is very likely that the overall decline in riding motorcycles has continued since 2011 as the number of motorcycle fatalities has continued to decline since 2010, apart from in the most recent year for which records are available (2013). In between Census years it is hard to know the possible reasons for any changes in road crash fatalities and how they are linked to wider changes in society. To begin to understand these changes, nuances such as increasing numbers of people becoming self-employed and officially working from home, but still travelling for work purposes, become more and more important to factor in.

Road crash fatalities of motorcyclists, Great Britain 2010–2013

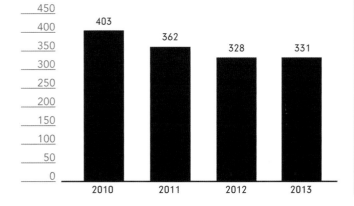

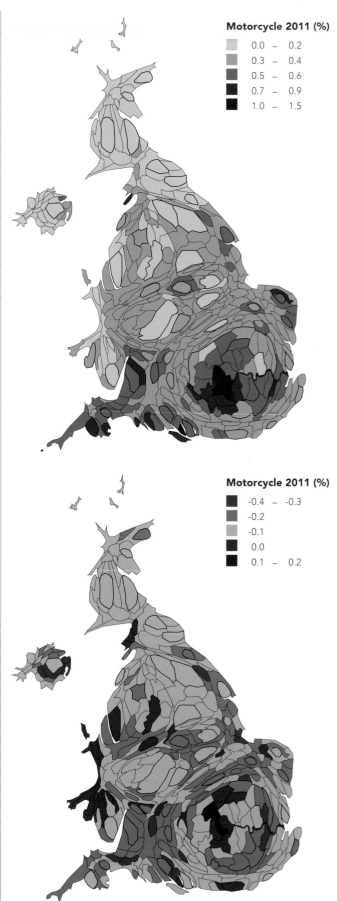

Motorcycle 2011 (%)

	0.0 – 0.2
	0.3 – 0.4
	0.5 – 0.6
	0.7 – 0.9
	1.0 – 1.5

Motorcycle 2011 (%)

	-0.4 – -0.3
	-0.2
	-0.1
	0.0
	0.1 – 0.2

OTHER METHOD OF COMMUTING

There are many other ways in which people can get to work that don't involve a conventional form of transport. In 2011, 0.2 million people travelled to work by a method not yet mapped and also not by taxi (which is mapped below). This is a rapid increase from a little over 0.1 million in 2001. The most common alternative method of travel to work is by boat, ferry or water taxi. This becomes obvious once these areas in which people are more likely to be travelling by alternative methods are listed in order: Isles of Scilly (2.6%, 2.1% excluding home-based workers); Orkney Islands (2.1%); Eilean Siar (2.0%); Aberdeenshire (1.8%); Moray (1.6%); Richmondshire and Shetland Islands (both 1.4%, and both possibly also involving helicopters and planes including for travel to oil rigs); Aberdeen (1.3%); Great Yarmouth, Isle of Wight and Angus (all 1.0%); City of London and South Tyneside (both 0.9%); Highland, Argyll & Bute and Kensington & Chelsea (all 0.8%); Waveney, Westminster and Gosport (all 0.7%); and South Hams and Inverclyde (both 0.6%).

The greatest increases have been in the Isles of Scilly (+1.3%, but only +0.6% excluding home-based workers); Eilean Siar (+0.6%); Moray and Orkney Islands (both +0.4%); and Richmondshire, Kensington & Chelsea and Greenwich (all +0.3%). Although all these small changes are interesting, it is worth remembering that they are dwarfed by the commuting behaviour of the large majority of the population.

The graph below shows how the Census reveals that almost one in seven of all students get to work or study as a passenger in a car or van each day, being driven by someone else – often a parent or another student as people aged 16 and above are included here. Less than 1 in 50 professionals or managers travel to work sharing a vehicle in that way.

Commutes as passenger in car or van, by job type (NS-SeC), England and Wales 2011 %

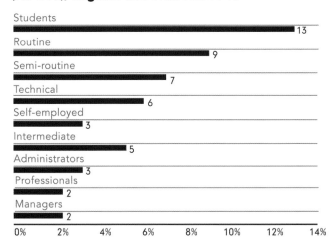

Job type	%
Students	13
Routine	9
Semi-routine	7
Technical	6
Self-employed	3
Intermediate	5
Administrators	3
Professionals	2
Managers	2

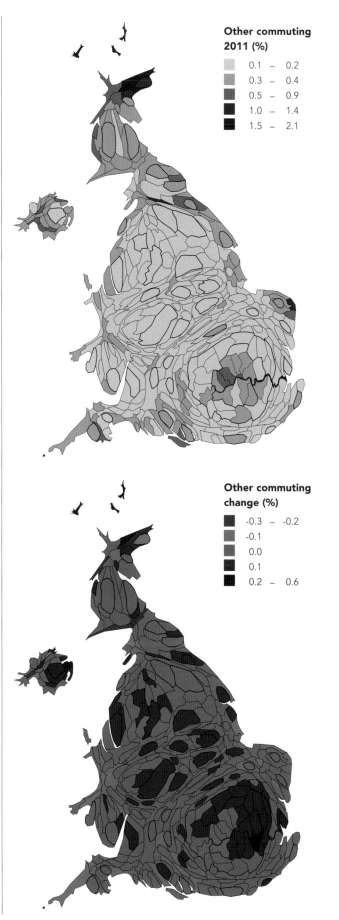

Other commuting 2011 (%)

- 0.1 – 0.2
- 0.3 – 0.4
- 0.5 – 0.9
- 1.0 – 1.4
- 1.5 – 2.1

Other commuting change (%)

- -0.3 – -0.2
- -0.1
- 0.0
- 0.1
- 0.2 – 0.6

COMMUTING BY TAXI

The least common way to get to work in the UK is by taxi. In 2011, 0.16 million people commuted this way, and 0.1% of that total were home-based workers. Many might be working unsocial hours and a taxi is the only way they can get home. In 2001, 0.15 million people used a taxi or a minicab to get to work. It can be a form of transport that is used disproportionally by those who cannot afford to run a car or who cannot drive because they have no driving licence. An increasing number of younger people in the UK have no car. Getting one may also be getting less attractive, both financially, with high insurance premiums for young drivers, and practically, if it is difficult to park near where they live or work.

The greatest increases in using taxis to get to work, as recorded between the Censuses, were in Middlesbrough (+0.4%, or +0.3% excluding home-based workers); Barrow-in-Furness (+0.3%); and Bolton, Antrim, Stoke-on-Trent, Hyndburn, Milton Keynes, Wakefield, Kirklees, Bradford, Merthyr Tydfil, Dungannon, Knowsley and Liverpool (all +0.2%). The largest reduction was in the City of London (-0.5%, although it is still the largest reduction, but only of -0.2%, if home-based workers are excluded). Clearly getting a taxi is no longer the preserve of the wealthy.

For some time using cheaper taxis to get to work in Northern Ireland has been more common than in the rest of the UK. Using a taxi to get to work in 2011 was most usual in Derry (1.2%); Belfast (1.1%); Kensington & Chelsea (1.0%); Antrim and Knowsley (both 0.9%); Blackburn with Darwen and Hartlepool (both 0.8%); and Westminster, Rochdale, Lisburn, Middlesbrough and Corby (all 0.7%). Rarely are such places all in the same list. When the Great Recession began, national estimates suggested that there was a sudden increase in taxi drivers as the graph below shows, but their numbers fell back below 200,000 in 2013. This count includes those who also work as chauffeurs that, interestingly, have been in steady decline since 2008.

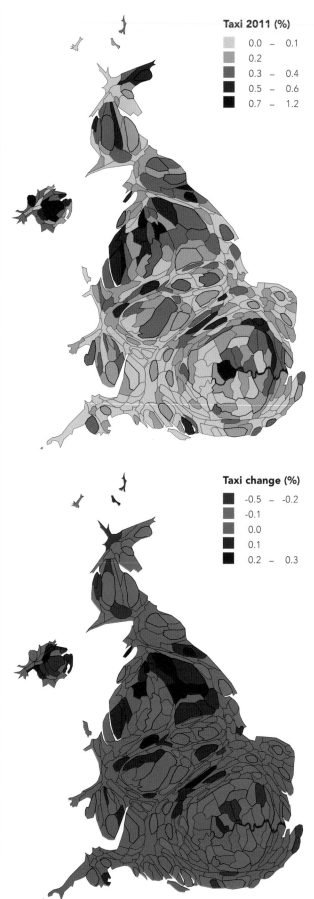

Taxi 2011 (%)

	0.0 – 0.1
	0.2
	0.3 – 0.4
	0.5 – 0.6
	0.7 – 1.2

Taxi change (%)

	-0.5 – -0.2
	-0.1
	0.0
	0.1
	0.2 – 0.3

People employed as taxi drivers and chauffeurs, Great Britain 2003–2014 thousands

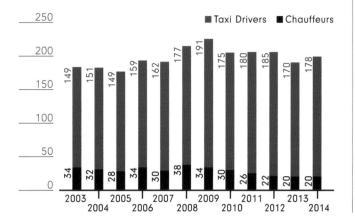

■ Taxi Drivers ■ Chauffeurs

OWNED OUTRIGHT

Moving from how people get to work to where they sleep at night, the Census is the main source of data on how people in the UK pay for their housing. When housing becomes more expensive, this can result in changing patterns of commuting, as workers often have to live further from where they work. In 2011, just over 15.9 million, mostly older, people owned the home they lived in outright; they had no debts to pay off on their home (on a mortgage at least), and no rent to pay. In 2001, that number had been 14.0 million. The increase was due to more older people coming to the end of their mortgage terms than the number of very elderly people who owned outright who were dying or moving to other tenures, and leaving a home that would usually be sold on the private market to become a rental or mortgaged property. The largest local increases in outright ownership were mostly in more remote areas: in the Isles of Scilly (+6.8%); East Dunbartonshire (+6.6%); Copeland (+6.3%); Inverclyde and Carrickfergus (both +5.8%); Moray and East Ayrshire (both +5.6%); and West Lothian (+5.5%). In contrast, the largest falls were often in better connected areas where many properties were being bought by landlords after the owners died or left the area: Bournemouth (-3.5%); Enfield and Slough (both -2.9%); Hammersmith & Fulham and Barnet (both -2.8%); Brent, Ealing and Barking & Dagenham (all -2.5%); Oxford (-2.4%); Newham (-2.3%); and Reading, Redbridge and Brighton & Hove (all -2.2%).

Outright ownership is now most common in Eilean Siar (41.7%) and the Orkney Islands (40.2%), and least common in Tower Hamlets (6.6%) and Hackney and Southwark (both 8.1%). Although the number of dwellings in the UK continues to rise, this rise is not keeping pace with new household formation. In 2010 an extra two-thirds of a per cent of property was added to the UK housing stock as new build exceeded demolitions. As the graph below shows, that rate of new building slowed down, and only just over an extra half a percentage point of the stock was added in 2013, net.

Owned outright 2011 (%)
- 6.6 – 19.9
- 20.0 – 24.9
- 25.0 – 29.9
- 30.0 – 34.9
- 25.0 – 41.7

Owned outright change (%)
- -3.5 – -2.0
- -1.9 – -0.1
- 0.0 – 1.9
- 2.0 – 3.9
- 4.0 – 6.8

All dwellings, net annual change, UK %

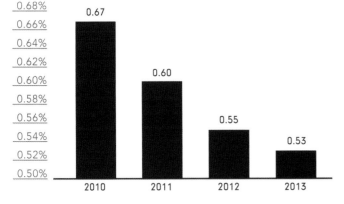

	2010	2011	2012	2013
	0.67	0.60	0.55	0.53

MORTGAGED

Having a mortgage here includes having a loan that, even if you pay it all off, will only ensure you have part ownership of a property. This is called *shared ownership*, a combination of buying and renting, and it is becoming increasingly popular because the cost of property in many areas is now so high. The number of people living in a home on which they had a mortgage fell from 27.0 million in 2001 to 25.0 million in 2011. That fall of 2 million people occurred at a time when the overall population was rising, especially of those in middle age who might be expected to have mortgages. The largest and most dramatic falls were recorded in Luton (-12.0%); Slough (-10.9%); Enfield (-10.8%); Milton Keynes (-10.7%); Brent (-10.6%); Eastleigh (-10.4%); Medway (-10.2%); Redditch (-10.1%); and Harrow (-10.0%). Nowhere experienced a rise, with the slowest declines being in Southwark (-0.4%); Falkirk (-0.6%); Strabane (-1.3%); and Barnsley (-1.5%).

By 2011 there were only 10 areas where more than half the population lived in a mortgaged property, and even then in each case it was only just a majority: East Renfrewshire (54.0%); Wokingham (52.3%); Blaby (52.1%); Carrickfergus (51.7%); East Dunbartonshire and Newtownabbey (both 51.0%); Rochford and South Northamptonshire (both 50.9%); Hart (50.5%); and Castlereagh (50.3%). By 2011 less than a fifth of the population lived in a mortgaged property in the Isles of Scilly (12.5%); Westminster (13.7%); Kensington & Chelsea (15.0%); Camden (16.1%); Tower Hamlets (16.5%); Hackney (17.7%); Islington (18.3%); and the City of London (18.8%). Nationally the proportion of dwellings that are both owned outright and mortgaged by their occupiers has fallen rapidly since 2010, from just under two-thirds of all dwellings to less than 63.5% in 2013. As yet there is no sign of a slowdown in this fall, and it is all due to the decline in the number of those with a mortgage.

Owner occupied dwellings, UK %

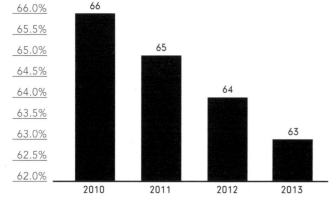

	2010	2011	2012	2013
	66	65	64	63

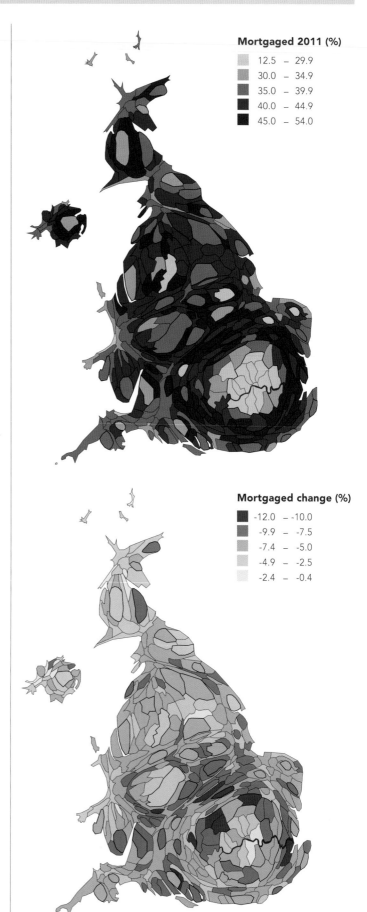

Mortgaged 2011 (%)

- 12.5 – 29.9
- 30.0 – 34.9
- 35.0 – 39.9
- 40.0 – 44.9
- 45.0 – 54.0

Mortgaged change (%)

- -12.0 – -10.0
- -9.9 – -7.5
- -7.4 – -5.0
- -4.9 – -2.5
- -2.4 – -0.4

LOCAL AUTHORITY HOUSING

After owning the property you live in outright (a tenure group that grew by 1.9 million people between Censuses) and living in a home on which your family is paying a mortgage and might eventually own (a group that shrunk by 2.0 million people), the next largest tenure group in the UK is made up of people living in a household where the home is rented from the Local Authority or, in the case of Northern Ireland, the Housing Executive. In 2001, 7.6 million people lived in Local Authority housing in the UK. By 2011 that number had fallen to 5.7 million, a massive drop of 1.9 million, or a quarter of all Local Authority stock in just 10 years, bringing the total *decline* in the numbers of people living in owner-occupied or state-owned housing in the UK to a *net* fall of 2.0 million in 10 years in these, the traditionally largest three, tenures.

Local Authority housing is not in decline everywhere, partly because there is a little building going on, but mainly because in some areas when housing associations fail the dwellings the associations are responsible for are often transferred to the care of the local council. However, Right to Buy purchases mean that the overall proportion of people living in this tenure has continued to decline rapidly between 2010 and 2013. The largest declines in the 2000s were where almost all the stock was transferred to a housing association between Census years: Glasgow (-23.6%) and Inverclyde (-22.2%); or where the Right to Buy has been exercised and then the bulk of the properties sold on to private landlords, while some older flats have been emptied and demolished with the new land going to the private sector: Tower Hamlets (-21.1%); Manchester (-13.6%); Liverpool (-11.7%); and Lewisham (-11.2%).

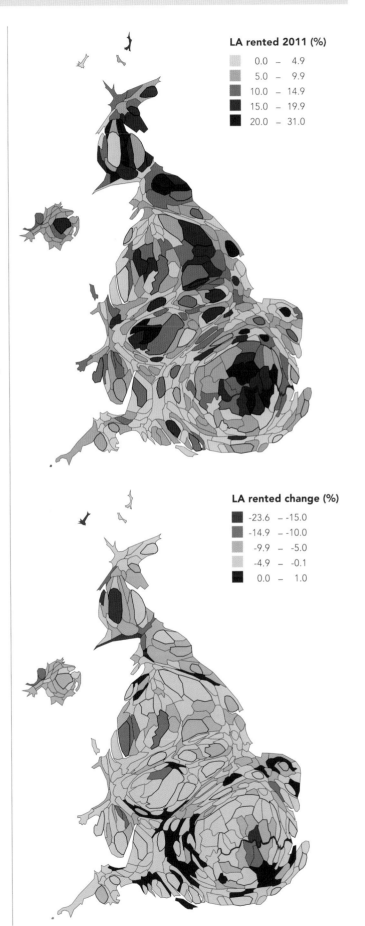

LA rented 2011 (%)
- 0.0 – 4.9
- 5.0 – 9.9
- 10.0 – 14.9
- 15.0 – 19.9
- 20.0 – 31.0

LA rented change (%)
- -23.6 – -15.0
- -14.9 – -10.0
- -9.9 – -5.0
- -4.9 – -0.1
- 0.0 – 1.0

Local Authority dwellings, UK %

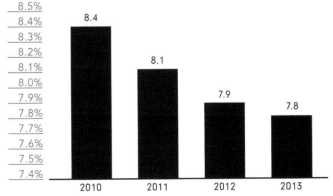

2010: 8.4, 2011: 8.1, 2012: 7.9, 2013: 7.8

HOUSING ASSOCIATIONS

Housing associations have grown rapidly in the 2000s, providing homes for 4.7 million people by 2011 compared to housing just 3.1 million people in 2001. A few decades before this, they housed a negligible proportion of the population of the UK and were a tenure that was almost disappearing. Their growth, which is mostly in England and Scotland, has been due to the national (Westminster) government's distrust of Local Authorities as landlords, and so this semi-private, in theory not-for-profit, sector, has been aided by considerable state intervention over recent years, most obviously when the entire stock of local councils is transferred to a housing association so that the local council no longer manages that stock.

By 2011 the highest proportions of local people housed by these charities were living in Glasgow (32.9%); Tower Hamlets (23.9%); Inverclyde (23.0%); Hackney (20.0%); Liverpool (19.9%); Scottish Borders (19.5%); Halton (19.1%); Dumfries & Galloway (17.8%); Argyll & Bute (16.7%); Basingstoke & Deane (16.2%); Eilean Siar (16.2%); Manchester (15.5%); Allerdale (14.9%); Kensington & Chelsea (14.8%); Lewisham and Hammersmith & Fulham (both 14.7%); Lambeth and Islington (both 14.6%); and Tameside and Westminster (both 14.0%).

In Glasgow by 2011 a larger proportion of the local population was housed in housing association tenure (32.9%) than in Local Authority housing in the district where that is most common still, which is Southwark (31.0%, down 11.0% on 2001). A 'stock transfer' created the Glasgow Housing Association in 2003. Since 2010 the proportion of the national population housed by these charities has risen, although it appeared to be levelling off in 2013, and in 2015 associations were threatened by the Right to Buy also being imposed on them.

HA rented 2011 (%)
- 0.5 – 4.9
- 5.0 – 9.9
- 10.0 – 14.9
- 15.0 – 19.9
- 20.0 – 32.9

HA rented change (%)
- -2.3 – -0.1
- 0.0 – 2.4
- 2.5 – 4.9
- 5.0 – 9.9
- 10.0 – 20.7

Housing association dwellings, UK %

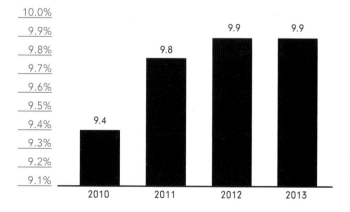

	2010	2011	2012	2013
	9.4	9.8	9.9	9.9

PRIVATE RENTING

Although housing associations saw a net increase in tenants of 1.6 million over the course of the 2000s, this was dwarfed by the rise in the number of people who were privately renting by 2011, 10.1 million, compared to 5.1 million private renters in 2001. A rise of 5 million tenants in just 10 years is unprecedented. Even those hardened to surprises in Census data have described the revealed increase as 'amazing'. By 2012 the continuation of this rise and the continued decline in Local Authority rented housing meant that more people were renting from private landlords than from all charities and the state combined. In 2001 there was twice as much social rented housing as private rented housing; a decade earlier almost three times as much. Since council housing was first built in the UK, most has now been privatised, and much of that stock is now in the hands of private landlords. The largest rises in the 2000s in private renting were recorded in Newham (+19.6%); Tower Hamlets (+16.1%); Slough (+15.6%); Brent (+14.7%); Hackney (+14.4%); Enfield (+14.3%); and Barking & Dagenham and Waltham Forest (both +14.0%). The only decline and the smallest rises have been recorded on islands, especially where the law on crofting changed in Scotland: Isles of Scilly (-0.7%); Eilean Siar (+0.5%); Orkney Islands (+1.6%); and Shetland Islands (+1.9%).

Private renting remains least common in parts of Scotland, although everywhere at least 1 in 20 people are now the tenant of a private landlord: East Renfrewshire (5.0%); East Dunbartonshire (5.2%); and West Dunbartonshire (5.8%). It is now the most common tenure in central London, and in most London areas at least an extra percentage point of property transfers to private landlords a year. The highest rates are found in Westminster (37.5%); Newham (37.1%); Wandsworth and the City of London (both 33.4%); and Kensington & Chelsea and Hammersmith & Fulham (both 33.3%). Within two or three years, one of these areas will become majority private renting if the current increase continues. Nationally there has been no slowdown since 2010 in the rise of private landlords and their tenants. If anything, the increase slightly accelerated in the most recent year for which there is data (2013).

Privately rented dwellings, UK %

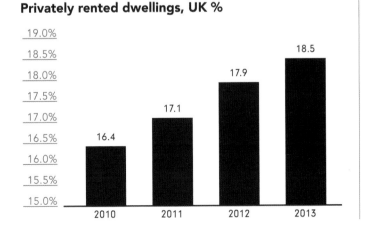

Private rented 2011 (%)

5.0 – 9.9
10.0 – 14.9
15.0 – 19.9
20.0 – 24.9
25.0 – 37.5

Private rented change (%)

-0.7
0.0 – 4.9
5.0 – 9.9
10.0 – 14.9
15.0 – 19.6

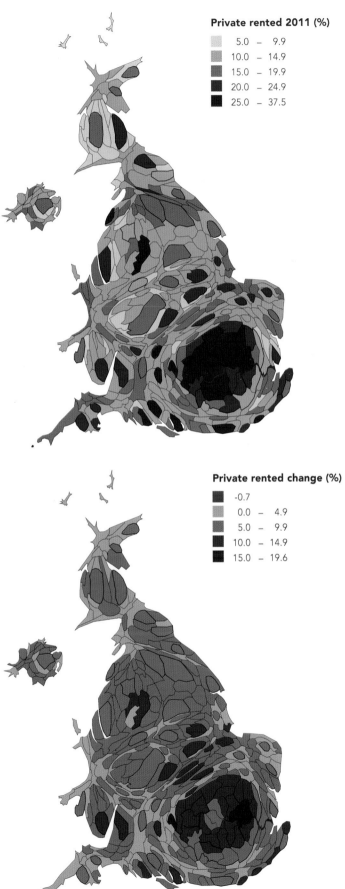

RENT FREE

Finally we look at a very small and dwindling proportion of the population of the UK who do not own where they live but who live rent free by dint of their occupation. This could have included many clergy in the past and sometimes firefighters and nurses who might have been given accommodation or just somewhere to sleep in a dormitory very near where they were required to work. Members of the armed forces (not living in communal barracks) or school teachers in private boarding schools and vice chancellors in universities might have been given grace-and-favour housing, or might still enjoy it. The prime minister, chancellor and a few other senior government officials, as well as many members of the royal family, live, in effect, rent free in some of their homes. You can also live rent free if a friend or relative chooses not to charge you rent. Servants, hotel and holiday park staff and on-site caretakers may also be housed in this way.

Across all of the UK, 1.0 million people lived rent free in 2001. This fell to 0.7 million by 2011. The areas with the most people living rent free in 2011 were the Isles of Scilly (9.2%); City of London (4.4%); Forest Heath (3.9%); Kensington & Chelsea (3.0%); Westminster and the Orkney Islands (both 2.9%); and the Scottish Borders and the Cotswolds (both 2.6%). The largest falls in people renting free probably coincide with the decamping of military barracks and US air force bases, but also people living in council housing whose benefit-covered rent was previously paid directly to the council might have called it rent-free, although technically it was not. These falls have been largest in Forest Heath (-5.2%); Glasgow (-3.0%); and East Ayrshire (-2.5%). Since 2011 there has been a slight increase in the total number of dwellings in the UK owned by government departments (for the police, prison officers, the armed forces and so on), but not in the total number of those owned by Local Authorities.

Rent free 2011 (%)

	0.5 – 0.9
	1.0 – 1.4
	1.5 – 1.9
	2.0 – 2.9
	3.0 – 9.2

Rent free change (%)

	-5.2 – -2.0
	-1.9 – -1.0
	-0.9 – -0.5
	-0.4 – -0.1
	0.0 – 1.0

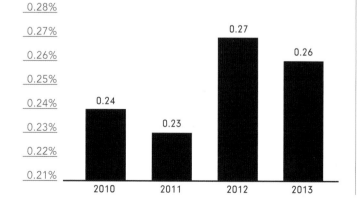

Other public sector dwellings, UK %

Year	Value
2010	0.24
2011	0.23
2012	0.27
2013	0.26

COMMUNAL ESTABLISHMENTS

A significant number of people in the UK do not live in residential dwellings, but in communal establishments such as military barracks, students' halls of residence, prisons, hostels for the homeless, or nursing homes for the ill and infirm. In the previous chapter, the 2011 distribution of the 0.4 million elderly residents aged 65 or over living in these establishments and the change in their distribution since 2001 was shown. Here, all 1.1 million people living in communal establishments in 2011 are mapped, up from 0.96 million in 2001. Some of these people will also live in households for part of the year, such as younger university students who often live with their family out of term time (about 0.25 million appear to live in both communal establishments and households).

The greatest concentrations of communal residents in the UK in 2011 were living in Cambridge (13.3%); Oxford (12.3%); Richmondshire (8.9%); Rutland (8.3%); Lancaster (6.5%); Lincoln (6.1%); Ceredigion (5.9%); Canterbury (5.7%); Nottingham (5.2%); and Exeter (5.1%). All of these are places with university halls of residence, apart from Richmondshire, which contains Catterick garrison, and Rutland, within which lies Stocken prison. The areas experiencing the largest increases in people living in communal establishments (between 2001 and 2011) were Lincoln (+3.9%); Preston and Ceredigion (both +2.3%); Oxford (+2.2%); and Nottingham (+2.0%). The largest decreases have been in areas where a few army barracks, nurses' homes or similar establishments have closed, including in the City of London (-1.2%). The majority of residents of communal establishments are either students or people who have never worked, which may include many young prisoners, as well as many long-term severely disabled people.

Communal establishment residents by job type (NS-SeC), England and Wales 2011 %

Job type	%
Students	38
Long-term unemployed	1
Never worked	22
Routine	8
Semi-routine	7
Technical	4
Self-employed	4
Intermediate	7
Administrators	8
Professionals	2
Managers	1

0%   5%   10%   15%   20%   25%   30%   35%   40%

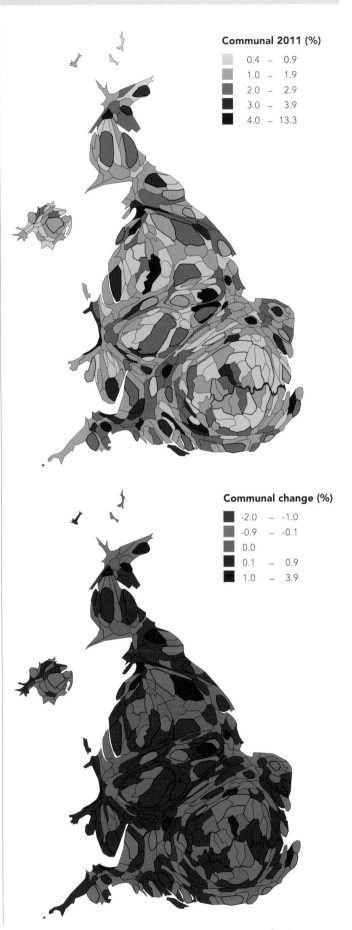

Communal 2011 (%)
- 0.4 – 0.9
- 1.0 – 1.9
- 2.0 – 2.9
- 3.0 – 3.9
- 4.0 – 13.3

Communal change (%)
- -2.0 – -1.0
- -0.9 – -0.1
- 0.0
- 0.1 – 0.9
- 1.0 – 3.9

HOUSES

For the vast majority of the population who live in flats or houses, the availability of such dwellings affects many things, ranging from how overcrowded people are, to the cost of renting or buying. There were 51.6 million people living in houses in the UK in 2011, up from 49.4 million in 2001, and a huge proportion given that only 63.2 million people were living in the UK that year. Of course many other houses will have been empty, some awaiting renovation. Others will have been (and will almost all still be) second or third homes or holiday homes and only occupied part of the year, and these are not counted here as the counting is by residents. They include bungalows, detached, semi-detached and terraced houses. The areas where people are most likely to live in a house are all in Northern Ireland, led by Strabane and Magherafelt (both 97.9%). It is least common to live in a house in London, especially in the City of London (2.7%); Westminster (13.6%); Tower Hamlets (18.5%); Camden (19.1%); and Kensington & Chelsea (22.4%).

The most rapid falls in the share of people living in houses has been where many were converted into flats between the Census years or where houses have been demolished and flats put up in their place, most obviously in Manchester (-6.9%); Cardiff (-6.2%); Lincoln (-5.9%); and Salford (-5.8%). The proportion of people living in houses has increased the most in a few areas where more have been built, especially in Scotland in Argyll & Bute (+2.7%), but also by the wealthiest in England in Kensington & Chelsea (+1.2%), where many houses that in the past had been divided up into flats have now been made very large town houses again. Almost three-quarters of households who live in houses, as opposed to flats, either own them outright or are buying their home with a mortgage.

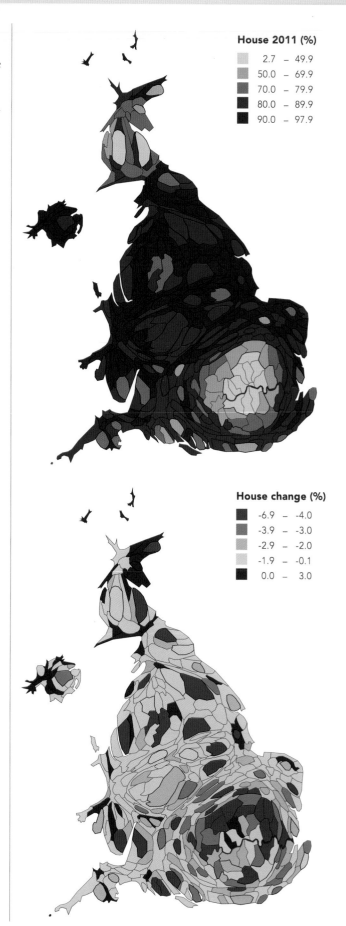

House 2011 (%)

	2.7 – 49.9
	50.0 – 69.9
	70.0 – 79.9
	80.0 – 89.9
	90.0 – 97.9

House change (%)

	-6.9 – -4.0
	-3.9 – -3.0
	-2.9 – -2.0
	-1.9 – -0.1
	0.0 – 3.0

Households in houses by tenure, England and Wales 2011 %

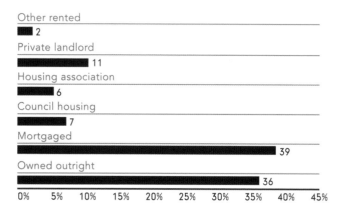

Other rented
2

Private landlord
11

Housing association
6

Council housing
7

Mortgaged
39

Owned outright
36

0%   5%   10%   15%   20%   25%   30%   35%   40%   45%

FLATS

In 2011, 10.1 million people lived in flats, a large increase from 8.1 million in 2001. Part of this increase will have come about as a result of the building of new blocks of flats, and partly due to the conversion of existing houses into flats, but a larger part of the increase is almost certainly due to the greater crowding of people into existing flats as the distribution of people between larger and smaller homes became more uneven over the course of the 2000s. The Census identifies different types of flats by whether they have been created by converting existing dwellings, purpose-built and so on, so further detailed analysis would be possible. By 2011 the most common tenure for those living in flats was to be renting from a private landlord. Living in flats, maisonettes, tenements or other apartments, by 2011, was the norm in the City of London (94.4%); Westminster (82.0%); Tower Hamlets (78.9%); Camden (74.8%); Islington (73.1%); Kensington & Chelsea (72.7%); Hackney (68.8%); Southwark (67.8%); Lambeth (64.3%); Hammersmith & Fulham (63.0%); Glasgow (62.2%); Wandsworth (55.9%); and Edinburgh (54.5%). It was least common across almost all of Northern Ireland, and North Kesteven and Broadland in England (both 2.5%).

The greatest increases in flat occupancy between the 2001 and 2011 Censuses were recorded in Manchester (+6.5%); Watford (+6.4%); Bournemouth (+6.2%); Bristol (+6.0%); Salford (+5.9%); Crawley and Reading (both +5.7%); Slough (+5.6%); Hounslow and Cardiff (both +5.4%); Ipswich (+5.3%); Southampton and Brent (both +5.2%); and Barnet (+5.1%). The largest decreases in local populations living in flats have been in Dundee (-3.1%), where many were demolished, and Kensington & Chelsea (-1.8%), where former subdivided houses have in many cases been turned back into town houses. Only just over a quarter of all flats are owned outright or being bought with a mortgage, even as shared ownership.

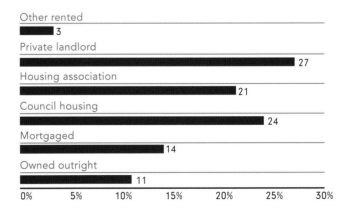

Households in flats by tenure, England and Wales 2011 %

Tenure	%
Other rented	3
Private landlord	27
Housing association	21
Council housing	24
Mortgaged	14
Owned outright	11

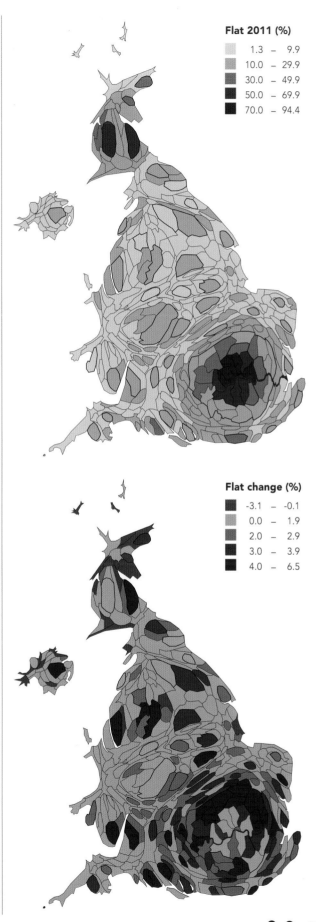

Flat 2011 (%)

	1.3 – 9.9
	10.0 – 29.9
	30.0 – 49.9
	50.0 – 69.9
	70.0 – 94.4

Flat change (%)

	-3.1 – -0.1
	0.0 – 1.9
	2.0 – 2.9
	3.0 – 3.9
	4.0 – 6.5

TEMPORARY DWELLINGS

The number of people living in temporary dwellings has stayed the same between Censuses at 0.16 million, and thus the proportion will have fallen slightly as the population has increased between the two Censuses. These homes include caravans and other mobile structures. Almost half the temporary dwellings in England and Wales are and were privately rented from a landlord. In only just over a quarter of cases do households living in a temporary dwelling own their own temporary home outright. The largest concentrations of people living in temporary dwellings and mobile structures in 2011 were found to be living in Runnymede (2.0%); Castle Point (1.8%); East Dorset (1.6%); Teignbridge (1.4%); Mole Valley, East Lindsey and Wyre Forest (all 1.3%); Tewkesbury, Bracknell Forest, South Staffordshire, Purbeck, Fylde and Wyre (all 1.2%); New Forest, South Bucks and South Oxfordshire (all 1.1%); and Cornwall and Stratford-upon-Avon (1.0%). The largest increases in people living in these kinds of home were recorded in Castle Point (+1.0%); Wyre Forest and Ribble Valley (both +0.5%); and Dover, East Lindsey and West Lancashire (all +0.3%). Castle Point in Essex contains many caravan/mobile home parks, those in Runnymede tend to be smaller, but its population is lower, and since 2012 an eco-village of temporary structures has also been built there.

In many areas, most prominently in Runnymede, attempts to build new caravan parks, or to allow travellers (especially Irish travellers), have been thwarted by local councils who have moved people on. The largest falls in local populations living in temporary accommodation between the Censuses were recorded in Runnymede and Armagh (-0.7%); Tewkesbury (-0.6%); and Dungannon and Newry & Mourne (-0.4%).

Households in temporary acommodation or commercial building by tenure, England and Wales 2011 %

Other rented
12

Private landlord
47

Housing association
2

Council housing
3

Mortgaged
9

Owned outright
27

0%　5%　10%　15%　20%　25%　30%　35%　40%　45%　50%

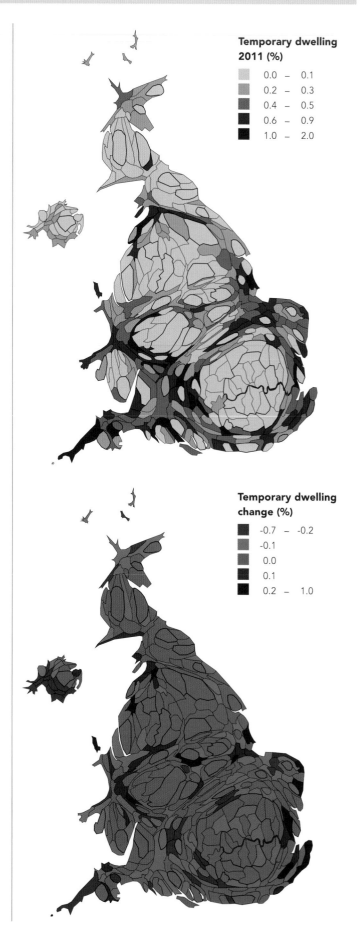

Temporary dwelling 2011 (%)

- 0.0 – 0.1
- 0.2 – 0.3
- 0.4 – 0.5
- 0.6 – 0.9
- 1.0 – 2.0

Temporary dwelling change (%)

- -0.7 – -0.2
- -0.1
- 0.0
- 0.1
- 0.2 – 1.0

SHARED DWELLINGS

As the proportion of people living in temporary dwellings in the UK fell, the proportion of those who are living more than one family to a dwelling rose. The number of people living in households that have to share a dwelling increased from 0.10 million in 2001 to 0.13 million in 2011. It will be much higher now than it was in 2011, as pressures on housing have continued to rise, but the pressure is likely to be greatest in much the same areas as in 2011. The greatest concentrations of sharing in 2011 were all reported in London: Kensington & Chelsea (3.1%); Camden (2.4%); Hackney and Hammersmith & Fulham (both 2.0%); Haringey (1.7%); Westminster and Lambeth (both 1.6%); Islington (1.4%); Brighton & Hove (1.3%); Bournemouth (1.2%); Tower Hamlets (1.1%); and Southwark (1.0%). In the rest of the UK sharing dwellings is most common in Bristol and Eastbourne (0.6%); and Worthing, Hastings, Cambridge, Liverpool, Southampton, Oxford and Shepway (all 0.5%).

In 19 districts, mostly in Northern Ireland, no family is sharing a dwelling with a separate household. The largest increases in sharing a dwelling between 2001 and 2011 were recorded in Kensington & Chelsea (+1.1%); Hammersmith & Fulham (+1.0%); Brighton & Hove and Camden (both +0.7%); Bournemouth and Haringey (both +0.6%); Islington and Lambeth (both +0.4%); Bristol, Liverpool, Wandsworth, Lewisham and Shepway (all +0.3%); and Westminster, Hastings, Hackney, Southwark and Greenwich (all +0.2%). The largest decreases were in areas where local housing officials have often intervened to prevent the illegal letting of unlicensed houses in multiple occupation. These falls in households sharing dwellings between Census years were greatest in Tower Hamlets (-0.4%); Leeds and Dundee (both -0.3%); and Cambridge and Oxford (both -0.2%). A majority of households sharing a dwelling with other households rent privately.

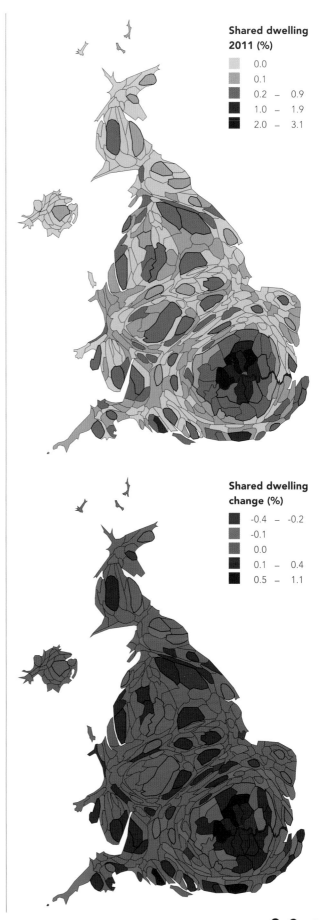

Shared dwelling 2011 (%)

- 0.0
- 0.1
- 0.2 – 0.9
- 1.0 – 1.9
- 2.0 – 3.1

Shared dwelling change (%)

- -0.4 – -0.2
- -0.1
- 0.0
- 0.1 – 0.4
- 0.5 – 1.1

Households in shared dwellings (including bedsits), England and Wales 2011 %

Other rented
4

Private landlord
51

Housing association
10

Council housing
6

Mortgaged
19

Owned outright
10

0%   10%   20%   30%   40%   50%   60%

HAVE A SECOND ADDRESS ELSEWHERE

Finally, when looking at homes and commuting it helps to have an idea of where people who have a second home live, and if those additional homes are used for work purposes, or if they are holiday homes. These are called second addresses and were first carefully enumerated in 2011 when 0.19 million people in England and Wales declared they had a second address elsewhere within England and Wales that they used for work purposes. Many of these people, people who had addresses elsewhere that they said they used for work, lived in quiet, picturesque places at their Sunday Census address. Their first address may include barracks and city flats. Here are the most common places for people saying they had a second address because of work: Richmondshire (1.1%); City of London (1.0%); South Hams, Gosport, North Kesteven and Cotswold (all 0.9%); West Dorset, West Devon, Rutland, Purbeck and North Dorset (all 0.8%); and South Somerset, North Devon, Herefordshire, Gwynedd, Plymouth, Wiltshire and West Somerset (all 0.7%).

A further 0.17 million people living in England and Wales said that the second address was a holiday home and that they lived there for at least 30 days a year. People with these holiday homes more often had first addresses in the City of London (2.9%); Kensington & Chelsea (2.3%); Isles of Scilly (1.3%); Westminster (1.2%); Richmond upon Thames and Hammersmith & Fulham (both 1.1%); and Camden (1.0%).

A remarkable 10.4% of residents of the City of London also had second addresses used for some purpose other than work or holidaying; these were possibly 'the family home', but such residents may have had more than one such home.

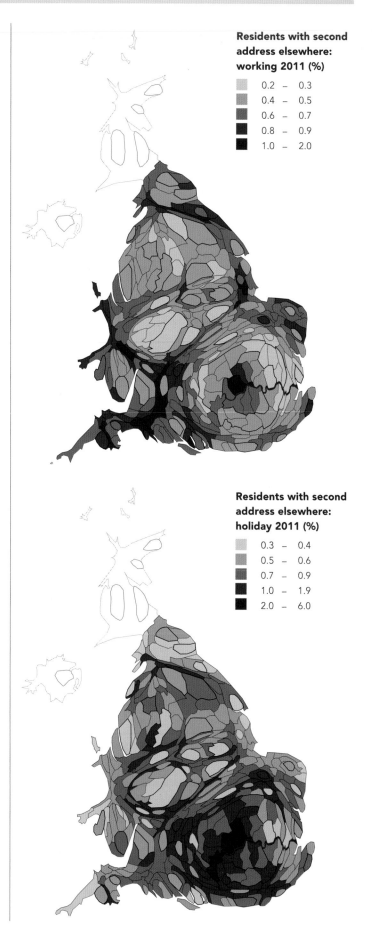

Residents with second address elsewhere: working 2011 (%)

- 0.2 – 0.3
- 0.4 – 0.5
- 0.6 – 0.7
- 0.8 – 0.9
- 1.0 – 2.0

Residents with second address elsewhere: holiday 2011 (%)

- 0.3 – 0.4
- 0.5 – 0.6
- 0.7 – 0.9
- 1.0 – 1.9
- 2.0 – 6.0

People living in households with a second address elsewhere by region of first address, England and Wales 2011 %

Region	%
London	6.1
South East	5.7
South West	5.7
Yorkshire and The Humber	5.2
East Midlands	5.1
Wales	5.0
North East	4.6
East	4.5
North West	4.6
East Midlands	4.3

4.0% 4.5% 5.0% 5.5% 6.0% 6.5%

By 2011 it was clear that the greatest population increase
since 2001 has been in the Centre of London, followed by
London Core, and what we call Inner London: all these
aggregate places having between two and almost 5 times
faster population increases than those seen in both the
Core and the Suburbs of the Archipelago.

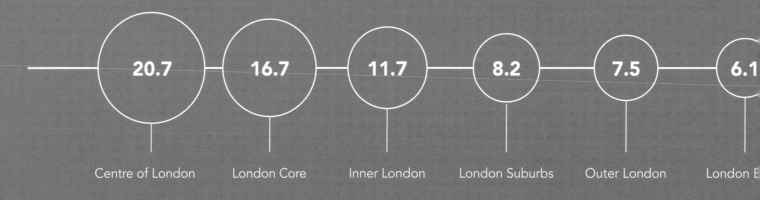

Centre of London	London Core	Inner London	London Suburbs	Outer London	London E
20.7	16.7	11.7	8.2	7.5	6.1

POPULATION GROWTH 2001–2011

Conclusion

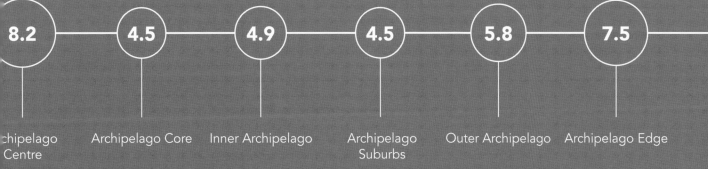

8.2	**4.5**	**4.9**	**4.5**	**5.8**	**7.5**
...chipelago Centre	Archipelago Core	Inner Archipelago	Archipelago Suburbs	Outer Archipelago	Archipelago Edge

Interestingly, the Outer Archipelago and the Archipelago Edge did not see such slower population growth, with the Archipelago Edge experiencing the national rise of 7.5%.

Conclusion

Over 10 years ago we came to the end of the last edition of this atlas and drew a map. Here is that map again, but now shown on a different projection with the 2011 population distribution underlying it. We renamed the South as the *London Areas* and the North as the *Archipelago*. Thus in the rest of this chapter, when we talk of the London Areas we mean what you might think of as Southern England.

The division into the 12 regions shown in the map was because we came to the conclusion that the 2001 Census had revealed the UK to be dividing very quickly and very abruptly. What mattered above all else in trying to explain change in any place since 1991 was how far that place was from London, especially from the centre of the old City of London and the borough of Westminster. The map we created was fantasy, but was based on what those last two (1991 and 2001) Censuses appeared to be telling us, and what the change over time trends were hinting at. Each region was defined, principally, by how far away it was from London's centre.

The first six of our 12 regions all had London in their titles: *Centre of London, London Core, Inner London, London Suburbs, Outer London* and *London Edge*. None of the last three of these regions actually included any area that was or is formally part of London, but London was included in their titles because distance to London had such a dominant effect on their recent fortunes. Thus, all of the South of England was labelled the London Areas, stretching as far North as Lincolnshire and as far West as Cornwall.

Londoners retired to Lincolnshire and holidayed in Cornwall. The most affluent had their second homes there, the poorest might one day end their days in these cheaper parts of the great metropolis' outer edges, but there was a distinct lack of much out-migration North and West of the outer border of the London Areas – what had been the old North/South divide. Occasionally a reporter from a Southern newspaper would venture out of their Southern comfort zone and do a little tour of the North. Politicians mostly only headed out of these areas when they needed votes. The affluent youth of the South might venture North for a few years to be university students, but in general, the traffic was mostly the other way round – far more Northerners moved South than Southerners ever crossed North and West.

The remaining six regions of the UK we termed the *Archipelago*. These were places centred on a string of urban centres in 'the provinces'. The largest of these is centred on what is now called the *Northern Powerhouse* of Manchester, connected

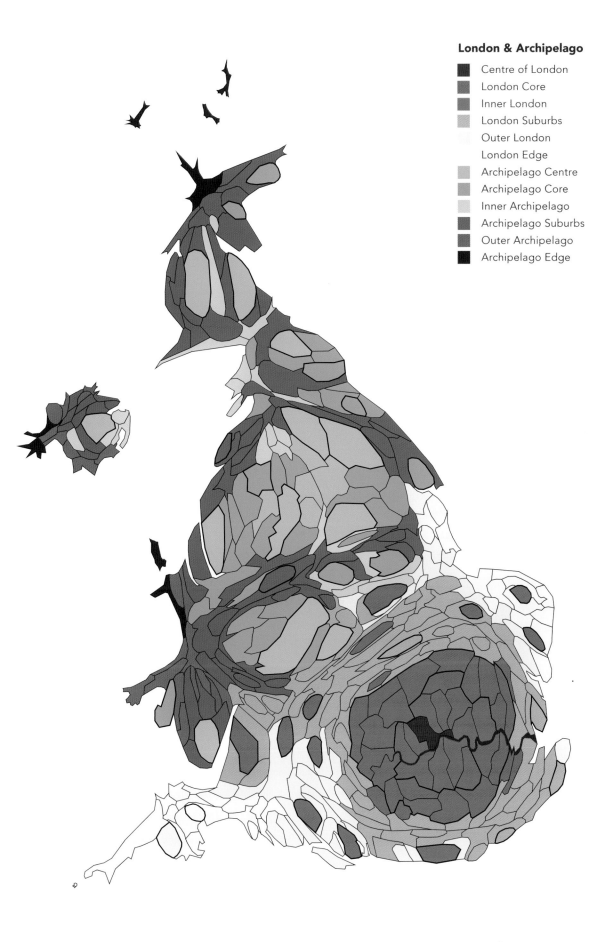

London & Archipelago

- Centre of London
- London Core
- Inner London
- London Suburbs
- Outer London
- London Edge
- Archipelago Centre
- Archipelago Core
- Inner Archipelago
- Archipelago Suburbs
- Outer Archipelago
- Archipelago Edge

by worn-out old railway lines through to Leeds and Sheffield. Less well connected again are the islands of Cardiff, Birmingham, Liverpool, Newcastle, Belfast, Glasgow and Edinburgh, all situated in the sea of peripheral places. Around many of these places is what we called the *Archipelago Core* – economically lower-lying land but still part of this string of islands. Then there was the *Inner Archipelago* that you can see defined on the map, places a little less well connected again; then the large mass of *Archipelago Suburbs*, places from which you might commute to a peripheral centre; and then there is the beginnings of the land that time appeared to have forgotten, the *Outer Archipelago*; and finally, the most isolated places of all – *Archipelago Edge*. These are areas that were most often being left behind in the past, places that appeared to be behind the times.

London and the Archipelago was how we summed up the new human geography that the 2001 Census had revealed. It did not matter where a place was in the South, or what people did there. Irrespective of all that, in the 1990s it would prosper just because it was in the South, was part of these essentially London Areas, prospering more the nearer to the centre of London it was. At the same time, living in the new expanded London Areas became less easy, more overcrowded and more stressful, a trend that showed no sign of abating when we were last writing about a Census (back in 2003 and 2004). Back then, life in the Archipelago was changing more slowly, economic prosperity was less sure, illness and unemployment rates remained stubbornly high, and the last gasps of old industries could still be heard and measured in those Censuses. Today we cannot even draw a map of where former miners and ship-workers retired to because the numbers surviving are just too few. We can only see their ghosts in terms of the far lower numbers of people living into extreme old age in the Archipelago.

Testing the theory

A good test of any theory is to see whether predictions based on it come true. If the UK had been splitting along the geographical lines we described back in 2004, using data from 2001, and if those splits were continuing to widen, then that should be evident in the continued change in the same direction that has occurred through to 2011 and beyond.

The most basic change is in the numbers of people living in each part of the UK. By 2011 it was clear that the greatest population increases since 2001 were in the Centre of London (+20.7%), followed by London Core (+16.7%), and what we called Inner London (+11.7%): all these places having between two and almost five times faster population increases than those seen in both the Core and the Suburbs of the Archipelago (+4.5%). Interestingly the outer regions of the Archipelago and the Edge did not see such slower population growth, with the Edge experiencing the national average rise of 7.5%, the same change as in what we termed the new Outer London (the area just *outside* of the Greater London Authority). The following table and graph show the number of people living in each region and how that changed between the Censuses.

Population, UK 2011–2011 % change

Archipelago Edge
7.5
Outer Archipelago
5.8
Archipelago Suburbs
4.5
Inner Archipelago
4.9
Archipelago Core
4.5
Archipelago Centre
8.2
London Edge
6.1
Outer London
7.5
London Suburbs
8.2
Inner London
11.7
London Core
16.7
Centre of London
20.7

| 0% | 5% | 10% | 15% | 20% | 25% |

Population by region, 2001 and 2011, absolute and relative change

		2001	2011	Increase	%
1	Centre of London	188,000	227,000	39,000	20.7
2	London Core	2,841,000	3,316,000	475,000	16.7
3	Inner London	6,973,000	7,792,000	819,000	11.7
4	London Suburbs	9,902,000	10,711,000	809,000	8.2
5	Outer London	4,603,000	4,946,000	343,000	7.5
6	London Edge	3,760,000	3,989,000	229,000	6.1
7	Archipelago Centre	6,903,000	7,468,000	565,000	8.2
8	Archipelago Core	7,778,000	8,129,000	351,000	4.5
9	Inner Archipelago	2,346,000	2,460,000	114,000	4.9
10	Archipelago Suburbs	11,217,000	11,725,000	508,000	4.5
11	Outer Archipelago	1,722,000	1,822,000	100,000	5.8
12	Archipelago Edge	556,000	598,000	42,000	7.5
	UK	**58,789,000**	**63,183,000**	**4,394,000**	**7.5**

The population change that has occurred in each of our 12 regions can be broken down in many ways. We can look at the change in people working in each part of the country, the qualifications they have, the kinds of jobs they have, where they come from and what kinds of families they form, if any. Increasing numbers of young people in the London Areas have to delay forming families because the cost of housing there has risen so much, and we can begin to see the implications of this in all kinds of other trends. However, the simplest breakdown is by age. Where are the young going to, and where are the very old now?

There are advantages to viewing the UK as split between two groups of regions. Areas are viewed differently from the stereotypical idea of where they are and hence how the population within them might normally be expected to behave given the traditional regional typology.

Age 90+, UK 2011 %

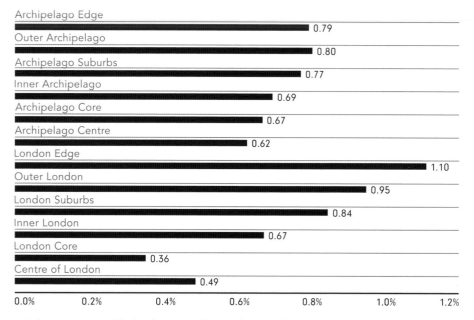

There is an established geography to the age distribution of the UK that is itself slowly changing. The graph above shows how, by 2011, in all but one region, less than 1% of the population were aged 90 or older. Nationally the share was just 0.7%, up from 0.6% a decade earlier. By 2011 the proportion of people aged 90+ exceeded 1% only in what we called the Edge of the London Areas, the most outer parts of the South East of England. There is a steady increase in the local proportion of the population who are very elderly, from just under 0.4% in the very heart of London through to 1.1% on its far outer Southern English edges. Very elderly people are now three times more likely to be found at the Edge of the South than at the Centre.

Outside of the South, outside what we now term the London Areas, there is again a linear increase, more gradual now, from 0.6% of the residents of the Archipelago Centre being very elderly to 0.8% at the Archipelago Edge. It is as if the UK is increasingly coming to be made up of two separate nations – North/South – Archipelago/London – and in each there is a continuum. A narrow majority of the very elderly live in the South (52.0%), a share that is slowly growing despite the very Centre of London becoming much younger. There are so many elderly on the periphery of the London Areas partly because there are so few in its centre.

The change in the geographical distribution of those aged 90 or over in the South has been very marked since 2001. Despite higher than average life expectancy, there have been actual falls in the London Core region in the proportion of people who are aged 90 or over, while the greatest increases across all of the UK have been at what is now the London Edge. When people in the South move in retirement, they tend to try to stay in the South, or at least to go no further than to its outer edges.

Even in extreme old age, connections to London matter, if only to allow families to visit without too long a journey. In the Archipelago a similar but far more muted process has been gathering steam. As the graph below shows, the slowest growth in terms of proportions of people being in this very elderly group was recorded in the Archipelago Centre in the 2000s, partly reflecting the poorer life expectancy in those areas, with greater growth towards the edges. Some of the very elderly will, of course, cross the North/South divide, but that divide is itself becoming clearer through their overall lack of movement beyond the London Areas on retirement and during retirement.

Age 90+, UK 2001–2011 % change

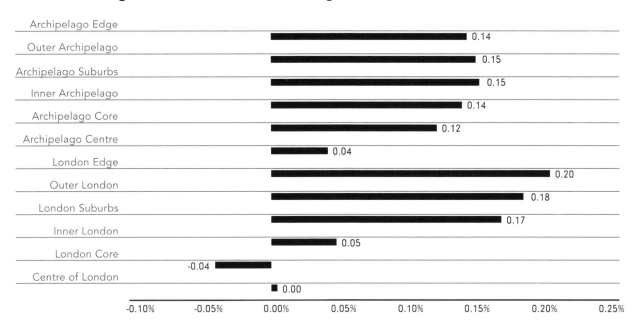

Archipelago Edge	0.14
Outer Archipelago	0.15
Archipelago Suburbs	0.15
Inner Archipelago	0.14
Archipelago Core	0.12
Archipelago Centre	0.04
London Edge	0.20
Outer London	0.18
London Suburbs	0.17
Inner London	0.05
London Core	-0.04
Centre of London	0.00

-0.10% -0.05% 0.00% 0.05% 0.10% 0.15% 0.20% 0.25%

The North/South divide

Up to now in this chapter we have only used basic demographic information and aggregated that by our 12 regions to see whether the patterns we observed before have strengthened. There are others ways in which the different regions of the UK are becoming more distinct from each other than in the continued concentration of the very elderly towards the edges at greater rates than possibly ever before seen, and to the two distinct edges of these two parts of the UK (the London Areas and the Archipelago). One example, drawn from data first presented in the *Religion and Ethnicity* chapter of this atlas, concerns how the geography of the UK is changing as far as ethnicity is concerned.

By the 12 broad regions used in this conclusion, everywhere there are more people who categorise themselves as not being of a White ethnicity, but the greatest increases in the multifarious types of non-White groupings between 2001 and 2011 were in Central London (+11.4%) and the smallest increases (*13 times smaller*) were on the Archipelago Edge (+0.9%). Again, and just as for the very elderly, a similar pattern of change is seen each side of the North/South divide, and again the changes are far greater within the heart of London, where only 55% of the residents of Core London were White in 2011. In contrast, 98% of both London Edge and the Archipelago Edge residents were White in that same year. The changes since 2011 that the graphs in the *Religion and Ethnicity* and *Birthplace and Nationality* chapters document suggest that this widening by ethnicity will have increased in at least 2012, 2013 and 2014.

Non-White ethnicity, UK 2001–2011 % change

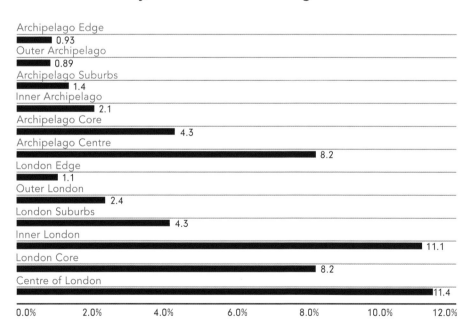

Region	% change
Archipelago Edge	0.93
Outer Archipelago	0.89
Archipelago Suburbs	1.4
Inner Archipelago	2.1
Archipelago Core	4.3
Archipelago Centre	8.2
London Edge	1.1
Outer London	2.4
London Suburbs	4.3
Inner London	11.1
London Core	8.2
Centre of London	11.4

When the population change that has occurred between 2001 and 2011 is analysed by country of birth, it becomes clear that a majority of the London Areas population growth that has occurred in recent years has been due to an increase in people living in the South of England who were not born in the UK. In 2001 there were 4.9 million people living in the UK who were not born in the UK. That number rose to 8.0 million by 2011. Of the net increase of 3.1 million non-UK-born people living in the UK by 2011, 2.0 million was of a rise in the non-UK-born population within the six London Areas. This contrasts with only a 0.7 million increase in the UK-born population of the London Areas over that same decade.

Only at the London Edge and in what we here call Outer London (which, remember, is outside traditional London) has the bulk of the increase in population been of people born in the UK. Even in the London Suburbs a majority of population increase has been due to a greater increase in the non-UK-born population. Further out from the London Suburbs you find that the rising UK-born population are mostly of elderly people moving away from London, but managing to still remain in the South, if only on its edge. It is true that even on the Archipelago Edge there has been an increase in non-UK-born that is considerable. But proportionally it is *eight times* smaller than the increase in non-UK-born in the Centre of London. The figures in the graph shown here are the increase in population of each group as a proportion of the total population of both groups combined (in others words, all people) in 2001. The only area to see a reduction in just one group is Inner London, where the UK-born population fell fractionally.

Population by birthplace, UK 2001–2011 % change

■ Born outside of UK   ■ Born in the UK

Archipelago Edge	2.4 · 5.1
Outer Archipelago	2.1 · 3.7
Archipelago Suburbs	2.0 · 2.6
Inner Archipelago	2.0 · 2.8
Archipelago Core	3.6 · 0.9
Archipelago Centre	7.0 · 1.1
London Edge	2.0 · 4.1
Outer London	3.4 · 4.1
London Suburbs	4.6 · 3.5
Inner London	-0.3% · 12.0
London Core	15.6 · 1.1
Centre of London	20.0 · 0.3

-5.0%   0.0%   5.0%   10.0%   15.0%   20.0%   25.0%

By country of birth there are fascinating patterns as to who moved into the very heart of the British Capital in the 2000s. France, the second nearest neighbour to the UK after Ireland, provided and continues to provide a disproportionate number of the new arrivals in London. Increasing numbers of France-born people living in the UK have added ever so slightly to the overall picture of multicultural cosmopolitan London, but each sliver of the pie tells a story that when added to all the other slivers creates a picture of great and growing diversity.

An extra 40,000 France-born people lived in the UK in 2011 compared to 2001, and thus at least that number must have been in-migrants within the last decade. Over half of this increase was seen in the very heart of London, with the proportionate rise in London Core being over 200 times greater than at the Archipelago Edge. This increase is only an extra 2,900 people in the Centre of London, and another 19,700 in the rest of London Core. So it is not the size of the absolute numbers that matters, but what the concentration in particular places reveals – the lack of movement to other parts of the UK from France.

By 2011, 59% of France-born people living in the UK lived within the (official) Greater London boundary; in 2001 that proportion had been 51%. Because of their very distinctive and increasing clustering, the France-born living in the UK are one of the most distinctive birthplace groups when it comes to this kind of increasingly selective migration, but in general, almost all overseas-born groups now living in the UK have had a tendency to concentrate near to the heart of London, and this is rapidly changing what London is, and what it is to be a Londoner.

France-born, England and Wales 2001–2011 % change

Archipelago Edge
0.00
Outer Archipelago
0.01
Archipelago Suburbs
0.00
Inner Archipelago
0.01
Archipelago Core
0.01
Archipelago Centre
0.02
London Edge
0.01
Outer London
0.02
London Suburbs
0.02
Inner London
0.07
London Core
0.48
Centre of London
0.99

0.0%   0.2%   0.4%   0.6%   0.8%   1.0%   1.2%

A very similar pattern to the changes in France-born living in England and Wales (the UK countries for which there was comparable data) is seen when we turn to look at the USA-born change (across all of the UK), although the increases are less dramatic because there were already 6,000 USA-born residents of London Centre and a further 25,000 in London Core in 2001. These populations grew, net, in the 10 years to 2011 and swelled by more than 15,000 in total, or 0.3% of the existing total populations of those areas. Such percentage increases might look small, but they are much larger than that experienced anywhere else in the UK. Added on to all the other migrants born outside the UK arriving in London, the Americans and the mainland Europeans and those from everywhere else have helped to change London, and especially its Centre, hugely. They also contrast greatly with the only decline in regional USA-born populations, due to a net reduction of just over 2,000 such people in London Edge, around where former military US airbases have tended to be located.

In the Archipelago, after the attraction of its centres and their universities are discounted, the further away from things the slightly greater the increases in USA-born living here have been. Even with this increase only one in every 530 people living on the Archipelago Edge was born in the US compared to one in every 28 living in London Core by 2011.

USA-born, UK 2001–2011 % change

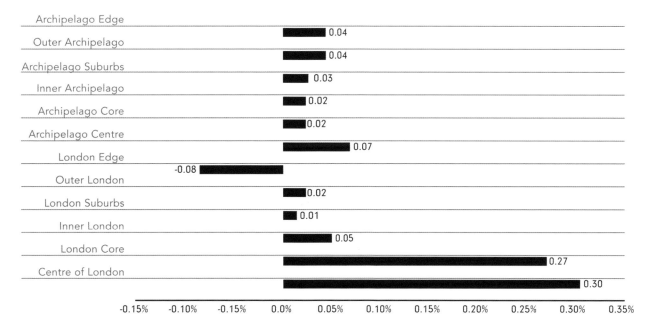

Everything is connected

Everything is connected to everything else. As the elderly leave London in ever greater numbers, as more migrants arrive, and as the population of London begins to grow by more and more than ever before (getting to growth rates last seen in Victorian times), the nature of work changes and it changes most the nearer the Centre of London you are.

Every one of the 12 regions we defined back in 2004 using 2001 data has experienced a growth in the number of people who are self-employed, but the growth in self-employment in London Core, the 13 boroughs that surround Westminster and the City, is almost two-and-a-half times greater, proportionately, than that experienced in what we call here London Suburbs, areas now outside of (but in close orbit of) London. And by 2011 London Suburbs themselves had experienced a slightly greater shift towards self-employment than any area of the Archipelago had yet seen.

It is as if London is pointing towards the future for the country as a whole and moving there faster than everywhere else, especially faster than further away places that are always playing catch-up. Many cities are now as ethnically diverse as some London boroughs were in 1991 and others in 2001, but most of London became more diverse again in 2011. While other cities are playing a game of catch-up, some rural areas are hardly in the game at all. However, in the very heart of London, in London Centre, that growth in self-employment is slower, so possibly by looking into the Centre we can see even further ahead – possibly even towards a time when the current growth in self-employment might abate.

Self-employment, UK 2001–2011 % change

Archipelago Edge
0.66
Outer Archipelago
0.73
Archipelago Suburbs
0.80
Inner Archipelago
0.75
Archipelago Core
0.91
Archipelago Centre
1.03
London Edge
0.82
Outer London
0.91
London Suburbs
1.07
Inner London
1.58
London Core
2.41
Centre of London
1.09

0.0%   0.5%   1.0%   1.5%   2.0%   2.5%   3.0%

We have no way of knowing if the Centre of London is currently some kind of UK crystal ball or not, but what we do know is that for several decades now, what happens first in the Centre of London tends to spread, but never quite as quickly as change occurs in the Centre of London itself, which becomes increasingly distinctive. In 2001, 18.1% of all self-employed people in the UK lived within the Greater London boundary; by 2011 that proportion had risen to 20.8%. The detailed maps of this change are shown in the *Qualifications and Employment* chapter. Here the graph below simply summarises that London is moving away and the Core of London has been moving away much faster than the periphery.

Sometimes we see very different regional breaks and the divide is between the Core of London and the rest, or to put it another way, there is far more variation within the London Areas than between their average and the Archipelago. The *Qualifications and Employment* chapter of this atlas also included a description and mapping of the number of hours people work and the changes in the hours worked over time. For the group who work the very longest hours each week there have been falls in their prevalence in almost every region except for the Core, and especially not in the Centre. These are people working at least 49 hours a week, an average of seven each day, although few work like that, many working 12 hours a day for fewer days. Increasingly, the reason to live in the very middle is often to have enough time to work for most of that waking time and not to have to waste time commuting. Others increasingly have to work very long hours to be able to afford to live there.

Working 49+ hours a week, UK 2001–2011 % change

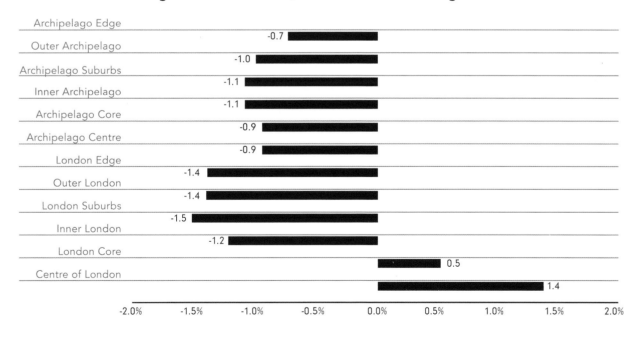

And then there are the qualifications people hold that were also mapped in the *Qualifications and Employment* chapter. Take the group that is declining most in number, those with no qualifications at all. London, as officially defined, had only 14.8% of its population aged 16–64 unqualified in 2001. By 2011 this share had risen to 20.1%. So what is going on? Part of the rise might be in people who have qualifications that are not recognised in the UK. However, this does not include university graduates with their degrees, and they have been flocking into London in ever greater numbers decade after decade.

Could it be that as well as gaining more highly skilled people, the Centre of London is also seeing the rise of a new, very lowly or completely unqualified group of people, many working very long hours? An army of cleaners, washers, porters, security guards, among whom are a disproportionate section with no recognised qualifications at all? Could these be some of the people working on average more than seven hours a day, every day? More detailed analysis of the Census data could be used to try to answer such questions, but the Census does not ask people how many jobs they have. Possibly more people in London are doing two or three very low-paid jobs. How else could they afford to live in the very Centre and do jobs that require no qualifications? The Census can only point to where to look and at what it might be most profitable to look further into if we are to discover more and understand better.

People aged 16–64 with no qualifications, UK 2001–2011 % change

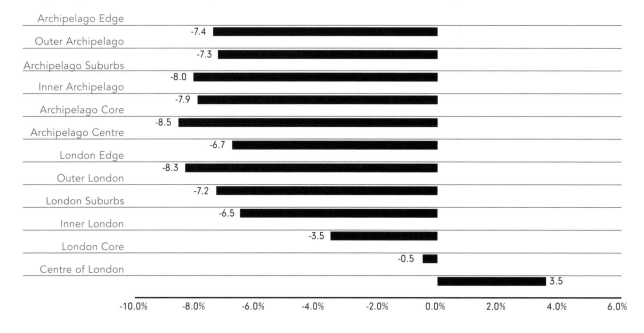

So let's look at how the work people are doing across the UK has changed according to the changing rates of activity in various groups of occupations in those 12 regions.

What has happened to the share of people working in the lowest paid jobs in each of our regions, the elementary occupations? Nationally this share has fallen by 0.1% of the population, from 5.4% of all people to 5.3% of the total. However, those Core London boroughs bucked the trend and the local share of elementary jobs increased there by 0.8% of total local populations (of total residents), a massive jump compared to jumps seen in any other area. The only other rises to 2011 in the proportions being recorded are in the surrounding Inner London boroughs (officially Outer London), and a much smaller rise in the Archipelago Centre. London itself is slowly splitting in two, but socially more than geographically: into the haves and the have-nots, who together increasingly crowd into its Core.

People aged 16–74 in elementary occupations, UK 2001–2011
% change

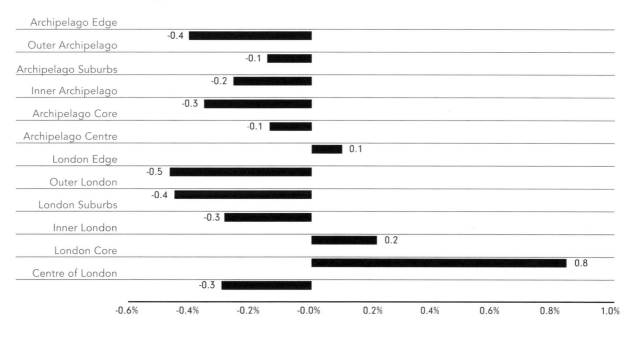

The heart of finance

The industry we now look to first to determine where the 'haves' might be is banking, finance and insurance, and between 2001 and 2011 it was in the Centre of London that these jobs became more common. To be exact, it was in the very heart of London that the proportion of people holding these jobs was increasingly likely to be sleeping on Census Day, Sunday 27 March 2011. The rises of 2.6% and 0.6% recorded in the heart of the Capital shown in the following graph are what now underpin the huge differences between average salaries and wages seen in these parts of London and those enjoyed or just survived on elsewhere. The Census shows us the changes that underlie so much more.

People aged 16–74 working in finance and insurance, UK 2001–2011 % change

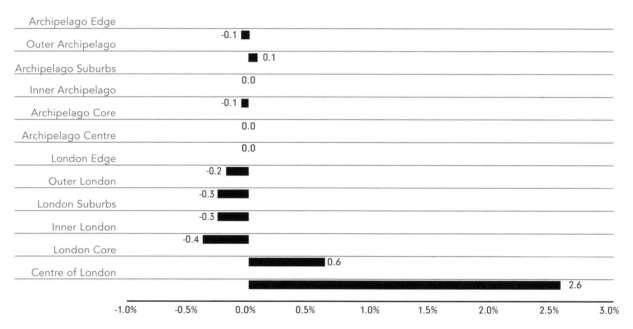

The Centre of London changed as the financiers concentrated in its heart and as their numbers in the suburbs fell. Those bankers culled in the crash were much more likely to be living in the suburbs, to be middle management. What London was left with by 2011 were only a few more financiers than there had been in 2001, but ones who were far better-off than they had ever been, and who would soon come to take even more.

Many financiers declare themselves as self-employed, which is why the mean average income of all the self-employed in the Centre of London exceeded £100,000 by the 2010/11 tax year (see the Introduction to this atlas). Census data can be used to merge these HMRC figures into our regions, but not to show change further back in time, as HMRC data for 2001 are not available.

Average annual income of the self-employed, UK 2010/2011 £

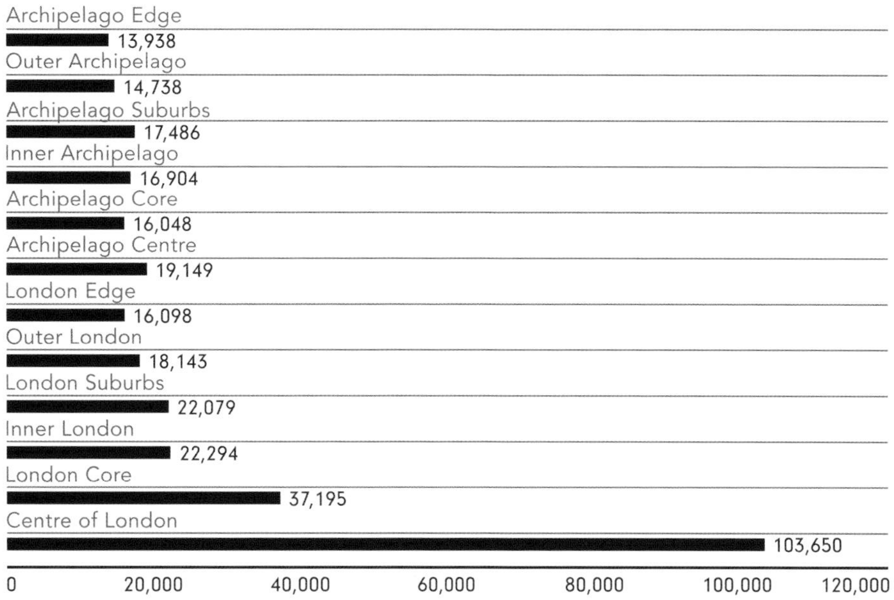

Archipelago Edge
13,938
Outer Archipelago
14,738
Archipelago Suburbs
17,486
Inner Archipelago
16,904
Archipelago Core
16,048
Archipelago Centre
19,149
London Edge
16,098
Outer London
18,143
London Suburbs
22,079
Inner London
22,294
London Core
37,195
Centre of London
103,650

| 0 | 20,000 | 40,000 | 60,000 | 80,000 | 100,000 | 120,000 |

The income of the self-employed in the heart of London is so high that it distorts national averages. Those employed in the Centre of London had a mean average annual income of £72,350 by 2010/11; those in London Core, £36,500 each, if employed. These sums are far higher than found anywhere else in the UK and result in the six London Areas taking 64% of all self-employment income and 56% of all employed people's incomes in the UK despite having only 56% of all the self-employed and 50% of all UK employees.

Outside of London Core and the Centre of London the large majority of people receive far less than the national average income of £25,000, even if they are in work as shown in the following graph. This is because just a few people, especially those concentrated in just the two Central London Areas, get so much.

Average annual income of the self-employed, employed, and pensioners, UK 2010/2011 £

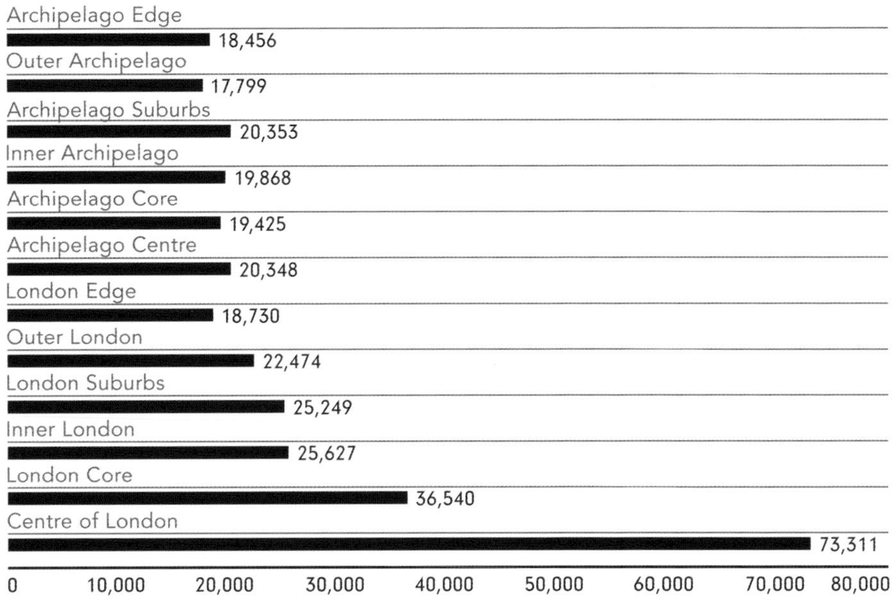

Area	Income (£)
Archipelago Edge	18,456
Outer Archipelago	17,799
Archipelago Suburbs	20,353
Inner Archipelago	19,868
Archipelago Core	19,425
Archipelago Centre	20,348
London Edge	18,730
Outer London	22,474
London Suburbs	25,249
Inner London	25,627
London Core	36,540
Centre of London	73,311

0   10,000   20,000   30,000   40,000   50,000   60,000   70,000   80,000

Not everyone is better-off the nearer they get to the heart of London. The six London Areas are home to just 45% of UK pensioners, and those pensioners take 48% of all pensioner income, only slightly more than an equal share with Northern pensioners. Some costs of living expenses are higher in the South, and so pensioners in the North may well be better-off despite having slightly lower average incomes.

In all but two areas the mean average income of pensioners is below £15,000 a year. The median is even lower. And once you are out of London's Core, it is pensioners in the London Suburbs – places all a long way away from what is currently thought of as London – who are best off in terms of having slightly higher average incomes. Pensioners living in the shadows of the City's skyscrapers tend, even when measured on mean average, to be worse off than those who have escaped further from the centre of the City. But they are not hugely worse off, and the differences within the Archipelago regions are greater.

A similar pattern is found in the Archipelago, where the lowest mean average annual pensions, being just a fraction over £12,000 a year by 2011, are what occur in the Archipelago's Core. The best-off non-London-based pensioners live in the Archipelago's Suburbs, with a minority of those pensioners enjoying an income of £13,300 a year. These are averages, so most of the pensioners in the better-off parts of the North live on less, with a few living on much more.

When it comes to income, the biggest divide is between London Core and the rest of the UK. If a wall had to be built to defend the highly paid, it would be built within London itself. However, rather than cut London in half, the wall would encircle its Core, and if the richest pensioners also wanted to be separated from the rest, then another wall would have to be built around the very centre within the Core, creating a kind of citadel of extreme affluence within a city of riches, surrounded nearby by the millions of people with far less. In many ways these walls have already been built, it is just that they are invisible. They exist when the market says you are too poor to move towards the Centre.

Average annual income of pensioners, UK 2010/2011 £

Region	Income
Archipelago Edge	13,277
Outer Archipelago	12,826
Archipelago Suburbs	13,317
Inner Archipelago	12,871
Archipelago Core	12,103
Archipelago Centre	12,579
London Edge	13,454
Outer London	14,154
London Suburbs	15,027
Inner London	14,039
London Core	14,829
Centre of London	24,528

12,000   14,000   16,000   18,000   20,000   22,000   24,000   26,000

The haves and the have-nots

To look at real wealth we have to turn to what comes after drawing a pension, to death, and again, we are now using data first presented in the Introduction to this atlas. Around the date of the last Census, in the tax year 2010/11, 15,600 people died with enough wealth to qualify for paying inheritance tax. During the calendar year 2011, 552,000 people's deaths were registered in the UK. Thus only 2.8% of the population paid inheritance tax. In many cases this includes monies that have been passed on tax-free from a spouse or partner who has died a few years earlier. It will be an even lower proportion that will pay that tax in the future as the inheritance tax threshold has been raised to a million pounds in the 2015 budget.

There are only four regions of our 12 that exceed the 2.8% average proportion of people who die who actually pay the tax, starting at the London Suburbs. In all the Archipelago areas, less than 1.5% of the population ever pay inheritance tax, and today almost nobody there is very wealthy. Within the six London regions the proportion of those that are that wealthy on death rises from 2.4% of those living in London Edge to 12.9% in the Centre of London. A centripetal process is under way, with the money spinning over time towards the middle.

People paying inheritance tax on death, UK 2010/2011 %

Archipelago Edge
0.7
Outer Archipelago
0.7
Archipelago Suburbs
1.1
Inner Archipelago
0.5
Archipelago Core
0.7
Archipelago Centre
1.4
London Edge
2.4
Outer London
2.8
London Suburbs
3.9
Inner London
4.3
London Core
5.6
Centre of London
12.9

0%   2%   4%   6%   8%   10%   12%   14%

To end, we turn to a few mundane Census counts. First, we consider rooms. Despite all the overcrowding in London and the complaints about lack of housing, there are actually more rooms available in residential dwellings per person in the Centre and Core of London than in the Centre of the Archipelago. In five of the areas there are, on average, over three rooms per person (not counting bathrooms, toilets, halls, landings or large storage cupboards).

In the very heart of London, in Westminster and the City of London, so many apartments are empty, so many mansions under-occupied that there are 1.36 rooms for every resident. Even if couples in the Centre of London did not share bedrooms, there would still be more than enough space for them all. In reality, poorer Londoners are the most overcrowded people in the UK while richer Londoners have rooms to spare.[9] Meanwhile, in the Archipelago Core, and just to underline how different the North is, there are only 0.58 rooms per person – no scope there for spare bedrooms, studies, dining rooms, sitting rooms, music rooms, playrooms or walk-in wardrobes as large as a room.

Rooms per person, UK 2011

Area	Rooms per person
Archipelago Edge	3.50
Outer Archipelago	2.69
Archipelago Suburbs	2.19
Inner Archipelago	4.23
Archipelago Core	1.94
Archipelago Centre	0.58
London Edge	3.40
Outer London	3.63
London Suburbs	3.09
Inner London	1.20
London Core	0.92
Centre of London	1.36

0   1   2   3   4   5

Between 2001 and 2011, 13.5 million more rooms (net) were added to houses and flats in the UK, or in some cases, were in new houses and flats. This increase in the amount of space we had occurred everywhere, but the growth was fastest in London Core (+16% more rooms in 2011 compared to 2001) and slowest in the Inner Archipelago (+9% rooms). However, once population change is taken into account, the average number of rooms available per person has actually fallen in Inner, Core and Central London. Everywhere else the number of rooms available per person has been raised, in many cases substantially – partly because the population is not rising as quickly as the number of extensions that are being added. And despite a little more pressure in the Centre of London, it remains the case that there are more than twice as many rooms there per resident compared to the Archipelago Centre.

Rooms per person, UK 2001–2011 % change

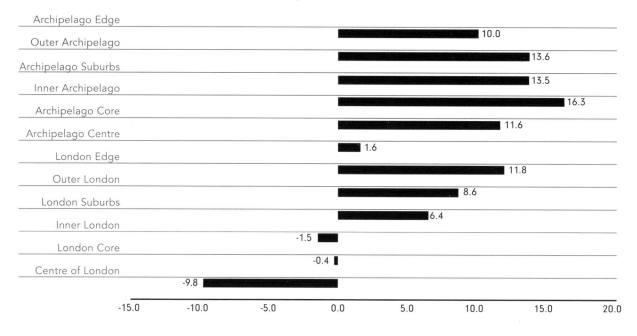

By 2011, in some ways the Archipelago had become more uniform while London was dividing more and more, and so becoming more distinct by looking more and more as a series of very different concentric rings. Life near the Centre of London looks bleak for many. More than two in five of all the households in the Centre of London were living in poverty, the highest proportion to be found in any region other than in the surrounding London Core, but nowhere do fewer than one in five households live in poverty.

It is grim down South for just as many people as it is grim up North, however. It is just that there are also richer people living down South, and much more variation both between and within areas. Move from the Centre of London out to the Suburbs, and you could soon be living in areas where fewer people are poor than can be found anywhere in the North, in the Archipelago. For most people, this is realistically the most that aspiration can get you to – not to be rich, but to at least avoid or escape poverty. And escaping poverty is more likely if you move to or are in the London Areas, and get to its new outer London Suburbs. However, fail to escape poverty there, as at least a fifth of the population do almost everywhere, and you might well have been better remaining in or moving to the Archipelago.

Households living in poverty, UK 2011 %

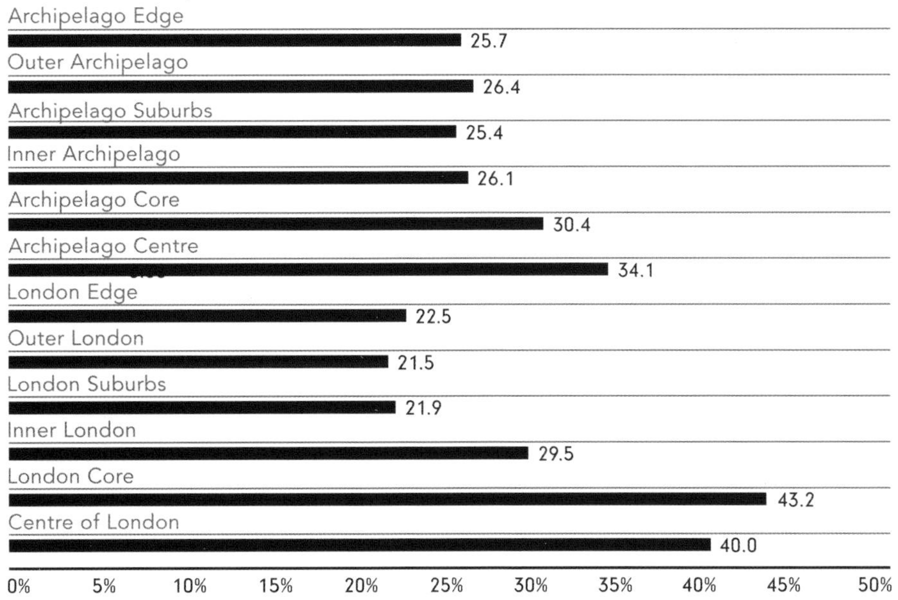

Region	%
Archipelago Edge	25.7
Outer Archipelago	26.4
Archipelago Suburbs	25.4
Inner Archipelago	26.1
Archipelago Core	30.4
Archipelago Centre	34.1
London Edge	22.5
Outer London	21.5
London Suburbs	21.9
Inner London	29.5
London Core	43.2
Centre of London	40.0

The pattern to the change in poverty is remarkable, and shows how hard it is to escape having too little simply by moving towards where people have more. Over the course of the 2000s, poverty rates were raised the most inside London, and in every part of London apart from the outer Edge.

In London more people now have less (poverty has risen), as well as others having more possessions than anyone owned in the past (wealth has also risen for others). Fewer are average in London anymore. In great contrast, poverty rates fell most in the Archipelago in the 2000s, sometimes by as much as 2.6 fewer households in every 100 being poor by the measure we first used to count such things in 2001. Absolute rises in overcrowding, in having to rent from a private landlord, and in families splitting up in the South, have meant that such improvements have been more concentrated in the North. And yet this measure of poverty does not measure the things that best indicate whether a household is poor today – whether they have debts and can't save £10 a month, or whether they can have no holiday at all, even for a week, just once a year – because they cannot afford it. The Census did not ask about holidays or debt or income or wealth. If it had done so, we would see poverty to have risen everywhere, and wealth to have become more and more concentrated.

Households living in poverty, UK 2001–2011 % change

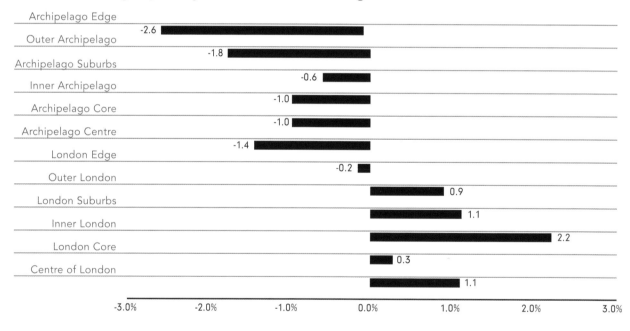

Of everything that the 2011 Census revealed, it was perhaps the rise in private renting and where that was concentrated that was most revealing. The number of people who had a private landlord almost doubled in what we define as Inner London to become more than a fifth of all residents by 2011, and there was a relative 70% increase in London's Core. In the Core, an additional eighth of the population were renting just 10 years on from 2001. In contrast, the rise in private renting on the Archipelago Edge was the slowest in the UK, but still over 40%.

People living in privately rented households, UK 2001 and % change 2001–2011

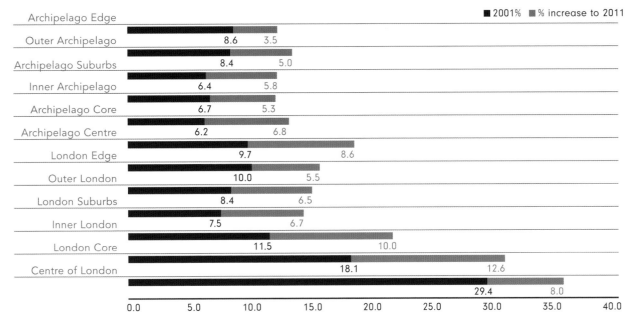

By just concentrating on the increase in private renting alone, the very different patterns and new diverging trends within London and the Archipelago become clear. And these changes are reinforcing all the other changes shown above. More people are becoming very wealthy in the South, partly because a small group of the wealthy can now collect rent from a much larger group who have no choice but to pay it; rent on average of a far greater monthly amount and greater proportion of their incomes than was charged before for identical properties. At the very same time, the numbers of families who can qualify for a mortgage have been falling, as has the availability of any non-private rented housing.

The number of rooms available for people to sleep in has never been higher, but those rooms have become far less equitably shared out. This is compared to how they used to be shared out, and so overcrowding is rising despite the addition of rooms outstripping population increases.

Average incomes might look high, and those averages in London often appear to be astronomical, until the cost of becoming a resident and renting or buying is factored in. London is filling up with the very rich, a tiny group of very wealthy people, a very large group of the extremely poor, and a dwindling group of people struggling in between, those on modest, average or even just slightly affluent (but not rich) incomes. In contrast, both very highly paid professional jobs and very lowly paid elementary occupations became more common in the heart of the capital during 2001–11, to the detriment of almost all other possible occupations. And although the percentage changes have been greatest within London in absolute terms, the rise in people having to rent privately has been almost as great within many Northern regions. As the graph below illustrates, more than half a million extra people are now renting privately in London's Core, and in Inner London, and in Outer London, and in the Centre of the Archipelago, and in its Core and in its Suburbs.

People living in privately rented households, UK 2001–2011 absolute change

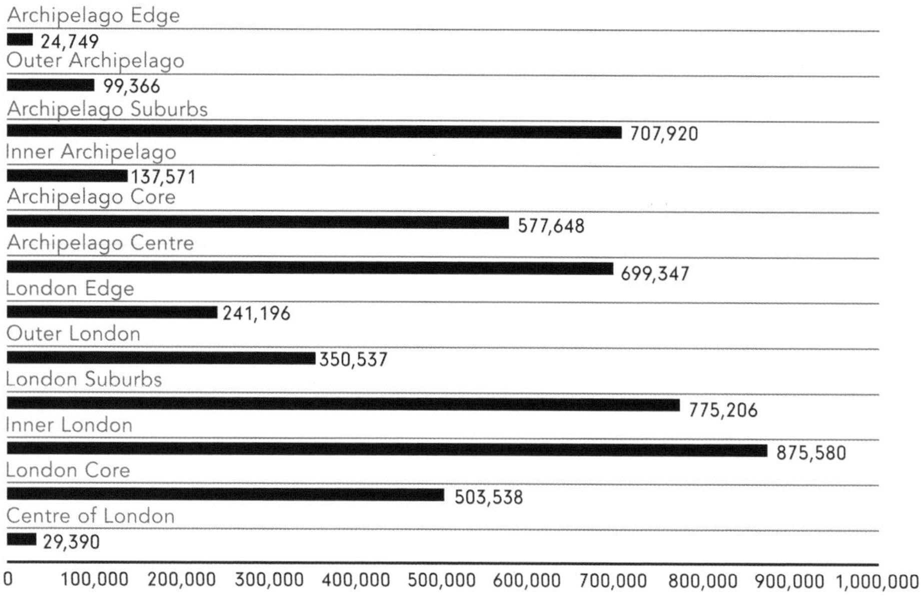

Archipelago Edge
24,749
Outer Archipelago
99,366
Archipelago Suburbs
707,920
Inner Archipelago
137,571
Archipelago Core
577,648
Archipelago Centre
699,347
London Edge
241,196
Outer London
350,537
London Suburbs
775,206
Inner London
875,580
London Core
503,538
Centre of London
29,390

0   100,000 200,000 300,000 400,000 500,000 600,000 700,000 800,000 900,000 1,000,000

Polarisation within London

There has been a rise in people with no qualifications working in the capital, and a rise in people working the equivalent of at least seven hours a day for seven days, more than 49 hours a week. Self-employment has risen, mostly in London's heart, as has immigration, and population increase in all but the elderly. And many of these increases are a continuation of trends first established most strongly in the 1990s with some antecedent seen in the 1980s but which are now progressing at a pace never observed before. Increases in the proportion of people living in privately rented stock of over 10% in a decade have to come to an end within a few decades, or very soon almost everyone will be renting from a private landlord.

And all the time the divide between the London Areas and the rest of the UK in most aspects of life grows and the divides within London grow, often faster than in decades before. The divide really did begin to widen many decades ago. It could first be seen when the 1981 and 1991 Censuses were compared. Unemployment and illness rose then and persisted longer in the North, especially in the Archipelago Core, whereas population turnover was rising in the South and the young and highly qualified were arriving in greater and greater numbers. It became more obvious by 2001, which was why we were able to define these regions shortly after that Census had been taken. By 2011 the divergences in the rates of change were clear enough to allow the 25 graphs in this chapter of so many different aspects of life to be drawn illustrating this divide.

Governments may manipulate the statistics – in summer 2015 a bill was read before Parliament to change the definition of 'child poverty'. People may try to avoid paying their taxes, and so the income data revealed in this chapter may well underestimate the growing extent of the divide by income and wealth. Entire Censuses can be cancelled to save money, or supposedly save it, if you believe that planning for schools to be built where they will be most needed is unnecessary and that there is no need to know much else about the population, other than what might be useful to financial markets and others in the private sector. The 2010 Coalition government considered cancelling the 2011 Census, but found that it was too late and the contracts had been signed. The 2015 Conservative government, however, may well not pass the Census Act in 2019 to allow the 2021 Census to take place.

Whatever is done, no matter how the statistics are reduced and manipulated, there will always be a way of unearthing what is happening. It is true that politicians instruct their civil servants to no longer count what they think doesn't matter – or worse, what they think you'd be better off not worrying about. But often the civil servants resist and eventually new politicians take over. Bodies such as the ONS have a little more independence than other groups of public servants, but they are still obliged to produce some things by law, and if their overall budget is cut, that supposed independence is of little use given little leeway to use it.

The 1951, 1970 and 1979 Conservative administrations all cut spending on official statistics. There is no reason to believe that the 2015 administration will be any different, but also no reason to believe it need last more than a year longer than the 1970 administration did, which was voted out of office in 1974, allowing the release of funds for the 1971 Census to be analysed and the 1981 Census planned for. Those Censuses allowed us to see many things. One thing was just how many more graduates were moving to London, so that by 2011, more than a third of all people living in the Core and Centre of London combined held a university degree.

People aged 16–64 holding a university degree, UK 2011 %

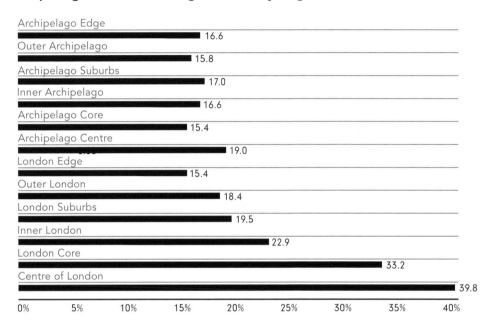

One day the divides will narrow. One day the prosperity of the few in the heart of London will no longer be assured. The value of property will fall, and/or new property be built, as it has always been in the past. Nothing stays dividing ever wider forever; the disadvantages, especially for those who are not rich but who live in the South, are now becoming too great. Eventually regions full of renters will vote against the interests of their landlords. At some point London will become part of the Archipelago again, or the Archipelago will become more like London – because there is only so much division you can take and make.

The future is another place

Whether all the constituent parts of the UK stay attached in the process is another matter. Scotland may leave, and Northern Ireland has suffered greatly economically in the 2000s, as the maps in this volume reveal. The Archipelago Centre has experienced deeper cuts to services than anywhere else in the UK has ever suffered before. The bailout of the banks has saved the wealth of the Centre of London. So much can happen in a decade.

If we don't look back it becomes easy to think it was always like this. But it was not, and London cannot separate itself off. London cannot build a wall within itself, to actually prevent those who have less and less to lose from living within the Centre. London needs their seven+ hours-a-day-seven-days-a-week labour, it needs the rent they pay, and it needs more and more resources, people and goods to spend all its money on. London makes hardly anything that it consumes, and yet a few of its citizens demand greater and greater tribute for their activities. There are already a few signs within the very centre of the Capital of a slowdown of this growing divide – we may never again see such divisions as we see now.

People aged 16–64 holding a university degree, UK 2001–2010 % change

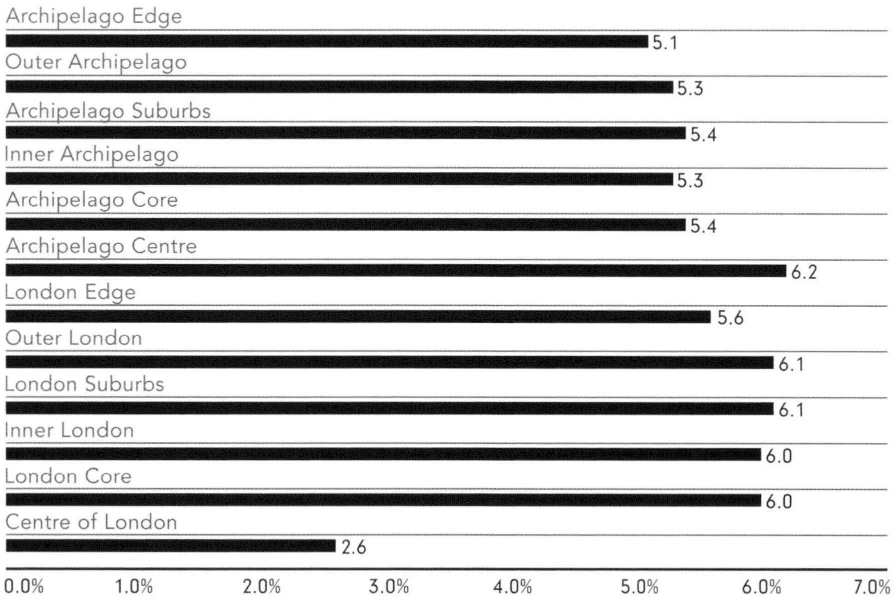

Region	% change
Archipelago Edge	5.1
Outer Archipelago	5.3
Archipelago Suburbs	5.4
Inner Archipelago	5.3
Archipelago Core	5.4
Archipelago Centre	6.2
London Edge	5.6
Outer London	6.1
London Suburbs	6.1
Inner London	6.0
London Core	6.0
Centre of London	2.6

0.0% 1.0% 2.0% 3.0% 4.0% 5.0% 6.0% 7.0%

Just as a week is a long time in politics, a decade is a long time in demography. Come 2021 we may not have a Census, or we may have just conducted what the previous government suggested might be the last traditional Census. But what matters most to people is change, whether things are getting better or worse, are there new problems, or are difficulties receding. And just as we had no way of knowing if the description we painted in 2001 would strengthen, so, too, we have no way of knowing if we are at a crossroads now – or if the divides will continue to grow. All we can do is show what has been happening, and look out for signs of change in long-established trends. So let's end with two different graphs (shown above and below), including one that suggests that the current divide need not continue forever.

Let's look at the change in the number of graduates in each part of the UK. Almost everywhere the number of graduates has risen by around 5 or 6 percentage points, apart from in one place, the place that was always increasing the most in the past, the very Centre of London. Every trend has to come to an end sometime, somewhere. There will eventually be a tipping point. Empires rise and fall.

Now look at the proportion of graduates in each place who arrived there (or stayed there) in the last decade, the relative change. The final graph in this book shows that a third of the university graduates living and working in almost the entire Archipelago in 2011 were not there in 2001. The same is true of London Edge, Outer London and London Suburbs, but in Inner London, the rise in graduates during the 2000s was of just a quarter more than its 2001 total, in London Core it was less than a fifth more, and in the Centre of London graduate growth was less than one extra graduate arriving by 2011 for every 15 already there in 2001. Maybe the Centre of London's growth is coming to an end. Or maybe being a graduate is not quite what it used to be. And maybe it is when this is realised that the change begins. Perhaps even the value of people without degrees, or without second or third university degrees, will start to be appreciated. But without the statistics we might not see that the tide has turned until many decades after the actual event.

Relative increase in people aged 16–64 holding a university degree, UK 2001–2011 % change

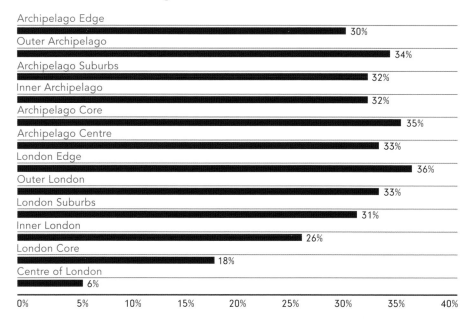

Appendix and Endnotes

Appendix
Ranking districts by wealth and poverty

There are five tables in this appendix. The first shows the Local Authority districts with the highest proportion of wealthy households; the second the Local Authority districts with highest proportion of middling households; and the third the Local Authority districts with the highest proportion of poor households. These are followed by two seperate lists of all 406 Local Authorities, one in the standard geographical order used by ONS and the other in alphabetical order.

The proportion of households that are wealthy in each district is estimated to be the same as the proportion of people who pay inheritance tax on death each year in the district. To reduce the effects of chance variation, three years of data have been used here so that all estates paying inheritance tax in the period 6 April 2010 to 5 April 2013 are included. This figure is divided by the total number of people whose deaths were registered there in the three years 2010–12 to produce the percentage shown. This number is low because the large majority of people in the UK have no way of amassing enough significant wealth to be eligible to pay inheritance tax. Furthermore, of the few who at some moment in their lives might control assets, especially housing, that would qualify them to pay this tax if they were to die, most are only just over the inheritance tax threshold and spend much of their capital long before they actually die. It is only the truly wealthy who pay inheritance tax. Because three years of data has been used here, these figures differ slightly from those used to produce the map in the Introduction of this atlas, which is based on one year's data.

The proportion of households that are poor in each Local Authority district is calculated using the same formula mentioned in the Introduction where this estimate of 2011 poverty rates is mapped. The formula is 57.6% of overcrowded households (more than one person per room) +35.7% of households renting from local authorities or housing associations +32.4% of lone-parent households +30.3% of households with an unemployed household reference person (HRP) +18.4% of households with no car +16.5% of households renting from private landlords +16.1% of households with a member with a limiting long-term illness + 13.5% of households with no central heating or without sole use of amenities +11.3% of households with HRP in a low social class (NS-SeC 6, 7 or 8). Individually the actual proportions of each of these types of households who are poor will be higher, but to offset the inevitable double counting, this formula, derived from regression analysis of the 2001 Census,[10] adjusts the proportions to produce results that are comparable to the Breadline Britain survey.

The proportion of the population who are poor in many districts will have risen by 2015 as overcrowding has increased significantly in the South East of England with rising housing prices, because private renting has increased faster than social renting has decreased, because there has been no fall in lone parent families and possibly a rise due to couples living apart as a result of changes to benefit rules and caps on benefits, because rates of mental illness, anxiety and depression have risen and the population is ageing so rates of limiting long-term illness should not be expected to be falling. Rates of recorded poor health rose abruptly after 2010/11 across the UK. The government programme of improving housing to a decent standard was cancelled in 2010 with the election of the Coalition government, so there will have been few improvements to the state housing stock since. In the private sector, as more and more housing is privately rented, quality falls because more repairs are neglected. And finally, more and more people, often despite qualifications, are being forced to work in lower status jobs (NS-SeC 6, 7 and 8) where wages tend to be low and the risk of being part of the working poor is highest. In short, we underestimate poverty. However, because so few are wealthy in most areas, most are still middling – that middling group. When you have fewer wealthy and fewer poor, there is greater equality.

Local Authority districts with the highest proportion of wealthy households

Local Authority	Region/ country	Classification	Wealthy %	Wealthy rank	Middling %	Middling rank	Poor %	Poor rank
Kensington & Chelsea	London	London Core	18.25	1	45.56	406	36.19	30
Richmond upon Thames	London	Inner London	15.41	2	63.31	369	21.29	286
Elmbridge	South East	Inner London	14.11	3	69.32	312	16.56	400
Westminster	London	Centre of London	12.19	4	47.44	404	40.37	14
Chichester	South East	London Suburbs	11.74	5	67.72	335	20.54	311
Barnet	London	Inner London	11.71	6	59.76	384	28.53	112
South Bucks	South East	London Suburbs	11.46	7	71.70	262	16.84	397
Epsom & Ewell	South East	Inner London	10.96	8	71.89	254	17.16	389
Guildford	South East	London Suburbs	10.53	9	71.19	268	18.29	373
Waverley	South East	London Suburbs	10.51	10	72.59	228	16.91	395
Camden	London	London Core	10.28	11	47.54	403	42.17	10
Mole Valley	South East	London Suburbs	10.25	12	72.39	237	17.36	386
Harrow	London	Inner London	9.76	13	64.11	362	26.14	161
Wandsworth	London	London Core	9.56	14	58.48	389	31.95	55
St Albans	East	London Suburbs	9.51	15	72.52	231	17.97	378
Kingston upon Thames	London	Inner London	9.46	16	67.54	337	23.00	243
Chiltern	South East	London Suburbs	9.40	17	74.01	179	16.59	399
Hammersmith & Fulham	London	London Core	9.33	18	50.40	400	40.27	15
Winchester	South East	Outer London	9.12	19	71.80	259	19.08	356
South Oxfordshire	South East	London Suburbs	8.91	20	73.71	189	17.38	385

Local Authority districts with the highest proportion of middling households

Local Authority	Region/ country	Classification	Wealthy %	Wealthy rank	Middling %	Middling rank	Poor %	Poor rank
Harborough	East Midlands	Outer London	0.00	313	83.92	1	16.08	403
Fareham	South East	Outer London	0.00	294	83.18	2	16.82	398
Rochford	East	London Suburbs	0.00	290	83.02	3	16.98	394
Ribble Valley	North West	Archipelago Suburbs	0.00	307	82.95	4	17.05	392
Blaby	East Midlands	London Suburbs	0.00	312	82.73	5	17.27	388
Rutland	East Midlands	Outer London	0.00	265	82.19	6	17.81	380
Maldon	East	Outer London	0.00	289	81.92	7	18.08	377
Rushcliffe	East Midlands	Inner Archipelago	1.03	209	81.87	8	17.11	390
North Kesteven	East Midlands	Outer London	0.00	319	81.54	9	18.46	370
Castle Point	East	London Suburbs	0.00	287	81.35	10	18.65	367
Broadland	East	London Edge	1.73	178	81.23	11	17.04	393
Richmondshire	Yorkshire & the Humber	Inner Archipelago	0.00	329	80.89	12	19.11	355
Uttlesford	East	London Suburbs	1.60	182	80.89	13	17.51	383
Oadby & Wigston	East Midlands	Outer London	0.00	316	80.84	14	19.16	354
South Northamptonshire	East Midlands	London Suburbs	3.06	134	80.82	15	16.12	401
Staffordshire Moorlands	West Midlands	Archipelago Suburbs	0.00	342	80.76	16	19.24	351
Eastleigh	South East	Outer London	0.00	293	80.57	17	19.43	344
Craven	Yorkshire & the Humber	Archipelago Suburbs	0.00	328	80.54	18	19.46	341
South Derbyshire	East Midlands	Inner Archipelago	0.00	282	80.43	19	19.57	336
Lichfield	West Midlands	Archipelago Suburbs	0.00	339	80.34	20	19.66	334

Local Authority districts with the highest proportion of poor households

Local Authority	Region/ country	Classification	Wealthy %	Wealthy rank	Middling %	Middling rank	Poor %	Poor rank
Hackney	London	London Core	3.12	126	45.75	405	51.13	1
Newham	London	London Core	0.00	237	50.72	397	49.28	2
Tower Hamlets	London	London Core	0.00	238	51.02	396	48.98	3
Southwark	London	London Core	3.57	106	49.05	401	47.38	4
Islington	London	London Core	5.43	61	47.94	402	46.63	5
Lambeth	London	London Core	5.58	59	50.45	398	43.97	6
Barking & Dagenham	London	Inner London	0.00	236	56.40	392	43.60	7
Glasgow	Scotland	Archipelago Centre	0.94	213	55.83	393	43.23	8
Haringey	London	London Core	7.19	32	50.43	399	42.37	9
Camden	London	London Core	10.28	11	47.54	403	42.17	10
Brent	London	London Core	5.28	65	53.36	395	41.36	11
Lewisham	London	London Core	3.26	120	55.78	394	40.96	12
Manchester	North West	Archipelago Centre	1.06	207	58.05	390	40.89	13
Westminster	London	Centre of London	12.19	4	47.44	404	40.37	14
Hammersmith & Fulham	London	London Core	9.33	18	50.40	400	40.27	15
Greenwich	London	Inner London	1.93	169	57.92	391	40.14	16
Liverpool	North West	Archipelago Centre	0.54	230	59.59	387	39.86	17
West Dunbartonshire	Scotland	Archipelago Suburbs	0.00	367	60.60	382	39.40	18
Nottingham	East Midlands	Archipelago Core	0.44	232	60.61	380	38.96	19
Belfast	Northern Ireland	Archipelago Centre	1.75	177	59.62	386	38.63	20

Households that are wealthy, middling or poor, Local Authority districts % and rank in 2011 (ONS order)

Region/country	Local Authority	Classification	Wealthy %	Wealthy rank	Middling %	Middling rank	Poor %	Poor rank
North East	**County Durham UA**	Archipelago Suburbs	0.69	227	70.56	287	28.75	110
	Darlington UA	Archipelago Core	0.00	258	72.39	236	27.61	130
	Hartlepool UA	Archipelago Core	0.00	254	65.76	356	34.24	38
	Middlesbrough UA	Archipelago Core	0.00	255	64.09	363	35.91	33
	Northumberland UA	Archipelago Suburbs	2.26	159	72.21	244	25.52	180
	Redcar & Cleveland UA	Archipelago Core	0.00	256	70.28	294	29.72	86
	Stockton-on-Tees UA	Archipelago Core	0.00	257	72.63	226	27.37	136
	Tyne & Wear (Met county)							
	Gateshead	Archipelago Core	0.00	248	66.28	352	33.72	45
	Newcastle upon Tyne	Archipelago Centre	1.84	174	62.45	373	35.71	36
	North Tyneside	Archipelago Core	0.00	249	70.95	279	29.05	101
	South Tyneside	Archipelago Core	0.00	250	63.42	367	36.58	27
	Sunderland	Archipelago Core	0.00	251	66.00	354	34.00	42
North West	**Blackburn with Darwen UA**	Inner Archipelago	0.00	260	68.84	319	31.16	65
	Blackpool UA	Archipelago Suburbs	0.00	261	68.57	322	31.43	63
	Cheshire East UA	Archipelago Suburbs	3.52	109	76.42	84	20.06	319
	Cheshire West & Chester UA	Archipelago Core	2.49	151	74.87	142	22.64	254
	Halton UA	Archipelago Core	0.00	259	68.31	324	31.69	60
	Warrington UA	Archipelago Core	1.27	197	75.33	126	23.39	232
	Cumbria							
	Allerdale	Inner Archipelago	0.91	217	73.82	185	25.27	188
	Barrow-in-Furness	Inner Archipelago	0.00	275	72.64	225	27.36	137
	Carlisle	Archipelago Core	0.00	276	74.57	159	25.43	185
	Copeland	Inner Archipelago	0.00	277	74.26	172	25.74	173
	Eden	Inner Archipelago	1.90	172	78.82	39	19.28	350
	South Lakeland	Archipelago Suburbs	5.25	67	75.74	108	19.01	359
	Greater Manchester (Met county)							
	Bolton	Archipelago Core	0.92	215	69.01	317	30.06	79
	Bury	Archipelago Core	0.57	228	73.93	182	25.50	182
	Manchester	Archipelago Centre	1.06	207	58.05	390	40.89	13
	Oldham	Archipelago Centre	0.00	239	68.19	326	31.81	58
	Rochdale	Archipelago Core	0.00	240	67.14	341	32.86	50
	Salford	Archipelago Centre	0.00	241	64.09	364	35.91	32
	Stockport	Archipelago Core	2.39	152	74.36	169	23.24	235
	Tameside	Archipelago Centre	0.00	242	69.26	314	30.74	69
	Trafford	Archipelago Core	3.50	111	72.43	235	24.07	222
	Wigan	Archipelago Core	0.00	243	72.05	247	27.95	125
	Lancashire							
	Burnley	Inner Archipelago	0.00	302	69.41	310	30.59	71
	Chorley	Archipelago Suburbs	0.00	303	78.59	42	21.41	282
	Fylde	Archipelago Suburbs	1.32	195	78.70	41	19.98	322
	Hyndburn	Inner Archipelago	0.00	304	71.48	264	28.52	113
	Lancaster	Archipelago Core	2.72	142	73.44	198	23.84	226
	Pendle	Archipelago Suburbs	0.00	305	72.38	238	27.62	128
	Preston	Archipelago Suburbs	0.00	306	70.13	295	29.87	85

Region/country	Local Authority	Classification	Wealthy %	Wealthy rank	Middling %	Middling rank	Poor %	Poor rank
	Ribble Valley	Archipelago Suburbs	0.00	307	82.95	4	17.05	392
	Rossendale	Inner Archipelago	0.00	308	74.76	147	25.24	191
	South Ribble	Archipelago Suburbs	0.00	309	80.04	25	19.96	325
	West Lancashire	Archipelago Suburbs	0.00	310	76.31	86	23.69	229
	Wyre	Archipelago Suburbs	0.00	311	79.28	37	20.72	304
	Merseyside (Met county)							
	Knowsley	Archipelago Core	0.00	244	63.13	370	36.87	26
	Liverpool	Archipelago Centre	0.54	230	59.59	387	39.86	17
	Sefton	Archipelago Suburbs	1.91	170	71.01	274	27.08	142
	St Helens	Archipelago Core	0.00	245	70.58	286	29.42	92
	Wirral	Archipelago Suburbs	1.80	176	70.03	299	28.17	119
Yorkshire & the Humber	**East Riding of Yorkshire UA**	Archipelago Suburbs	2.09	164	77.94	53	19.97	323
	Kingston upon Hull, City of UA	Archipelago Core	0.00	262	61.70	379	38.30	21
	North East Lincolnshire UA	London Edge	0.00	263	70.81	280	29.19	99
	North Lincolnshire UA	London Edge	0.00	264	75.12	134	24.88	201
	York UA	Archipelago Suburbs	2.97	136	73.40	199	23.63	230
	North Yorkshire							
	Craven	Archipelago Suburbs	0.00	328	80.54	18	19.46	341
	Hambleton	Archipelago Suburbs	2.78	138	78.17	47	19.05	357
	Harrogate	Archipelago Suburbs	6.06	51	75.01	140	18.93	362
	Richmondshire	Inner Archipelago	0.00	329	80.89	12	19.11	355
	Ryedale	Archipelago Suburbs	3.37	118	75.89	103	20.74	303
	Scarborough	Archipelago Suburbs	0.96	211	72.77	223	26.27	158
	Selby	Archipelago Suburbs	0.00	330	80.10	24	19.90	327
	South Yorkshire (Met county)							
	Barnsley	Archipelago Core	0.00	246	70.41	291	29.59	89
	Doncaster	Archipelago Core	0.33	234	70.76	281	28.91	106
	Rotherham	Archipelago Core	0.00	247	70.74	282	29.26	97
	Sheffield	Archipelago Centre	1.52	188	66.78	348	31.70	59
	West Yorkshire (Met county)							
	Bradford	Archipelago Centre	1.84	173	68.20	325	29.96	82
	Calderdale	Archipelago Centre	0.53	231	72.31	239	27.16	141
	Kirklees	Archipelago Centre	1.47	189	71.13	271	27.40	135
	Leeds	Archipelago Centre	1.54	187	67.89	329	30.57	73
	Wakefield	Archipelago Core	0.32	235	69.76	305	29.92	83
East Midlands	**Derby UA**	Archipelago Core	1.57	185	68.44	323	30.00	81
	Leicester UA	Inner London	0.42	233	62.27	376	37.31	25
	Nottingham UA	Archipelago Core	0.44	232	60.61	380	38.96	19
	Rutland UA	Outer London	0.00	265	82.19	6	17.81	380
	Derbyshire							
	Amber Valley	Archipelago Suburbs	0.83	221	76.65	76	22.52	258
	Bolsover	Archipelago Suburbs	0.00	278	72.43	234	27.57	131
	Chesterfield	Archipelago Core	0.00	279	70.64	285	29.36	93
	Derbyshire Dales	Archipelago Suburbs	3.52	108	76.91	70	19.57	337

Region/country	Local Authority	Classification	Wealthy %	Wealthy rank	Middling %	Middling rank	Poor %	Poor rank
	Erewash	Archipelago Suburbs	0.00	280	75.66	110	24.34	214
	High Peak	Inner Archipelago	1.21	200	76.48	83	22.31	265
	North East Derbyshire	Inner Archipelago	0.00	281	75.71	109	24.29	215
	South Derbyshire	Inner Archipelago	0.00	282	80.43	19	19.57	336
	Leicestershire							
	Blaby	London Suburbs	0.00	312	82.73	5	17.27	388
	Charnwood	Inner Archipelago	0.95	212	77.93	54	21.12	290
	Harborough	Outer London	0.00	313	83.92	1	16.08	403
	Hinckley & Bosworth	Outer London	1.08	206	79.60	31	19.31	348
	Melton	Outer London	0.00	314	80.03	26	19.97	324
	North West Leicestershire	Inner Archipelago	0.00	315	78.42	43	21.58	279
	Oadby & Wigston	Outer London	0.00	316	80.84	14	19.16	354
	Lincolnshire							
	Boston	Outer London	0.00	317	73.01	216	26.99	145
	East Lindsey	London Edge	0.74	225	76.29	87	22.98	245
	Lincoln	London Edge	0.00	318	69.25	315	30.75	68
	North Kesteven	Outer London	0.00	319	81.54	9	18.46	370
	South Holland	Outer London	4.40	89	73.59	193	22.01	273
	South Kesteven	Outer London	1.81	175	76.80	73	21.39	283
	West Lindsey	London Edge	0.00	320	79.52	32	20.48	312
	Northamptonshire							
	Corby	London Suburbs	0.00	323	69.54	308	30.46	75
	Daventry	London Suburbs	0.00	324	80.32	21	19.68	333
	East Northamptonshire	London Suburbs	0.00	325	79.61	30	20.39	313
	Kettering	London Suburbs	0.00	326	76.92	69	23.08	237
	Northampton	Inner London	0.77	224	71.82	257	27.41	134
	South Northamptonshire	London Suburbs	3.06	134	80.82	15	16.12	401
	Wellingborough	London Suburbs	0.00	327	73.63	191	26.37	157
	Nottinghamshire							
	Ashfield	Archipelago Suburbs	0.00	331	73.11	212	26.89	148
	Bassetlaw	Archipelago Suburbs	0.00	332	75.38	124	24.62	207
	Broxtowe	Inner Archipelago	0.00	333	78.28	44	21.72	276
	Gedling	Archipelago Suburbs	0.00	334	78.16	48	21.84	275
	Mansfield	Archipelago Suburbs	0.00	335	71.89	253	28.11	121
	Newark & Sherwood	Archipelago Suburbs	0.87	219	76.09	94	23.03	239
	Rushcliffe	Inner Archipelago	1.03	209	81.87	8	17.11	390
West Midlands	**Herefordshire, County of UA**	Archipelago Suburbs	3.85	97	73.80	186	22.34	263
	Shropshire UA	Archipelago Suburbs	3.18	123	75.28	128	21.53	280
	Stoke-on-Trent UA	Archipelago Suburbs	0.00	267	66.75	349	33.25	46
	Telford & Wrekin UA	Archipelago Suburbs	0.00	266	72.50	232	27.50	132
	Staffordshire							
	Cannock Chase	Archipelago Suburbs	0.00	337	74.43	165	25.57	178
	East Staffordshire	Archipelago Suburbs	0.00	338	75.61	113	24.39	213
	Lichfield	Archipelago Suburbs	0.00	339	80.34	20	19.66	334
	Newcastle-under-Lyme	Archipelago Core	0.00	340	74.39	166	25.61	177
	South Staffordshire	Archipelago Suburbs	0.00	341	80.30	22	19.70	331
	Stafford	Archipelago Suburbs	0.81	222	78.23	46	20.95	297
	Staffordshire Moorlands	Archipelago Suburbs	0.00	342	80.76	16	19.24	351

Region/country	Local Authority	Classification	Wealthy %	Wealthy rank	Middling %	Middling rank	Poor %	Poor rank
	Tamworth	Archipelago Suburbs	0.00	343	73.51	195	26.49	156
	Warwickshire							
	North Warwickshire	London Suburbs	0.00	346	77.78	56	22.22	269
	Nuneaton & Bedworth	London Suburbs	0.00	347	74.53	161	25.47	184
	Rugby	London Suburbs	0.00	348	77.75	57	22.25	267
	Stratford-upon-Avon	London Suburbs	5.00	70	76.20	90	18.80	364
	Warwick	London Suburbs	4.11	94	74.61	155	21.28	288
	West Midlands (Met county)							
	Birmingham	Archipelago Centre	1.34	193	62.21	377	36.45	29
	Coventry	Archipelago Centre	0.88	218	67.81	332	31.31	64
	Dudley	Archipelago Core	1.24	198	71.30	267	27.46	133
	Sandwell	Archipelago Core	0.00	252	63.50	366	36.50	28
	Solihull	Archipelago Core	4.41	87	72.79	220	22.79	251
	Walsall	Archipelago Core	0.00	253	67.51	338	32.49	51
	Wolverhampton	Archipelago Core	0.97	210	62.85	372	36.18	31
	Worcestershire							
	Bromsgrove	Archipelago Suburbs	2.24	160	80.27	23	17.49	384
	Malvern Hills	Archipelago Suburbs	4.20	92	75.75	106	20.05	320
	Redditch	Archipelago Suburbs	0.00	350	72.93	219	27.07	143
	Worcester	Archipelago Suburbs	0.00	351	74.86	143	25.14	195
	Wychavon	Archipelago Suburbs	4.41	88	75.55	116	20.04	321
	Wyre Forest	Archipelago Suburbs	0.00	352	76.21	89	23.79	227
East	**Bedford UA**	London Suburbs	3.10	130	71.88	255	25.03	197
	Central Bedfordshire UA	London Suburbs	2.61	148	77.52	61	19.88	330
	Luton UA	London Suburbs	0.73	226	68.12	327	31.15	66
	Peterborough UA	London Suburbs	0.00	269	70.98	277	29.02	103
	Southend-on-Sea UA	London Suburbs	3.24	121	70.98	278	25.78	170
	Thurrock UA	London Suburbs	0.00	270	73.15	210	26.85	149
	Cambridgeshire							
	Cambridge	Inner London	7.52	29	63.41	368	29.07	100
	East Cambridgeshire	Outer London	2.64	147	77.82	55	19.55	338
	Fenland	Outer London	0.00	274	76.01	96	23.99	225
	Huntingdonshire	London Suburbs	2.34	155	77.97	52	19.68	332
	South Cambridgeshire	London Suburbs	5.35	64	76.83	71	17.82	379
	Essex							
	Basildon	London Suburbs	0.00	286	73.10	213	26.90	147
	Braintree	London Suburbs	2.27	158	75.03	139	22.70	253
	Brentwood	Inner London	6.62	44	74.74	149	18.64	368
	Castle Point	London Suburbs	0.00	287	81.35	10	18.65	367
	Chelmsford	London Suburbs	3.44	115	76.68	75	19.89	328
	Colchester	Outer London	3.73	101	73.28	203	22.99	244
	Epping Forest	London Suburbs	6.38	47	72.54	230	21.08	295
	Harlow	London Suburbs	0.00	288	67.59	336	32.41	52
	Maldon	Outer London	0.00	289	81.92	7	18.08	377
	Rochford	London Suburbs	0.00	290	83.02	3	16.98	394
	Tendring	London Edge	1.29	196	74.68	150	24.03	224
	Uttlesford	London Suburbs	1.60	182	80.89	13	17.51	383

Region/country	Local Authority	Classification	Wealthy %	Wealthy rank	Middling %	Middling rank	Poor %	Poor rank
	Hertfordshire							
	Broxbourne	London Suburbs	0.00	297	76.77	74	23.23	236
	Dacorum	London Suburbs	4.47	84	71.83	256	23.69	228
	East Hertfordshire	London Suburbs	5.60	58	76.12	92	18.28	374
	Hertsmere	London Suburbs	7.29	31	69.78	304	22.93	247
	North Hertfordshire	London Suburbs	3.84	98	73.63	190	22.53	257
	St Albans	London Suburbs	9.51	15	72.52	231	17.97	378
	Stevenage	London Suburbs	0.00	298	70.50	288	29.50	91
	Three Rivers	London Suburbs	8.41	22	71.46	265	20.13	318
	Watford	Inner London	1.97	168	72.21	243	25.82	168
	Welwyn Hatfield	London Suburbs	4.50	82	68.58	320	26.92	146
	Norfolk							
	Breckland	London Edge	0.93	214	76.65	77	22.42	261
	Broadland	London Edge	1.73	178	81.23	11	17.04	393
	Great Yarmouth	London Edge	0.00	321	70.68	284	29.32	94
	King's Lynn & West Norfolk	London Edge	1.42	191	76.11	93	22.47	259
	North Norfolk	London Edge	3.47	112	74.94	141	21.59	278
	Norwich	Inner London	0.00	322	64.99	358	35.01	37
	South Norfolk	London Edge	3.72	102	77.98	51	18.30	372
	Suffolk							
	Babergh	Outer London	5.05	69	75.03	138	19.92	326
	Forest Heath	London Edge	0.00	344	76.62	78	23.38	233
	Ipswich	Inner London	0.00	345	69.54	307	30.46	76
	Mid Suffolk	London Edge	2.58	149	79.29	36	18.12	376
	St Edmundsbury	Outer London	2.38	154	75.39	122	22.22	268
	Suffolk Coastal	London Edge	4.80	76	75.89	102	19.31	349
	Waveney	London Edge	1.91	171	73.00	217	25.10	196
London	**Inner London**							
	Camden	London Core	10.28	11	47.54	403	42.17	10
	City of London	Centre of London	3.12	128	65.35	357	31.53	62
	Hackney	London Core	3.12	126	45.75	405	51.13	1
	Hammersmith & Fulham	London Core	9.33	18	50.40	400	40.27	15
	Haringey	London Core	7.19	32	50.43	399	42.37	9
	Islington	London Core	5.43	61	47.94	402	46.63	5
	Kensington & Chelsea	London Core	18.25	1	45.56	406	36.19	30
	Lambeth	London Core	5.58	59	50.45	398	43.97	6
	Lewisham	London Core	3.26	120	55.78	394	40.96	12
	Newham	London Core	0.00	237	50.72	397	49.28	2
	Southwark	London Core	3.57	106	49.05	401	47.38	4
	Tower Hamlets	London Core	0.00	238	51.02	396	48.98	3
	Wandsworth	London Core	9.56	14	58.48	389	31.95	55
	Westminster	Centre of London	12.19	4	47.44	404	40.37	14
	Outer London							
	Barking & Dagenham	Inner London	0.00	236	56.40	392	43.60	7
	Barnet	Inner London	11.71	6	59.76	384	28.53	112
	Bexley	Inner London	3.01	135	72.29	240	24.70	205
	Brent	London Core	5.28	65	53.36	395	41.36	11
	Bromley	Inner London	7.35	30	69.85	302	22.80	250
	Croydon	Inner London	5.35	62	62.97	371	31.68	61
	Ealing	Inner London	7.11	35	58.73	388	34.16	40

Region/country	Local Authority	Classification	Wealthy %	Wealthy rank	Middling %	Middling rank	Poor %	Poor rank
	Enfield	Inner London	5.67	56	60.58	383	33.76	44
	Greenwich	Inner London	1.93	169	57.92	391	40.14	16
	Harrow	Inner London	9.76	13	64.11	362	26.14	161
	Havering	Inner London	2.57	150	73.17	208	24.26	216
	Hillingdon	Inner London	4.72	78	67.12	342	28.16	120
	Hounslow	Inner London	5.35	63	60.60	381	34.06	41
	Kingston upon Thames	Inner London	9.46	16	67.54	337	23.00	243
	Merton	Inner London	8.51	21	63.87	365	27.62	129
	Redbridge	Inner London	4.56	79	66.95	343	28.49	115
	Richmond upon Thames	Inner London	15.41	2	63.31	369	21.29	286
	Sutton	Inner London	5.19	68	70.69	283	24.12	221
	Waltham Forest	Inner London	2.39	153	59.63	385	37.98	23
South East	**Bracknell Forest UA**	Outer London	0.00	272	79.35	33	20.65	308
	Brighton & Hove UA	Inner London	6.21	48	64.57	359	29.23	98
	Isle of Wight UA	Outer London	3.52	107	72.27	241	24.21	218
	Medway UA	London Suburbs	0.00	271	74.76	146	25.24	192
	Milton Keynes UA	London Suburbs	1.65	179	72.55	229	25.79	169
	Portsmouth UA	Inner London	1.98	167	67.44	339	30.58	72
	Reading UA	Inner London	3.99	96	67.81	331	28.20	117
	Slough UA	London Suburbs	0.00	273	66.85	346	33.15	48
	Southampton UA	Inner London	0.91	216	67.15	340	31.94	57
	West Berkshire UA	Outer London	4.91	73	76.08	95	19.01	360
	Windsor & Maidenhead UA	London Suburbs	8.38	23	72.67	224	18.95	361
	Wokingham UA	Outer London	6.65	43	79.33	35	14.01	405
	Buckinghamshire							
	Aylesbury Vale	London Suburbs	3.51	110	77.08	65	19.40	345
	Chiltern	London Suburbs	9.40	17	74.01	179	16.59	399
	South Bucks	London Suburbs	11.46	7	71.70	262	16.84	397
	Wycombe	London Suburbs	5.76	55	74.36	170	19.88	329
	East Sussex							
	Eastbourne	London Suburbs	4.74	77	68.58	321	26.68	155
	Hastings	London Suburbs	0.00	285	68.92	318	31.08	67
	Lewes	Outer London	5.99	53	72.62	227	21.39	284
	Rother	London Suburbs	5.00	71	74.03	178	20.97	296
	Wealden	London Suburbs	5.54	60	77.60	60	16.86	396
	Hampshire							
	Basingstoke & Deane	Outer London	3.34	119	75.16	132	21.50	281
	East Hampshire	Outer London	6.01	52	76.35	85	17.64	381
	Eastleigh	Outer London	0.00	293	80.57	17	19.43	344
	Fareham	Outer London	0.00	294	83.18	2	16.82	398
	Gosport	Outer London	0.00	295	74.32	171	25.68	174
	Hart	Outer London	6.48	46	79.73	29	13.80	406
	Havant	Outer London	2.05	166	72.10	246	25.85	167
	New Forest	Outer London	6.49	45	74.50	163	19.02	358
	Rushmoor	Outer London	0.00	296	76.97	67	23.03	240
	Test Valley	Outer London	4.89	74	75.64	111	19.47	340
	Winchester	Outer London	9.12	19	71.80	259	19.08	356
	Kent							
	Ashford	London Suburbs	3.15	124	74.68	151	22.16	271

Region/country	Local Authority	Classification	Wealthy %	Wealthy rank	Middling %	Middling rank	Poor %	Poor rank
	Canterbury	London Suburbs	3.13	125	73.50	196	23.36	234
	Dartford	Inner London	0.00	299	75.87	104	24.13	219
	Dover	London Suburbs	1.10	204	73.36	200	25.54	179
	Gravesham	Inner London	0.00	300	72.77	222	27.23	140
	Maidstone	London Suburbs	3.40	117	75.32	127	21.27	289
	Sevenoaks	London Suburbs	8.15	24	73.15	209	18.69	366
	Shepway	London Suburbs	0.85	220	73.88	184	25.27	189
	Swale	London Suburbs	0.00	301	75.08	137	24.92	198
	Thanet	Outer London	1.40	192	69.57	306	29.02	102
	Tonbridge & Malling	London Suburbs	2.83	137	76.50	81	20.67	305
	Tunbridge Wells	London Suburbs	7.15	33	70.99	276	21.86	274
	Oxfordshire							
	Cherwell	London Suburbs	4.55	80	74.63	153	20.82	301
	Oxford	Inner London	7.14	34	62.32	375	30.54	74
	South Oxfordshire	London Suburbs	8.91	20	73.71	189	17.38	385
	Vale of White Horse	London Suburbs	5.95	54	75.50	118	18.55	369
	West Oxfordshire	London Suburbs	6.13	50	75.61	114	18.26	375
	Surrey							
	Elmbridge	Inner London	14.11	3	69.32	312	16.56	400
	Epsom & Ewell	Inner London	10.96	8	71.89	254	17.16	389
	Guildford	London Suburbs	10.53	9	71.19	268	18.29	373
	Mole Valley	London Suburbs	10.25	12	72.39	237	17.36	386
	Reigate & Banstead	London Suburbs	8.10	25	73.47	197	18.43	371
	Runnymede	London Suburbs	6.78	42	73.72	188	19.51	339
	Spelthorne	London Suburbs	3.46	113	76.29	88	20.25	314
	Surrey Heath	London Suburbs	7.01	39	77.42	62	15.58	404
	Tandridge	London Suburbs	7.76	26	75.18	131	17.05	391
	Waverley	London Suburbs	10.51	10	72.59	228	16.91	395
	Woking	London Suburbs	7.54	28	73.02	215	19.44	343
	West Sussex							
	Adur	Outer London	1.43	190	75.97	97	22.60	256
	Arun	London Suburbs	4.44	85	74.48	164	21.08	294
	Chichester	London Suburbs	11.74	5	67.72	335	20.54	311
	Crawley	London Suburbs	0.00	349	71.50	263	28.50	114
	Horsham	London Suburbs	7.10	36	75.55	117	17.36	387
	Mid Sussex	London Suburbs	6.85	41	75.61	112	17.55	382
	Worthing	Outer London	3.64	103	73.33	202	23.03	241
South West	**Bath & North East Somerset UA**	London Suburbs	5.63	57	71.74	261	22.63	255
	Bournemouth UA	Outer London	4.07	95	70.04	298	25.90	164
	Bristol, City of UA	Inner London	3.07	133	66.87	345	30.06	80
	Cornwall UA	London Edge	3.12	127	73.92	183	22.96	246
	Isles of Scilly UA	London Edge	3.12	129	66.51	350	30.37	77
	North Somerset UA	London Suburbs	3.61	104	76.17	91	20.22	316
	Plymouth UA	Outer London	0.57	229	70.12	296	29.31	95
	Poole UA	Outer London	5.26	66	73.14	211	21.60	277
	South Gloucestershire UA	London Suburbs	3.09	131	78.06	50	18.86	363
	Swindon UA	Inner London	0.00	268	75.25	130	24.75	203
	Torbay UA	London Edge	2.74	140	71.79	260	25.48	183
	Wiltshire UA	Outer London	4.54	81	74.57	158	20.89	299

Region/country	Local Authority	Classification	Wealthy %	Wealthy rank	Middling %	Middling rank	Poor %	Poor rank
	Devon							
	East Devon	London Edge	6.16	49	74.60	156	19.24	352
	Exeter	London Edge	2.67	145	70.48	290	26.85	150
	Mid Devon	London Edge	0.00	283	78.90	38	21.10	293
	North Devon	London Edge	2.18	162	75.47	120	22.35	262
	South Hams	London Edge	7.06	38	73.62	192	19.32	347
	Teignbridge	London Edge	3.82	99	75.95	100	20.23	315
	Torridge	London Edge	2.69	143	75.95	99	21.36	285
	West Devon	London Edge	4.94	72	75.86	105	19.20	353
	Dorset							
	Christchurch	Outer London	1.57	184	77.64	59	20.79	302
	East Dorset	London Edge	4.17	93	79.73	28	16.10	402
	North Dorset	London Edge	7.56	27	72.98	218	19.46	342
	Purbeck	London Edge	2.09	165	77.35	63	20.55	310
	West Dorset	London Edge	6.91	40	72.44	233	20.64	309
	Weymouth & Portland	London Edge	0.00	284	74.50	162	25.50	181
	Gloucestershire							
	Cheltenham	London Suburbs	4.22	91	73.34	201	22.44	260
	Cotswold	London Suburbs	7.08	37	73.52	194	19.40	346
	Forest of Dean	London Suburbs	0.00	291	79.33	34	20.67	306
	Gloucester	London Suburbs	0.00	292	75.10	135	24.90	200
	Stroud	London Suburbs	4.50	83	75.92	101	19.58	335
	Tewkesbury	London Suburbs	1.23	199	80.02	27	18.74	365
	Somerset County							
	Mendip	Outer London	3.78	100	75.12	133	21.10	292
	Sedgemoor	Outer London	1.18	202	76.50	82	22.33	264
	South Somerset	London Edge	4.23	90	74.66	152	21.12	291
	Taunton Deane	London Edge	4.42	86	72.77	221	22.81	249
	West Somerset	London Edge	0.00	336	76.92	68	23.08	238
Wales	Isle of Anglesey	Archipelago Edge	0.00	353	75.44	121	24.56	209
	Gwynedd	Archipelago Edge	2.13	163	72.25	242	25.62	176
	Conwy	Outer Archipelago	1.33	194	74.54	160	24.13	220
	Denbighshire	Outer Archipelago	0.00	354	75.08	136	24.92	199
	Flintshire	Archipelago Suburbs	0.00	355	76.53	80	23.47	231
	Wrexham	Archipelago Core	0.00	356	71.81	258	28.19	118
	Powys	Outer Archipelago	3.43	116	74.37	168	22.20	270
	Ceredigion	Outer Archipelago	2.67	146	75.27	129	22.05	272
	Pembrokeshire	Outer Archipelago	3.21	122	72.05	248	24.74	204
	Carmarthenshire	Outer Archipelago	1.11	203	74.04	177	24.86	202
	Swansea	Archipelago Core	1.62	181	70.36	292	28.01	123
	Neath Port Talbot	Outer Archipelago	0.00	357	71.15	270	28.85	107
	Bridgend	Outer Archipelago	0.00	358	74.59	157	25.41	186
	The Vale of Glamorgan	Archipelago Suburbs	3.08	132	74.20	174	22.72	252
	Cardiff	Archipelago Centre	2.34	156	69.37	311	28.29	116
	Rhondda Cynon Taf	Archipelago Suburbs	0.00	359	72.12	245	27.88	126
	Merthyr Tydfil	Outer Archipelago	0.00	360	67.86	330	32.14	54
	Caerphilly	Archipelago Suburbs	0.00	361	71.37	266	28.63	111
	Blaenau Gwent	Outer Archipelago	0.00	362	66.07	353	33.93	43
	Torfaen	Archipelago Suburbs	0.00	363	70.49	289	29.51	90
	Monmouthshire	Outer Archipelago	1.09	205	78.07	49	20.84	300

Region/country	Local Authority	Classification	Wealthy %	Wealthy rank	Middling %	Middling rank	Poor %	Poor rank
	Newport	Archipelago Suburbs	0.00	364	70.34	293	29.66	88
Scotland	Aberdeen City	Archipelago Core	3.44	114	67.80	333	28.76	109
	Aberdeenshire	Archipelago Suburbs	2.23	161	76.83	72	20.94	298
	Angus	Archipelago Suburbs	1.04	208	71.91	252	27.05	144
	Argyll & Bute	Outer Archipelago	0.00	365	73.74	187	26.26	159
	Clackmannanshire	Inner Archipelago	0.00	366	68.05	328	31.95	56
	Dumfries & Galloway	Inner Archipelago	2.77	139	69.91	301	27.31	139
	Dundee City	Archipelago Core	0.00	368	62.40	374	37.60	24
	East Ayrshire	Archipelago Suburbs	0.00	369	66.83	347	33.17	47
	East Dunbartonshire	Archipelago Suburbs	2.73	141	76.61	79	20.66	307
	East Lothian	Archipelago Suburbs	2.31	157	70.03	300	27.66	127
	East Renfrewshire	Archipelago Suburbs	1.55	186	78.24	45	20.20	317
	Edinburgh City of	Archipelago Centre	4.86	75	66.32	351	28.82	108
	Eilean Siar	Archipelago Edge	0.00	381	74.74	148	25.26	190
	Falkirk	Archipelago Suburbs	0.00	370	69.81	303	30.19	78
	Fife	Archipelago Suburbs	1.57	183	69.13	316	29.30	96
	Glasgow City	Archipelago Centre	0.94	213	55.83	393	43.23	8
	Highland	Archipelago Edge	0.00	371	74.37	167	25.63	175
	Inverclyde	Archipelago Suburbs	0.00	372	64.28	360	35.72	35
	Midlothian	Archipelago Suburbs	0.00	373	70.10	297	29.90	84
	Moray	Archipelago Suburbs	0.00	374	74.78	145	25.22	193
	North Ayrshire	Archipelago Suburbs	0.00	375	65.80	355	34.20	39
	North Lanarkshire	Inner Archipelago	0.00	376	64.26	361	35.74	34
	Orkney Islands	Archipelago Edge	0.00	377	77.69	58	22.31	266
	Perth & Kinross	Archipelago Suburbs	3.60	105	71.93	251	24.47	211
	Renfrewshire	Archipelago Suburbs	0.00	378	67.74	334	32.26	53
	Scottish Borders	Inner Archipelago	2.68	144	71.18	269	26.14	160
	Shetland Islands	Archipelago Edge	0.00	379	73.95	181	26.05	162
	South Ayrshire	Archipelago Suburbs	1.65	180	71.00	275	27.35	138
	South Lanarkshire	Archipelago Suburbs	0.80	223	69.50	309	29.70	87
	Stirling	Archipelago Suburbs	1.19	201	73.04	214	25.77	172
	West Dunbartonshire	Archipelago Suburbs	0.00	367	60.60	382	39.40	18
	West Lothian	Archipelago Suburbs	0.00	380	69.29	313	30.71	70
Northern Ireland	Antrim	Archipelago Suburbs	0.00	382	75.56	115	24.44	212
	Ards	Inner Archipelago	0.00	383	75.96	98	24.04	223
	Armagh	Outer Archipelago	0.00	384	75.48	119	24.52	210
	Ballymena	Archipelago Suburbs	0.00	385	75.38	123	24.62	208
	Ballymoney	Outer Archipelago	0.00	386	74.11	176	25.89	165
	Banbridge	Archipelago Suburbs	0.00	387	77.13	64	22.87	248
	Belfast	Archipelago Centre	1.75	177	59.62	386	38.63	20
	Carrickfergus	Archipelago Suburbs	0.00	388	74.11	175	25.89	166
	Castlereagh	Inner Archipelago	0.00	389	77.00	66	23.00	242
	Coleraine	Archipelago Suburbs	0.00	390	73.19	207	26.81	151
	Cookstown	Archipelago Suburbs	0.00	391	73.95	180	26.05	163
	Craigavon	Inner Archipelago	0.00	392	71.08	272	28.92	105
	Derry	Outer Archipelago	0.00	393	61.78	378	38.22	22
	Down	Outer Archipelago	0.00	394	74.82	144	25.18	194
	Dungannon	Outer Archipelago	0.00	395	73.19	206	26.81	152
	Fermanagh	Archipelago Edge	0.00	396	75.37	125	24.63	206
	Larne	Archipelago Suburbs	0.00	397	74.23	173	25.77	171
	Limavady	Outer Archipelago	0.00	398	71.03	273	28.97	104

Region/country	Local Authority	Classification	Wealthy %	Wealthy rank	Middling %	Middling rank	Poor %	Poor rank
	Lisburn	Archipelago Suburbs	0.00	399	73.28	204	26.72	154
	Magherafelt	Archipelago Suburbs	0.00	400	75.75	107	24.25	217
	Moyle	Archipelago Suburbs	0.00	401	72.00	249	28.00	124
	Newry & Mourne	Outer Archipelago	0.00	402	71.95	250	28.05	122
	Newtownabbey	Archipelago Suburbs	0.00	403	74.63	154	25.37	187
	North Down	Inner Archipelago	0.00	404	78.72	40	21.28	287
	Omagh	Outer Archipelago	0.00	405	73.26	205	26.74	153
	Strabane	Archipelago Edge	0.00	406	66.91	344	33.09	49

Households that are wealthy, middling or poor, Local Authority districts % and rank in 2011 (alphabetical order)

Local Authority	Region/country	Classification	Wealthy %	Wealthy rank	Middling %	Middling rank	Poor %	Poor rank
Aberdeen	Scotland	Archipelago Core	3.44	114	67.80	333	28.76	109
Aberdeenshire	Scotland	Archipelago Suburbs	2.23	161	76.83	72	20.94	298
Adur	South East	Outer London	1.43	190	75.97	97	22.60	256
Allerdale	North West	Inner Archipelago	0.91	217	73.82	185	25.27	188
Amber Valley	East Midlands	Archipelago Suburbs	0.83	221	76.65	76	22.52	258
Angus	Scotland	Archipelago Suburbs	1.04	208	71.91	252	27.05	144
Antrim	Northern Ireland	Archipelago Suburbs	0.00	382	75.56	115	24.44	212
Ards	Northern Ireland	Inner Archipelago	0.00	383	75.96	98	24.04	223
Argyll & Bute	Scotland	Outer Archipelago	0.00	365	73.74	187	26.26	159
Armagh	Northern Ireland	Outer Archipelago	0.00	384	75.48	119	24.52	210
Arun	South East	London Suburbs	4.44	85	74.48	164	21.08	294
Ashfield	East Midlands	Archipelago Suburbs	0.00	331	73.11	212	26.89	148
Ashford	South East	London Suburbs	3.15	124	74.68	151	22.16	271
Aylesbury Vale	South East	London Suburbs	3.51	110	77.08	65	19.40	345
Babergh	East	Outer London	5.05	69	75.03	138	19.92	326
Ballymena	Northern Ireland	Archipelago Suburbs	0.00	385	75.38	123	24.62	208
Ballymoney	Northern Ireland	Outer Archipelago	0.00	386	74.11	176	25.89	165
Banbridge	Northern Ireland	Archipelago Suburbs	0.00	387	77.13	64	22.87	248
Barking & Dagenham	London	Inner London	0.00	236	56.40	392	43.60	7
Barnet	London	Inner London	11.71	6	59.76	384	28.53	112
Barnsley	Yorkshire & the Humber	Archipelago Core	0.00	246	70.41	291	29.59	89
Barrow-in-Furness	North West	Inner Archipelago	0.00	275	72.64	225	27.36	137
Basildon	East	London Suburbs	0.00	286	73.10	213	26.90	147
Basingstoke & Deane	South East	Outer London	3.34	119	75.16	132	21.50	281
Bassetlaw	East Midlands	Archipelago Suburbs	0.00	332	75.38	124	24.62	207
Bath & North East Somerset	South West	London Suburbs	5.63	57	71.74	261	22.63	255
Bedford	East	London Suburbs	3.10	130	71.88	255	25.03	197
Belfast	Northern Ireland	Archipelago Centre	1.75	177	59.62	386	38.63	20
Bexley	London	Inner London	3.01	135	72.29	240	24.70	205
Birmingham	West Midlands	Archipelago Centre	1.34	193	62.21	377	36.45	29
Blaby	East Midlands	London Suburbs	0.00	312	82.73	5	17.27	388
Blackburn with Darwen	North West	Inner Archipelago	0.00	260	68.84	319	31.16	65
Blackpool	North West	Archipelago Suburbs	0.00	261	68.57	322	31.43	63
Blaenau Gwent	Wales	Outer Archipelago	0.00	362	66.07	353	33.93	43
Bolsover	East Midlands	Archipelago Suburbs	0.00	278	72.43	234	27.57	131
Bolton	North West	Archipelago Core	0.92	215	69.01	317	30.06	79
Boston	East Midlands	Outer London	0.00	317	73.01	216	26.99	145
Bournemouth	South West	Outer London	4.07	95	70.04	298	25.90	164
Bracknell Forest	South East	Outer London	0.00	272	79.35	33	20.65	308
Bradford	Yorkshire & the Humber	Archipelago Centre	1.84	173	68.20	325	29.96	82
Braintree	East	London Suburbs	2.27	158	75.03	139	22.70	253
Breckland	East	London Edge	0.93	214	76.65	77	22.42	261
Brent	London	London Core	5.28	65	53.36	395	41.36	11
Brentwood	East	Inner London	6.62	44	74.74	149	18.64	368
Bridgend	Wales	Outer Archipelago	0.00	358	74.59	157	25.41	186
Brighton & Hove	South East	Inner London	6.21	48	64.57	359	29.23	98
Bristol	South West	Inner London	3.07	133	66.87	345	30.06	80
Broadland	East	London Edge	1.73	178	81.23	11	17.04	393
Bromley	London	Inner London	7.35	30	69.85	302	22.80	250

Local Authority	Region/country	Classification	Wealthy %	Wealthy rank	Middling %	Middling rank	Poor %	Poor rank
Bromsgrove	West Midlands	Archipelago Suburbs	2.24	160	80.27	23	17.49	384
Broxbourne	East	London Suburbs	0.00	297	76.77	74	23.23	236
Broxtowe	East Midlands	Inner Archipelago	0.00	333	78.28	44	21.72	276
Burnley	North West	Inner Archipelago	0.00	302	69.41	310	30.59	71
Bury	North West	Archipelago Core	0.57	228	73.93	182	25.50	182
Caerphilly	Wales	Archipelago Suburbs	0.00	361	71.37	266	28.63	111
Calderdale	Yorkshire & the Humber	Archipelago Centre	0.53	231	72.31	239	27.16	141
Cambridge	East	Inner London	7.52	29	63.41	368	29.07	100
Camden	London	London Core	10.28	11	47.54	403	42.17	10
Cannock Chase	West Midlands	Archipelago Suburbs	0.00	337	74.43	165	25.57	178
Canterbury	South East	London Suburbs	3.13	125	73.50	196	23.36	234
Cardiff	Wales	Archipelago Centre	2.34	156	69.37	311	28.29	116
Carlisle	North West	Archipelago Core	0.00	276	74.57	159	25.43	185
Carmarthenshire	Wales	Outer Archipelago	1.11	203	74.04	177	24.86	202
Carrickfergus	Northern Ireland	Archipelago Suburbs	0.00	388	74.11	175	25.89	166
Castle Point	East	London Suburbs	0.00	287	81.35	10	18.65	367
Castlereagh	Northern Ireland	Inner Archipelago	0.00	389	77.00	66	23.00	242
Central Bedfordshire	East	London Suburbs	2.61	148	77.52	61	19.88	330
Ceredigion	Wales	Outer Archipelago	2.67	146	75.27	129	22.05	272
Charnwood	East Midlands	Inner Archipelago	0.95	212	77.93	54	21.12	290
Chelmsford	East	London Suburbs	3.44	115	76.68	75	19.89	328
Cheltenham	South West	London Suburbs	4.22	91	73.34	201	22.44	260
Cherwell	South East	London Suburbs	4.55	80	74.63	153	20.82	301
Cheshire East	North West	Archipelago Suburbs	3.52	109	76.42	84	20.06	319
Cheshire West & Chester	North West	Archipelago Core	2.49	151	74.87	142	22.64	254
Chesterfield	East Midlands	Archipelago Core	0.00	279	70.64	285	29.36	93
Chichester	South East	London Suburbs	11.74	5	67.72	335	20.54	311
Chiltern	South East	London Suburbs	9.40	17	74.01	179	16.59	399
Chorley	North West	Archipelago Suburbs	0.00	303	78.59	42	21.41	282
Christchurch	South West	Outer London	1.57	184	77.64	59	20.79	302
City of London	London	Centre of London	3.12	128	65.35	357	31.53	62
Clackmannanshire	Scotland	Inner Archipelago	0.00	366	68.05	328	31.95	56
Colchester	East	Outer London	3.73	101	73.28	203	22.99	244
Coleraine	Northern Ireland	Archipelago Suburbs	0.00	390	73.19	207	26.81	151
Conwy	Wales	Outer Archipelago	1.33	194	74.54	160	24.13	220
Cookstown	Northern Ireland	Archipelago Suburbs	0.00	391	73.95	180	26.05	163
Copeland	North West	Inner Archipelago	0.00	277	74.26	172	25.74	173
Corby	East Midlands	London Suburbs	0.00	323	69.54	308	30.46	75
Cornwall	South West	London Edge	3.12	127	73.92	183	22.96	246
Cotswold	South West	London Suburbs	7.08	37	73.52	194	19.40	346
County Durham	North East	Archipelago Suburbs	0.69	227	70.56	287	28.75	110
Coventry	West Midlands	Archipelago Centre	0.88	218	67.81	332	31.31	64
Craigavon	Northern Ireland	Inner Archipelago	0.00	392	71.08	272	28.92	105
Craven	Yorkshire & the Humber	Archipelago Suburbs	0.00	328	80.54	18	19.46	341
Crawley	South East	London Suburbs	0.00	349	71.50	263	28.50	114
Croydon	London	Inner London	5.35	62	62.97	371	31.68	61
Dacorum	East	London Suburbs	4.47	84	71.83	256	23.69	228
Darlington	North East	Archipelago Core	0.00	258	72.39	236	27.61	130
Dartford	South East	Inner London	0.00	299	75.87	104	24.13	219
Daventry	East Midlands	London Suburbs	0.00	324	80.32	21	19.68	333
Denbighshire	Wales	Outer Archipelago	0.00	354	75.08	136	24.92	199
Derby	East Midlands	Archipelago Core	1.57	185	68.44	323	30.00	81
Derbyshire Dales	East Midlands	Archipelago Suburbs	3.52	108	76.91	70	19.57	337

Local Authority	Region/country	Classification	Wealthy %	Wealthy rank	Middling %	Middling rank	Poor %	Poor rank
Derry	Northern Ireland	Outer Archipelago	0.00	393	61.78	378	38.22	22
Doncaster	Yorkshire & the Humber	Archipelago Core	0.33	234	70.76	281	28.91	106
Dover	South East	London Suburbs	1.10	204	73.36	200	25.54	179
Down	Northern Ireland	Outer Archipelago	0.00	394	74.82	144	25.18	194
Dudley	West Midlands	Archipelago Core	1.24	198	71.30	267	27.46	133
Dumfries & Galloway	Scotland	Inner Archipelago	2.77	139	69.91	301	27.31	139
Dundee	Scotland	Archipelago Core	0.00	368	62.40	374	37.60	24
Dungannon	Northern Ireland	Outer Archipelago	0.00	395	73.19	206	26.81	152
Ealing	London	Inner London	7.11	35	58.73	388	34.16	40
East Ayrshire	Scotland	Archipelago Suburbs	0.00	369	66.83	347	33.17	47
East Cambridgeshire	East	Outer London	2.64	147	77.82	55	19.55	338
East Devon	South West	London Edge	6.16	49	74.60	156	19.24	352
East Dorset	South West	London Edge	4.17	93	79.73	28	16.10	402
East Dunbartonshire	Scotland	Archipelago Suburbs	2.73	141	76.61	79	20.66	307
East Hampshire	South East	Outer London	6.01	52	76.35	85	17.64	381
East Hertfordshire	East	London Suburbs	5.60	58	76.12	92	18.28	374
East Lindsey	East Midlands	London Edge	0.74	225	76.29	87	22.98	245
East Lothian	Scotland	Archipelago Suburbs	2.31	157	70.03	300	27.66	127
East Northamptonshire	East Midlands	London Suburbs	0.00	325	79.61	30	20.39	313
East Renfrewshire	Scotland	Archipelago Suburbs	1.55	186	78.24	45	20.20	317
East Riding of Yorkshire	Yorkshire & the Humber	Archipelago Suburbs	2.09	164	77.94	53	19.97	323
East Staffordshire	West Midlands	Archipelago Suburbs	0.00	338	75.61	113	24.39	213
Eastbourne	South East	London Suburbs	4.74	77	68.58	321	26.68	155
Eastleigh	South East	Outer London	0.00	293	80.57	17	19.43	344
Eden	North West	Inner Archipelago	1.90	172	78.82	39	19.28	350
Edinburgh	Scotland	Archipelago Centre	4.86	75	66.32	351	28.82	108
Eilean Siar	Scotland	Archipelago Edge	0.00	381	74.74	148	25.26	190
Elmbridge	South East	Inner London	14.11	3	69.32	312	16.56	400
Enfield	London	Inner London	5.67	56	60.58	383	33.76	44
Epping Forest	East	London Suburbs	6.38	47	72.54	230	21.08	295
Epsom & Ewell	South East	Inner London	10.96	8	71.89	254	17.16	389
Erewash	East Midlands	Archipelago Suburbs	0.00	280	75.66	110	24.34	214
Exeter	South West	London Edge	2.67	145	70.48	290	26.85	150
Falkirk	Scotland	Archipelago Suburbs	0.00	370	69.81	303	30.19	78
Fareham	South East	Outer London	0.00	294	83.18	2	16.82	398
Fenland	East	Outer London	0.00	274	76.01	96	23.99	225
Fermanagh	Northern Ireland	Archipelago Edge	0.00	396	75.37	125	24.63	206
Fife	Scotland	Archipelago Suburbs	1.57	183	69.13	316	29.30	96
Flintshire	Wales	Archipelago Suburbs	0.00	355	76.53	80	23.47	231
Forest Heath	East	London Edge	0.00	344	76.62	78	23.38	233
Forest of Dean	South West	London Suburbs	0.00	291	79.33	34	20.67	306
Fylde	North West	Archipelago Suburbs	1.32	195	78.70	41	19.98	322
Gateshead	North East	Archipelago Core	0.00	248	66.28	352	33.72	45
Gedling	East Midlands	Archipelago Suburbs	0.00	334	78.16	48	21.84	275
Glasgow	Scotland	Archipelago Centre	0.94	213	55.83	393	43.23	8
Gloucester	South West	London Suburbs	0.00	292	75.10	135	24.90	200
Gosport	South East	Outer London	0.00	295	74.32	171	25.68	174
Gravesham	South East	Inner London	0.00	300	72.77	222	27.23	140
Great Yarmouth	East	London Edge	0.00	321	70.68	284	29.32	94
Greenwich	London	Inner London	1.93	169	57.92	391	40.14	16
Guildford	South East	London Suburbs	10.53	9	71.19	268	18.29	373
Gwynedd	Wales	Archipelago Edge	2.13	163	72.25	242	25.62	176
Hackney	London	London Core	3.12	126	45.75	405	51.13	1
Halton	North West	Archipelago Core	0.00	259	68.31	324	31.69	60

Local Authority	Region/country	Classification	Wealthy %	Wealthy rank	Middling %	Middling rank	Poor %	Poor rank
Hambleton	Yorkshire & the Humber	Archipelago Suburbs	2.78	138	78.17	47	19.05	357
Hammersmith & Fulham	London	London Core	9.33	18	50.40	400	40.27	15
Harborough	East Midlands	Outer London	0.00	313	83.92	1	16.08	403
Haringey	London	London Core	7.19	32	50.43	399	42.37	9
Harlow	East	London Suburbs	0.00	288	67.59	336	32.41	52
Harrogate	Yorkshire & the Humber	Archipelago Suburbs	6.06	51	75.01	140	18.93	362
Harrow	London	Inner London	9.76	13	64.11	362	26.14	161
Hart	South East	Outer London	6.48	46	79.73	29	13.80	406
Hartlepool	North Eat	Archipelago Core	0.00	254	65.76	356	34.24	38
Hastings	South East	London Suburbs	0.00	285	68.92	318	31.08	67
Havant	South East	Outer London	2.05	166	72.10	246	25.85	167
Havering	London	Inner London	2.57	150	73.17	208	24.26	216
Herefordshire	West Midlands	Archipelago Suburbs	3.85	97	73.80	186	22.34	263
Hertsmere	East	London Suburbs	7.29	31	69.78	304	22.93	247
High Peak	East Midlands	Inner Archipelago	1.21	200	76.48	83	22.31	265
Highland	Scotland	Archipelago Edge	0.00	371	74.37	167	25.63	175
Hillingdon	London	Inner London	4.72	78	67.12	342	28.16	120
Hinckley & Bosworth	East Midlands	Outer London	1.08	206	79.60	31	19.31	348
Horsham	South East	London Suburbs	7.10	36	75.55	117	17.36	387
Hounslow	London	Inner London	5.35	63	60.60	381	34.06	41
Huntingdonshire	East	London Suburbs	2.34	155	77.97	52	19.68	332
Hyndburn	North West	Inner Archipelago	0.00	304	71.48	264	28.52	113
Inverclyde	Scotland	Archipelago Suburbs	0.00	372	64.28	360	35.72	35
Ipswich	East	Inner London	0.00	345	69.54	307	30.46	76
Isle of Anglesey	Wales	Archipelago Edge	0.00	353	75.44	121	24.56	209
Isle of Wight	South East	Outer London	3.52	107	72.27	241	24.21	218
Isles of Scilly	South West	London Edge	3.12	129	66.51	350	30.37	77
Islington	London	London Core	5.43	61	47.94	402	46.63	5
Kensington & Chelsea	London	London Core	18.25	1	45.56	406	36.19	30
Kettering	East Midlands	London Suburbs	0.00	326	76.92	69	23.08	237
King's Lynn & West Norfolk	East	London Edge	1.42	191	76.11	93	22.47	259
Kingston upon Hull	Yorkshire & the Humber	Archipelago Core	0.00	262	61.70	379	38.30	21
Kingston upon Thames	London	Inner London	9.46	16	67.54	337	23.00	243
Kirklees	Yorkshire & the Humber	Archipelago Centre	1.47	189	71.13	271	27.40	135
Knowsley	North West	Archipelago Core	0.00	244	63.13	370	36.87	26
Lambeth	London	London Core	5.58	59	50.45	398	43.97	6
Lancaster	North West	Archipelago Core	2.72	142	73.44	198	23.84	226
Larne	Northern Ireland	Archipelago Suburbs	0.00	397	74.23	173	25.77	171
Leeds	Yorkshire & the Humber	Archipelago Centre	1.54	187	67.89	329	30.57	73
Leicester	East Midlands	Inner London	0.42	233	62.27	376	37.31	25
Lewes	South East	Outer London	5.99	53	72.62	227	21.39	284
Lewisham	London	London Core	3.26	120	55.78	394	40.96	12
Lichfield	West Midlands	Archipelago Suburbs	0.00	339	80.34	20	19.66	334
Limavady	Northern Ireland	Outer Archipelago	0.00	398	71.03	273	28.97	104
Lincoln	East Midlands	London Edge	0.00	318	69.25	315	30.75	68
Lisburn	Northern Ireland	Archipelago Suburbs	0.00	399	73.28	204	26.72	154
Liverpool	North West	Archipelago Centre	0.54	230	59.59	387	39.86	17
Luton	East	London Suburbs	0.73	226	68.12	327	31.15	66
Magherafelt	Northern Ireland	Archipelago Suburbs	0.00	400	75.75	107	24.25	217
Maidstone	South East	London Suburbs	3.40	117	75.32	127	21.27	289
Maldon	East	Outer London	0.00	289	81.92	7	18.08	377
Malvern Hills	West Midlands	Archipelago Suburbs	4.20	92	75.75	106	20.05	320
Manchester	North West	Archipelago Centre	1.06	207	58.05	390	40.89	13

Local Authority	Region/country	Classification	Wealthy %	Wealthy rank	Middling %	Middling rank	Poor %	Poor rank
Mansfield	East Midlands	Archipelago Suburbs	0.00	335	71.89	253	28.11	121
Medway	South East	London Suburbs	0.00	271	74.76	146	25.24	192
Melton	East Midlands	Outer London	0.00	314	80.03	26	19.97	324
Mendip	South West	Outer London	3.78	100	75.12	133	21.10	292
Merthyr Tydfil	Wales	Outer Archipelago	0.00	360	67.86	330	32.14	54
Merton	London	Inner London	8.51	21	63.87	365	27.62	129
Mid Devon	South West	London Edge	0.00	283	78.90	38	21.10	293
Mid Suffolk	East	London Edge	2.58	149	79.29	36	18.12	376
Mid Sussex	South East	London Suburbs	6.85	41	75.61	112	17.55	382
Middlesbrough	North East	Archipelago Core	0.00	255	64.09	363	35.91	33
Midlothian	Scotland	Archipelago Suburbs	0.00	373	70.10	297	29.90	84
Milton Keynes	South East	London Suburbs	1.65	179	72.55	229	25.79	169
Mole Valley	South East	London Suburbs	10.25	12	72.39	237	17.36	386
Monmouthshire	Wales	Outer Archipelago	1.09	205	78.07	49	20.84	300
Moray	Scotland	Archipelago Suburbs	0.00	374	74.78	145	25.22	193
Moyle	Northern Ireland	Archipelago Suburbs	0.00	401	72.00	249	28.00	124
Neath Port Talbot	Wales	Outer Archipelago	0.00	357	71.15	270	28.85	107
New Forest	South East	Outer London	6.49	45	74.50	163	19.02	358
Newark & Sherwood	East Midlands	Archipelago Suburbs	0.87	219	76.09	94	23.03	239
Newcastle upon Tyne	North East	Archipelago Centre	1.84	174	62.45	373	35.71	36
Newcastle-under-Lyme	West Midlands	Archipelago Core	0.00	340	74.39	166	25.61	177
Newham	London	London Core	0.00	237	50.72	397	49.28	2
Newport	Wales	Archipelago Suburbs	0.00	364	70.34	293	29.66	88
Newry & Mourne	Northern Ireland	Outer Archipelago	0.00	402	71.95	250	28.05	122
Newtownabbey	Northern Ireland	Archipelago Suburbs	0.00	403	74.63	154	25.37	187
North Ayrshire	Scotland	Archipelago Suburbs	0.00	375	65.80	355	34.20	39
North Devon	South West	London Edge	2.18	162	75.47	120	22.35	262
North Dorset	South West	London Edge	7.56	27	72.98	218	19.46	342
North Down	Northern Ireland	Inner Archipelago	0.00	404	78.72	40	21.28	287
North East Derbyshire	East Midlands	Inner Archipelago	0.00	281	75.71	109	24.29	215
North East Lincolnshire	Yorkshire & the Humber	London Edge	0.00	263	70.81	280	29.19	99
North Hertfordshire	East	London Suburbs	3.84	98	73.63	190	22.53	257
North Kesteven	East Midlands	Outer London	0.00	319	81.54	9	18.46	370
North Lanarkshire	Scotland	Inner Archipelago	0.00	376	64.26	361	35.74	34
North Lincolnshire	Yorkshire & the Humber	London Edge	0.00	264	75.12	134	24.88	201
North Norfolk	East	London Edge	3.47	112	74.94	141	21.59	278
North Somerset	South West	London Suburbs	3.61	104	76.17	91	20.22	316
North Tyneside	North East	Archipelago Core	0.00	249	70.95	279	29.05	101
North Warwickshire	West Midlands	London Suburbs	0.00	346	77.78	56	22.22	269
North West Leicestershire	East Midlands	Inner Archipelago	0.00	315	78.42	43	21.58	279
Northampton	East Midlands	Inner London	0.77	224	71.82	257	27.41	134
Northumberland	North East	Archipelago Suburbs	2.26	159	72.21	244	25.52	180
Norwich	East	Inner London	0.00	322	64.99	358	35.01	37
Nottingham	East Midlands	Archipelago Core	0.44	232	60.61	380	38.96	19
Nuneaton & Bedworth	West Midlands	London Suburbs	0.00	347	74.53	161	25.47	184
Oadby & Wigston	East Midlands	Outer London	0.00	316	80.84	14	19.16	354
Oldham	North West	Archipelago Centre	0.00	239	68.19	326	31.81	58
Omagh	Northern Ireland	Outer Archipelago	0.00	405	73.26	205	26.74	153
Orkney Islands	Scotland	Archipelago Edge	0.00	377	77.69	58	22.31	266
Oxford	South East	Inner London	7.14	34	62.32	375	30.54	74
Pembrokeshire	Wales	Outer Archipelago	3.21	122	72.05	248	24.74	204
Pendle	North West	Archipelago Suburbs	0.00	305	72.38	238	27.62	128

Local Authority	Region/country	Classification	Wealthy %	Wealthy rank	Middling %	Middling rank	Poor %	Poor rank
Perth & Kinross	Scotland	Archipelago Suburbs	3.60	105	71.93	251	24.47	211
Peterborough	East	London Suburbs	0.00	269	70.98	277	29.02	103
Plymouth	South West	Outer London	0.57	229	70.12	296	29.31	95
Poole	South West	Outer London	5.26	66	73.14	211	21.60	277
Portsmouth	South East	Inner London	1.98	167	67.44	339	30.58	72
Powys	Wales	Outer Archipelago	3.43	116	74.37	168	22.20	270
Preston	North West	Archipelago Suburbs	0.00	306	70.13	295	29.87	85
Purbeck	South West	London Edge	2.09	165	77.35	63	20.55	310
Reading	South East	Inner London	3.99	96	67.81	331	28.20	117
Redbridge	London	Inner London	4.56	79	66.95	343	28.49	115
Redcar & Cleveland	North East	Archipelago Core	0.00	256	70.28	294	29.72	86
Redditch	West Midlands	Archipelago Suburbs	0.00	350	72.93	219	27.07	143
Reigate & Banstead	South East	London Suburbs	8.10	25	73.47	197	18.43	371
Renfrewshire	Scotland	Archipelago Suburbs	0.00	378	67.74	334	32.26	53
Rhondda Cynon Taf	Wales	Archipelago Suburbs	0.00	359	72.12	245	27.88	126
Ribble Valley	North West	Archipelago Suburbs	0.00	307	82.95	4	17.05	392
Richmond upon Thames	London	Inner London	15.41	2	63.31	369	21.29	286
Richmondshire	Yorkshire & the Humber	Inner Archipelago	0.00	329	80.89	12	19.11	355
Rochdale	North West	Archipelago Core	0.00	240	67.14	341	32.86	50
Rochford	East	London Suburbs	0.00	290	83.02	3	16.98	394
Rossendale	North West	Inner Archipelago	0.00	308	74.76	147	25.24	191
Rother	South East	London Suburbs	5.00	71	74.03	178	20.97	296
Rotherham	Yorkshire & the Humber	Archipelago Core	0.00	247	70.74	282	29.26	97
Rugby	West Midlands	London Suburbs	0.00	348	77.75	57	22.25	267
Runnymede	South East	London Suburbs	6.78	42	73.72	188	19.51	339
Rushcliffe	East Midlands	Inner Archipelago	1.03	209	81.87	8	17.11	390
Rushmoor	South East	Outer London	0.00	296	76.97	67	23.03	240
Rutland	East Midlands	Outer London	0.00	265	82.19	6	17.81	380
Ryedale	Yorkshire & the Humber	Archipelago Suburbs	3.37	118	75.89	103	20.74	303
Salford	North West	Archipelago Centre	0.00	241	64.09	364	35.91	32
Sandwell	West Midlands	Archipelago Core	0.00	252	63.50	366	36.50	28
Scarborough	Yorkshire & the Humber	Archipelago Suburbs	0.96	211	72.77	223	26.27	158
Scottish Borders	Scotland	Inner Archipelago	2.68	144	71.18	269	26.14	160
Sedgemoor	South West	Outer London	1.18	202	76.50	82	22.33	264
Sefton	North West	Archipelago Suburbs	1.91	170	71.01	274	27.08	142
Selby	Yorkshire & the Humber	Archipelago Suburbs	0.00	330	80.10	24	19.90	327
Sevenoaks	South East	London Suburbs	8.15	24	73.15	209	18.69	366
Sheffield	Yorkshire & the Humber	Archipelago Centre	1.52	188	66.78	348	31.70	59
Shepway	South East	London Suburbs	0.85	220	73.88	184	25.27	189
Shetland Islands	Scotland	Archipelago Edge	0.00	379	73.95	181	26.05	162
Shropshire	West Midlands	Archipelago Suburbs	3.18	123	75.28	128	21.53	280
Slough	South East	London Suburbs	0.00	273	66.85	346	33.15	48
Solihull	West Midlands	Archipelago Core	4.41	87	72.79	220	22.79	251
South Ayrshire	Scotland	Archipelago Suburbs	1.65	180	71.00	275	27.35	138
South Bucks	South East	London Suburbs	11.46	7	71.70	262	16.84	397
South Cambridgeshire	East	London Suburbs	5.35	64	76.83	71	17.82	379
South Derbyshire	East Midlands	Inner Archipelago	0.00	282	80.43	19	19.57	336
South Gloucestershire	South West	London Suburbs	3.09	131	78.06	50	18.86	363
South Hams	South West	London Edge	7.06	38	73.62	192	19.32	347
South Holland	East Midlands	Outer London	4.40	89	73.59	193	22.01	273
South Kesteven	East Midlands	Outer London	1.81	175	76.80	73	21.39	283
South Lakeland	North West	Archipelago Suburbs	5.25	67	75.74	108	19.01	359
South Lanarkshire	Scotland	Archipelago Suburbs	0.80	223	69.50	309	29.70	87
South Norfolk	East	London Edge	3.72	102	77.98	51	18.30	372

Local Authority	Region/country	Classification	Wealthy %	Wealthy rank	Middling %	Middling rank	Poor %	Poor rank
South Northamptonshire	East Midlands	London Suburbs	3.06	134	80.82	15	16.12	401
South Oxfordshire	South East	London Suburbs	8.91	20	73.71	189	17.38	385
South Ribble	North West	Archipelago Suburbs	0.00	309	80.04	25	19.96	325
South Somerset	South West	London Edge	4.23	90	74.66	152	21.12	291
South Staffordshire	West Midlands	Archipelago Suburbs	0.00	341	80.30	22	19.70	331
South Tyneside	North East	Archipelago Core	0.00	250	63.42	367	36.58	27
Southampton	South East	Inner London	0.91	216	67.15	340	31.94	57
Southend-on-Sea	East	London Suburbs	3.24	121	70.98	278	25.78	170
Southwark	London	London Core	3.57	106	49.05	401	47.38	4
Spelthorne	South East	London Suburbs	3.46	113	76.29	88	20.25	314
St Albans	East	London Suburbs	9.51	15	72.52	231	17.97	378
St Edmundsbury	East	Outer London	2.38	154	75.39	122	22.22	268
St Helens	North West	Archipelago Core	0.00	245	70.58	286	29.42	92
Stafford	West Midlands	Archipelago Suburbs	0.81	222	78.23	46	20.95	297
Staffordshire Moorlands	West Midlands	Archipelago Suburbs	0.00	342	80.76	16	19.24	351
Stevenage	East	London Suburbs	0.00	298	70.50	288	29.50	91
Stirling	Scotland	Archipelago Suburbs	1.19	201	73.04	214	25.77	172
Stockport	North West	Archipelago Core	2.39	152	74.36	169	23.24	235
Stockton-on-Tees	North East	Archipelago Core	0.00	257	72.63	226	27.37	136
Stoke-on-Trent	West Midlands	Archipelago Suburbs	0.00	267	66.75	349	33.25	46
Strabane	Northern Ireland	Archipelago Edge	0.00	406	66.91	344	33.09	49
Stratford-upon-Avon	West Midlands	London Suburbs	5.00	70	76.20	90	18.80	364
Stroud	South West	London Suburbs	4.50	83	75.92	101	19.58	335
Suffolk Coastal	East	London Edge	4.80	76	75.89	102	19.31	349
Sunderland	North East	Archipelago Core	0.00	251	66.00	354	34.00	42
Surrey Heath	South East	London Suburbs	7.01	39	77.42	62	15.58	404
Sutton	London	Inner London	5.19	68	70.69	283	24.12	221
Swale	South East	London Suburbs	0.00	301	75.08	137	24.92	198
Swansea	Wales	Archipelago Core	1.62	181	70.36	292	28.01	123
Swindon	South West	Inner London	0.00	268	75.25	130	24.75	203
Tameside	North West	Archipelago Centre	0.00	242	69.26	314	30.74	69
Tamworth	West Midlands	Archipelago Suburbs	0.00	343	73.51	195	26.49	156
Tandridge	South East	London Suburbs	7.76	26	75.18	131	17.05	391
Taunton Deane	South West	London Edge	4.42	86	72.77	221	22.81	249
Teignbridge	South West	London Edge	3.82	99	75.95	100	20.23	315
Telford & Wrekin	West Midlands	Archipelago Suburbs	0.00	266	72.50	232	27.50	132
Tendring	East	London Edge	1.29	196	74.68	150	24.03	224
Test Valley	South East	Outer London	4.89	74	75.64	111	19.47	340
Tewkesbury	South West	London Suburbs	1.23	199	80.02	27	18.74	365
Thanet	South East	Outer London	1.40	192	69.57	306	29.02	102
The Vale of Glamorgan	Wales	Archipelago Suburbs	3.08	132	74.20	174	22.72	252
Three Rivers	East	London Suburbs	8.41	22	71.46	265	20.13	318
Thurrock	East	London Suburbs	0.00	270	73.15	210	26.85	149
Tonbridge & Malling	South East	London Suburbs	2.83	137	76.50	81	20.67	305
Torbay	South West	London Edge	2.74	140	71.79	260	25.48	183
Torfaen	Wales	Archipelago Suburbs	0.00	363	70.49	289	29.51	90
Torridge	South West	London Edge	2.69	143	75.95	99	21.36	285
Tower Hamlets	London	London Core	0.00	238	51.02	396	48.98	3
Trafford	North West	Archipelago Core	3.50	111	72.43	235	24.07	222
Tunbridge Wells	South East	London Suburbs	7.15	33	70.99	276	21.86	274
Uttlesford	East	London Suburbs	1.60	182	80.89	13	17.51	383
Vale of White Horse	South East	London Suburbs	5.95	54	75.50	118	18.55	369
Wakefield	Yorkshire & the Humber	Archipelago Core	0.32	235	69.76	305	29.92	83
Walsall	West Midlands	Archipelago Core	0.00	253	67.51	338	32.49	51

Local Authority	Region/country	Classification	Wealthy %	Wealthy rank	Middling %	Middling rank	Poor %	Poor rank
Waltham Forest	London	Inner London	2.39	153	59.63	385	37.98	23
Wandsworth	London	London Core	9.56	14	58.48	389	31.95	55
Warrington	North West	Archipelago Core	1.27	197	75.33	126	23.39	232
Warwick	West Midlands	London Suburbs	4.11	94	74.61	155	21.28	288
Watford	East	Inner London	1.97	168	72.21	243	25.82	168
Waveney	East	London Edge	1.91	171	73.00	217	25.10	196
Waverley	South East	London Suburbs	10.51	10	72.59	228	16.91	395
Wealden	South East	London Suburbs	5.54	60	77.60	60	16.86	396
Wellingborough	East Midlands	London Suburbs	0.00	327	73.63	191	26.37	157
Welwyn Hatfield	East	London Suburbs	4.50	82	68.58	320	26.92	146
West Berkshire	South East	Outer London	4.91	73	76.08	95	19.01	360
West Devon	South West	London Edge	4.94	72	75.86	105	19.20	353
West Dorset	South West	London Edge	6.91	40	72.44	233	20.64	309
West Dunbartonshire	Scotland	Archipelago Suburbs	0.00	367	60.60	382	39.40	18
West Lancashire	North West	Archipelago Suburbs	0.00	310	76.31	86	23.69	229
West Lindsey	East Midlands	London Edge	0.00	320	79.52	32	20.48	312
West Lothian	Scotland	Archipelago Suburbs	0.00	380	69.29	313	30.71	70
West Oxfordshire	South East	London Suburbs	6.13	50	75.61	114	18.26	375
West Somerset	South West	London Edge	0.00	336	76.92	68	23.08	238
Westminster	London	Centre of London	12.19	4	47.44	404	40.37	14
Weymouth & Portland	South West	London Edge	0.00	284	74.50	162	25.50	181
Wigan	North West	Archipelago Core	0.00	243	72.05	247	27.95	125
Wiltshire	South West	Outer London	4.54	81	74.57	158	20.89	299
Winchester	South East	Outer London	9.12	19	71.80	259	19.08	356
Windsor & Maidenhead	South East	London Suburbs	8.38	23	72.67	224	18.95	361
Wirral	North West	Archipelago Suburbs	1.80	176	70.03	299	28.17	119
Woking	South East	London Suburbs	7.54	28	73.02	215	19.44	343
Wokingham	South East	Outer London	6.65	43	79.33	35	14.01	405
Wolverhampton	West Midlands	Archipelago Core	0.97	210	62.85	372	36.18	31
Worcester	West Midlands	Archipelago Suburbs	0.00	351	74.86	143	25.14	195
Worthing	South East	Outer London	3.64	103	73.33	202	23.03	241
Wrexham	Wales	Archipelago Core	0.00	356	71.81	258	28.19	118
Wychavon	West Midlands	Archipelago Suburbs	4.41	88	75.55	116	20.04	321
Wycombe	South East	London Suburbs	5.76	55	74.36	170	19.88	329
Wyre	North West	Archipelago Suburbs	0.00	311	79.28	37	20.72	304
Wyre Forest	West Midlands	Archipelago Suburbs	0.00	352	76.21	89	23.79	227
York	Yorkshire & the Humber	Archipelago Suburbs	2.97	136	73.40	199	23.63	230

1   (Page 31) Beaujouan, E and Ní Bhrolcháin, M, 2011, Cohabitation and marriage in Britain since the 1970s, Population Trends, 145.

2   (Page 50) Coleman, D A, 1987, UK statistics on immigration: development and limitations, International Migration Review, xxi, 4, Winter, 1138–69. Quote from p 1144.

3   (Page 50) Jivraj, S and Simpson, L, eds, 2015, Ethnic identity and inequalities in Britain: The dynamics of diversity, Bristol: Policy Press.

4   (Page 51) Doughty, S, 2014, Just 800,000 worshippers attend a Church of England service on an average Sunday, The Daily Mail, 22 March, www.dailymail.co.uk/news/article-2586596/Just-800-000-worshipers-attend-Church-England-service-average-Sunday.html

5   (Page 88) Dorling, D, 2009, Migration: A long-run perspective, London: Institute for Public Policy Research.

6   (Page 136) There is a tendency on the right of UK politics to cut census and survey funding because of a dislike of the public being confused by the disclosure of facts. Official statistics agencies saw their funding cut by the incoming Conservative government of 1951, resulting in a much-depleted 1961 Census. Large cuts were introduced to the OPCS by Margaret Thatcher's government in 1979, and to the ONS by David Cameron's in 2010. There was even a proposal to scrap the 2011 Census, but the data collection contracts had been signed before 2010, and scrapping the census would have cost more than running it. The 2021 Census remains under great threat.

7   (Page 140) Studies of long-term changes in the proportion of people working in various classes of occupation from 1841 through to 2001 have been undertaken. They show that the most rapid changes have been in the period after 1981. See Vision of Britain for more details (www.visionofbritain.org.uk/).

8   (Page 170) Dorling, D, 2014, Why are the old dying before their time? How austerity has affected mortality rates, New Statesman, 7 February.

9   (Page 243) See Tunstall, B, 2015, Relative housing space inequality in England and Wales, and its recent rapid resurgence, International Journal of Housing Policy, 15, 2, 105–26.

10 (Page 256) Fahmy, E, Dorling, D, Rigby, J, Wheeler, B, Ballas, D, Gordon, D and Lupton, R, 2008, Poverty, wealth and place in Britain, 1968–2005, Radical Statistics, 97, 11–30.